MW00789715

CONTINUING BONDS IN BEREAVEMENT

The introduction of the continuing bonds model of grief near the end of the 20th century revolutionized the way researchers and practitioners understand bereavement. *Continuing Bonds in Bereavement* is the most comprehensive, state-of-the-art collection of developments in this field since the inception of the model. As a multi-perspectival, nuanced, and forward-looking anthology, it combines innovations in clinical practice with theoretical and empirical advancements. The text traces grief in different cultural settings, asking questions about the truth in our interactions with the dead and showing how new cultural developments like social media change the ways we relate to those who have died. Together, the book's four sections encourage practitioners and scholars in both bereavement studies and in other fields to broaden their understanding of the concept of continuing bonds.

Dennis Klass, PhD, is on the editorial boards of *Death Studies* and *Omega: Journal of Death and Dying* and is professor emeritus at Webster University in St. Louis, Missouri. He is the author of *The Spiritual Lives of Bereaved Parents*, coauthor of *Dead but Not Lost: Grief Narratives in Religious Traditions*, and coeditor of *Continuing Bonds: New Understandings of Grief*. A licensed psychologist, he has been active in the study of death, dying, and bereavement since 1968.

Edith Maria Steffen, PsychD, is a lecturer in counseling psychology at the University of Roehampton, London, UK. Her research focuses on sense of presence experiences in bereavement and meaning-oriented group grief therapy. She has published articles in journals such as *Death Studies*, *Omega: Journal of Death and Dying*, and *Mental Health, Religion & Culture*, and has contributed a number of chapters to anthologies.

THE SERIES IN DEATH, DYING, AND BEREAVEMENT

Robert A. Neimeyer and Darcy L. Harris, Series Editors

For a complete list of all books in this series, please visit the series page at: https://www.routledge.com/series/SE0620

CONTINUING BONDS IN BEREAVEMENT

New Directions for Research and Practice

Edited by Dennis Klass and
Edith Maria Steffen

Routledge
Taylor & Francis Group

NEW YORK AND LONDON

First edition published 2018
by Routledge
711 Third Avenue, New York, NY 10017

and by Routledge
2 Park Square, Milton Park, Abingdon, Oxon, OX14 4RN

Routledge is an imprint of the Taylor & Francis Group, an informa business

© 2018 Dennis Klass and Edith Maria Steffen

The right of the editors to be identified as the authors of the editorial
material, and of the authors for their individual chapters, has been asserted
in accordance with sections 77 and 78 of the Copyright, Designs and
Patents Act 1988.

All rights reserved. No part of this book may be reprinted or reproduced
or utilised in any form or by any electronic, mechanical, or other means,
now known or hereafter invented, including photocopying and recording,
or in any information storage or retrieval system, without permission in
writing from the publishers.

Trademark notice: Product or corporate names may be trademarks or
registered trademarks, and are used only for identification and explanation
without intent to infringe.

Library of Congress Cataloging-in-Publication Data
Names: Klass, Dennis, editor. | Steffen, Edith, editor.
Title: Continuing bonds in bereavement : new directions for research and
    practice / edited by Dennis Klass, Edith Steffen.
Description: New York, NY : Routledge, 2018. | Series: Death, dying, and
    bereavement | Includes bibliographical references and index.
Identifiers: LCCN 2017026244| ISBN 9780415356190
    (hardcover : alk. paper) | ISBN 9780415356206 (pbk. : alk. paper) |
    ISBN 9781315202396 (e-book)
Subjects: LCSH: Grief. | Bereavement—Psychological aspects. |
    Attachment behavior.
Classification: LCC BF575.G7 C669 2017 | DDC 155.9/37—dc23
LC record available at https://lccn.loc.gov/2017026244

ISBN: 978-0-415-35619-0 (hbk)
ISBN: 978-0-415-35620-6 (pbk)
ISBN: 978-1-315-20239-6 (ebk)

Typeset in Bembo
by Swales & Willis Ltd, Exeter, Devon, UK

IN MEMORY OF
PHYLLIS ROLFE SILVERMAN
JULY 10, 1927–JUNE 10, 2016
WHO INITIATED THE CONVERSATION
THAT CONTINUES IN THIS BOOK

CONTENTS

Contents

Contents

Contents

SERIES FOREWORD

As Thomas Kuhn once famously recognized, normal science—including social science—tends to proceed as "bit and piece puzzle-solving," as the great majority of researchers work comfortably within the prevailing paradigm, taking up its implicit assumptions, usually unconsciously, as they concentrate on applying its analytic and methodological framework to an ever-expanding range of problems. This approach, which takes for granted the adequacy of foundational commitments within the paradigm, works well . . . until it doesn't. At that point anomalies begin to accumulate that call for a revolutionary paradigm shift that promises a fuller, deeper, and more useful means of conceptualizing the subject matter. Whether at the over-arching level of shifting from a Newtonian mechanics to a unified field theory, or at the more specific level of transitioning from a pathology-focused psychotherapy to one that emphasizes client strengths and resilience, the emergence of a new paradigm marks a sea change in the field, for scholars as well as practitioners working within it.

In the past two decades just such a paradigm shift has occurred in the field of bereavement research and practice. Where once psychologists, psychiatrists, and related professionals labored under the largely unquestioned assumption that adaptation to the death of a significant person required "decathexis," "letting go," or the "withdrawal of emotional investment" in the one who had died in order to "move on" in a healthy way, the predecessor of this book (Klass, Silverman, & Nickman, 1996) persuasively argued that the natural course of bereavement involves not relinquishing bonds with the dead, but rather retaining them. In a remarkably short time this "new look" in the study of grief has emerged as a major challenger to the dominant paradigm, generating a sizable body of research and practice substantiating, extending, and applying its insights in both scholarly and practical contexts of support and therapy.

Just how revolutionary the continuing bonds model has been in reorienting scholarship and practice in the field of bereavement studies is clearly documented in this intriguing successor volume edited by Dennis Klass and Edith Maria Steffen. Amply sampling the breadth and depth of contemporary contributions to the field, various chapters demonstrate how the ongoing relationship with the deceased is woven into the fabric of leading models of grief, including two-track, posttraumatic growth, narrative, attachment, and meaning reconstruction approaches. Similarly, historical and cultural scholarship documents the pervasive role of relations between the living and dead in sustaining social, political, and religious systems of meaning and power, and the investment that cultural stakeholders have in regulating their expression. Complementing these more macro perspectives on the phenomenon, other contributions provide penetrating close-ups of the unique significance of continuing bonds for such populations as parents mourning children, college students using social media, immigrants seeking cultural continuity, and users of ritual to narrate and validate profound transitions. Collectively, these chapters convincingly argue for the centrality of relations between the living and the dead for scholars and researchers in a great variety of disciplines, whose joint consideration of the phenomenon adds texture and dimensions to a cardinal feature of the human encounter with loss.

But even beyond this wealth of understanding, the book provides critical commentary on such pressing questions as the ontological status of continuing bonds as "real" or constructed, the related issue of survival in an afterlife, and the role of medium-assisted after-death communication. Less controversial but no less daunting are problems addressed by other chapters, such as welcome and unwelcome senses of presence reported by the bereaved, how bonds might be used to address the need for post-mortem forgiveness, the difference between internalized and externalized bonds, positive and negative dimensions of ongoing connection, and how these might be creatively reconstructed in the intimate theatre of psychotherapy.

In sum, in *Continuing Bonds in Bereavement*, Klass and Steffen offer a sweeping and substantial successor to the pioneering volume that initiated a paradigm shift in the study of grief and its therapeutic implications, consolidating a perspective that is likely to remain ascendant as the field of bereavement matures. Of equal relevance to serious scholars and practitioners alike, this is a volume I recommend highly to others like myself who want to deepen their conceptual grasp of the role of ongoing attachment to the dead on the part of the living, and how this can inform our efforts to ease human suffering in the face of life's ultimate transition.

Robert A. Neimeyer, PhD, University of Memphis
Editor, *Routledge Series on Death, Dying and Bereavement*

Reference

Klass, D., Silverman, P., & Nickman, S. (1996). *Continuing bonds: New understandings of grief.* New York, NY: Routledge.

PROLOGUE
A Personal History

Dennis Klass

When Edith Maria Steffen and I sent invitations to authors we hoped would contribute to this anthology, we said this book would be the second edition of *Continuing Bonds: New Understandings of Grief* (1996), an anthology I coedited with Phyllis Silverman and Steven Nickman. As the book took shape, however, we realized the themes in the book went beyond what could be legitimately called a second edition. This is a new book. The authors in the 1996 book made the same case over and over: the model of grief that was dominant in both the scholarly literature and in popular culture over most of the 20th century was wrong. Bereaved people did not sever the bonds with significant people who had died as the accepted theory said they should. Rather, people continued the attachment, albeit in new circumstances. The then-dominant theory said that maintaining a bond was evidence of pathological grief. Some theorists even said it was the cause of pathological grief. Author after author in *Continuing Bonds: New Understandings of Grief* presented evidence that maintaining bonds with the dead is not pathological; indeed, they could play a positive part in the survivors' ongoing lives.

If ever a book was successful, *Continuing Bonds: New Understandings of Grief* was one of them. Within a few years, the great majority of bereavement researchers accepted its thesis. Continuing bonds are now regarded as a common aspect of bereavement in virtually all psychiatric and psychological models of grief. This model has been incorporated into many techniques of professional and pastoral support and help for grieving people. As some chapters in this book demonstrate, the continuing bonds model is increasingly established in sociological and anthropological understandings of grief.

Developing the continuing bonds model has always been a cooperative venture. I had written about how dead children remained important in bereaved parents' lives and as the parents shared their lives in a self-help group. The first time I met Phyllis Silverman was at a conference in New York. She said that her data from bereaved children was much like mine from the bereaved parents.

She pulled transcripts of interviews out of her briefcase and we slowly went over them together. Yes, we had found the same thing. Phyllis suggested we write a book, so we began planning. She asked Steven Nickman, who had studied adopted children, to join us. We knew the book should be an anthology because many other researchers also had found that bereaved people did not sever their ties to the dead the way the then-dominant bereavement theory said they should. Phyllis, Steve, and I never claimed we had invented a new idea, but we said our anthology was to give voice to an emerging consensus among bereavement scholars.

When we began planning this book, I thought Phyllis should be involved in the expanded collaboration, but we learned that she was further along in the aging process than I was. She died after we assembled the contributors, but before most of the new anthology was written. We have dedicated this book to her.

The continuing bonds model of bereavement is an example of a common phenomenon in academic work: multiple discovery, sometimes called simultaneous invention. Multiple discovery describes the fact that many, perhaps most, scientific discoveries and inventions are made independently and almost at the same time by more than one person, or more than one group.

Two authors in this book published the continuing bonds model independent from Phyllis, Steve, and me.

Simon Shimshon Rubin's two-track model of bereavement (1981) that he here outlines and updates in the chapter he coauthored with Ruth Malkinson and Eliezer Witztum is essentially the same as the continuing bonds model Phyllis, Steve, and I proposed. The strength of Simon's two-track model is the clear relationship he draws between a positive continuing bond and a better adjustment to the changed social environment. I think we implied that connection, but Simon made it explicit.

Tony Walter had written an article for the first issue of *Mortality* (1996) in which he crisply stated the continuing bonds model. I have quoted his article many times.

> The purpose of grief is . . . the construction of a durable biography that enables the living to integrate the memory of the dead into their ongoing lives; the process by which this is achieved is principally conversation with others who knew the deceased.

I wish we had said it that well.

Shortly after his article was published, Tony wrote a review of our anthology. He could have stated, correctly, that he actually published the idea first, but he did not say that. Rather, he wrote a glowing review of *Continuing Bonds*, simply noting he had written something similar, but that we had more data. I still consider his response as incredibly generous.

The term "continuing bonds" came out of a very different intellectual and personal collaboration. The anthology Phyllis, Steve, and I were editing was well along, but we still did not have a good phrase for the phenomena we were describing, and we needed a satisfying title for the book. Simon Rubin recently reminded me that when Phyllis and I approached him to contribute a chapter, we called the project "Detachment Revisited." So, we had a name for what we were rejecting in the then-dominant model, but we had no name for what we would put in its place. Sociologist David Unruh (1983) had used the terms "continued bonding activities" and "continued attachment," but his work had not made its way into the psychological literature in which Phyllis, Steve, and I were grounded.

I asked my wife Carol to help me. We tried out some terms for a week, but none seemed right. Then one morning while we were putting groceries away she said, "continuing bonds." We said it back and forth to each other in different sentences, and we both knew it was right. I called Phyllis, she asked Steve, and that is what we have called it ever since.

There is a rich history of conversation between my wife and me as well as a history of me looking for the right words to describe what she named that morning in the kitchen.

In 1979, bereaved parents who were founding a local chapter of a self-help group asked me to be their professional advisor. I used the opportunity to do ethnographic research. The sociology of education was a significant component in my wife's doctoral studies. She knew the methodological literature on ethnography well and became my tutor and consultant. I have written elsewhere (Klass, 1999) about my roles in the group and the ways I used the ethnographic method. I spent several years listening to bereaved parents to make sure I understood their stories and also understood the self-help group's dynamics and how they were coming to terms with their children's deaths.

A prominent feature of the parents' grief was that the children were still a significant part of the parents' lives. The first term we used to describe the phenomenon was "inner representation of the deceased." The definition of inner representation came from the psychoanalytic writing of the time. It was, we said, the parts of the self-actualized in the bond with the person, characterizations and thematic memories of the person, and the emotional states connected with the characterizations and memories (Fairbairn, 1952; Kernberg, 1976; see also Benedek, 1975). The term still works well when describing any bonds with a person, living or dead, but focusing only on one individual, not on all the people in the relationship.

It soon became obvious, however, that the word "inner" in inner representation was wrong. Their dead children were an important inner reality to the parents, but an important element in the self-help process was that they worked hard to make the reality they felt so strongly within themselves into a social reality within the group, and within their extended families and other social networks. A couple who were on the group's national board wrote a song: "Our children live on in the love that we share."

As I tried to make sense of the data I was gathering from the bereaved parents, I sorted through the academic literature of grief then available. I had been an assistant in Elisabeth Kübler-Ross's seminar in death and dying at the University of Chicago Hospitals, and it was obvious to me, after just one meeting of the group, that the parents' grief could not be described in terms of her five stages of grief. Kübler-Ross said the end of dying and grieving is acceptance, but while these parents might accept the deaths of their children in the sense that they knew it was true, it was not acceptance as defined by Kübler-Ross. I wrote an article showing the historical roots of her idea of acceptance (Klass, 1981), and turned to other scholarship into which the data from bereaved parents might fit.

John Bowlby published the third volume in his trilogy, *Attachment and Loss* (1969–80), just as I began listening to the bereaved parents. In it he developed the attachment model of grief he had sketched in his 1961 essay "Processes of Mourning." I read his work carefully, but my data did not fit into the Bowlby model, or into the growing body of scholarship on grief that grew from Bowlby's work (Parkes, 1972; Parkes & Weiss, 1983). As I wrote up my first extended report of my observations with the parents, I included an appendix detailing the problems with the Bowlby model (1988), and edited the appendix into an article (Klass, 1986–7).

Briefly, the problem with Bowlby's attachment model is that he excluded what we later called continuing bonds from any notion of the healthy resolution of grief. When he rejected the psychoanalysis of his day, Bowlby replaced Freud's drive theory and metapsychology with the attachment instinct. Bowlby used the word attachment in place of the psychoanalytic term cathexis. In Freud, the paradigmatic grief is the young child's loss of its immediate cathexis with its mother in the Oedipus drama. The resolution of the Oedipus drama was the internalization of the parent. Internalization made the representation of the parent part of the ego in that the child identified with the parent. The internalization was thus a split in the ego, creating the ego ideal in the earlier version of Freud's metapsychology, the superego in the later version. The internalization/identification was the conscience, the internalized parent who monitors a person's thoughts and actions.

In psychoanalytic theory, then, a continued bond with a dead person would be an identification. In rejecting the Oedipus idea, Bowlby also rejected anything in grief that smacked of identification. The title of my article on Bowlby's model was "John Bowlby's Model of Grief and the Problem of Identification" (Klass, 1986–7). He said that grief without identification might seem like Hamlet without the prince, but that was, he said, his conclusion. In the long period between the first and third volumes of *Attachment and Loss* Bowlby found other ways to describe the resolution of grief. Much of what he said foreshadowed Robert Neimeyer's (2001) constructivist model. But he never connected his rejection of internalization with those newer thoughts.

As I continued in my efforts to understand the bereaved parents, rather than stay within psychological studies in the West, I turned to ancestor rituals in Japan that showed so many similarities to the narratives and rituals the parents developed in the self-help group (Klass, 1996). In retrospect, the move into cross-cultural studies was fortuitous for the development of the continuing bonds model. Many authors in this book use continuing bonds in cultural settings well beyond those in which Phyllis and I first observed them.

In not staying with the Bowlby model, however, I missed a term that later seemed so obvious. Mary Ainsworth was among Bowlby's earliest collaborators (Ainsworth & Bowlby, 1953). Without challenging him directly, she transformed his understanding of attachment into mother–child bonding. Ainsworth's modification was not a radical innovation. Donald Winnicott's (1966) catchphrase that there is no such thing as a baby was common both in and outside psychiatric circles in those days. There is, Winnicott said, always a baby and someone else, the mother or a significant caregiver. Thus, Winnicott said, the mother and baby function together as one unit. Ainsworth simply brought Winnicott's observation into the Bowlby attachment model.

A bond is, in common parlance, love. Love is not a thing. It is not a feeling or emotional state within the self. Love is a relationship between two or more people. If we are to understand love, even loves that seem pathological to us, we need to include all the parties in our observations.

Bowlby used Ainsworth's findings on children's stranger anxiety, but he does not seem to have recognized how significantly she had revised his model. Bowlby's own history might help us understand why he continued to see attachment as a psychiatric construct (see Van Dijken, 1998). He was raised by nannies. He had almost no connection with his own mother. She was away for long stretches, and when she was home, he saw her only an hour a day after teatime. When he was three years old, the nurturing nanny who had cared for him from infancy left the family and was replaced by a nanny who was emotionally distant. When he was 10, he was sent away to boarding school. Thus, Bowlby's own biography made him sensitive to the children separated from their mothers, but did not provide him with the basis to deeply understand the intersubjective nature of the mother–child bond. He continued to see attachment as an instinct that can be described in individual behaviors.

The caregiver–child bond made its way quickly into early childhood education and child psychology that was outside psychoanalysis. Bonding was central to my wife's graduate studies in child development and to her work, especially as she implemented an out-of-home daycare program for children at risk of abuse and neglect, and then as she was research director for a home visiting program. Carol's book on home visiting (Klass, 2008) is about strengthening a healthy bond between parents and children. She and I often talked about the similarities between what she observed in her work with parents and children and what I observed among bereaved parents.

As I reflect on it now, I am astonished that I missed appropriating the term bond that was so central to the intellectual and professional component of our marriage, but that's what happened. Indeed at a conference when Carol described my interest in ancestor worship to a child development expert from Japan, the Japanese woman gave Carol references to research that studied differences in mother–child bonding in Japan and North America. Those studies helped me understand how the dynamics of grief are different in traditional Japan when the cultural value is dependence compared with when the cultural value is autonomy, as it is in the developed West (Klass, 1996; see Goss & Klass, 2005). Thus, although I was using scholarship based on mother–child bonding, I did not use the term bonds to describe what I observed in the bereaved parents until that Saturday morning when we were putting away the groceries.

I have been gratified over the last 20 years as the term has taken on a life of its own and been useful to so many scholars and clinicians. I hope that by putting so much scholarly and clinical work in one volume, we can foster the kind of cross-fertilization and collaboration that has characterized the continuing bonds model of grief from its beginning.

References

Ainsworth, M.D.S. (1983). Mary D. Salter Ainsworth. In A.N. O'Connell & N.F. Russo (Eds) *Models of Achievement: Reflections of Eminent Women in Psychology* (pp. 200–219). New York: Columbia University Press.

Ainsworth, M.D.S., & Bowlby, J., (1953). *Research Strategy in the Study of Mother–child Separation*. Paris: Courrier de la Centre International de L'Enfance.

Benedek, T. (1975). Discussion of parenthood as a developmental phase. *Journal of the American Psychoanalytic Association, 23*, 154–165.

Bowlby, J. (1961). Processes of mourning. *International Journal of Psychoanalysis, 42*, 317–340.

Bowlby, J. (1969–80). *Attachment and Loss*. New York: Basic Books.
    Volume 1: 1969 *Attachment*.
    Volume 2: 1973 *Separation: Anxiety and Anger*.
    Volume 3: 1980 *Loss: Sadness and Depression*.

Fairbairn, W.R.D. (1952). *Psychological Studies of the Personality*. London: Routledge & Kegan Paul

Goss, R., & Klass, D. (2005). *Dead but Not Lost: Grief Narratives in Religious Traditions*. Walnut Creek, CA: AltaMira Press.

Kernberg, O.F. (1976). *Object–Relations Theory and Clinical Psychoanalysis*. New York: Aronson.

Klass, C.S. (2008). *The Home Visitor's Guidebook: Promoting Optimal Parent and Child Development*, 3rd edition. Baltimore, MD: Paul Brooks Publishing Company (first edition 1996, second edition 2003).

Klass, D. (1981). Elisabeth Kübler-Ross and the traditions of the private sphere: An analysis of symbols. *Omega, Journal of Death and Dying, 12*, 241–267.

Klass, D. (1986–7). John Bowlby's model of grief and the problem of identification. *Omega, Journal of Death and Dying, 18*, 13–32.

Klass, D. (1988). *Parental Grief: Solace and Resolution*. New York: Springer Publishing Company.

Klass, D. (1996). Ancestor worship in Japan: Dependence and the resolution of grief. *Omega, Journal of Death and Dying, 33*, 279–302.

Klass, D. (1999). *The Spiritual Lives of Bereaved Parents*. Philadelphia, PA: Brunner/Mazel.

Klass, D., Silverman, P.R., & Nickman, S.L. (Eds) (1996). *Continuing Bonds: New Understandings of Grief*. London, UK: Taylor & Francis.

Neimeyer, R.A. (Ed.). (2001). *Meaning Reconstruction and the Experience of Loss*. Washington, D.C.: American Psychological Association.

Parkes, C.M. (1972). *Bereavement: Studies of Grief in Adult Life*. London: Tavistock Publications (2nd edition 1986, 3rd edition 1996).

Parkes, C.M., & Weiss, R.W. (1983). *Recovery from Bereavement*. New York: Basic Books.

Rubin, S.S. (1981). A two-track model of bereavement: Theory and research. *American Journal of Orthopsychiatry*, *51*(1), 101–109.

Unruh, D.R. (1983). Death and personal history: Strategies of identity preservation. *Social Problems*, *30*(3) 240–251.

Van Dijken, S. (1998). *John Bowlby: His Early Life – A Biographical Journey into the Roots of Attachment Theory*. London: Free Association Books.

Walter, T. (1996). Bereavement and Biography. *Mortality*, *1*(1), 7–25.

Winnicott, D.W. (1996). *The Family and Individual Development*. New York: Basic Books.

CONTRIBUTORS

David E. Balk is a professor at Brooklyn College where he chairs the Department of Health and Nutrition Sciences and directs graduate studies in thanatology. His research has examined adolescent bereavement following the death of siblings. For the past several years his primary focus has been on bereavement and college students.

Julie Beischel received her doctorate in pharmacology and toxicology in 2003. She is the cofounder and director of research at the Windbridge Institute where she performs research examining mediums' accuracy, experiences, psychology, and physiology, and the potential social applications of mediumship readings. She is the author of *Investigating Mediums*.

Mia W. Biran was born in Haifa, Israel. She completed her PhD degree in clinical psychology at Rutgers University, New Jersey. She is currently professor emeritus at Miami University, Ohio, and a faculty member of the Cincinnati Psychoanalytic Institute where she teaches and supervises psychoanalysis trainees.

Mark Boccuzzi is a cofounder and researcher at the Windbridge Institute where he conducts empirical after-death communication research. He is a recipient of grants from the Helene Reeder Memorial Fund for Research into Life after Death and the Parapsychological Association's Gilbert Roller Fund. He is the author of *Visualizing Intention*.

Harold K. Bush is a professor of English at Saint Louis University and author most recently of *Continuing Bonds with the Dead: Parental Grief and Nineteenth-Century American Authorship*. He is also lead editor of *The Letters of Mark Twain and Joseph H. Twichell*. His first novel, *The Hemingway Files*, appeared in the summer of 2017.

Contributors

Celia H.Y. Chan is associate professor of the Department of Social Work and Social Administration at the University of Hong Kong. Her major areas of research and evidence-based practice include developing an integrated body–mind–spirit model on health and mental health issues, counselling on sex and reproductive health, and regulating assisted reproduction technologies and third-party conception.

Ide S.F. Chan is a clinical psychologist at Queen Elizabeth Hospital in Hong Kong. She has worked in the field for more than 20 years and deals with a number of clinical problems like pain management, trauma, cardiac rehabilitation, and bereavement. Her doctoral thesis focused on continuing bonds after death.

Amy Y.M. Chow is an associate professor in the Department of Social Work and Social Administration at the University of Hong Kong, and project coordinator of the Jockey Club End-of-Life Community Care Project. She is chairperson of the International Workgroup of Death, Dying and Bereavement. Her research interests include bereavement, end-of-life care, and death and dying.

Callum E. Cooper is based at the University of Northampton within its Centre for the Study of Anomalous Psychological Processes. He is the author of over 30 papers in psychology and parapsychology, a dozen book chapters, and four edited and authored books. He received the 2009 Eileen J. Garrett Scholarship Award. His teaching and research interests include thanatology, parapsychology, positive psychology, sexual behavior, and research methods.

Michael Robert Dennis is an associate professor in the Department of Communication at Emporia State University. He investigates prevention of loss from health communication perspectives, cognition and communication in surviving loss, eulogies, elegies, and grief self-help books. He introduced the study of the "grief account" in 2008.

Candy H.C. Fong is a senior training officer in the Faculty of Social Sciences at the University of Hong Kong. Her areas of research interests include integrative body–mind–spirit intervention, psychosocial oncology, palliative and end-of-life care, grief, and bereavement care.

Elizabeth A. Gassin is a professor of psychology at Olivet Nazarene University and a licensed counselor. She received her PhD from the University of Wisconsin-Madison. Her recent research focuses on linking forgiveness and various bereavement processes. She has also written in the area of ritual studies.

Jacqueline Hayes is a lecturer in counseling psychology and a humanistic psychotherapist at the University of Roehampton, London. For her doctoral studies she investigated experiences of continuing presence in bereavement, focusing on the phenomenological and pragmatic characteristics of these as well as how the bereaved make sense of them.

Lorraine Hedtke teaches about a narrative approach to death and bereavement throughout the United States and internationally. She is a professor of counseling at California State University San Bernardino and an Associate of the Taos Institute. She has written several books about the philosophical and practical intersections of narrative counseling and grief psychology.

Hani M. Henry is an associate professor of psychology and chair of the Sociology, Anthropology, Psychology and Egyptology Department at the American University in Cairo, Egypt. He received his PhD in clinical psychology from Miami University of Ohio. He has published numerous journal articles on diversity-related issues, such as immigration, acculturation, women's empowerment, and cultural sensitivity in psychotherapy.

Samuel M.Y. Ho is an associate provost and professor of psychology at the City University of Hong Kong. His primary research interest is in traumatology and resilience under adversity. As a registered clinical psychologist and researcher, Ho conducts basic research to further the understanding of applied problems as well as using applied issues to explore empirical research.

An Hooghe is a clinical psychologist and marriage and family therapist working in Belgium. Besides her clinical practice with bereaved couples and families, she conducts research on couples talking and not talking with each other about their grief. She is also a trainer in marriage and family therapy at the University of Leuven, Belgium.

Jack Hunter is an anthropologist of consciousness, religion, and the paranormal. His doctoral research with the University of Bristol examines spirit mediumship and its influence on the development of self-concepts. He is the editor of *Talking with the Sprits*, *Strange Dimensions*, and *Damned Facts*. He currently teaches A-level religious studies and sociology.

Melissa D. Irwin is a doctoral candidate in sociology at Kansas University. She specializes in thanatology and online social networking behavior. Her work on Facebook memorial pages appeared in *Omega: Journal of Death and Dying*, and pending publications explore the role of nouveau spiritualism and technology in after-death communication.

Elaine Kasket is a counseling psychologist with a particular interest in psychology and digital-age technologies. She has written and spoken extensively on how the digital era is transforming grieving and memorialization. In addition to her private practice, she is principal lecturer and head of programs for counseling psychology at Regent's University London.

Dennis Klass is professor emeritus at Webster University. He first studied bereavement in 1968 when he was an assistant in Elisabeth Kübler-Ross's Death and Dying Seminar at the University of Chicago Hospitals. Klass is the author of *Parental Grief: Solace and Resolution, The Spiritual Lives of Bereaved Parents*, and coauthor of *Dead but not Lost: Grief Narratives in Religious Traditions*. He coedited *Continuing Bonds: New Understandings of Grief*.

Phyllis S. Kosminsky is a clinical social worker specializing in life-threatening illness and grief. Over the past 22 years, Dr. Kosminsky has provided individual counseling to hundreds of bereaved individuals and has conducted trainings for mental health professionals nationally and internationally on the treatment of normal and problematic grief. She coauthored *Attachment-Informed Grief Therapy: The Clinician's Guide to Foundations and Applications*.

Adrianne Kunkel is a professor in the Department of Communication Studies at the University of Kansas. Her research focuses on emotional support/coping processes in personal relationships and support group settings, grief and communication, romantic relationship (re)definition processes, sex/gender similarities and differences, sexual harassment, and domestic violence intervention.

Bobo H.P. Lau is an educator and researcher of health psychology and gerontology. After obtaining her doctorate in health psychology, she worked as a senior training officer in a community end-of-life care project at the Faculty of Social Sciences of the University of Hong Kong and then as a post-doctoral researcher in the same institution. Her research interests include end-of-life care, caregiving, mind–body interventions, and reproductive loss.

Paisley Lewis is a doctoral student in the health psychology program at the University of North Carolina, Charlotte. Her research interests involve the role of exercise in natural environments in assisting trauma survivors and promoting posttraumatic growth.

Renata MacDougal brings an archaeological understanding to ancient ritual practices, with a particular interest in mortuary ritual and the development of belief systems. MacDougal has participated in several archaeological expeditions and teaches university courses on ancient women, ritual, history, religion, and magic. She holds degrees in the ancient Near East and a doctorate in archaeology from the University of Leicester.

Ruth Malkinson is director of training at the International Center for the Study of Loss, Bereavement and Resilience, University of Haifa. She is past president of the Israeli Association for Family and Marital Therapy. Her field of expertise is cognitive-behavioral therapy/rational emotive behavior therapy in bereavement and trauma with individuals, couples, and families.

Chad Mosher lives in Tucson, Arizona and works as a clinical coordinator for a community mental health agency. In addition, Mosher is a research associate with the Windbridge Institute. His clinical expertise focuses on gender identity, sexuality, spirituality, and culturally responsive integrated healthcare practices.

Robert A. Neimeyer is a professor of psychology at the University of Memphis, where he also maintains an active clinical practice. Neimeyer has published 30 books, including *Techniques of Grief Therapy: Creative Practices for Counseling the Bereaved*, and serves as editor of the journal *Death Studies*. The author of nearly 500 articles and book chapters and a frequent workshop presenter, he is currently working to advance a more adequate theory of grieving as a meaning-making process.

Ana I. Orejuela-Dávila is a doctoral student in the Health Psychology Program at the University of North Carolina, Charlotte. Her research interests include the role of emotion regulation in posttraumatic growth, as well as how ethnic and racial minorities experience growth within the context of oppression.

Simon Shimshon Rubin is director of the International Center for the Study of Loss, Bereavement and Human Resilience at the University of Haifa in Israel where he is chairman of the Postgraduate Psychotherapy Program and professor of psychology. An active clinician and researcher, his work focuses on ethics, loss, and psychotherapy.

Anastasia (Tasia) Philippa Scrutton is an associate professor in philosophy and religion at the University of Leeds. She works on philosophy of religion and religion and mental health. Recent publications include "Two Christian theologies of depression" and "Why not believe in an evil God?"

Edith Maria Steffen is a lecturer in counseling psychology at the University of Roehampton, London, as well as a practicing counseling psychologist. Her doctoral research focused on sense of presence experiences in bereavement and meaning-making. Collaborating with Robert Neimeyer and colleagues, she currently undertakes research into meaning-oriented group grief therapy.

William B. Stiles is professor emeritus of psychology at Miami University, Oxford, Ohio, USA, and adjunct professor of psychology at Appalachian State University. He has been president of Division 29 (Psychotherapy) of the American Psychological Association and of the Society for Psychotherapy Research. He has served as editor of *Psychotherapy Research* and *Person-Centered and Experiential Psychotherapies*. He has published more than 300 journal articles and book chapters.

Richard Tedeschi is a professor in the Department of Psychological Science at the University of North Carolina, Charlotte. He is a practicing clinical psychologist with a specialty in trauma and bereavement, and conducts research on posttraumatic growth and how people may experience personal transformation in the aftermath of trauma.

Christine Valentine is a member of the Centre for Death and Society at the University of Bath. Her research and publications include continuing bonds in Britain and Japan, funeral welfare systems for people on low incomes, funeral directing in the 21st century, and bereavement following drug or alcohol-related deaths.

Mary Alice Varga is an assistant professor of educational research and the director of the School Improvement Doctoral Program in the Department of Leadership, Research, and School Improvement at the University of West Georgia. She currently serves on the Board for the Association of Death and Education Counseling and conducts research on student grief and online grief support.

Tony Walter is honorary professor of death studies at the University of Bath. His most recent books are *Social Death* (coauthored with Jana Králová) and *What Death Means Now: Thinking Critically About Dying and Grieving*.

Eliezer Witztum is a professor in the Division of Psychiatry, Faculty of Health Sciences, Ben-Gurion University of the Negev and Director of the School for Psychotherapy, Mental Health Center, Beer Sheva. He specializes in cultural psychiatry, trauma and bereavement, strategic and short-term dynamic psychotherapy, treatment of pedophiles, and the history of psychiatry.

1

INTRODUCTION

Continuing Bonds—20 Years On

Dennis Klass and Edith Maria Steffen

Since the continuing bonds model of grief was introduced into bereavement studies in *Continuing Bonds: New Understandings of Grief* (1996), it has been extended from its origins in psychology into other disciplines and adopted in a surprising range of cross-cultural studies. In turn, developments in other cultures and disciplines have fed back into the psychological study and treatment of grief. We think the far-flung developments provide a solid basis for new directions in research and practice. The purposes of this anthology are, first, to show the range of ways the continuing bonds model has been used; second, to trace how the model has been expanded and enriched through this process of cross-fertilization and proliferation; and third, to encourage further cross-fertilization by having so many of the developments together in the same book.

While there appears to be a consensus that continuing bonds are a central aspect of grief, some active discussions and ongoing controversies remain. For example, there are disagreements about the nature of the bonds, how they fit into cultural narratives, and how "adaptive" they are when viewed in the context of Western mental health. We find stark differences in the scholarly discourses, as well as in lay opinion about the reality status of the deceased people with whom the living remain bonded and sharp differences about the empirical reality of the experiences through which continuing bonds are often experienced.

Most sides of the disagreements are represented by authors in this book. We do not think it is helpful, however, to cast the differences in either/or statements or in oppositional language. We are bringing together many developments and perspectives because we hope that by having so diverse a collection in one place, readers will find connections across disciplines, across populations, and across cultures. Furthermore, we hope that by presenting the broad range of settings in which continuing bonds are present and the variety of ways scholars and clinicians think about them, we can begin to develop a broader synthesis in which the views that now seem opposed to each other can all have a place.

In this Introduction we first give a short overview of the continuing bonds model of grief. We have written it especially for readers from outside bereavement studies. Second, we set the developments in the continuing bonds model in the context of other developments in bereavement studies. Third, we describe four overarching themes that struck us as significant threads running through many of the book's chapters. Finally, we outline how the chapters are organized. At the beginning of each of the book's sections we have a brief introduction of the topic and chapters in that section.

The Origins of the Continuing Bonds Model of Grief

The book's Prologue is a personal account of the origins of the term continuing bonds. The next few pages briefly sketch an overview of the scholarly background for readers who are unfamiliar with the history of the continuing bonds model of grief.

Even though scholarship and clinical work on continuing bonds are now grounded in many cultures, the model grew out of the discovery that the then-dominant Western model of grief did not account for important aspects of the experiences of bereaved people. This model replaced the theory of grief work that was rooted in an exaggerated, if not, some might say, obsessive adoption of some passages in Freud's (1961) essay *Mourning and Melancholia*, published in 1917. He said that in the work of grief:

> Reality-testing has shown that the loved object no longer exists, and it proceeds to demand that all libido shall be withdrawn from its attachments to that object. This demand arouses understandable opposition . . . people never willingly abandon a libidinal position, not even, indeed, when a substitute is already beckoning to them. This opposition can be so intense that a turning away from reality takes place and a clinging to the object through the medium of a hallucinatory wishful psychosis.
>
> *(p. 223)*

In *Mourning and Melancholia*, Freud did not present any case material on the resolution of grief. When his daughter Sophie died, and later when her son died, Freud did not use the idea of grief work to understand his sorrow (see Klass, 2014). Right after Sophie died Freud connected how he responded to his lack of any religious sense.

> Since I am profoundly irreligious there is no one I can accuse, and I know there is nowhere to which any complaint could be addressed. . . . Quite deep down I can trace the feelings of a deep narcissistic hurt that is not to be healed. My wife and Annerl are terribly shaken in a more human way.
>
> *(Jones, 1957, p. 20)*

Nine years after Sophie died, on what would have been her thirty-sixth birthday, he wrote to Ludwig Binswanger whose child had just died. He said he remained unconsoled (*ungetröstet*).

> One knows that the acute grief after such a loss will lapse, but one will remain unconsoled, never find a substitute. (*Man weiß, daß die akute Trauer nach einem solchen Verlust ablaufen wird, aber man wird ungetröstet bleiben, nie einen Ersatz finden.*)
>
> (Freud, 1960, p. 383)

Yet, for the next seven decades the overwhelming consensus among psychologists and psychiatrists was that for successful mourning to take place the mourner must disengage from the deceased, let go of the past, and move on.

The psychoanalytic idea of grief work was a radical change from the sentimental attachment to the dead in the middle and upper classes before the First World War. In "Footsteps of Angels," a poem that was republished several times over the nineteenth century, Henry Wadsworth Longfellow described a visit from his wife, Mary, who died during a miscarriage in 1835:

> With a slow and noiseless footstep
> Comes that messenger divine,
> Takes the vacant chair beside me,
> Lays her gentle hand in mine.
>
> . . .
>
> Uttered not, yet comprehended,
> Is the spirit's voiceless prayer,
> Soft rebukes, in blessings ended,
> Breathing from her lips of air.

In the Freudian model, the poem would be evidence of Longfellow's incomplete grieving.

Freud's concept of grief work remained largely within the psychoanalytic circle until 1944, when Erich Lindemann (1979) began the contemporary discourse about grief. He defined acute grief as a psychiatric syndrome. Lindemann, who was a leader in the mental health movement in psychiatry, accepted the grief work model uncritically. That is, he thought that the task of grief was to sever the bonds with the dead, thus freeing the survivors to form new relationships that served individuals in their changed social environment. The concept passed quickly into popular usage. Lindemann thus codified the underdeveloped ideas about grieving of Freud's essay, thereby giving the culture the concepts to make grief an individual matter for which psychiatric and psychological concepts and diagnoses provided the best explanations and paths to resolution.

Within the psychological/psychiatric hegemony, continuing an attachment with the dead was regarded as pathological grief. Widows beginning to date or marrying again was counted as evidence that they were over their grief. It was as if a woman could develop a new relationship with a man only if her deceased husband was fully out of her life.

That theory proved inadequate to the data. In the 1980s, several researchers reported that seemingly well-adjusted survivors did not sever their bonds with the dead. People who continued their bonds said their ongoing relationship with a significant dead person helped them cope with the death, and supported their better self. Tony Walter put it succinctly:

> The purpose of grief is . . . the construction of a durable biography that enables the living to integrate the memory of the dead into their ongoing lives; the process by which this is achieved is principally conversation with others who knew the deceased.
>
> *(1996, p. 7)*

A bond with the deceased continues, but also changes the multi-dimensional bond with the living person. All the history in bonds between people when they were living continues into the bond after they die, although as we see in several of this book's chapters, survivors may have opportunities to reshape the bond that they did not have when the person was living.

Phenomena that indicate active continuing bonds are a sense of presence, experiences of the deceased person in any of the senses, belief in the person's continuing active influence on thoughts or events, or a conscious incorporation of the characteristics or virtues of the dead into the self. In individuals a continuing bond includes the part of the self actualized in the bond with the person, characterizations and thematic memories of the deceased person, and the emotional states connected with the characterizations and memories. Living people play roles, often complex, within the family and psychic system. After they die, roles change, but the dead can still be significant members of families and communities. Continuing bonds are, then, not simply mental constructs – that is, they are not just an idea, or a feeling.

The editors of *Continuing Bonds: New Understandings of Grief* never said they had developed a new model. They said their book articulated the consensus that had emerged among many bereavement scholars. Most psychological models of grief now accept that continuing bonds are a normal aspect of grief. George Hagman's edited book (2016) shows that even some psychoanalysts accept that continuing bonds are normal.

Continuing Bonds in Bereavement Studies and Interventions

Although *Continuing Bonds: New Understandings of Grief* did not contain any chapters specifically addressing how continuing bonds may present themselves or be worked with in the consulting room, the book's very inception was first and foremost a response to clinical perspectives, to the psychoanalytic theories that had informed them, and to the clinical practices that had arisen as a result of how these theories had been received, interpreted, and passed on. The grief work model became increasingly simplistic, one-sided, and removed from either scientific or human truths.

The 1996 book became, then, a call to the clinical community to stop, look around, and take note of the clinical evidence that did not fit into the dominant model. Within a few years continuing bonds were an accepted aspect of grief in the psychological descriptions of grief and in clinical practice.

Not surprisingly, the early questions for clinicians and psychological research-ers were whether continuing bonds contributed to "healthy" resolutions of grief, and then to what kinds of bonds were better for the bereaved than others. An early empirical strand of research investigated the "adaptiveness" of not breaking bonds to the dead. The research used measures of grief intensity and the attach-ment styles identified in Ainsworth's stranger anxiety studies that were noted in the Prologue, but retained Bowlby's understanding of attachment as a psychiat-ric construct measurable in individuals (e.g. Field et al., 2003; Stroebe & Schut, 2005). By searching for what may be "maladaptive" or "unhealthy" about contin-uing bonds (without, however, making transparent who decides what is healthy or unhealthy), that strand of research preserved a prescriptive medical model. The chapter by Samuel Ho and Ide Chan in this book shows the limitations of this research strand in a Chinese cultural setting.

It was tempting to move from the idea of continuing bonds being pathologi-cal, to continuing bonds as normal, and then to continuing bonds as good. Ten years on, in a response to the contributions in a special issue of *Death Studies* on continuing bonds, one of us (Klass, 2006) reminded readers that it was never the intention to replace old simplistic and prescriptive formulas with new ones. As many chapters in this book show, we have now moved to a more nuanced understanding of how the bonds function in individual and family life in different cultural settings, as well as how they function in the therapy process itself.

At the same time that the continuing bonds model was being enlarged, a group of researchers, largely quantitative, was pressing to define grief that merited treatment by mental health professionals. Rather than call it pathological, it was labeled prolonged grief disorder or complicated grief. Defining grief as a psychiat-ric diagnosis is part of what Heidi Rimke and Deborah Brock call "the shrinking spectrum of normalcy":

> The idea that some people are psychologically sick or disordered reflects the growth of the pathological approach, a distinctly Western and recent historical phenomenon, in which it is assumed that personal problems are individual and caused by biological and/or psychological factors.
>
> *(2012, p. 182)*

As we decided whom to invite as contributors to *Continuing Bonds: New Directions for Research and Practice*, we did not want to isolate the experience of those seek-ing help from clinicians from those who do not, nor did we want to paint a picture of "healthy grieving" versus "pathological grieving" or of "adaptive" versus "maladaptive" continuing bonds. Instead, we wanted to open windows on the complex interweavings within diverse manifestations of continuing and discontinuing bonds in a nuanced way. We did not want to separate the psychological from the social and cultural but to see these as interlinked in complex ways. The scholarship, well represented in this book, that has grown around the construct of continuing bonds from disciplines other than psychology is as important for clinical practice as the latest empirical research in clinical and counseling psychology.

The authors in this book are, then, for the most part reluctant to see pathology in grief as anything more than a cultural matter. That is, all cultures have guidelines for grieving and expectations of bereaved people. Among the book's authors, the underlying viewpoint is that we should avoid drawing simplistic causal relationships and should be particularly careful when it comes to telling people how they should live – and grieve. By and large, then, scholars and clinicians who are extending and clarifying the continuing bonds model avoid getting involved in the questions of clinical diagnosis. The issues involved in labeling pathology show up in a few chapters in this book, but most of the chapters leave the matter aside.

Four Themes in the Book

A lot has happened in the way we understand continuing bonds and the issues to which the continuing bonds model has been applied since it was introduced. Few of the developments have happened in a straight line. Rather, as the chapters in this book show, the idea has been incorporated into a widely diverse set of clinical, cultural, and scholarly discourses.

We invited chapters from people we think have interesting, important, and novel contributions to the model. When we sent out invitations we had a provisional table of contents, but it was quite different from what we now have. As authors sent proposals and as we received drafts, we tried to let the structure of the book develop from the ground up rather than by fitting chapters into a preconceived order. The contributions we received in response to our invitations often surprised us in the directions they took and in the new insights they generated. One of the delights of editing the book has been our correspondence with many of the book's authors as we responded to early drafts, and they helped us understand the implications of what they had written. In the conversations, however, we cannot claim to have found an outline in which all the ideas and directions in the chapters neatly fit. The book reflects the far-flung developments in the idea of continuing bonds.

In the next parts of this Introduction we try to articulate four overarching themes that struck us as significant threads running through many of the chapters. Obviously, the themes interweave and overlap in interesting ways, but we think it is useful to separate out themes as a way of facilitating conversations. We hope that as readers make their way through the book, they will find themes and connections that did not occur to us as we edited. The continuing bonds model of grief has been crowd-sourced from its beginning. We invited contributors who, we thought, would keep the process going. We hope the authors' ideas and writing styles encourage readers to join the process of expanding and deepening how we understand continuing bonds.

Theme 1: Continuing Bonds Are Intersubjective

As was noted in the Prologue, the term continuing bonds comes from the way Mary Ainsworth's word "bond" is used in the field of child development. The mother–child bond is not the individual instinct. It is intersubjective. We can define intersubjectivity simply as the experience or reality that exists between two or more conscious minds, whether two people in the therapy room or all the citizens of a nation. Grieving is a relationship between the bereaved and the dead who are now, in varying degrees, both absent and present. As lonely as we might feel in grief, the longing is itself a relationship with the person who used to fill the now-empty place.

Grief, with its continuing bonds, is intersubjective between the individual griever and community of people to whom they are bonded. Even at the biological level grief is characterized by intersubjectivity. One side of the biological response is expressed by crying and withdrawal. The other side is reaching out to others for a close intimate connection. Crying elicits a response from others. A grieving person's words and feelings often prompt a hug or other culturally appropriate comforting gestures from those around them, thus inviting them back into communion with others. Grief thus creates the intersubjective spaces described in many of the book's chapters.

When the idea of continuing bonds was first introduced, researchers and clinicians recognized them in individual grief. A theme that weaves though many chapters in this anthology is that bonds with the dead are not individual; they are interpersonal: they are woven into the complex bonds individuals maintain with intimate others within the communities and the overarching narratives that structure the culture in which their lives and bonds are set. Intersubjectivity is relevant not only for culturally focused disciplines such as anthropology or religious studies, but perhaps even more so for mental health professionals who too often regard continuing bonds as individual psychic phenomena. The bonds are, as we see in this book, a great deal more than an attachment between two separate entities, one of which is merely a "representation." It seems that conceptualizing continuing bonds as individual phenomena is demonstrably misleading, because our ongoing relationships with the dead are elements in our larger social and cultural attachments, and form part of our personal and social identities.

Many of the chapters in this book are set in grief's intersubjective spaces. Rituals and religious beliefs in every culture provide intersubjective spaces. In contemporary Western culture, counseling and psychotherapy, the setting for many chapters in this book, is a socially sanctioned intersubjective space. Many cultures, including our own, have specialists such as mediums who can call back the dead, communicate what the dead need from the living, or speak for the dead. In one sense psychological counseling/therapy has moved into the intersubjective space that was previously the province of mediums. Recognizing that continuing bonds are real and true, in whatever sense, brings us to a question in the book of how the work of mediums is like, unlike, or can be coordinated with grief counseling/therapy.

The intersubjective spaces in which bonds continue have been expanded by the introduction of social media such as Facebook. In the last Section in the book, three chapters argue that the new technology creates new forms of relationships between the living and the dead, and new forms of an intersubjective community of grief. A few chapters in the book move beyond person-to-person interactions to continuing bonds, to the continuing bonds that are part of our larger cultural memberships and our ethnic, national, and religious membership.

Theme 2: Continuing Bonds Are an Important Aspect of Finding or Constructing Meaning

Some deaths present a challenge to individual, family, and sometimes larger cultural narratives because the deaths seem to make no sense. They can throw survivors into an existential crisis that requires them to engage in a search for meaning (Balk, 1999; Benore & Park, 2004; Frankl, 1959). Making meaning is making sense of the events leading to the death and around the death, making sense of our relationship to the deceased, and making sense of our ongoing lives after the death. Meaning and meaning-making in bereavement have always had an important place in the continuing bonds model, for example in the cultural meanings that are invoked in the narratives on which we draw to frame our connections with the deceased.

We know that meaning-making is not an individual process. Meaning is created, transformed, and sustained within communities. Communities, ranging from groups of friends to nations and religions, offer narratives that are the templates from which individuals construct their individual and family narratives. In other words, meaning is socially constructed. Robert Neimeyer, Dennis Klass, and Michael Robert Dennis, one of the co-editors of this book and two of the authors, sketched what appears to be the emerging social constructionist model of bereavement that defines grief as a *situated interpretive and communicative activity*:

> By "situated," we mean to emphasize that mourning is a function of a given social, historical and cultural context; by "interpretive," we draw attention to the meaning-making processes it entails; by "communicative," we stress the essential embeddedness of such processes in written, spoken, and nonverbally performed exchanges with others; and by "activity," we underscore that grieving and mourning are active verbs, not merely states to be endured. In sum, "the work of grief," in our view, involves reaffirmation or reconstruction of a world of meaning that has been challenged by loss, at social as well as individual levels, in a specific cultural and historical frame.
>
> *(2014, p. 486)*

The best way to understand grief, then, is as an interaction between interior, interpersonal, communal, and cultural narratives by which individuals and communities construct the meaning of the deceased's life and death, as well as the post-death status of the bereaved within the broader community.

To understand continuing bonds, it matters how we conceptualize interactions with the dead ontologically, i.e. in what ways our cultural and personal narratives permit us to perceive and experience the relationship as real. As we will see in some contributions to this volume, for example in Anastasia Scrutton's chapter, meanings are not just belief and ideas, but are often experienced within ritual and shared experience. While continuing bonds appear to be a cross-cultural phenomenon, the meanings ascribed vary significantly from context to context. A number of chapters in this book focus on culturally mediated diverse understandings of continuing bonds. This includes not only the diversity of meaning across broader cultural frameworks but also the creation of different meanings across a diversity of cultural channels, for example eulogy patterns, communication styles of mediums, or novel social conventions about how to maintain bonds with the deceased and what they mean as practiced in social media.

At a more micro level, meanings can also be seen as depending on the nature and history of the relationship with the deceased who is still present and alive for the bereaved. Some chapters, particularly in Section II, show how specific continuing bonds between persons play out, how difficulties in such a relationship may impact on the survivor who comes to counseling, and how working on the relationship can lead to active – and beneficial – changes in the meanings that are made.

Meaning-making, and meaning reconstruction, are frequently central processes in bereavement (Neimeyer, 2016). Both meaning-as-comprehensibility and meaning-as-significance, or sense-making and benefit-finding (Davis, Nolen-Hoeksema, & Larson, 1998), can be enhanced through the continuing bond with the deceased. A number of chapters in the clinical section of this book explicitly deal with this aspect. Grief therapy techniques can be employed to access what Robert Neimeyer calls the back story of the relationship with the deceased in order for the bereaved to regain attachment security and address unfinished business in the relationship. There is an intertwinement here of meaning-making and continuing bonds in which each helps the other.

The importance of continuing bonds for meaning-making is not only relevant within clinical contexts. The experience of continuing bonds also invites us to rethink our understandings about what are often considered to be polar opposites: life and death, presence and absence, mind and matter, self and other. The paradox of continuing bonds seems to cut through this dialectic and may stimulate openness to different existential possibilities in a consciousness-expanding way, something that is further elaborated in the chapter on posttraumatic growth and continuing bonds by Richard Tedeschi and his colleagues.

Theme 3: The Continuing Bonds Model Raises Questions about the Sense in which Continuing Bonds with the Dead Are Real and/or in What Sense They Are True

When we say continuing bonds are a part of normal short-term and long-term grief, the question almost all Western bereaved people ask is also the scholarly question: Are those whose presence we feel really there? Are the voices we hear or the glimpses we catch of them just our imagination? Can we trust the deep truths continuing bonds seem to have for our lives? The answers to these questions are the focus of many chapters in the book, and assumptions about the answers are found in all the chapters. The theme, then, is about the ontology of continuing bonds. Ontology is the philosophical study of what exists and what does not. The word literally means *the study of being.*

When the purpose of grief was to detach from the dead because, as Freud said, "the object no longer exists" (1961, p. 223), the phenomena by which people continued their bonds were not real. If the grief process is completed, the dead are gone. Continuing bonds might be hallucinations, evidence of longing, perhaps necessary illusions that compensate for the loss, but they are only real in the bereaved person's mind.

The continuing bonds model does not allow us so easily to foreclose the ontological status of the dead and the experiences by which we interact with the dead. The question the continuing bonds model raises for philosophers, as well as for lay bereaved people, is: What is the ontological status of continuing bonds?

The question is not an idle one. In both research and counseling, the beliefs of the person asking questions influence how the bereaved people report their experience. If, for example, a researcher thinks hearing a dead person is a hallucination, either consciously or unconsciously the bereaved person knows that some things should be left out of the story. If the counselor thinks the sense of presence is an imagined compensation for the loss, very little in the patient–professional interactions will help bereaved people deal with the ambivalences in the relationship with the person that died, or to stabilize the continuing bond in a way that can be helpful and solace-giving for the rest of their years.

We find a good deal of variation in different cultural contexts in how problematic the ontological status of continuing bonds is. Ontological reality is, for example, more of a problem in contemporary Western culture than in Japan. In the West, the strong inner truth that the survivor is interacting with the dead usually calls forth the claim that the spirits are, in some way, objectively present. Matthew Hamabata, a Japanese-American studying ancestor rituals in a Japanese business family, found that he kept asking about the "real" existence of the dead. He was constantly frustrated because the replies were "It really doesn't matter, does it?" or, "I don't know." Hamabata finally realized, he said, that his questions were framed in Western scientific rationalism. His informants answered in the same framework, so none could say that they believed in the real presence of the dead in an unqualified way. "However, just because they could not claim belief under my scientifically oriented interrogation, it does not necessarily follow that they did not believe in the presence of the dead in the realm of the ritual" (Hamabata, 1990, p. 83).

Section III of the book is devoted to three scholars asking the ontological question, but the ontological theme runs through every chapter either as a focus of study or in the assumptions that undergird the research questions.

Theme 4: Continuing Bonds Are Best Understood within their Cultural Setting and Are Very Useful as We Develop a Model of Grief that Can Be Applied to All Cultures

Continuing bonds have a rich history. We find them from the earliest human narratives we have. They are as culturally diverse as any form of human expression. They constitute a dimension of human experience that can be both challenging and enriching for the bereaved, as well as for those supporting them.

Continuing bonds has proven a useful way to see differences in grief as it is experienced, expressed, and resolved in different cultures. While culture has multiple meanings, as we use the term, culture is how a people or group of peoples construe their world. Cultures provide the map of both visible and invisible reality on which individuals and communities within the culture locate external and internal events, from which individuals discover or choose religious, political, or ideological affiliations, and upon which individuals and communities base moral judgments and actions. That is, cultures provide the templates for how people represent their experience and are, thus, the basis for their actions.

Earlier attempts at cross-cultural studies of grief focused on cultural guidelines for how the emotions of grief should be expressed, or on the meaning systems from which individuals and communities construct grief narratives. Some of those studies were fascinating. Cultural guidelines and meaning systems are, however, so deeply embedded in larger cultural narratives that it is extremely difficult to find broad cross-cultural comparisons (see Klass, 1999).

The introduction of continuing bonds into bereavement studies quickly opened the door to cultural differences. If the dead are included in some cultural narratives and excluded from others, we can look at the reasons in larger cultural dynamics. For example, when a new group takes political power we sometimes find that bonds with the dead support loyalty to the old arrangements of political power; thus, the new group must suppress continuing bonds to foster loyalty to the new holders of political power (see Goss & Klass, 2005).

If the dead are still with us, it is easy to ask in different cultural settings what roles the dead play in individual, family, and community narratives, and to ask by what means the living and the dead communicate with each other. None of those cross-cultural questions were possible when bereavement studies regarded continuing bonds as illusions.

In his chapter Tony Walter begins the project of defining different cultural frames in which the living can experience continuing bonds. He looks at frames that encourage or resist normalizing intercourse between the living and the dead. He also looks at frames that define the dead as needing our care, or needing our remembrance. While Walter's project might seem esoteric to some readers, he makes a strong case that if grief counselors or therapists do not understand the different frames, they risk imposing their own unexamined frame on bereaved people who are using other frames.

The chapters in Section II, on intervention, use a variety of frames to understand people seeking grief therapy as well as the frames of those who offer therapy. Cultural frames set the limits and possibilities in the relationship between the living and the dead. The frames define possible solutions when the continuing bond becomes complicated or problematic for one of the parties.

Using continuing bonds as a lens led to some dramatic changes in the way we look at the writings and artifacts of some cultures. For example, Renata MacDougal's chapter on ancestor rituals in Mesopotamia four thousand years ago challenges over a century of anthropological interpretation. The chapter by Hani Henry and his colleagues shows how continuing bonds helps us understand the grief that is part of migrating from one cultural frame to a new one. The book concludes with chapters on social media as a new cultural frame for continuing bonds.

The Structure of the Book

The four chapters of Section I: Overview of the Continuing Bonds Model shine different lights on the model: theoretical, clinical, historical, sociological, philosophical, literary, and personal, highlighting different facets of the phenomenon, yet sharing an underlying valuing of the complexity, relationality, situatedness, and non-pathological nature of grieving and living with loss. We could have chosen others, but we think that these four together orient readers to the continuing bonds model as it has developed in all its depth and breadth over the first decades of the twenty-first century.

Having situated the subject matter in its broader context, Section II: Continuing Bonds and Clinical Contexts takes the phenomenon back into the consulting room. We hope readers will not lose sight of the complexity and depth elaborated in the opening chapters as we consider different ways of working with continuing bonds in grief therapy and counseling. The chapters draw both on practitioner experience and practice-relevant research to present state-of-the-art innovative practices and research findings.

The clinical section is divided into two subsections. The first, Innovations for Working with Continuing Bonds, consists of six chapters that bring together work from theoretical perspectives based in narrative therapy, meaning reconstruction, positive psychology, and attachment theory. The second, Specific Perspectives for Working with Sense of Presence, houses two chapters which examine therapeutic work around sensing the presence of the deceased. The first chapter studies spontaneous experience of presence and the second advocates for including mediums who induce the sense of presence and assist people with after-death communication.

The contributions in Section II, we think, do some pioneering work. While the 1996 book called for new ways of working, we now have a growing corpus of clinical knowledge that can provide practitioners with information and inspiration for their own work. We hope the clinical section provides practitioners with tastes of the broad fields that may constitute rich resources for their work. We tried, in our invitations to authors in this section, to show innovative approaches and new ideas that can be taken forward into developing practices.

We have already noted that when we regard continuing bonds as normal, not pathological, we cannot avoid asking whether or how the dead are real. The chapters in Section III: The Truth Status and Reality Status of Continuing Bonds focus on the ontological question. We hope readers find these chapters useful as they think through the question for themselves. We also think that readers will find these chapters useful as they look at how authors of the book's other chapters answer the ontological question, and therefore how the reality of continuing bonds determines how the authors structure their research and theory, or how continuing bonds plays a role in counseling techniques.

In Section IV: Continuing Bonds in Cultural Contexts, the authors discuss continuing bonds in cultural narratives. We have divided this Section into two. The first Subsection, Continuing Bonds' Complex Roles in Cultures, explores the relationship of continuing bonds to cultural narratives. The three chapters in the second Subsection, A New Cultural Context: Social Media, discuss the new culture of social media that, the authors claim, create different ways for bereaved people to continue their bond and to have a community that shares the bond.

References

Balk, D.E. (1999). Bereavement and spiritual change. *Death Studies, 23*, 485–493.

Benore, E.R., & Park, C.L. (2004). Death-specific religious beliefs and bereavement: Belief in an afterlife and continued attachment. *The International Journal for the Psychology of Religion, 14*, 1–22.

Davis, C.G., Nolen-Hoeksema, S., & Larson, J. (1998). Making sense of loss and benefiting from the experience: Two construals of meaning. *Journal of Personality and Social Psychology, 75*, 561–574.

Field, N.P., Gal-Oz, E., & Bonanno, G.A. (2003). Continuing bonds and adjustment at 5 years after the death of a spouse. *Journal of Consulting and Clinical Psychology, 71*, 110–117.

Frankl, V.E. (1959). *Man's search for meaning.* New York: Pocket Books.

Freud, E.L. (ed.). (1960). *Sigmund Freud, Briefe 1873–1939.* Frankfurt am Main: Fischer Verlag.

Freud, S. (1961). Mourning and melancholia. In J. Strachey (ed. and trans.), *The standard edition of the complete psychological works of Sigmund Freud* (Vol. 14, pp. 243–258). London: Hogarth Press. (Original work published 1917.)

Goss, R., & Klass, D. (2005). *Dead but not lost: Grief narratives in religious traditions.* Walnut Creek, CA: AltaMira.

Hagman, G. (ed.). (2016). *New models of bereavement theory and treatment: New mourning.* New York: Routledge.

Hamabata, M.M. (1990). *Crested kimono: Power and love in the Japanese business family.* Ithaca, NY: Cornell University Press.

Johnstone, L. (2014). *A straight talking introduction to psychiatric diagnosis.* Monmouth: PCCS Books.

Jones, E. (1957). *Sigmund Freud: Life and work. Vol 3: The last phase 1919–1939.* London: Hogarth Press.

Klass, D. (1999). Developing a cross-cultural model of grief: The state of the field. *Omega, Journal of Death and Dying, 39*(3), 153–178.

Klass, D. (2006). Continuing conversation about continuing bonds. *Death Studies, 30,* 1–16.

Klass, D. (2014). Grief, consolation, and religions: A conceptual framework. *Omega, Journal of Death and Dying, 69*(1), 1–18.

Klass, D., Silverman, P.R., & Nickman, S.L. (eds) (1996). *Continuing bonds: New understandings of grief.* Washington DC: Taylor & Francis.

Lindemann, E. (1979). Symptomatology and management of acute grief. In Erich Lindemann & Elizabeth Lindemann (eds), *Beyond grief: Studies in crisis intervention.* New York: Aronson.

Neimeyer, R.A. (2016). Meaning reconstruction in the wake of loss: Evolution of a research programme. *Behaviour change.* doi: 10.2017/bec.2016.4.

Neimeyer, R.A., Klass, D., & Dennis, M.R. (2014). A social constructionist account of grief: Loss and the narration of meaning. *Death Studies, 38,* 485–498.

Rimke, H., & Brock, D. (2012). The culture of therapy: Psychocentrism in everyday life. In M. Thomas, R. Raby, & D. Brock (eds), *Power and everyday practices* (pp. 182–202). Toronto: Nelson.

Stroebe, M., & Schut, H. (2005). To continue or relinquish bonds: A review of consequences for the bereaved. *Death Studies, 29,* 477–494.

Walter, T. (1996). Bereavement and biography. *Mortality, 1*(1), 7–25.

SECTION I

Overview of the Continuing Bonds Model

Introduction

The four chapters in this Section provide a preview for the rest of the book. We could have chosen others, but we think that these four together give readers an overview of the continuing bonds model as it has developed over the first decades of the twenty-first century.

The chapter by Simon Shimshon Rubin, Ruth Malkinson, and Eliezer Witztum shows how continuing bonds fits into the psychological study of grief. Significant deaths can disrupt how a person functions in their social environment that may be radically changed. A death can also disrupt the relationship between the bereaved and the one who died. Continuing bonds are centered in the second, but, as the authors show, how well people function on one track affects how well they function on the other. A case study by the authors offers a clear description of where continuing bonds fits in both the assessment and the help we can provide for the bereaved.

Richard Tedeschi, Ana Orejuela-Davila, and Paisley Lewis show how therapeutic work in bereavement can be characterized by a movement toward greater tolerance of seemingly irreconcilable paradoxes. In fact, the authors posit that dialectical thinking and acceptance of paradox open the door toward a narrative assimilation process which allows for the development and meaningful integration of a continuing bond with the deceased in the ongoing lives of the bereaved, in a process that often suggests post-traumatic growth. This focus on dialectics is very much in keeping with the drive behind the continuing bonds model and invites further development.

Tony Walter expands the study of continuing bonds to sociology and anthropology as he discusses how bonds fit into larger cultural narratives. He describes how the cultural frames in the relationships between the living and the dead are experienced. In some frames, for example, the dead are excluded from the world of the living; in others, the dead need our care; and in others, the dead only require remembrance. In setting out the frames, Walter is laying the groundwork on which we can construct a theory of grief that can be applied cross-culturally.

The Section ends with Harold Bush's chapter in which all the themes intersect. He describes how the theme of suffering and redemption in his own theological journey to find meaning in his son's death helps him describe how suffering and redemption move significant nineteenth-century authors to create significant cultural narratives, for example Abraham Lincoln's restatement of the American narrative in his Gettysburg Address. He moves to contemporary bereaved parents, for example Mamie Till-Bradley, an Afro-American whose son was murdered in Mississippi in 1955. Her response was one of the beginning points for the Civil Rights Movement.

2

THE TWO-TRACK MODEL OF BEREAVEMENT AND CONTINUING BONDS

Simon Shimshon Rubin, Ruth Malkinson, and Eliezer Witztum

In this fourth decade of the existence of the Two-Track Model of Bereavement, we begin with case material, followed by a history and orientation to the model (Rubin, 1981, 1999; Rubin, Malkinson, & Witztum, 2012). Next, we return to the case and its unfolding over time as viewed through the twin lenses of the model. We conclude with attention to some of the current challenges to the Continuing Bonds field in general, and the Two-Track Model of Bereavement in particular.

Bereavement is most often understood as both an event of loss and a process of adjusting to that loss. The death of a significant other typically sets in motion processes of grief and mourning. While the onset of bereavement is usually relatively easy to identify, determining if and when an end point has been reached is far more difficult. In this chapter, we shall refer to both grief and mourning to describe the response to the loss of a significant other, such as a close family member, to death. While no human being can avoid exposure to loss and bereavement, the ways in which people understand, experience, and respond to loss vary greatly.

In the Two-Track Model of Bereavement, the bereavement response is conceptualized as occurring along two main multidimensional tracks. The first track focuses on how people function on a variety of dimensions of their biopsychosocial functioning. It considers how this functioning is affected by the cataclysmic life experience that loss may entail. The second track is concerned with how people maintain and transform their relationship bond to the highly significant person of the deceased. Often the story of the death as it is narrated becomes part of the organization and regulation of accessibility and affect regarding the deceased and so should also be included in the focus on this relational track. Prior to our fuller exposition of the Two-Track Model of Bereavement, we open with a bereaved family's request for assistance, and the ways in which we might think about their experience of loss.

Case Study: A Family's Loss to Suicide – The Initial Contact

The office phone rings, and I, Simon Shimshon Rubin, answer the call. A Human Resource coordinator asks if I would be willing to see a recently bereaved family. The facts are sparse, but from the call, I learn that Mr. Shammai Levy had died by suicide in the home two days earlier. His body was discovered by his wife, Mrs. Dasi Levy. Three generations of the family are observing the Shiva, the seven-day mourning period in the Jewish tradition, and are available for a family meeting. With the company agreeing to fund the contacts and to respect the family's privacy and the treatment's confidentiality, evaluation and treatment will begin within days. For the initial meeting, a co-therapist will be present.

First Thoughts

Although there is very little by way of description of the family and individuals bereaved, even the little information we have calls to mind a number of parameters in response to loss. Three generations are responding to the death of this son, husband, and father. The different kinship relationships, genders, and stages of maturity and development can be assumed to process loss differently. Death by suicide influences the unfolding of grief differently than death by other causes. The cultural and religious social organization of the communal response to this loss, and the ways in which members of the social fabric of this family will come to support the bereaved, are factors in grief as well. The passage of time, in this case a matter of days, is a major influence in the response to bereavement. And yet, perhaps the most important questions for professionals and laypersons alike might be these: What are the markers of adaptive response to bereavement? What behaviors and interventions might assist the bereaved to achieve a more adaptive response to their loss? Let us now turn to the Two-Track Model of Bereavement to see how it can assist our conceptualization of bereavement and the questions it raises.

The Model and Its Background

Bereavement is the process of adjusting to the death of a loved one. Psychologically, behaviorally, interpersonally, and socially, life changes for the bereaved. From the psychological and relational point of view, the Two-Track bereavement paradigm assists clinicians, researchers, and the bereaved themselves to understand and focus on the significance of death on that relationship and the life of the bereaved. All relationships are an amalgam of past, present, and future (anticipated) behaviors and the memories, feelings, and mental representations of self and other. While it is obvious that the physical interaction with the deceased ends with death, it is by no means obvious what happens to the emotional and psychological relationship as it is encoded in memories, emotions, and mental representations linking the deceased to the bereaved. When the significant other is alive, the relationship to him or her is one relationship among many. Following death, the relationship is maintained in the inner world of the bereaved in ways that are similar, but not identical, to how other relationships are encoded and experienced at conscious and unconscious levels (Bar-Nadav & Rubin, 2016). Particularly in the initial period following death, the relationship and its acutely felt significance are accompanied by strong emotions that reflect the unattainability of connection in life.

It is easiest to explain the Two-Track Model of Bereavement (Rubin, 1999) and its analysis of bereavement by looking at is history. The model grew out of the doctoral research of Simon Shimshon Rubin and the study of recently and non-recently bereaved mothers who had lost children to Sudden Infant Death (Rubin, 1981). In preparation for the research, Rubin felt that two literatures were central to the examination of the loss experience.

The first body of clinical and research literature considered the separation from the deceased as the essence of the response to loss and drew from the original formulation by Freud that conceptualized mourning as the dissolution of the tie to the deceased leading to the investment in new love relationships (1917). The focus on the relationship to the deceased was the key. Observation of the bereaved, together with theory and clinical interventions, showed repeatedly that the centrality of the relationship to the deceased, and the nature of the bond with him or her, were most significant for understanding dysfunction in adaptation to loss. Despite the many changes in the understanding of human behavior, Freud's original framing of the significance of the relationship remained central to the psychology of bereavement. At the same time, this perspective came with the premise that withdrawal of active emotional involvement in the relationship to the deceased was the harbinger of successful adaptation to loss. Thus, the severance of the bond and withdrawal of attachment and emotional investment to the significant other were cast as goals of the mourning process.

The second body of scientific literature on loss was rooted in the worldview of stress and life change. Here, the outcome of the bereavement experience was assessed for affective, biological, behavioral, and cognitive outcomes in a manner indistinguishable from how persons responded to other major life crises, traumas, and stressors. A range of unwelcome changes and difficulties, including incidence and prevalence of emotional, mental, and physical illness, were assessed without regard to their relationship context. Mapping functioning and psychopathology following loss recognized that bereavement was a stressful event, but effectively treated loss as merely one more stressor amidst a long list of stressful life events.

Rubin's research used both objective and narrative measures of functioning and relationship to study the impact of loss. Based on the psychological literature, the presumption was that only a minority of bereaved mothers four years post-loss would continue to show significant involvement in their relationship with the deceased, and that this response pattern would be reflected in problematic functioning. The results turned this hypothesis on its head. The most striking finding of the research demonstrated unequivocally that essentially all of the bereaved women remained involved and invested in ongoing relationships to their deceased children months and years after the death. Indeed, despite the death, there was no end to their relationships. A second feature was the finding that these women felt that they were no longer the same person they had been prior to the loss. The changes were not of pathology or dysfunction but rather of changes in values of what was important. Often they mentioned the greater significance attached to the family following loss.

Faced with empirical data that contradicted the models of grief and mourning then extant, it was not at all an easy task to respect the data that pulled in other directions. And yet, the interview and objective measures demanded no other conclusion but that an ongoing relationship was normative and not indicative of pathology. As a result of the data obtained in his research, combined with his personal and cultural experiences of loss, Simon rejected major tenets of the presumption that "successful" mourning meant disconnection from the deceased. In so doing, he entered a lonely place shared with a small minority of clinicians and researchers who were "discovering" that an ongoing relationship with the deceased was the norm, and not an indication of disordered mourning or psychopathology (Klass, 1988; Klass, Silverman, & Nickman, 1996). Ultimately, Simon proposed a new paradigm and model to organize and encompass the essence of bereavement. This bifocal approach was proposed as the Two-Track Model of Bereavement with application to theory, clinical material, research, and cultural aspects of loss (Rubin, 1999). The two independent scientific and clinical literatures were, separately and together, essential to this comprehensive understanding of loss and its aftermath. It was the combination of the perspectives on relationship and life change that would lend clarity to the experiences of the bereaved mothers in this study, as well as to the many aspects of the field in general.

This new model incorporated a range of biopsychosocial factors which expanded the purview of functioning beyond the medical model of grief complications. At the same time, the focus on the significance and centrality of the relationship to the deceased as it evolved post-bereavement retained fidelity to the significance of the relationship. This relationship, pre- and post-loss, would determine the nature of the continuing bond between the griever and his or her loved one, and its implications for life after loss. Over the years, clinical, research, and theoretical contributions expanded and broadened the model. A close collaboration with Ruth Malkinson and Eliezer Witztum further developed aspects of the model and its relevance for clinicians and researchers alike (Malkinson, 2007; Rubin, Malkinson, & Witztum, 2012, 2016). In recent years, a set of Two-Track Bereavement Questionnaires has been developed for clinical and research use (Rubin & Bar-Nadav, 2016; Rubin et al., 2009).

One can summarize the Two-Track Model of Bereavement paradigm as follows:

1   The Two-Track Model of Bereavement directs our focus to biopsychosocial functioning and the continuing relationship and bond to the deceased following loss.

2   Response to loss involves conscious as well as out-of-awareness attention to issues related to biopsychosocial functioning as well as a focus on the relationship to the deceased, the pain of loss, and the implications of the death for the continuing bond with the deceased and its meaning for the self. The model emphasizes the co-existence of coping with the demands of life alongside the thoughts, memories, and emotions that accompany the reworking of the bond with the deceased. In the complex and multi-tiered process of responding to loss, one or the other aspects of functioning and relationship to the deceased may be in the forefront of consciousness. Whether predominant in one's experience or less so, when one is grieving, both the demands of functioning and the involvement with the relational bond are active and requiring cognitive and emotional resources.

3   Understanding the levels of response to loss on each of the two tracks of the model is helped by using a metaphor from the world of computers and smartphones. The Two-Track Model posits a continually running bereavement "application" that is active during the active grieving process. On the one hand, this process must deal with biopsychosocial features of life functioning, while at the same time, this process also has an open "'relationship-to-the-deceased' application", which reorganizes and relates to the memories, thoughts, associations, and degrees of preoccupation connected to the bond with the deceased. In a matter similar to our most basic homeostatic functions that run outside our awareness, the involvement and preoccupation with the memories, relationship, and continuing bond to the deceased are not a function of consciousness alone. This involvement makes claims on our attention and freedom to attend to other things, even when it may not be at the forefront of our attention. We know that multi-tasking is associated with lowered performance on many tasks. Grief and mourning make demands on our conscious attention and our "out-of-awareness" and unconscious processes that are highly significant in understanding and tracking bereavement. Until a new level of homeostasis around function and relationship is reached, the psychological processes of grief and mourning can be thought of as operant, impacting both tracks of the model, with the potential to reach a more or less satisfactory outcome. These processes take their toll on the life experience and energy of the bereaved, and on their experience of the grief process.

4   The implications of the Two-Track Model of Bereavement and its bifocal orientation are relevant for theory, research, clinical work, and counseling interventions. Assessment of the bereaved's response is always done along each of the multidimensional tracks following loss. As such, the model allows for assessment of the state of the response to loss at any point across the life span. In normal grief, whether 3 months, 2 years, or 40 years after the death, considering both the adequacy of biopsychosocial functioning

(Track I) and the nature of the ongoing relationship to the deceased and the death story (Track II) remains valid to understanding bereavement and its impact on the bereaved.

5   The clinical implications of the model derive directly from the focus on both the functional and relational aspects of the response to loss. The extent to which interventions focus and titrate the attention to one or both domains of the response to loss is an outcome of the binocular lenses of the Two-Track Model of Bereavement. A schematic visual representation of the model in clinical use and relevant texts is contained in Figure 2.1 and Table 2.1. A more complete presentation on how to assess loss using this model in clinical practice follows the briefer presentation seen here.

Track I addresses functioning and assesses the individual's adaptive and disrupted life functioning (see Table 2.1). For the clinician, researcher, and the bereaved themselves, the two basic questions addressed here are: What is the nature and degree of potential maladaptive responses? And where are the areas of new growth and successful adaptation? The loss event and the experience of interpersonal loss are examined here for their impact on the broad schemas of biopsychosocial function. The ranges of domains include affective-cognitive, intrapersonal, social-interpersonal, somatic, and psychiatric indicators as well as the experience of self and the organization of meaning systems. Each of the 10 domains listed has received attention in the literature and figures prominently in response to bereavement.

Track II is focused on the psychological construction and relationship regarding the deceased and the death story (see Table 2.1). The questions we ask include:

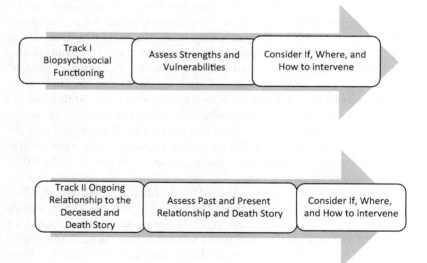

Figure 2.1 The Two-Track Model of Bereavement in Clinical Use

22

Table 2.1 The Two-Track Model of Bereavement: Overview

Track I: Biopsychosocial Functioning		Track II: Relationship to the Deceased and Death Story	
1	Anxious affect	1	Reconnection wishes and longing for the deceased
2	Depressive affects and cognitions	2	Imagery, memory, and physical experience of the deceased
3	Somatic concerns	3	Degree of emotional involvement and closeness
4	Traumatic responses (e.g., PTSD)	4	Positive perceptions and affects associated with the deceased
5	Familial relationships	5	Preoccupation with loss event and/or the deceased
6	General interpersonal relationships	6	Negative perceptions and affects associated with the deceased
7	Self-esteem and self-system	7	Conflict surrounding the deceased, the relationship, and/or the loss event
8	General meaning structure	8	The loss trajectory: degree of each in present: shock, searching, disorganization, and reorganization
9	Work or similar roles	9	Self-system experience vis-à-vis the deceased
10	Investment in life tasks	10	Memorialization and transformation of relationship with the deceased

To what degree is the relationship to the deceased sought out and a focus for the bereaved both in and outside conscious awareness? The content and organization of the cognitive and affective psychological memories and construction of these vis-à-vis the deceased are what we wish to understand. These elements reflecting features of the relationship are summarized in the table. Here, too, the organization is broken down into 10 domains that capture the salient features of the interpersonal relationship to the deceased. They address the questions regarding who and what did and does the deceased represent for the bereaved. The accessibility and the nature of the imagery, sensations, and memories that constitute the bereaved's experience of the relationship bond with the deceased are the focus (Rubin, 1999). The inclusion of the death story as significant for Track II reflects what we have learned about the ways in which some loss events effectively and disproportionately impact the reworking of the relationship to the deceased. Likewise, depending upon the circumstances (suicide, homicide, natural disaster, etc.), the death story is objectively seen as a traumatic bereavement, but it is also important to note that any death story can be subjectively experienced as traumatic by the bereaved with equal implications for the bereavement process.

The fact that the painful longing and pining for the other are so hard to bear can lead to the mistaken assumption that successful mourning is the absence of undue longing for the deceased. From the Continuing Bonds framework, however, the adaptive task or goals of working thorough loss on Track II is to achieve a way to live on with the memories and feelings associated with the deceased. Finding one's balance of neither too great nor too little a connection to the memories of the deceased is a challenge for the bereaved. In practice, this translates into achieving a connection and accessibility to the complex of mental events associated with the deceased without being trapped there.

Intervention following bereavement assesses difficulties and strengths on both tracks of the model to allow interventions to be tailored to the needs of the bereaved. One whose functioning has been severely disrupted following loss may well benefit from interventions aimed at assisting the return to some level of adaptive homeostasis of biological, psychological, and social dimensions. The "ideal" as well as idealized outcome of adaptation to loss is the expectation that the bereaved will choose and be helped to live in as full and rich a manner as possible. Parallel to the consideration of the need for intervention that can assist the bereaved in their biopsychosocial domain, both researchers and clinicians need to pay attention to the nature and role of the continuing bond to the deceased (Silverman, Baker, Cait, & Boerner, 2003). Grief and mourning combine emotional, cognitive, and somatic responses that serve to reorder how the bereaved manage their connection both to the world and to the deceased. When proceeding adaptively, the accommodation and assimilation will allow for the reworking and re-integration of the bonds with the deceased into the bereaved's past, present, and future life narrative.

It is a truism today that psychological engagement in supportive and positive relationships with significant meaningful figures provides psychological support for the individual (Mikulincer & Shaver, 2003). Emotional flexibility and positive life energy are byproducts of this as well. Loss and bereavement have the potential to upset the inner psychological relationship with these persons to whom we have important connections. The connection to the one who was loved and alive and is no longer so is a dyadic story as told, communicated, and experienced by the survivor.

In dealing with bereavement, we believe that interventions need to focus on biopsychosocial functioning (Track I) as well as upon the relationship to the deceased and its meaning for the bereaved (Track II). Our thesis is that reworking relationships with the person who died is as important as attending to biopsychosocial functioning. Interventions attending to both can assist the bereaved in resuming the ongoing creation of their life narratives as they live fully in the world with themselves and others, while being open to the continuing bond and connection to the deceased. In practical terms, this perspective means that on every research and clinical report on the bereaved, we seek out attention to the nature of the past and present relationship to the deceased alongside attention to function. We now return to the case we opened with and consider how the Two-Track Model was used to tailor the response to this family following the suicide of Mr. Levy.

Case Consultations and Three-Year Follow-Up of Loss

The Initial Consultation

Three generations of bereaved family members were present for the initial meeting, but we will consider only the parent and children meetings. Our focus was on listening to the bereaved, making sure that each individual was spoken to, and being sure that we heard their stories. We sought to learn how the family made sense of what had happened and was happening. Initially, we spoke to everyone together, explained our focus and clarified that we would be making time to speak with various members separately. We explained how sorry we were to be meeting them under these unfortunate circumstances but hoped that we could serve as consultants to them. The initial visit to the family in their home was open-ended and was concluded after three hours.

We sat first with Mrs. Dasi Levy, aged 39, who began by talking of her husband's emotional distress in the weeks prior to his suicide. She related how she had found her husband sprawled at the entrance to the bathroom and what a shock that had been. After the ambulance had left, she had explained to the children that Dad was "sick and that he had not gone out for help" despite her strong recommendation to that effect, and now he was dead. She had not yet told her 7-year-old the cause of death but believed she may already have understood. Mrs. Levy said she had explained to her three children that they were not to blame and that, indeed, no one in the family had contributed to or caused the death. She gave voice to her shock and the horror of finding her husband with his wrists slit in the bloodied bathroom and felt that the image of him lying in a large pool of congealed blood would always remain with her.

In sitting with Mrs. Levy alone, we listened as she moved from emotion state to emotion state; from calm and composed to anxious, confused, and distraught; from overwhelmed to angry; from trusting herself to feeling inadequate and unable to manage. She was able to give us a history of her husband's depression and work difficulties, his rebuff of her suggestions for treatment, her years of happiness with him and, intertwined with these, to talk about what it was like for her to go to the upstairs bathroom and find her husband's body with blood dripping down the staircase "over there." Her questions included: What to share with the children. Would she ever be able to go down the staircase without seeing her husband's lifeless body in her mind's eye? How would she cope financially? How could he do this to her? Didn't he love her and the children? In addition to listening, we also reiterated what she knew but did not feel, that response to loss, and particularly to loss due to suicide, was a painful process that would take time. Although by no means a profound statement, it did serve to reassure her, to normalize her feelings, and to give her hope for the future.

Next, we sat with the children, aged 17, 12, and 7. Despite the age spread, we were able to make room for both joint and individual discussions as we sat with them. The children spoke of their father as someone who had invested greatly in spending time with them and talking to them. We asked them if they had questions or things that they wanted to know or talk about but were not sure they could ask or discuss either together, with us, or with their mom. Initially hesitant, they responded to our talking about "other children had shared with us questions such as . . ." The things we opened with included differences between children's and adults' expression of grief and emotion; crying or its absence; concerns about the surviving parent; what they were supposed to say to people about how their father had died; and whether it was ok to have fun and play. In response to this opening, the children raised some of their own concerns, a number of which related to their mother and whether she would be strong enough to take care of them and how they might take care of her. We asked the children if it would be okay to discuss this together with their mother when we returned to sit together with the family. They agreed.

Their next set of questions related to their father, their relationship, and the fact that he had died by his own hand. "Did he not love us enough? Was it something that we did to make him leave us? Is there a part of him that still lives somewhere? Is there a heaven where the souls of dead people go? Can he see us? Does he care about us? Do people who take their own life go to Hell? Is there such a place?" The latter set of questions, related directly to the organization of their relationship and bond with their father, were very important, and we encouraged them to include this as part of the discussion when we returned to the conjoint family session. In closing this part of the meeting, we stressed the ongoing nature of the grief and mourning process, and how it would take time to sort out the mix of emotions, thoughts, and questions. We told them that based on our impressions of them as individuals and as a family, we believed they would find the resources to get through this very difficult and painful time. After a short break, we reconvened the conjoint family session to facilitate the discussion and strengthen the family functioning.

Comment

Despite the press of emotion and the rapid swirling of issues, one can see in the consultation with Mrs. Levy issues clearly related to Track I's biopsychosocial domain. These included her role as a parent, the extent to which the trauma of seeing her husband's body would remain a stimulus for her, and how she would cope overall with the new demands upon her. At a period so early in the bereavement process, listening and providing a general orientation to the bereavement process in general, and bereavement following suicide in particular, can be helpful. On Track II, the continuing bond to the deceased, we see a mixture of their pre-loss relationship, the story of the crisis of the depression, and the shock of the death together with a rollercoaster of emotions. Ultimately, these themes will figure in the reworking and reconstruction of her memories and organization of her relationship with her husband over time. The nature of the continuing bond, its accessibility, and its affective valence will be a significant part of her grief and mourning. At the same time that she attends to her own experiences, Dasi Levy also wonders how to help her children structure their memories and relationship with their father. These issues are also very much related to the nature of the continuing bond and relationship with the deceased as well as to her parenting role. We spoke with her about her belief system and her thoughts on the soul and its continuity with an eye to how these would figure in the way in which the younger children would think about their father and his "location". Finally, because of the traumatizing suicidal nature of the death, we believed it would be particularly important to monitor and address over time how the suicide would be woven into the story of the father/husband's life and his death. At this early stage, we could not predict the extent to which it would complicate and dominate their experiences, but by facilitating discussion, it would be easier for them to work on it together over time. Because of the immediacy of the meeting, coming so close to the death itself, the consideration of the issues and topics under discussion emerged in a relatively fluid and dynamic state. Typically, as time from loss passes, there is a greater ability for both the bereaved and the therapist to attend to one domain or the other in talking with the bereaved at different junctures in the discussion.

With the children as well, in addition to attention to such Track I features of biopsychosocial functioning related to questions about whether they "should" be crying, what feelings were to be expected, and how to manage with their friends and classmates, many of their questions related to the Track II axis of their relationship with their father. They were concerned with their relationship to him, and this sometimes merged with questions about what death by his own hand meant for their relationship. At this initial meeting, the reworking of that relationship was in its earliest stage and would continue to evolve over time. In the weeks, months, and years to come, what they would understand about their relationship, their understanding of him, and how the death by suicide would interact with those aspects of their bond is a process that in most cases will shift and evolve across a lifetime. In our initial consultation, their questions had included attention to where he or his essence might be and about his love for them, and they had begun to try to understand his choice of death by suicide. As individuals, and as a family, these questions invite conjoint discussions and individual construction mediated by developmental, kinship, and personality variables.

Follow-Up

Mrs. Levy was not interested in entering a regular psychotherapy or in joining groups for survivors of suicide. She maintained irregular contact with SSR, the primary therapist. The family story unfolded as follows: Overwhelmed by the traumatic memories that the house contained for her, Dasi Levy relocated with her family to another city within a matter of months to make "a new start". The first months after the death were very hard for her and the two younger children. The oldest child had been drafted by the military and was no longer living regularly at home. For the first year, she was on "auto-pilot" in her work, her parenting, and her self-care. For a time she experienced vivid flashbacks to the bathroom death scene, but these subsided over time. More surprising to her was the gradual reemergence of memories, triggered by songs, smells, and occasional "Shammai-like" gestures by her children that brought back sadness and warm feelings all "mixed up together".

Briefly in the first year, and more noticeably in the second, things were changing. Holidays, birthdays, the anniversary of the death, and news of suicides and deaths of husbands with young children continued to trigger waves of sadness and despair. Yet initially little by little, and then more noticeably, she found herself remembering the good years with Shammai and could think of him and their lives together before the depression and before his suicide. As she explained when we met for our final session three years after the death, Dasi Levy felt that she had regained much of herself that had disappeared when she discovered Shammai's body. She described the feeling of rediscovering the strong sense of connection to the Shammai she had married and lived with before his depression, and a strong connection to the woman she had been before Shammai's depression and death. She was no longer the same person, she said, but she had reconnected to things she thought had disappeared forever. Her interest in art, her passion for reading, her energy for her work, and her availability for her friends and children had returned, as had her ability to remember many of the things that made her feel close to Shammai. They were not as robust as before, she said, but they were definitely back. For herself and her children, she had come to accept that Shammai's wish to be the best husband, father, son, and breadwinner he could be made it intolerable for him to "fail". Depression for Shammai was failure, and despite her and his parents' urging to see a doctor, Shammai had been too overwhelmed to try to get help. "I used to think that Shammai's senseless, traumatic, and unnecessary death had taken him away from me forever – but now I find that I and the children have a place for him in our hearts. I, and also they, feel a connection to the strong, optimistic, and caring Shammai that he had been before his depression". In the final meeting, Dasi thanked the therapist SSR for having been willing to accept her pacing of their contacts, and for being a support system available in times of need. For the therapist, the goodbye involved appreciating her thanks, and accepting the limits of what she wanted from the irregular consultation/therapy contacts over the years.

Closing Case Comments

The follow-up consultation sessions give a picture of Mrs. Levy's return to bio-psychosocial functioning and a reconnection to the relational bond with the deceased that reflect adaptation on both domains of the Two-Track Model. The narrative that the family has constructed to deal with Shammai's depression and death by suicide should be seen as a way to free up the connection to the memories and connections with him for his wife and family. For the Levy family, we note that the continuing bond and the way in which Shammai is remembered as well as the facilitated reworking of the death story allow his wife to reclaim important parts of herself that were intertwined with her memories of the deceased (Track II). Despite the highly traumatic nature of the death by suicide and its potential to derail adaptive grief and mourning, the grief and mourning process allowed reworking of the relationship. This yielded a renewed adaptive connection to her husband without the need to intervene around the traumatic imagery (Rynearson, 2006). The way that Dasi Levy described her ability to reconnect and find closeness to the memories and presence of her husband (Track II) came together with what she described as her reconnection and rediscovery of qualities in herself

(Track I) that she thought had disappeared along with Shammai. While difficulties and negative emotions remain, the overall renewal of her ability to connect to herself, and at the same time to connect to the memories and bond with her husband, is positive. This outcome illustrates the distinctiveness, and the potential connection, of the twin domains of the Two-Track Model of Bereavement.

Concluding Remarks: Continuing Bonds and Life-Long Connections

The Continuing Bonds framework has successfully changed much of the language about the "goals" of the grief and mourning process from detachment to ongoing connection. Although the relationship to the deceased remains central across the bereaved's life cycle, it has remained surprisingly underappreciated among professionals and lay people. Too often, professional and lay considerations of loss and bereavement recast the question of how we remain connected with others (both living and dead) across the life cycle into questions and discussions about coping, growing, healing, moving on, and finding new meanings in life after loss. In the healthcare field, the language and conceptualizations of trauma and post-trauma can obscure the centrality of interpersonal connection in the investigation of adaptive and maladaptive responses to the death of significant others. Future research into the field of bereavement will benefit from the use of measures designed to measure adaptive living as well as the nature of the relational bond and connection to the deceased. We believe that the Continuing Bonds paradigm will only be fully integrated into the field of bereavement when a much greater emphasis on the complex, but central, nature of the pre-loss and post-loss relational bond to the deceased is achieved. The Two-Track Model of Bereavement, in the past and in the present, remains a beacon stressing the significance of recognizing that biopsychosocial functioning is significant (Track I), but not isomorphic with successful adaptation to loss. The model underscores that conceptualizing and assessing the bereavement response always requires a parallel focus on the nature of the relationship to the deceased (Track II), the continuing bond, as equally central to the understanding of bereavement.

References

Bar-Nadav, O., & Rubin, S. S. (2016). Love and bereavement: Life functioning and relationship to partner and spouse in bereaved and non-bereaved young women. *Omega*, 74(1), 62–79.

Freud, S. (1917/57). Mourning and melancholia. In J. Strachey (Ed. and Trans.), *SE of the complete psychological works of S. Freud* (Vol. 14, pp. 237–258). London: Hogarth. (Originally published 1917.)

Klass, D. (1988). *Parental grief: Solace and resolution.* New York, NY: Springer.

Klass, D., Silverman, P., & Nickman, S. (Eds). (1996). *Continuing bonds: New understandings of grief.* New York, NY: Taylor and Francis.

Malkinson, R. (2007). *Cognitive grief therapy.* New York, NY: W. W. Norton.

Malkinson, R., Rubin, S. S., & Witztum, E. (Eds). (2000). *Traumatic and nontraumatic loss and bereavement: Clinical theory and practice.* Madison, CT: Psychosocial Press.

Mikulincer, M., & Shaver, P. R. (2003). The attachment behavioral system in adulthood. In M. P. Zanna (Ed.), *New York: Advances in experimental social psychology, Vol. 35* (pp. 56–152). New York, NY: Academic Press.

Rubin, S. (1981). A two-track model of bereavement: Theory and research. *American Journal of Orthopsychiatry, 51*(1), 101–109.

Rubin, S. S. (1999). The Two-Track Model of Bereavement: Overview, retrospect and prospect. *Death Studies, 23*(8), 681–714.

Rubin, S. S., & Bar-Nadav, O. (2016). The Two-Track Bereavement Questionnaire for complicated grief (TTBQ-CG31). In R. Neimeyer (Ed.), *Techniques of grief therapy, Vol. 2*. New York, NY: Routledge.

Rubin, S. S., Malkinson, R., & Witztum, E. (2012). *Working with the bereaved: Multiple lenses on loss and mourning*. New York, NY: Routledge.

Rubin, S. S., Malkinson, R., & Witztum, E. (2016). *The many faces of loss and bereavement: Theory and therapy*. Haifa: University of Haifa Press and Pardes Publishers.

Rubin, S. S., Bar Nadav, O., Malkinson, R., Koren, D., Gofer-Shnarch, M., & Michaeli, E. (2009). The Two-Track Model of Bereavement Questionnaire (TTBQ). *Death Studies, 33*, 1–29.

Rubin, Z. (1973). *Liking and loving: An invitation to social psychology*. New York, NY: Holt, Rinehart and Winston.

Rynearson, E. K. (Ed.). (2006). *Violent death*. New York, NY: Routledge.

Silverman, P. R., Baker, J., Cait, C. A., & Boerner, K. (2003). The effects of negative legacies on children's adjustment after parental death. *Omega, 64*, 359–376.

3

POSTTRAUMATIC GROWTH AND CONTINUING BONDS

Richard Tedeschi, Ana I. Orejuela-Dávila,
and Paisley Lewis

This chapter will explore the relationship between continuing bonds and the process of posttraumatic growth (PTG) in bereaved persons. Bereavement can usher into a person's life new considerations of how to live, as a loss requires changes in perspective, habits, and relationships. Managing these changes can challenge people to greater personal development, i.e., PTG. At the same time, the challenge of navigating the emotional connection to the deceased person also requires new perspectives. In this chapter, the ability to think dialectically—that is, to appreciate paradox—will be considered as an important common element in PTG and the holding of a continuing bond. In this way, PTG and continuing bonds can work together to mitigate the distress of bereavement, and ultimately produce benefits for others as bereaved persons find ways to carry forward the bonds with their loved ones into acts of service.

PTG and Bereavement

The human struggle with grief due to the death of a loved one has always been present throughout history. However, the systematic attempt to understand the process of grief and bereavement is a relatively new concept. Thus far, research on bereavement has typically focused on the many negative effects of loss. There is no doubt that the death of a loved one can be a truly devastating experience that can lead to a variety of negative outcomes, including emotional distress (Gamino & Sewell, 2004), externalizing symptoms (Wolchik, Coxe, Tein, Sandler, & Ayers, 2008), substance use (Suar, Das, & Alat, 2015), and depression (Edelstein, Drozdick, & Ciliberti, 2010). Yet despite these negative outcomes, research has also shown that bereavement may also provide a context in which PTG and other positive outcomes can occur (Calhoun, Tedeschi, Cann, & Hanks, 2010; Michael & Cooper, 2013).

Using the PTG model (Tedeschi & Calhoun, 1995) within the context of bereavement, the death of a loved one is a deeply devastating event that can greatly challenge or even shatter one's core beliefs about the world, one's self, and others (Michael & Cooper, 2013). Such a challenge to one's beliefs can make the world appear unjust and unpredictable (Janoff–Bulman, 1992), especially if the death is unexpected. Research has shown that a "natural death" (i.e., one at the end of a long life) is much easier to accept and facilitates the process of meaning finding (Gillies & Neimeyer, 2006), so there tends to be little cognitive work required. On the other hand, an "unexpected death" (such as the death of a child) is less consistent with assumptive world views, thus causing more distress and posing a greater challenge to one's core beliefs.

This disruption to core beliefs can add to the distress caused by the death itself, which would then require bereaved individuals to find ways of managing their emotional distress. It is assumed that individuals will oscillate between wanting to confront and wanting to avoid this distress (Stroebe & Schut, 1999), and for some people the grieving process can last for many years (Carnelley, Wortman, Bolger, & Burke, 2006; Rogers, Floyd, Seltzer, Greenberg, & Hong, 2008). However, it should be noted that not all individuals experience profound or prolonged distress as a result of bereavement. For some individuals, if their core beliefs have not been seriously challenged by the death, then they may deal with their loss and survive the distress fairly easily and quickly, thus displaying resilience (Bonanno, 2004).

For those individuals whose core beliefs are disrupted and who subsequently experience greater distress, they may also oscillate between experiencing intrusive and deliberate rumination related to the event. Intrusive rumination (or repetitive unwanted negative thoughts about the loss) related to the death may further per- petuate distress (Cann et al., 2011) and also cause the individual to disengage from previously significant goals, so that they can then focus on grieving. At some point in this process, bereaved individuals may begin engaging in more deliberate forms of rumination, which is purposeful reflection that allows them to extract mean- ing out of the loss and to begin rebuilding their core beliefs (Cann et al., 2010). Ideally, this deliberate rumination will also decrease the frequency and impact of intrusive negative thoughts.

PTG, Dialectical Thinking, Wisdom, and Continuing Bonds

At the heart of PTG is the paradox that one may experience gains even amidst the deepest of losses. Engaging with such a paradox requires dialectical thinking, which has been described as "the ability to recognize and work effectively with contradictions" (Daloz, Keen, Keen, & Parks, 1996, p. 120). As explored in the literature on continuing bonds, experiencing the death of a loved one is also fundamentally paradoxical:

> The deceased are both present and not present at the same time. It is possible to be bereft and not bereft simultaneously, to have a sense of continuity and yet to know that nothing will ever be the same . . . What has traditionally been called the mourning period may simply be the period in which the survivor is learning to live within this paradox.
>
> *(Klass, Silverman, & Nickman, 1996, p. 351)*

Those who think dialectically work through the contradictions of a loss, and go on to experience significant growth following a traumatic event, which may be described as having attained some degree of wisdom (Calhoun & Tedeschi, 1998). In other words, they may have a better understanding of the "quintessential aspects of the human condition and human life" (Baltes, Staudinger, Maercker, & Smith, 1995, p. 155), including more specific functions such as dilemma resolution, perspective taking, and spiritual growth. Wisdom has been theorized to contain two aspects of "knowing" (Kramer, 1990): a more cognitive, intellectual component (e.g., ability to think dialectically), as well as an affective, experiential component (e.g., having grown from a traumatic event). As wisdom cannot be achieved through intellectual work alone, the affective experience is crucial. After all, humans understand on an intellectual level that trauma is possible, but we also believe, on an affective level, that we are protected from such possibilities. The occurrence of real traumatic events wrests us from our comforting illusions, sending a shock that may serve as "the beginning of an affectively based knowing of truth that had been denied" (Tedeschi & Calhoun, 2006a, p. 308).

Instead of viewing paradoxes as irreconcilable, a "wise" individual understands and appreciates the value of integrating seemingly opposing ideas and beliefs (Tedeschi & Calhoun, 1995). Wisdom requires recognition of both the positive and negative aspects of life, as well as the awareness that "attention to one does not belie the existence of the other" (Janoff-Bulman, 2006, p. 94). Likewise, attention to continuing bonds does not belie the fact that a loved one has passed away; nor does attention to the loved one's death belie the truth that connection—in one way or another—is still possible. Therefore we see that the maintenance of a continuing bond with the deceased and the experience of PTG are both supported by an ability to think dialectically.

Domains of Growth Following Bereavement

Through deliberate rumination that involves dialectical thinking and acceptance of paradox, bereaved persons assimilate the experience of loss into their lives, and their narrative of their lives (Neimeyer, Burke, Mackay, & van Dyke Stringer, 2010). This narrative allows for a continuing bond with the person who has been lost, as they are woven into the life story of the bereaved person in a meaningful way. Through this process, the bereaved individual may then begin to experience one or more domains of PTG: a greater appreciation for life, developing closer relationships with others, having a greater sense of personal strength, identifying new opportunities, and experiencing spiritual growth (Tedeschi & Calhoun, 2004).

Although the death of a loved one may cause a bereaved individual to realize that they are vulnerable to experiencing great suffering, this experience can also cause them to tap into a well of strength that they were previously unaware of possessing. In a systematic review of PTG and bereavement, Michael and Cooper (2013) found that one of the key themes to emerge was positive personal growth as evidenced by a greater sense of personal strength. Several studies have revealed that bereaved individuals tend to report positive transformations in terms of their own self-concept, and this transformation is enabled as a result of the struggle to cope with the loss. Specifically, bereaved individuals have described becoming more courageous, self-confident, self-reliant, tolerant, and patient as a result of their experiences with loss (Carnelley et al., 2006; Matthews, 1991; Oltjenbruns, 1991; Parappully, Rosenbaum, van den Daele, & Nzewi, 2002). For example, Calhoun, Tedeschi, Cann, and Hanks (2010) cite a bereaved parent who stated "I've been through the absolute worst that I know. And no matter what happens, I'll be able to deal with it" (p. 127). This statement implies that surviving bereavement can offer individuals evidence of their own personal strength, while also providing them with the knowledge that they will be able to tackle any subsequent challenges that life presents them with.

In their review, Michael and Cooper (2013) also found that another key theme to emerge was reappraisal of priorities in life, as evidenced by being able to identify new possibilities for oneself. This is accomplished, in part, because bereaved individuals may make a greater effort to live in the present moment and not postpone things, which then allows them to discover new strengths and talents that they did not previously know they had (Hogan, Morse, & Tason, 1996; Lieberman, 1996). Sometimes a death may also force bereaved individuals into doing things that they had not done previously. In the case of spousal bereavement, the bereaved spouse may have to suddenly take over the responsibilities of the deceased spouse. For example, Calhoun and Tedeschi (1989–90) examined how widows found themselves having to take over the responsibilities of their husbands (such as finances and physical labor). Although many of the widows had never done these things before, they found enjoyment in doing them.

Bereaved individuals may also experience growth by developing a greater appreciation for life. When a death occurs, a bereaved individual's own mortality can become more salient, and this may serve as an impetus for making the most out of the time they have left to live. Therefore, the death of a loved one may paradoxically highlight the life of the bereaved, thus prompting them to live more fully and deliberately. Studies have shown that bereaved individuals may evaluate their lives as more meaningful as a result of coping with the loss, and this then leads to finding greater fulfillment and pleasure in everyday life (Hogan et al., 1996; Malinak, Hoyt, & Patterson, 1979).

Growth after a loss can also be experienced in the form of new and closer relationships with others. While the death of a loved one may cause strain among relationships, this difficult experience also has the power to deepen emotional connections as a result of surviving individuals' attempts to cope with the loss. In fact, research has shown that the death of a loved one can prompt an individual to re-evaluate his or her relationships with friends and family, and to make those relationships be more open and intimate (Hogan et al., 1996; Lieberman, 1996; Malinak et al., 1979). Further, this greater closeness and intimacy may extend beyond significant others to include an enhanced sense of connection and compassion with human beings in general, especially with those who have experienced similar losses (Tedeschi, Calhoun, & Addington, 2011).

In addition, it also needs to be noted that close relationships can play a crucial role in how a bereaved individual copes with loss. In fact, there is evidence to suggest that systems of social support can play a critical role in promoting PTG within the context of bereavement (Wolchik et al., 2008). Bereavement is a socially constructed experience, and as such, it requires socially supportive contexts in which individuals can explore and mediate the meaning of the loss. Ideally, the bereaved individual's social environment will have the culturally appropriate conditions for emotional disclosure and exploration related to the loss. When there is a socially supportive environment, close relationships may not only help ameliorate bereavement-related distress; they may also stimulate constructive information processing that can help individuals find meaning and experience growth. In addition, having the support of someone who has experienced a similar loss can help facilitate growth for the newly bereaved individual (Cobb, Tedeschi, Calhoun, & Cann, 2006; Weiss, 2004).

Lastly, bereaved individuals may also experience growth in the domain of spiritual development (Balk, 1999; Bray, 2013; Rosenblatt, 2000). Specifically, bereavement can alter an individual's relationship with their religion and spirituality, which can then shape the experiences of the bereavement itself (Bray, 2013). Because of their experience with the death of a loved one, bereaved individuals may become more aware of their existence as mortal beings and engage in existential questioning (regardless of religious beliefs). For example, individuals might question their purpose in life, or wonder if there is an afterlife. This heightened existential awareness may provide a context in which the re-examination of core beliefs can occur. In addition, religion and spirituality can serve as a framework for promoting growth through a deepening of faith and conviction (Bray, 2013), which can then result in spiritual change that leads to an increased sense of meaning and purpose (Balk, 1999). However, the death of a loved one can also cause religious doubt (Ingersoll-Dayton, Krause, & Morgan, 2002), which can be conceptualized as a challenge to one's core beliefs. Thus, resolving this doubt could be a potential mechanism for growth (Patrick & Henrie, 2015).

For some individuals, religious and/or spiritual coping is crucial for dealing with the loss of a loved one (Pargament, Smith, Koenig, & Perez, 1998). For example, Znoj (2006) discovered that spiritual coping was actually one of the top three predictors of PTG among bereaved parents. This type of coping may influence adjustment to bereavement because it provides a meaning-making mechanism through which individuals can make sense of the death. Similarly, Parappully et al. (2002) found that faith in God, belief in an afterlife, and prayer aided bereaved parents in experiencing growth after the death of their children. In addition, religious beliefs can also help with reappraising the death of a loved one as less of a threatening situation and more of a challenge, thereby suggesting that something positive can be derived from the suffering caused by grief (Shaw, Joseph, & Linley, 2015).

In their discussion of the philosophical and spiritual aspects of PTG, Calhoun and Tedeschi (1999) describe spirituality as "the individual's experience of the transcendent, a higher force, or an existential state beyond the self" (p. 105). The loss of a loved one may serve as a "forced opportunity to change one's general philosophy of life" (Calhoun & Tedeschi, 1999, p. 107), often in regards to spirituality. In the words of Tedeschi and Calhoun (2006a), "Spiritual development occurs at a time when the deepest spiritual needs and questions are confronted" (p. 303). The death of a loved one, wrapped in existential dilemmas and reminders of one's own mortality, may indeed be a time of "deepest spiritual need," prompting reevaluations of one's conceptions of God and the meaning of life.

For some individuals, spiritual grappling may lead to unsatisfactory and cynical conclusions, and it may even result in persistent existential despair. Others may find their spiritual beliefs weakened in the immediate aftermath of a loved one's passing, only to discover strengthened spirituality after a process of questioning and embracing the dilemmas surrounding death (Calhoun & Tedeschi, 2006; Tedeschi & Calhoun, 1995). Even those who are non-spiritual may reconsider their perspective on the afterlife after experiencing an inexplicable and immaterial continuing bond with a deceased loved one (Klass et al., 1996).

Spirituality, Continuing Bonds, and PTG

In a qualitative study of bereaved parents, Sormanti and August (1997) explored parents' feelings of spiritual connection—often through "sensing" the presence of their deceased children—and its impact on the grieving process. Such presence-sensing experiences, thanks to their intangible and subjective nature, are difficult to describe; however, the overarching themes connecting these experiences include the feeling that the loved one is near, the awareness that such a feeling is distinguishable from a dream or memory, and the knowledge that the feeling is outside the control of the individual experiencing it (Steffen & Coyle, 2010).

Despite the painful knowledge that their deceased children were at once close and unreachable, most parents in Sormanti and August's study described the experiences of sensing their children's presence in positive terms, citing the power of these continued spiritual connections to promote feelings of peace and comfort; to bring parents closer to both their child and to God; to reassure their belief in the afterlife; and to inspire them to help others. Almost without exception, continued spiritual connections were associated with psychological benefits and were described as ways of accommodating paradoxical thoughts about life and death. Given their findings, the authors argue that spiritual factors, which have traditionally been overlooked in the scientific community, merit further inquiry by all who study bereavement (Sormanti & August, 1997).

While the work of Sormanti and August (1997) was not described explicitly in terms of PTG or continuing bonds, later researchers incorporated sense of presence into a framework that clearly integrates both concepts. Steffen and Coyle (2010), for instance, outlined the process by which presence-sensing experiences can influence both spiritual thought and PTG. The authors posit that presence-sensing may challenge existing beliefs about death and the afterlife, just as it challenges assumptions about the traditional, "breaking bonds" view of the grieving process. After all, some individuals who sense the presence of a deceased loved one find such experiences to be consistent with their worldviews, while others will find presence-sensing to be disturbingly at odds with their current understandings of the world we live in (Klass, 1999). Sensing the presence of the deceased may, for some bereaved individuals, pose challenges to existing worldviews—challenges that, when explored with an open mind, can provide the catalyst for meaning-making and PTG (Steffen & Coyle, 2010).

The presence of spiritual beliefs may aid in the process of meaning-making, a process believed to be twofold: Sense-making allows for the individual to explain the loss in a way that is consistent with his or her existing worldviews, and benefit-finding allows for the extraction of gain from an enormous loss (Davis, Nolen-Hoeksema, & Larson, 1998). Meaning-making during the process of bereavement may lead to PTG, especially when it occurs amidst a challenging of spiritual beliefs (Calhoun & Tedeschi, 2006). Challenges to one's belief system, in turn, are best faced within a supportive sociocultural context that allows for open exploration of spiritual issues and narrative reconstruction (Tedeschi & Calhoun, 2006b). Overall, sense of presence experiences may be invaluable tools for promoting PTG within a spiritual context:

> Apart from the potentially positive implications of enabling the continuing relationship with the deceased, these phenomena could expand the experiential horizon for the bereaved, allow for the creation of spiritual meaning and facilitate a new spiritually informed sense of identity.
>
> *(Steffen & Coyle, 2010, p. 282)*

Continuing Bonds and Facilitating PTG

A process of facilitating PTG has been described as incorporating five phases (Calhoun & Tedeschi, 2013): education about the trauma experience, help with emotional regulation, encouragement of disclosure, the development of a revised life narrative that incorporates the experience and domains of PTG, and the recognition that one has something to offer others, that can form the basis of a sense of service. Facilitating PTG is a delicate process when working with many bereaved persons, especially those who have experienced losses that are traumatic or seem "unnatural" (Tedeschi & Calhoun, 2004). It is difficult, for example, to encourage many bereaved parents to see that out of their child's death, there has emerged something of value. In many cases, a sense of a continuing bond may be important in the facilitation of PTG.

Considering the five phases of PTG facilitation, it is important to note that the person helping the bereaved person be expert in their ability to be a companion through this process. This *expert companionship* for the bereaved (Tedeschi & Calhoun, 2004) requires a sensitivity to listening to the story of the bereaved person, especially understanding who the deceased person was and what relationship the bereaved person had to the deceased. Before anything else can be accomplished, listening to and understanding who has been lost and what seems missing in the relationship is crucial. This kind of discussion immediately allows for a recognition that a continuing bond is present, at least through memory, but also through artifacts such as letters, recordings, and possessions. There may also be discussion of the continuing bond that some bereaved persons report in their experience of the deceased person in dreams and mystical encounters.

Out of this raw material, the expert companion can then help bereaved persons understand that their concerns and experiences are a normal expression of the bereavement experience, and move from the unpleasantness and distress of intrusive ruminations about their loss to a deliberate consideration of the way they will live in the aftermath of loss. Here, learning how to regulate the emotional reactions to loss is useful, since it is hard to think clearly about the future with the burdens of intrusive ruminations and emotional reactions.

By taking a sensitive and patient stance in listening to the story the bereaved person tells about who has died and what the relationship was with that person, disclosure of tender and difficult emotional material is encouraged. This is important as the continuing bond with the deceased may have elements of the living relationship while also now changed after death. Here we encounter the dialectical thinking necessary to appreciate the continuing bond, that the relationship is the same in some ways while at the same time changed. The expert companion may also help a bereaved person see that despite their loss, the changes may be of value, and this is a prerequisite to PTG. It is commonplace, it appears, for bereaved persons with continuing bonds to describe their relationship with the deceased to be less conflicted and more understanding. This may be because the deceased person is no longer suffering and seems to be returned to health, or that the deceased seems to have a spiritual presence or wisdom, or can better know the bereaved person's mind. The PTG facilitation phase that encourages disclosure is important since some bereaved persons are initially reluctant to describe thoughts and experiences such as these, because they might be seen as irrational. An accepting consideration of the way this relationship has changed, and how "real" it is, can allow the bereaved person to appreciate this new reality of relating that has never been considered before this death. The exercise of holding the apparently conflicting ideas of a person being dead but still alive in a way can also allow a person to appreciate the paradox that out of this sadness and loss there can be growth.

The expert companion who listens to the story of the life and death of the person who has died has encouraged an initial consideration of the life narrative that has to now be reworked to accommodate the loss. Now looking forward into the future, the bereaved person can be encouraged to consider what the next chapter of life will hold, and the degree to which this is a conscious decision on the part of a bereaved person. In this part of the narrative, there can be a consideration of what kind of relationship with the deceased person is possible and can be cultivated. In doing so, there may be questions to be answered such as "How can I be a mother to a dead child?" or, "In what ways can I make sure my child still lives?". In grappling with such questions, there are simultaneous considerations of the quality of a continuing bond and the possibility of PTG.

Using the Continuing Bond in a Mission to Serve

The final phase of PTG is a recognition that one has something to offer others. It is common for bereaved persons to think of themselves as having learned something about life that is worth passing on, or having a specific empathy for others going through a similar experience. These bereavement experiences that generate this type of empathy may be ones that separate the bereaved person from normative experiences, including such things as suicidal deaths, combat-related deaths, or deaths of children. Such experiences may give the impression of being socially isolated, misunderstood, or stigmatized, while also prompting a sense that there is a mission that can be taken on. The mission might be to educate the public, or to support others going through similar circumstances. These missions of service are often accomplished in the name of the deceased person, and in that sense also represent a continuing bond. This bond is one of honor and remembrance. It helps keep this person alive and the name used and can represent a furthering of the life narrative of the deceased person as well as the bereaved person. In this way, the bereaved person carries their loved one into the future as a living force for good and as a partner in making the world a better place. Acts of service by bereaved people then carry on various aspects of the PTG experience as well as a continuing bond. Through service, the bereaved person educates others, discloses their personal experience with what has been tragic, creates a new narrative about these events, and serves others. The death has been transformed, and the person who has been lost has also been transformed, as they lead a second life, providing the impetus and sometimes a name for the changes in society that can address those in similar circumstances to the bereaved.

Conclusion

In summary, the dialectical thinking surrounding the paradox of continuing bonds—the coexistence of past and present, life and death, presence and absence—may facilitate PTG in the wake of a loved one's death. For some, this growth could be particularly noticeable in the spiritual realm, as death may elicit both a confrontation of one's own mortality and a conflict with one's existing belief systems. The loss of a loved one, and the ensuing potential for paradoxical struggles and continued spiritual connections, may transport individuals "to a place where spiritual experiences provide pathways to accommodation and posttraumatic growth" (Bray, 2013, p. 901). The continuing bonds may also prompt bereaved persons through the PTG process, recognizing their own personal growth in other domains such as relationships with others, personal strength, appreciation of life, and new possibilities. All these changes may be expressed in many cases by ultimately developing a cause, a mission, or providing expert companionship to those in similar circumstances. In doing so, bereaved persons become partners with their deceased loved one in a new chapter in the narrative of lives that continue to be intertwined, but in a new way. This newly developed narrative serves to enliven the bereaved person, and keep alive the one who has been lost.

References

Balk, D. (1999). Bereavement and spiritual change. *Death Studies, 23,* 485–493.

Baltes, P. B., Staudinger, U. M., Maercker, A., & Smith, J. (1995). People nominated as wise: A comparative study of wisdom related knowledge. *Psychology and Aging, 10,* 155–166. doi: 10.1037/0882-7974.10.2.155.

Bonanno, G. A. (2004). Loss, trauma, and human resilience: Have we underestimated the human capacity to thrive after extremely aversive events? *American Psychologist, 59,* 20–28.

Bray, P. (2013). Bereavement and transformation: A psycho-spiritual and post-traumatic growth perspective. *Journal of Religion and Health, 52*(3), 890–903.

Calhoun, L. G., & Tedeschi, R.G. (1989–90). Positive aspects of critical life problems: Recollections of grief. *Omega, 20,* 265–272.

Calhoun, L. G., & Tedeschi, R. G. (1998). Posttraumatic growth: Future directions. In R. G. Tedeschi, C. L. Park, & L. G. Calhoun (Eds), *Posttraumatic growth: Positive changes in the aftermath of crisis* (pp. 215–238). Mahwah, NJ: Lawrence Erlbaum Associates.

Calhoun, L. C., & Tedeschi, R. G. (1999). *Facilitating posttraumatic growth: A clinician's guide.* Mahwah, NJ: Lawrence Erlbaum Associates.

Calhoun, L. C., & Tedeschi, R. G. (2006). The foundations of posttraumatic growth: An expanded framework. In L. C. Calhoun & R. G. Tedeschi (Eds), *Handbook of posttraumatic growth: Research and practice* (pp. 3–23). Mahwah, NJ: Lawrence Erlbaum Associates.

Calhoun, L. G., & Tedeschi, R. G. (2013). *Posttraumatic growth in clinical practice.* New York, NY: Routledge/Taylor & Francis Group.

Calhoun, L. G., Tedeschi, R. G., Cann, A., & Hanks, E. A. (2010). Positive outcomes following bereavement: Paths to posttraumatic growth. *Psychologica Belgica, 50*(1–2), 125–143.

Cann, A., Calhoun, L. G., Tedeschi, R. G., Triplett, K. N., Vishnevsky, T., & Lindstrom, C. M. (2011). Assessing posttraumatic cognitive processes: The Event Related Rumination Inventory. *Anxiety, Stress, & Coping, 24*(2), 137–156.

Carnelley, K. B., Wortman, C. B., Bolger, N., & Burke, C. T. (2006). The time course of grief reaction to spousal loss: Evidence from a national probability sample. *Journal of Personality and Social Psychology, 91,* 476–492.

Cobb, A. R., Tedeschi, R. G., Calhoun, L. G., & Cann, A. (2006). Correlates of posttraumatic growth in survivors of intimate partner violence. *Journal of Traumatic Stress, 19,* 895–903.

Daloz, L. A. P., Keen, C. H., Keen, J. P., & Parks, S. D. (1996). *Common fire: Lives of commitment in a complex world.* Boston, MA: Beacon.

Danhauer, S. C. (2010). The Core Beliefs Inventory: A brief measure of disruption in the assumptive world. *Anxiety, Stress, & Coping, 23*(1), 19–34.

Davis, C. G., Nolen-Hoeksema, S., & Larson, J. (1998). Making sense of loss and benefitting from the experience: Two construals of meaning. *Journal of Personality and Social Psychology, 75,* 561–574. doi: 10.1037/0022-3514.75.2.561.

Edelstein, B. A., Drozdick, L. W., & Ciliberti, C. M. (2010). Assessment of depression and bereavement in older adults. In P. A. Lichtenberg (Ed.), *Handbook of assessment in clinical gerontology* (pp. 3–43). San Diego, CA: Elsevier Academic Press.

Gamino, L. A., & Sewell, K. W. (2004). Meaning constructs as predictors of bereavement adjustment: A report from the Scott & White grief study. *Death Studies, 28*, 397–421.

Gillies, J., & Neimeyer, R.A. (2006). Loss, grief, and the search for significance: Toward a model of meaning reconstruction in bereavement. *Journal of Constructivist Psychology, 19*, 31–65.

Hogan, N., Morse, J. M., & Tason, M. C. (1996). Toward an experiential theory of bereavement. *Omega: Journal of Death and Dying, 33*, 45–65.

Ingersoll-Dayton, B., Krause, N., & Morgan, D. (2002). Religious trajectories and transitions over the life course. *The International Journal of Aging & Human Development, 55*(1), 51–70. doi: 10.2190/297Q-MRMV-27TE-VLFK.

Janoff-Bulman, R. (1992). *Shattered assumptions.* New York, NY: Free Press.

Janoff-Bulman, R. (2006). Schema-change perspectives on posttraumatic growth. In L. C. Calhoun & R. G. Tedeschi (Eds), *Handbook of posttraumatic growth: Research and practice* (pp. 81–99). Mahwah, NJ: Lawrence Erlbaum Associates.

Klass, D. (1999). *The spiritual lives of bereaved parents.* Philadelphia, PA: Brunner/Mazel.

Klass, D., Silverman, P. R., & Nickman, S. L. (1996). *Continuing bonds: New understandings of grief.* Washington, DC: Taylor & Francis.

Kramer, D. A. (1990). Conceptualizing wisdom: The primacy of affect-cognition relations. In R. J. Sternberg (Ed.), *Wisdom: Its nature, origins, and development* (pp. 279–313). Cambridge, UK: Cambridge University Press.

Lieberman, M. A. (1996). *Doors close, doors open: Widows, grieving, and growing.* New York, NY: G.P. Putnam & Sons.

Malinak, D. P., Hoyt, M. F., & Patterson, V. (1979). Adults' reactions to the death of a parent. *American Journal of Psychiatry, 136*, 1152–1156.

Matthews, A. M. (1991). *Widowhood in later life.* Toronto: Butterworths.

Michael, C., & Cooper, M. (2013). Post-traumatic growth following bereavement: A systematic review of the literature. *Counselling Psychology Review, 28*(4), 18–33.

Neimeyer, R. A., Burke, L. A., Mackay, M. M., & van Dyke Stringer, J. G. (2010). Grief therapy and the reconstruction of meaning: From principles to practice. *Journal of Contemporary Psychotherapy, 40*(2), 73–83.

Oltjenbruns, K. A. (1991). Positive outcomes of adolescent experience with grief. *Journal of Adolescent Research, 6*, 43–53.

Pargament, K. I., Smith, B. W., Koenig, H. G., & Perez, L. (1998). Patterns of positive and negative religious coping with major life stressors. *Journal for the Scientific Study of Religion, 37*, 711–725.

Parappully, J., Rosenbaum, R., van den Daele, L., & Nzewi, E. (2002). Thriving after trauma: The experience of parents of murdered children. *Journal of Humanistic Psychology, 42*, 33–70.

Patrick, J. H., & Henrie, J. A. (2015). Religious doubt and spiritual growth among adults bereaved of a grandparent. *Journal of Religion, Spirituality & Aging, 27*(2–3), 93–107.

Rogers, C. H., Floyd, F. J., Seltzer, M. M., Greenberg, J., & Hong, J. (2008). Long-term effect of the death of a child on parents' adjustment in midlife. *Journal of Family Psychology, 22*, 203–211.

Rosenblatt, P. C. (2000). *Parent grief: Narratives of loss and relationship.* Philadelphia, PA: Brunner/Mazel.

Shaw, A., Joseph, S., & Linley, A. (2015). Religion, spirituality, and posttraumatic growth: A systematic review. *Mental Health, Religion & Culture, 8*, 1–11.

Sormanti, M., & August, J. (1997). Parental bereavement: Spiritual connections with deceased children. *American Journal of Orthopsychiatry, 67*(3), 460–469. doi: 10.1037/h0080247.

Steffen, E., & Coyle, A. (2010). Can "sense of presence" experiences in bereavement be conceptualized as spiritual phenomena? *Mental Health, Religion & Culture, 13*(3), 272–291. doi: 10.1080/13674670903357844.

Stroebe, M., & Schut, H. (1999). The dual process model of coping with bereavement: Rationale and description. *Death Studies, 23,* 192–224.

Suar, D., Das, S. S., & Alat, P. (2015). Bereavement, postdisaster trauma, and behavioral changes in tsunami survivors. *Death Studies, 39*(4), 226–233.

Tedeschi, R. G., & Calhoun, L. C. (1995). *Trauma and transformation: Growing in the aftermath of suffering.* Thousand Oaks, CA: Sage.

Tedeschi, R. G., & Calhoun, L. G. (2004). *Helping bereaved parents: A clinician's guide.* New York, NY: Routledge.

Tedeschi, R. G., & Calhoun, L. C. (2006a). Expert companions: Posttraumatic growth in clinical practice. In R. G. Tedeschi, C. L. Park, & L. G. Calhoun (Eds), *Posttraumatic growth: Positive changes in the aftermath of crisis* (pp. 215–238). Mahwah, NJ: Lawrence Erlbaum Associates.

Tedeschi, R. G., & Calhoun, L. C. (2006b). Time of change? The spiritual challenges of bereavement and loss. *Omega: Journal of Death and Dying, 53*(1–2), 105–116. doi: 10.2190/7MBU-UFV9-6TJ6-DP83.

Tedeschi, R. G., Calhoun, L. G., & Addington, E. (2011). Positive transformations in response to the struggle with grief. In K. J. Doka & A. S. Tucci (Eds), *Beyond Kubler-Ross: New perspectives on death, dying, and grief* (pp. 61–75). Washington, DC: Hospice Foundation of America.

Weiss, T. (2004). Correlates of posttraumatic growth in married breast cancer survivors. *Journal of Social and Clinical Psychology, 23*(5), 733–746. doi: 10.1521/jscp.23.5.733.50750.

Wolchik, S. A., Coxe, S., Tein, J. Y., Sandler, I. N., & Ayers, T. S. (2008). Six-year longitudinal predictors of post-traumatic growth in parentally bereaved adolescents and young adults. *Omega: Journal of Death and Dying, 58,* 107–128.

Znoj, H. (2006). Bereavement and posttraumatic growth. In L. G. Calhoun & R. G. Tedeschi (Eds), *Handbook of posttraumatic growth: Research and practice* (pp. 176–196). Mahwah, NJ: Lawrence Erlbaum Associates.

4

HOW CONTINUING BONDS HAVE BEEN FRAMED ACROSS MILLENNIA

Tony Walter

Continuing bonds (CBs) with the dead became part of bereavement studies toward the end of the twentieth century in North America. CBs, however, are not new, for we find them in cultures through history and even in pre-history– but that does not mean that CBs are understood the same way in each culture. On the contrary. Every culture provides frameworks (or frames) that members use to make sense of events and experiences (Goffman, 1974; Jakoby, 2012). Frames can be informal as well as formal, unofficial as well as official, lay as well as pro- fessional, sub- or counter-cultural as well as cultural. Frames that structure and organize CBs derive from a culture's major narratives about personhood, God, life, death, and reality; they are therefore often political, tied to religious dogma or political positions that support–or sometimes resist–existing religious or politi- cal power (Goss & Klass, 2005). Frames help people interpret CBs, for example as acceptable or unacceptable, making sense or making no sense; some frames regu- late CBs, others anathematize them. CBs may be framed as internal or external, a psychological need of the living or a social obligation to the dead, a relationship with a real spiritual entity or a hallucination, etc., etc. Practitioners and researchers use frames to make sense of CBs, whether manifested by a contemporary client or in another society; thus we all risk imposing our own frame on another person or another culture. The chief safeguard against this is to be aware of the range of possible frames.

This chapter identifies six frames that promote and/or resist CBs. They are far from comprehensive, but they are reasonably representative of how human cultures have framed CBs. First I describe two frames–the dangerous dead, and ancestors–that go way back before the world religions. Then I consider the mono- theistic world religions–Judaism, Islam, and especially Christianity–before looking at a religion with a distinctive take on CBs, namely Buddhism. Finally, I consider two more recent frames–secular memory, and romantic love. Some frames allow the deceased some kind of personal existence and a relationship with the living. Other frames allow a post-mortem existence but disallow any relationship with the living, while others allow no post-mortem existence; in these latter cases, the dead exist for the living only through memory practices which may allow a continuing bond or attachment but not a continuing relationship.

Six Frames

The Dangerous Dead

In many societies the dead must be pushed away. Actively continuing a bond hinders the dead from moving on to the next world: they need to be prevented from returning to this world and helped on their rightful way. The tears of the living may be forbidden because tears make it hard for the dead to leave. Heavy stones may be placed on the grave to keep the dead from returning to haunt the living. Food offerings may sustain the dead on their journey. In some cultures and religions, the wellbeing of the living and/or the dead is best served by the living permanently letting go, so the dead can move on. In Tibetan Buddhism, for example, no appearances of the dead are beneficial; the dead are told to leave. In twentieth-century western grief theory and practice, "letting go" was often seen as the bereaved person's goal, achieved through the painful process of emotional disinvestment from the deceased. But for some peoples, such as the Shona of Zimbabwe, pushing the dead away is only temporary, followed some months later by a rite that–now both living and dead know their position–invites the dead back into the community. The spirits of Shona of evil disposition who could cause trouble, however, are ritually placed in a goat which is then driven out and set free to roam wild, never to return.

This idea that bonds with the dead are potentially dangerous to the community or to the individual, and therefore need to be broken temporarily or permanently, is widespread–in both traditional and modern societies.

Family Ancestors

In many agricultural societies, those whose social position in life commands respect continue to be respected in death as ancestors. In much of sub-Saharan Africa what becomes an ancestor is not the person, but the authority that the deceased had over their descendants (Fortes, 1965). We find the same in East Asia, though authority there has long been shared between ancestors and the state. So ancestors may reflect/support authority within kinship systems rather than personal attachment. Culturally required ancestor veneration is not necessarily an effective way to continue a bond to the beloved dead, especially if the deceased was a baby, a child, a woman, or another category of person that the culture deems ineligible for ancestorhood.

Ancestor veneration does, however, provide ample opportunity for interaction between the living and at least some of the dead. Ancestors' agency continues with them beyond the grave. In Chinese society, "every death produces a potentially dangerous spirit. Funeral rites . . . convert this volatile spirit into a tamed, domesticated ancestor" (Watson, 1988, p. 204)—a very different purpose from that of most contemporary western funerals. Living and dead interact in ritual processes of exchange. Gifts and prayers to the dead ensure that the dead aid, or at least do not harm, the living. An implicit threat underlies the logic of mutual care: if we look after you, you will look after us. Mediums (Emmons, 2003) and shamans (Vitebsky, 1992) often facilitate these ritual exchanges. Exchange continues not for eternity, but for a few generations until memory—of the person, or of the grave's location—fades, after which the ancestor become less known, less accessible, part of the ancestral collectivity, or they are simply forgotten. A few ancestors, however, gain mythic status as family or clan founders, their stories told for many generations, justifying the occupation of land or enabling distant kin to be identified. That said, who becomes an ancestor, what rites create ancestors, and how long it takes for the personally known ancestor to become subsumed into a more collective and impersonal body of ancestors vary considerably (Straight, 2006).

If venerating family ancestors is ancient and widespread, how does it fare when subsistence agriculture encounters larger-scale social forces such as markets, cities, empires, and formal religions? The answer is that ancestor veneration has been supported by some of these forces and undermined by others. In East Asia, ancestors have continued strongly into the modern era. Confucius, unconcerned about the dead themselves, used ancestral respect to encourage respect for the living older generation; many Chinese today still demonstrate filial piety in part through ancestral rites. Likewise Taoism and Japanese Shinto do not undermine exchanges with the family dead. Across East Asia today, however, as cultural values become more individualistic, ancestor veneration is increasingly used to connect with chosen beloved individuals rather than specified authority figures (e.g., Suzuki, 1998).

Other social forces, however, undermine ancestors. While many western colonists saw no conflict between modern rationality and Christian doctrines such as Jesus' virgin birth and physical resurrection, they considered indigenous spirit worship to be superstitious, backward, and even evil, as did postcolonial, capitalist, and Communist modernizers. In Mao's China, family loyalty—embodied in ancestor veneration—undermined loyalty to party and state, so ancestral rites were suppressed (Goss & Klass, 2005). In several South East Asian countries today, however, ancestral and other spirits are being revitalized (Endres & Lauser, 2011). A Chinese colleague described to me a medium-size business whose headquarters office block has a rooftop ancestral shrine where business decisions are checked out with the ancestors—communists consult ancestors to ensure capitalist profits.

Ancestral rites, therefore, may drastically limit CBs to particular authority-bearing older males, disenfranchising all but a minority of griefs (Doka, 2002). Or people may conduct the rites more flexibly to express CBs with a wide range of loved deceased. As we will see with religion, formal worldviews and informal practices are complex and varied, and rarely match exactly.

45

Monotheism

In the ancient Near East, for example in the Epic of Gilgamesh and Egyptian mortuary practices, some high-status individuals began to seek not just temporary ancestral status but immortality. It was the emergence of world religions, however, that really challenged ancestor veneration. These religions, especially as they developed over time, came to offer immortality forever (not just for two or three generations while kin survived to perform ancestral rites) to everyone (including the lower classes, women, children, and even slaves). World religions have therefore often proved attractive to people excluded from ancestral status.

As well as offering immortality, the monotheistic Abrahamic religions (Judaism, Christianity, Islam) actively attacked ancestor veneration. Ancestors possess agency, the power to affect social life on earth, but in monotheism only the one true God (plus his appointed angels and saints) has supernatural power. So ancestral spirits and shrines–along with animist nature spirits and shrines–posed a direct threat to monotheism (Douglas, 2004). In eighteenth and nineteenth-century Korea, as in many parts of the world, Catholic and Protestant missionaries were clear that converts could no longer worship their ancestors, so many converts were rejected by their family or even became martyrs (Park, 2010). Jesus, like Mao, demanded a total loyalty that can be undermined by familial love and loyalty (polytheisms, notably Hinduism, may be more accommodating). The CB that unites many across the globe is not with family ancestors but rather with their religious founder–Abraham, Jesus, the Prophet, the Buddha (Goss & Klass, 2005).

Family ancestors may also appear weak in the face of imperialism or colonialism. In twenty-first-century India, some young Sora–whose parents used shaman mediums to dialogue with deceased relatives to transform them into ancestors–have become Baptists, a religion they find attractive because of its association with western modernity. Others have embraced Hinduism, attractive for its association with Indian nationalism. Both Baptist and Hindu Sora, seeking to engage larger national and global forces, have turned their backs on local ancestors and mediums (Vitebsky, 2008). World religions and their global deity can seem more powerful than family ancestors to those seeking to participate in an increasingly global world. This is the attraction of Islam and Christianity in much of Africa.

Nevertheless, throughout the world–not least Africa–there are countless examples of syncretism between religious immortality and family ancestors. It is understandable if people want both eternal life/reincarnation/nirvana *and* to care for deceased family members and gain their advice and guidance. Sometimes this is encouraged by the religious hierarchy. In medieval Europe, millions paid the church to pray for the dead, while today's Mormon Church has a major program of posthumous conversion of family ancestors.

More often, syncretism and incorporation are found in lived, experienced, or "vernacular" religion rather than in the official religion. At best, priests, monks, and theologians tolerate, at worst attack, vernacular religious practice. In southern Thailand, Muslim and Buddhist villagers still believe in ancestor spirits, taking heed of both ancestral power and modern religion (Endres & Lauser, 2011). Many Shona are Christian, yet also use ancestral stories to trace the kin connections that enable them to survive in Zimbabwe's catastrophic economy (Walter, 2015). Many African Americans see death as a homecoming to the land of their ancestors across the ocean, linking this to biblical stories of exile and redemption (Parry & Ryan, 1995). In Catholicism throughout the world, not least in the Mexican Day of the Dead, saints and even the family dead can pray for the living and in turn be prayed to (Bryant, 2003). In the Church of England liturgy of the Eucharist in which believers symbolically ingest Christ through bread and wine, many people feel the presence of deceased relatives, finding an affinity between an absent/present Christ and an absent/present loved one (Davies, 1993). Though Christian theology speaks of the resurrected Christ dwelling within the believer, it discourages believers from contacting the spirits of the family dead; Christ is the only deceased human spirit believers are supposed to entwine with. Yet at the same time, as Davies (1993) shows, Christianity provides a liturgy symbolizing Christ within the believer that readily evokes in them the family dead.

Christian views of heaven, theological as well as vernacular, have for two millennia oscillated between a heaven where souls perpetually worship God and a heaven where souls enjoy the perpetual company of other family members (McDannell & Lang, 2001). Either way, the soul is central—as it is also in Islam and some forms of Hinduism. Though Christian theology teaches that deceased souls are inaccessible to the living except (in Catholicism) through the prayers of the church, and typically anathematizes mediums who offer direct access to the deceased, the very notion of the deceased having a soul provides an entity with whom the living can in practice continue to connect. As Hussein and Oyebode (2009, p. 908) say in their study of CBs among British Muslims of Pakistani origin: "The Islamic concept of the continuing existence of the soul allowed for a meaningful relationship with the deceased." Ambiguity also pervades Hinduism which provides rites both to reincarnate the soul in another body most likely in another family, and rites to transform the soul into its previous family's ancestor (Firth, 1997).

In sum, religions' relationships to CBs are complex and contradictory. They may ritualize CBs; they may anathematize them yet posit a soul that enables them; and informally, believers often find ways to channel CBs through religion.

Buddhism

Like contemporary western secularism and certain forms of Hinduism, Buddhism denies the existence of personal identity post-mortem. In Buddhism, everything is impermanent, most importantly the self. It may take many lifetimes to learn the hard truth that relationships are not forever (Gouin, 2015). It is not surprising therefore if many Buddhists at some level feel and act as though the deceased continues to exist in some way (the same may be true of some western atheists and secularists).

Like other religions, however, Buddhism does consider as beneficial certain actions performed after the death, whether by family or monks. Many Buddhists build merit that can be transferred to deceased family members. Ongoing attachment through remembering and memorializing is not unusual in Buddhism—memories remain even though the deceased is dead and gone. But continuous dwelling on memories, or talking to the deceased as though they exist somewhere, might indicate unenlightened clinging to the deceased, thus preventing the deceased from leaving the self and being reborn (Gouin, 2015). That said, in much of East Asia, Buddhist rites are used to create ancestors. Millions of urban Japanese pay Buddhist priests considerable sums to perform funeral rites whose main purpose is to turn the deceased into a family ancestor. Contemporary Japanese are not ashamed to talk to their ancestors—though whether that means they consider the deceased to "exist" varies from individual to individual (Árnason, 2012). From one point of view, Japanese Buddhism's encouragement of an ongoing relation between the living and the dead denies impermanence, a sop to those who require more lifetimes to learn the truth of impermanence. From another point of view, it simply reflects Buddhism's adaptability to different cultures.

Memory

This brief discussion of Buddhism raises the possibility that, in the absence of the deceased continuing as an immortal soul, bereaved people's ongoing attachment to the dead is expressed and experienced, if at all, as individual or group memory rather than as a bond to a person. If a continuing *relationship* with the deceased as a spiritual entity is impossible, it remains possible to cherish their memory; to uphold their values; to enjoy their social, emotional, and economic legacy. This would appear to fit Freud's view, shared by many modern westerners, that the mourner has to accept that the person is dead and the relationship at an end, however many memories may continue. In other words, "letting go" need not mean forgetting. In the west, this stance has long roots back to Judaism whose concept of a personal afterlife is rather weak, and more recently to Europe's sixteenth-century Protestant Reformation.

At the heart of the Reformation was Martin Luther's rejection of praying for the dead, and especially of paying priests to do the praying. In Luther's understanding of Scripture, there is nothing that the living can do for the dead. To enter heaven, all that is needed is pre-mortem faith and the grace of God; post-mortem, neither Church nor family can help. Radically undermining the Church's power by offering believers direct access to God, the new Protestant theology denied mourners access to those who had died. Erasing at a stroke the medieval funeral's task of assisting souls to heaven, it reduced funerals to mere acts of disposal (Gittings, 1984). And it left a puzzle. If there is nothing we can do to care for our dead, what can we do for them? How are we to relate to them?

Even if many ordinary folk in countries such as England continued after the Reformation to engage with their dead (Duffy, 1992), Protestantism itself had no answer. So the answers were secular. We can remember the dead. We can honor them (and before long, upper-class Protestant funerals were not shy about displaying social status). We can appreciate their legacy; they can live on in their children; their artistic, cultural, economic, or political legacy may continue to influence the living. But Protestantism allows no exchange with the dead, exiling them as an active presence. Thus, it was no secular social movement but Luther's intensely religious reform that secularized the relationship between north-west Europe's living and their dead.

So the most that those many north-western Europeans and North Americans who are cultural heirs to the Reformation can do for their dead is to remember them with respect, esteem, and/or affection. Memory thus offered a potentially secularizing and universalizing discourse—erupting in recent decades in the proliferation of talk about memory, reflected in the secular academy in the thriving field of memory studies.

Romantic Love

But memory is not secular, (post)Protestant western culture's only carrier of CBs (Stroebe, Gergen, Gergen, & Stroebe, 1996). Nineteenth-century Romanticism saw the meaning of life in intimate relationships, which leaves bereavement—losing the beloved—as death's greatest threat, even greater than my own death. In Romanticism love is eternal. It continues after death—the person may have died, but the relationship continues. As the inscription on a beautiful 1960 gravestone for an eleven-year-old boy in an English country churchyard states: "Brief is life, but love is long." Where are the dead? How do they survive? One romantic answer is that they live in our hearts. Another is that they continue in some external spiritual realm, illustrated in nineteenth-century America in sentimental forms of Protestantism, and on both sides of the Atlantic in Spiritualism whereby mediums could contact the dead. Spiritualism has continued to attract bereaved people through to the present day, especially after violent deaths which raise doubts that the dead are "okay" in their post-mortem existence—hence Spiritualism's popularity immediately after the First World War (Emmons, 2003).

In the twentieth century, by far the most popular afterlife belief in western societies was soul reunion (McDannell & Lang, 2001). Once released from the body, the soul goes to heaven where it joins, and will be joined by, other loved family members. The twentieth was the first century in which it became normal for death to occur not in childhood or childbirth but in old age, leaving a widow mourning the loss of a husband of maybe fifty or more years. With the elderly widow's own life expectancy no more than a few years, hope for reunion with her husband in heaven offered considerable comfort—assuming a good-enough marriage! Romanticism plus longevity plus the historic western concept of soul lent credence to soul reunion.

In many western countries, however, the early twenty-first century has witnessed a new imagined spiritual status for the loved dead: he or she is transformed into an angel. Souls are locked up in heaven, but angels fly back and forth, guarding and guiding the living–particularly attractive to younger mourners with fifty or sixty years left on earth before they themselves get to heaven and join their grand-parent, parent, child, or friend (Walter, 2016). The angel articulates an active CB in which, crucially, the dead as well as the living exert agency, guiding, and guarding. In other words, contemporary angels have assumed one of the main roles of traditional ancestors. Thus, in the twenty-first century, love across the grave continues for a couple of generations–for as long as there are people alive to be cared for by the dead–who then dissolve into little more than a name on the genealogist's family tree.

If a cultural milieu in which romantic love challenges the modernist/Protestant ban on relationships between the living and the dead re-introduces ancestor veneration, there are marked differences between traditional and contemporary ancestral interactions.

First, relationships between the living and the dead in the west today are not governed by expectations of reciprocal exchange (Valentine, 2008). As in tradi-tional ancestor veneration, we care for the dead and they guide us; but when they guide us, there is nothing we *need* do in return. And when we care for their grave, there is nothing they *need* do for us in return. Relationships with the dead are governed by personal feeling and personally chosen actions, not prescribed ritual.

Second, contemporary westerners like to see themselves as autonomous self-governing individuals who choose their relationships, in mourning as in the rest of life. Today's "ancestors" with whom survivors interact can be any deceased family member, irrespective of age or gender, or indeed someone outside the family.

Third, today's western dead have little or no power to meddle in the lives of the living. Survivors' relationships with them are almost entirely positive (Goss & Klass, 2005), motivated by loneliness and loss rather than by any practical services that the dead can offer (Emmons, 2003). Meanwhile, the troublesome dead are simply ignored, left behind, or forgotten, at least by those psychologically able to do so.

Fourth, talking about a connection to the dead, or the dead as a soul or an angel, is for many, especially in secular Europe compared to religious USA, often a way of articulating CBs rather than part of a formal belief system (Benore & Park 2004). In their 1979 song *I Have a Dream*, Abba depict their belief in angels as a dream, a fantasy that helps them through reality. Beliefs, ideas, and practices are articulated when needed to cope with adversity, with no desire to turn them into a coherent worldview (to the annoyance of some clergy and theologians). Such beliefs and practices are not creedal but situ-ational (Stringer, 2008).

We may conclude that contemporary western practices and imaginings do comprise ancestor veneration, but a veneration transformed by individualism and secularization. People increasingly derive their afterlife imaginings from personal experience of bereavement rather than from religious teaching.

Care or Memory?

A "bond" can be pictured either as a close connection between two separate objects or as two objects glued so tightly together that they become inseparable, fused into one. Árnason (2012) explores this ambiguity. The mourner can imagine her bond with a deceased who exists in some ancestral or spiritual realm. Or she may feel the deceased is within her, in her heart. Or both. The dead person can be external or internal, or both. This ambiguity mirrors the conflict in Christian history concerning the bond between the believer and that most significant (and for the believer, resurrected) dead person, Jesus Christ. Is Christ/God immanent (in me) or transcendent (out there)? As with Christians, so too mourners may have different expectations and experiences, shaped by culture. Silverman and Nickman (1996) found that bereaved American children able to locate the deceased parent in a place such as heaven could more readily construct a CB. Yet Árnason (2012) describes a Japanese widow who got to hate the daily rituals at her husband's *butsudan* (household shrine) and the yearly rites at the O'Bon (day of the dead) festival because they implied he was other, lost, gone, rather than residing deep within her heart.

This psychological contrast between external and internal CBs is mirrored culturally. I suggest it is helpful to think of *care cultures* in which living and dead are expected to look after one another in some kind of dynamic exchange, and *memory cultures* in which the living are expected to encounter the dead through memory and through the inspiration, role modeling, memento keeping, and story telling that memory gives rise to.

Care cultures externalize the attachment to the dead as a relationship with a person who continues in some spiritual realm. Memory cultures internalize the attachment within the remembering individual or group—even if, as in Protestantism, the deceased continues as an external spiritual entity (a soul). In care cultures, not least ancestor veneration, Hinduism, Roman Catholicism, and contemporary angelology, the transformed dead can enter into exchange with the living. In memory cultures they cannot, for, as Epicurus argued, death is the annihilation of life, or as Buddhism teaches, the dead have gone and are now reborn: either way, there is no way for them to connect with the living. Judaism too has generated a memory culture in which collective memory of the dead, from Abraham to the Holocaust, profoundly shapes Jewish identity.

The care/memory contrast was succinctly captured by Mayumi Sekizawa, a Japanese folklorist researching how Europeans and Japanese relate to their war dead. She told me, "You Europeans remember your war dead. We Japanese care for ours." British war remembrance (note the term "remembrance") is saturated with the language of memory: "We will remember them." "Lest we forget." By contrast, the Japanese war dead become *kami*, gods, who guide the living and are, in turn, cared for by them. What is true of the sacred war dead is true also of the ordinary family dead. In Japan there is ritual exchange of care and guidance. In secular/Protestant Europe, by contrast, memory is the language for speaking of the dead: memorial services, *in memoriam* newspaper columns, memorial benches, memory boxes. It is hard to talk about the European dead without using the language of memory.

Of course, memory often invokes kinship and care, and vice-versa. The popular English-language phrase "in loving memory" leaves its meaning tantalizingly open: Are the dead gone, but we can remember them with affection? Or do we continue to love by remembering? Despite such fuzziness between care and memory, and despite many humans both caring for and remembering their dead, most live in cultures that validate only one of these narratives (see Christine Valentine's chapter in this volume). Japanese do remember their dead, and some scholars argue that nowadays Japanese "ancestral" rites produce not ancestors but memory (Suzuki, 1998)–yet the language remains substantially that of ancestors. And secularized Protestant westerners often care for their dead, for example by tending the grave (Francis, Kellaher, & Neophytou, 2005), yet may be embarrassed to speak of practices that imply the dead can benefit from such tending. Grieving individuals whose practices or beliefs are culturally unspeakable keep silent, question their practices, re-cast them in culturally more acceptable terms, or use ambiguous phrases such as "in loving memory."

Discussion

This chapter has argued that CBs with the dead, though experienced personally, are framed by religion and/or culture which the individual embraces to a greater or lesser extent. The frames discussed are the dangerous dead, ancestors, monotheism, Buddhism, memory, and romantic love. I noted that the different frames can be divided into care cultures and memory cultures, although there is considerable crossover between the two. Throughout, I have distinguished frames which allow the deceased some kind of personal existence with which the living can connect and frames which allow no such post-mortem existence, or an existence that is out of reach, so the dead can exist only through private or shared memory and the practices memory promotes. Frames influence how people experience CBs and how they talk about them. They allow or disallow, invite or suppress, continuing relationships to the dead; they provide a lens through which such relationships can be viewed.

I will now briefly discuss some of the generic issues that arise, not least the complex relationship between formal frames, lived/vernacular frames, and personal experience.

1   Cultural or religious framing is not always experienced positively. We have already encountered the Japanese widow who resented rituals implying her husband was somewhere "out there" when she experienced him within her heart. Or, as this volume's chapters by Fong and Chow and Kosminsky note, relationships that are not positive in life are unlikely to be positive in death. Cultures which make it hard to leave difficult relationships, yet which expect mourners to venerate or respect the dead, can therefore be problematic for some members (Goss & Klass, 2005).

2   Frames give rise to what Valentine in her chapter calls "dominant scripts" which validate some experiences and enable them to be spoken of, but obscure and silence other experiences. I recall talking to a Protestant hospice chaplain about the phenomenon of sensing the presence of the dead. "Ah yes," he responded, "these hallucinations are an early stage in the grief process." His religious frame prevented him from acknowledging the dead's objective presence, while stage theory provided him with a secular script that psychologized the experience as, ontologically, a hallucination. Mourners may be out of step with their culture. Some who psychologically prefer to internalize the dead may resent cultural expectations ritually to care for the dead; mourners who prefer to externalize the dead may feel inhibited by a culture restricted to the language of memory.

3   Frames inviting or suppressing CBs are rarely neutral. They have often derived from religious dogma and/or have been used as powerful tools of control (Goss & Klass, 2005). Some religious hierarchies, including some varieties of Buddhism and the medieval Christian church, have provided channels through which bonds with the dead can be articulated, thereby enhancing the religious hierarchy's power and often its coffers. Is this supporting CBs? Or, by teaching that the living can relate to the dead only through the religious organization, undermining them? Vernacular practices may in turn subvert religious power; thus, an Irish Catholic may beseech a deceased aunt or grandmother as well as the Virgin Mary to pray to Jesus on behalf of the living. And cultural encouragement of CBs is not always taken up. A spouse who in life may be heir to Romanticism, embracing marital love, may in widowhood accept that love is not eternal, that the dead are dead, and that–good though the marriage was–everything comes to an end.

Religious rites that assist the soul's passage to the next world aim to help the dead, not the living. They may even exploit the living for the sake of bolstering religious power. Rites that provide a vehicle for the continuing of bonds usually do so as a side-effect: formal rites are more often driven by religion than by mourners' psychological needs. Informal rites or informal adaptation of formal rites, however, may more often be driven by psychological need. Pastorally, a priest may tolerate local indigenous practices perceived to have social or psychological benefits, even though the priest perceives such practices to be ineffective spiritually in helping the soul on its way or even to undermine his religion's authority.

Conclusion

Where do these historic frames leave mourners today? In Protestant-influenced western culture, which includes psychology/death studies/thanatology, the dominant frame is secular memory. In this frame, the dead live on in memory, as role models, as part of mourners' autobiographies, as legacy affecting various social groups. This makes experiences such as sensing the dead's presence hard to talk about as anything other than an illusion or, at best, psychologically comforting.

Tony Walter

Adherents in the west of other religions may express their care for the dead through, for example, traditional Catholic prayers for the soul, Hindu rites, or the Buddhist transfer of merit. These practices make sense only within the frame of the particular religion; outside, they may seem quaintly old-fashioned, misguided, or at best having value only psychologically to the living, not spiritually to the dead. Yet throughout the west, talking to the dead as though they continue to have some kind of external existence, which once may have been common in private or at the graveside when nobody else was around, is now routine, expected even, on social media–as is the idea of the dead as angels who can care for the living as well as be cared for. Technology affords a connection with the dead that culture denies (Cann, 2014).

In East Asia and the global South, by contrast, the dominant frame has long been care for the dead, with millennia of ancestor veneration continuing into the modern world. Millions who would not describe themselves as religious perform ritual practices of care for the dead, for example at the Japanese *butsudan* household shrine or at the annual Chinese hungry ghost festival. When talking to visiting westerners they may smile and describe their practices as "superstitious," but have no qualms continuing with such practices. In Africa and Latin America, ancestor veneration and Christianity often co-exist.

Because psychological bereavement care has not talked much about frames, those who would help can easily assume the bereaved person shares the helper's frame. This courts failure. I hope this chapter's delineation of some major frames will help practitioners identify where both they and each client are "coming from" as they explore CBs, and thus to see things through the client's eyes. One key question for practitioners is whether they and their clients inhabit a care culture or a memory culture. Does their culture's religion and/or communication technology give the deceased an existence, such that two-way social relationships can continue in some way across the grave? Or is post-mortem existence denied, so that mourners–individually or together–connect to the deceased only through memory and memory-enabled actions such as continuing the deceased's projects or upholding his values? Are CBs experienced and understood as external or internal? And a final question–is the person's own experience and belief in or out of step with their culture?

References

Árnason A. (2012). Individuals and relationships: On the possibilities and impossibilities of presence. In D. Davies & C.-W. Park (Eds), *Emotion, identity and death* (pp. 59–70). Aldershot: Ashgate.

Benore, E. R., & Park, C. L. (2004). Death-specific religious beliefs and bereavement. *International Journal for the Psychology of Religion, 14*, 1–22.

Bryant, C. D. (2003). Hosts and ghosts. In C. D. Bryant (Ed.), *Handbook of death and dying* (pp. 77–86). Thousand Oaks, CA: Sage.

Cann, C. K. (2014). *Virtual afterlives*. Lexington, KY: University Press of Kentucky.

Davies, D. (1993). The dead at the Eucharist. *Modern Churchman, 34*, 26–32.

Doka, K. J. (2002). *Disenfranchised grief*. Champaign, IL: Research Press.

Douglas, M. (2004). *Jacob's tear*. Oxford: Oxford University Press.

Duffy, E. (1992). *The stripping of the altars*. New Haven, CT: Yale University Press.

Emmons, C. F. (2003). The spiritualist movement. In C. D. Bryant (Ed.), *Handbook of death and dying* (pp. 57–64). Thousand Oaks, CA: Sage.

Endres, K. W., & Lauser, A. (2011). *Engaging the spirit world*. Oxford: Berghahn.

Firth, S. (1997). *Dying, death and bereavement in a British Hindu community*. Leuven: Peeters.

Fortes, M. (1965). Some reflections on ancestor worship in Africa. In M. Fortes & G. Dieterlen (Eds), *African systems of thought* (pp. 122–142). Oxford: Oxford University Press.

Francis, D., Kellaher, L., & Neophytou, G. (2005). *The secret cemetery*. Oxford: Berg.

Gittings, C. (1984). *Death, burial and the individual in early modern England*. London: Croom Helm.

Goffman, E. (1974). *Frame analysis*. Cambridge, MA: Harvard University Press.

Goss, R. E., & Klass, D. (2005). *Dead but not lost*. Walnut Creek, CA: AltaMira.

Gouin, M. (2015). The Buddhist way of death. In C. M. Parkes, P. Laungani, & B. Young (Eds), *Death and bereavement across cultures* (2nd ed., pp. 61–75). London: Routledge.

Hussein, H., & Oyebode, J. R. (2009). Influences of religion and culture on continuing bonds in a sample of British Muslims. *Death Studies, 33*, 890–912.

Jakoby, N. (2012). Grief as a social emotion. *Death Studies, 36*, 679–711.

McDannell, C., & Lang, B. (2001). *Heaven: A history*. New Haven, CT: Yale University Press.

Park. C.-W. (2010). Between God and ancestors. *International Journal for the Study of the Christian Church, 10*, 257–273.

Parry, J. K., & Ryan, A. S. (1995). *A cross-cultural look at death, dying and religion*. Chicago, IL: Nelson-Hall.

Silverman, P. R., & Nickman, S. L. (1996). Children's construction of their dead parents. In D. Klass, P. R. Silverman, & S. L. Nickman (Eds), *Continuing bonds: New understandings of grief* (pp. 199–215). Washington, DC: Taylor & Francis.

Straight, B. (2006). Becoming dead: The entangled agencies of the dearly departed. *Anthropology & Humanism, 31*, 101–110.

Stringer, M. D. (2008). Chatting with gran at her grave. In P. Cruchley-Jones (Ed.), *God at ground level* (pp. 23–39). Oxford: Peter Lang.

Stroebe, M., Gergen, M. M., Gergen, K. J., & Stroebe, W. (1996). Broken hearts or broken bonds? In D. Klass, S. L. Nickman, & P. Silverman (Eds), *Continuing bonds: New understandings of grief* (pp. 31–44). Philadelphia, PA: Taylor & Francis.

Suzuki, H. (1998). Japanese death rituals in transit. *Journal of Contemporary Religion, 13*, 171–188.

Valentine, C. (2008). *Bereavement narratives*. London/New York, NY: Routledge.

Vitebsky, P. (1992). *Dialogues with the dead*. New Delhi: Cambridge University Press.

Vitebsky, P. (2008). Loving and forgetting. *Journal of the Royal Anthropological Institute, 14*, 243–261.

Walter, T. (2015). Communication media and the dead. *Mortality, 20*, 215–232.

Walter, T. (2016). The dead who become angels: Bereavement and vernacular religion. *Omega, 73*, 3–28.

Watson, R. S. (1988). Remembering the dead. In J. L. Watson & E. S. Rawski (Eds), *Death ritual in late imperial and modern China* (pp. 203–227). Berkeley, CA: University of California Press.

5

CONTINUING BONDS, AUTHORSHIP, AND AMERICAN CULTURAL HISTORY

Harold K. Bush

Most Americans have never given much thought to the ways some of our stellar writers composed their greatest works in the context of their suffering as bereaved parents. But in the nineteenth century, many of our literary greats wrote masterpieces while trying to cope with parental grief—members of "the club" that nobody wants to join. Harriet Beecher Stowe, for example, wrote arguably the most influential novel of the century, *Uncle Tom's Cabin* (1852), largely as a response to the death of her beloved son Charley, who died of cholera a few years earlier. Abraham Lincoln memorialized for all time the deaths of countless sons at the Battle of Gettysburg while himself suffering the seemingly endless pain of his own loss: his son Willie, who died in the White House in February 1862. W. D. Howells, America's most powerful editor and literary mentor of some of the century's most famous masters, suffered the death of his adult daughter Winny in 1889, after which his work became haunted by psychological themes, while at the same time he became deeply immersed in social justice issues, largely as a tribute to her memory. One of Howells' good friends and literary protégés, Mark Twain, lost three of his children during his lifetime, the most impactful being the death of his own adult daughter Susy in 1896. Like Howells, Twain turned much of his own grief into constructive critique of his homeland. And W. E. B. Du Bois, whose masterpiece *The Souls of Black Folk* (1903) is filled with lengthy meditations on loss and grief over the death in 1899 of his own "first-born," similarly became deeply obsessed with righting the many wrongs perpetrated by white citizens against their African American neighbors. In particular, Du Bois' long-term campaign against public lynching, a barbaric practice that was carried out well into the twentieth century, most often against young black males, can be understood as a result of his desire to remember the legacy of his own deceased son.

As I argue in my latest work, *Continuing Bonds with the Dead* (2016), the grief experiences of these and other great authors impacted them in constructive and often lifelong ways. Ultimately, their struggles bore redemptive fruit in not just their own lives, but in America's ongoing attempt to achieve a better world for all its citizens. What they all shared was a profound acquaintance with grief coupled with a strong sense of how the bonds with the dead sustained and motivated them. All of them toiled in the shadows of the nearly total breakdown of their spouses, as well as suffering their own bouts of depression and doubts about God and religion. And yet, these brave survivors, like many bereaved parents before and after, and despite finding themselves in such a condition, plunged forward into their work, motivated by the memories of the dead. Their perceived bonds with the dead produced genuine influence in the ways these authors thought about their writing and career.

Our tendency is to mythologize the great artists, which seems understandable. However, all of these authors were living and breathing human beings, facing life's trials and disappointments like the rest of us. When I've spoken to groups large and small about the ways parental grief affected the lives of some of our nation's greatest authors, listeners are transfixed. Somehow, a deep acquaintance with grief, and in certain cases, trauma humanizes these great authors. Partly this is because many listeners have suffered from their own profound losses: if not a child, then a spouse, a parent, a sibling, or a mentor or good friend. The insights I tried to express in my book have become extremely important for me personally—perhaps even life-saving (at the risk of sounding melodramatic). Like these great authors, I too yearn to commune with, and listen to, what Stowe called "those hovering spirits"; the "cloud of witnesses" that is said to surround us (Hebrews 12). In particular, I've managed to hold onto my own bonds with my deceased son Daniel, to whom the book is a tribute in so many ways. His death in summer 1999 was the classic before-and-after moment for me and my wife. Honestly, my emotional stake in these areas as guilty survivor is crucial, and indeed formative; just as emotional turmoil affected those heroic exemplars listed above. As many readers might imagine, my decision to include in my own research some auto-biographical details about my own loss has produced a certain amount of critical backlash. But in truth, I now consider my book *Continuing Bonds with the Dead* to be a material outcome of my own continuing bonds with Daniel: it is frankly a tangible product of my own wrestling with grief. *Continuing Bonds with the Dead* represents, to some extent, additional evidence of what Lincoln called famously the "mystic chords of memory" binding all of us together—even the living and the dead.

At the time when my own tragedy struck in 1999, I had been working on the life and times of Mark Twain for the better part of a decade. Oddly, in all my reading about Twain over many years, it had literally never even occurred to me how the deaths of three of his four children had affected him. Evidently it had not seemed important to almost any of the other hundreds of Twain scholars, for some reason. But I have become convinced that Mark Twain's status as a bereaved parent is crucial to understanding him fully, and I've given a large amount of attention to this claim in the years since then. What fascinated and horrified me initially, as I was beginning my own descent into what seemed near-madness, was the discovery of Twain's striking comments, some of the most accurate I've ever read about the emotionally numbing first encounter with disaster, which he wrote soon after the death of his lovely, highly intelligent, adult daughter Susy in 1896:

> It is one of the mysteries of our nature that a man, all unprepared, can receive a thunderstroke like that and live. There is but one reasonable explanation of it. The intellect is stunned by the shock and but gropingly gathers the meaning of the words. The power to realize their full import is mercifully wanting. The mind has a dumb sense of vast loss— that is all. It will take mind and memory months, and possibly years, to gather together the details and thus learn and know the whole extent of the loss.
>
> *(Twain, 2010)*

I still consider Twain's remark to be a cornerstone statement, at least in my own experience, largely due to its nod toward latency: the fact that a full recognition of loss takes much time. Work was therapeutic for the grieving Mark Twain, as I would later discover it was for many other bereaved authors (and for me)—and despite feeling underwater and disconnected much of the time, Twain's writing, consisting of varying degrees of import and originality, did in fact get published, in those years after Susy's death. Some of Twain's writing in this period was scattershot and rambling, but some of it was very good indeed, especially the social criticism that became a near-obsession. Even so, he found himself wandering around in a sort of hopeless trance for at least the first several years, if not more. His wife Livy, never strong physically to begin with, fell into a decline from which she would never fully recover; she died eight years later, during which period Twain served as both consoler and caregiver. Her plight had similarities with other famous wives, including Mary Todd Lincoln, famously neurotic and even psychotic according to popular legend. But in the frame of parental loss, the erratic behavior and emotional decline of these spouses accentuates the sorrows and the struggles of their more famous husbands. Abraham Lincoln and Mark Twain are not commonly remembered as caregivers for their emotionally wrecked wives, but when we consider that aspect of their own grief experience, it both raises our admiration for them and helps us realize that their grief was a constant factor in both their everyday lives and their imaginative and creative lives as writers. Care for the inconsolable became an everyday feature. And as a result, I now firmly believe that a true accounting of this subject must begin with that aspect: the sheer torture of losing a child, and a view of life to come as hopeless and horrible, all summarized in what Mark Twain memorably described elsewhere as "this odious world" (2010). His wife Livy, like Lincoln's wife Mary, would face profound grief and chronic mental and physical illness for the rest of her life, as her well-meaning husband looked on helplessly.

After a couple of years of mental gyration (including my own share of caregiving), I began digging around into the research about parental grief. I discovered, initially, something that Twain and Lincoln had already discovered—that many parents never do seem to "recover"—at least not fully. One of the first and most disturbing clinical studies I came upon showed that for many, a psychological state of "overwhelming life meaninglessness" does not necessarily change with time; or if it does, it takes many years at least. In other words, there is clinical evidence that the old adage "Time heals all wounds" does not easily fit parental bereavement (Florian, 1989). (I was also beginning to realize that "healing" itself is a Freudian metaphor based upon the mistaken idea of grief as illness, and that "recovery" is a symptom of this metaphor of illness.) Actually, the opposite might be more accurate: there may be an intensification of pain, especially in the third or fourth year after the loss. Some studies show that parental grief often gets worse with time, at least in the initial years. I think I discovered that stunner near the end of my own second year of suffering, and it was depressing to think that I might not have even bottomed out yet.

Still, I plunged ahead, genuinely curious to learn how writers like Lincoln and Twain managed their own pain. What I learned mostly from their ordeals with grief was basically three-fold: first, both men experienced the deepest and most profound versions of hell on earth, and both wrote about that hell in a compelling manner that resonated deeply with me. Second, like almost all bereaved parents, Twain and Lincoln both confronted a profound crisis of meaning. Losing a child challenges one's view of the world, leading frequently into a kind of despair and hopelessness. A child evokes a connection with the past, an investment in the future, and an extension of self. To say it another way, a child is a concrete expression of hope in the future, and when a child dies, much of a person's hope dies as well. Lincoln and Twain both felt quite forlorn in the loss of a legacy for the future. Their losses challenged previous assumptions about the purpose and meaning of life. But their responses were significantly different: Lincoln turned heavenward, as I argue in my book; he returned in significant ways to a mystical vision of God that became a stunning feature of his most famous writings after 1862, especially the *Gettysburg Address* (1863) and the *Second Inaugural Address* of 1865. Both speeches pay tribute to the bonds with the dead, and gesture toward the fact that those dead did not suffer in vain. Twain, on the other hand, gravitated away from God or the sublime: his legendary anger and bitterness raged after Susy's death, to such an extent that this later version of Mark Twain would become the reigning stereotype of the great author. These two diametrically opposed responses to parental bereavement represent common responses: some parents move closer to God or the things of the spirit; others move dramatically and permanently away.

Finally, the continuing bonds with their beloved children haunted both men for the remaining years of their lives. Some of that connection bore some good fruit for both Lincoln and Twain. The pain softened both hearts in certain ways, even as it hardened them in other ways. Most importantly, Lincoln's loss of a son during the Civil War fostered a genuine sympathy for the thousands of other bereaved parents who, like him, never saw their sons again. Out of that sympathy for his countrymen came what many consider the greatest artistic renderings of an American political philosophy yet recorded. Meanwhile, the loss of Susy tended to exacerbate Twain's sense of moral outrage. And out of that moral outrage came some of the finest social criticism of Twain's long career—and indeed, some of the finest ever to be written by an American. Imperialism, political corruption, and lynching became favorite targets of his rage—along with sour and hypocritical religion. In both instances, and as different as their individual responses were to the death of a child, it is possible to chart the many ways that the extended grief of Lincoln and Twain bore redemptive fruit in their lives, their writing, and in the cultural history of the nation.

But why "redemptive"? I hesitate to attempt a summary of all the constructive or "redemptive" aspects that might emerge from different individuals' pain and suffering; and in fact, making that sort of argument to the newly bereaved can sound coarse or even sadly naïve. Many people are also very uncomfortable in general with invoking the religious term "redemption." So we should use the term advisedly. And yet, the concept of finding the redemptive effects of pain and suffering has become cemented into the everyday language of Americans. Even today one often hears survivors describe their stubborn resistance to the idea that their child has "died in vain." This concept, lifted from biblical passages like I Corinthians 15 and elsewhere, was a catchphrase in nineteenth-century America, and still is today. The key biblical promise is found in I Corinthians 15:58, which reminds us that, since death is to be defeated, one must be "steadfast, immovable, always abounding in the work of the Lord, knowing that your toil is not in vain in the Lord." The mystery of redemption, that our labor is "not in vain" (I Cor. 15:58), was captured for all time, and was framed most memorably and artfully at Gettysburg by our martyr president in fall 1863. The concept of the dead not "dying in vain" was a prominent theme in the nineteenth century.

But it would be a mistake to consider this response an artifact of an older cultural ethos. It has been invoked by grieving parents ever since. As challenging as it may be for some to believe it, many bereaved parents have in fact found terrific consolation in that idea—including all of the authors I've written about. Thus, in his volumes *The Stories We Live By* (1993) and *The Redemptive Self* (2006), psychologist Dan P. McAdams has shown that generativity is a key theme in American autobiography, and that Americans are particularly prone to seeing redemptive aspects come out of tragic circumstances. In some ways, a strong belief in the redemptive outcomes of suffering and pain seems to be somehow programmed into the American DNA. McAdams claims that in the American construction of self, redemption narratives featuring one's struggles, the overcoming of adversity, and generativity are central and common features. He describes the common themes in the stories of "highly regenerative" adults describing the "transformation of bad life scenes into good outcomes." Such stories highlight how "extremely bad events (e.g. death, loss, failure, frustration) are followed by good outcomes (e.g. revitalization, improvement, growth, enlightenment)." Some major expressions of these themes are the often repeated desires "to give something back" to family, friends, schools, organizations, or society in general; and he detects a variety of clichés to sum up this concept: from "it's always darkest before the dawn" to "turning lemons into lemonade" to "finding the silver lining of a dark cloud." Counter-intuitively, something constructive and lasting emerges out of life's worst tragedies.

In spiritual terms, this good can be called the "redemptive" outcomes that emerge from testing through adversity or tragedy. The key feature of the stories told by survivors, as documented by McAdams (2006), is an appeal to what he is calling redemption, which he defines as the ability to see something positive come out of tragic circumstances. Over two decades, McAdams has built on Erik Erikson's important earlier work by studying the ways that survivors of disaster and misfortune tell their stories, envisioning the ongoing effects of the dead, and commonly sensing the presence of the deceased. Redemptive stories or "sequences" are told when brave people, faced with tragedy, find ways to turn the pain into something powerful and perpetual. According to McAdams,

> Research findings suggest that highly generative American adults are statistically more likely than their less generative counterparts to make sense of their own lives through an idealized story script that emphasizes, among other themes, the power of human redemption. In the most general sense, redemption is *a deliverance from suffering to a better world.*

Moreover, McAdams explains, constructive approaches to suffering need not be limited to a Christian framework: "The general idea of redemption can be found in all of the world's major religions and many cultural traditions."

McAdams' work has been enormously helpful to me, as I've analyzed and unraveled these authors' complicated responses to the pain of losing a child. Moreover, his work has promising implications for further application in the fields of literary and cultural studies as well as narrative theory. Specifically, "redemption sequences" appear to be a very prominent motif in the fiction and non-fiction of Americans from all walks of life. My own claim is that the perception of a continuing bond with the dead child has often been one of the most inspiring motivations for the surviving parents, and thus a key manifestation of a redemptive view of the survivor's experience of grief. On one level, this assertion relies upon a pragmatic explanation of the bonds: when survivors perceive the bonds and act upon that perception, they can be said to be "real" to them. But despite this pragmatic response, the one question that still comes up constantly is that of ontology: "Yes, but are the bonds really real?" For many (but not all) of the parents described here and in my book, the answer is a definitive yes. This view depends also on theological and biblical belief, and there are other philosophical grounds for finding this position plausible, as well.

Obviously a solution to the quandary of the "reality" of continuing bonds is beyond the scope of this chapter, but the conception of "ontological flooding" presented elsewhere in this volume by Jack Hunter is intriguing: it allows researchers to avoid bracketing off this query and thus avoid responding to it.

As Hunter mentions (and I concur), it's the one question that comes up the most. Suffice it to say that for countless survivors, the bonds are real not simply because of their "perceptions," but because the deceased person does exist elsewhere, and the consolation of reunion is coming. Simply dismissing this metaphysical claim has offended and hurt many good people over the years. Thus, instead of bracketing off the possibility of phenomena or access to knowledge we are unable to prove, flooding allows clinicians and researchers to take seriously the claims of those survivors who believe in an afterlife.

Another specific problem with any appeal to a redemptive view, of course, even if it is a metaphysical reality, is that it can sound trite or glib to those in the throes of suffering. Under no circumstances should we discount the horrific element of these experiences; none of these authors did, certainly. But they were determined, to varying degrees, to find some solace in a constructive memory of the dead, inspiring them as they moved forward into some sort of hopeful future after grief. And this redemptive view became commonly incorporated into the story of grief and suffering subsequently told. If trauma consists, as Cathy Caruth has written, of the "story of a wound," then redemption has often been a major part of the story (1996).

Caruth's simple metaphor reminds me of a line from *The Gift of Pain* (1993) by Phillip Yancey and Paul Brand: "Think of pain as a speech your body is delivering about a subject of vital importance to you." The speech of pain often, though not always, records the motivational empowerment that derives from a sense of the bonds with the dead. In making such claims, continuing bonds theory has supplied much of the main theoretical and clinical grounds. In addition, I believe that my own approach to continuing bonds theory, as applied to the lives and writings of great American authors, can be greatly expanded to include the stories of many more Americans than I could possibly cover in a single book. The fields are ripe for harvest, in terms of uncovering the many "stories of a wound," in which a person's sense of a continuing bond with a deceased child has both inspired them but also changed, literally, some aspect of public opinion, or some element of our social institutions. In the remainder of this chapter, I will consider this powerful sense that our bonds continue with the dead, and I will sketch a few instances of individuals who have survived the death of a child and then gone on to bear redemptive fruits by drawing upon those bonds. By documenting how continuing bonds with the dead have shaped American culture for the good, I hope to inspire further biographical story-telling that will help light the way forward for those who find themselves, sadly, on the same path in the future.

Such redemptive effects of continuing bonds are not limited to the nineteenth century, of course. Even up to the present day, bereaved parents and sometimes entire communities are motivated by the desire to remember the dead in constructive ways, often at the strong appeal of a surviving parent. A magisterial redemption sequence can be witnessed in the actions of Mamie Till-Bradley, whose 14-year-old son Emmett Till was brutally murdered in Mississippi, in August 1955. But Mamie refused to let go of her bond with her son.[1]

Mamie's emphasis on finding some constructive meaning out of the horror of her son's death was in utter opposition to the advice of her friends and pastor, who resisted her proposal for an open-casket funeral in Chicago at the Roberts Temple Church of God in Christ. But Mamie's dogged insistence that the funeral include an open casket so that the world could witness "what they did to my son," even in the face of great pressure to do otherwise, is the remarkable detail of this redemption sequence (2004).

As a result, the swollen and disturbingly disfigured head and body of her son, encased in glass in the coffin, became emblazoned on the nation's consciousness through a series of reprints in major publications. Mamie asserted that the entire nation should face the horrific death personally, and behold the corpse along with her. Viewing the mangled remains of her dead son was, in Mamie's words, the "sledgehammer of God." These images became motivating factors of the movement to change America: Mamie's courage is now remembered as a genetic starting point in the emergence of a national Civil Rights Movement. Her sad story illustrates powerfully the way her continuing bond with her dead son Emmett could produce redemptive fruit.

In 2003, nearly a half-century later and just after her own death, Mamie's memoir of those historic events was published posthumously. The title of the book, *Death of Innocence: The Story of the Hate Crime that Changed America*, says a lot about Mamie's understanding of her son's legacy a half-century later: Emmett's death, according to the title, ended up changing America. Mamie's title echoed and agreed with what many commentators had already asserted: that national exposure of a single crime, the murder of her son, had marked the true beginning of the Civil Rights Movement. As Jesse Jackson puts it in the book's foreword, "If the men who killed Emmett Till had known his body would free a people, they would have let him live" (2003). These majestic words figure Emmett as a kind of martyr-savior. As Jackson puts it: "Mamie turned a crucifixion into a resurrection. Well done, Mamie, well done. You turned death into living. Well done. You awakened the world. Well done. You gave your son so a nation might be saved. Well done" (2004). Jackson is echoing here a biblical phrase, "well done, good and faithful servant," a phrase spoken by God that is said to greet the true believer into the heavenly kingdom (e.g., Matthew 25:21, 23). Jackson, like Mamie, is attributing massive historical changes to the death of this one boy, and consequently to the courage and long-suffering of the mother who publicized the atrocity.

In doing so, Jackson's tribute is more the rule than the exception: the cultural memory of Till's murder as a turning point is very common in memoirs of the period. This "sledgehammer" impact became a national phenomenon when pictures of the mutilated head and body of Emmett Till were published in magazines and newspapers. Particularly noteworthy were photos printed in *Jet* magazine. Many Americans have commented on the power of those images, and the dramatic effect that viewing them had in their lives. The sociologist Joyce Ladner, for instance, has stated that Emmett:

was about our age . . . When we saw the picture of his bloated body
in *Jet* magazine, we asked each other, "How could they do that to
him?" . . . [my] sister promised that she would become a lawyer and
fight to change things. I had decided to become a social worker so that
I could help black people.

(Whitfield, 1991)

Boxer Muhammad Ali remembered that as a young Cassius Clay on the streets
of Louisville,

I stood on the corner with a gang of boys, looking at pictures of him
in the black newspapers and magazines . . . his head was swollen and
bashed in . . . His mother had done a bold thing . . . I couldn't get
Emmett out of my mind.

(Ali, 1975)

Student Nonviolent Coordinating Committee (SNCC) activist Cleveland Sellers
recalled that

the atrocity that affected me the most was Emmett Till's lynching . . .
Many black newspapers and magazines carried pictures of the corpse. I
can still remember them. They showed terrible gashes and tears in the
flesh. It gave the appearance of a ragged, rotting sponge.

(Sellers, 1990)

Basketball star Kareem Abdul-Jabbar recalled

how Emmett Till's lynching affected me when it happened . . . I was
eight years old when I saw a photo of Emmett's body in *Jet* magazine.
It made me sick. His face was distorted, gruesomely bloated . . . the *Jet*
photo left an indelible image I could never forget . . . Emmett's mother
had insisted on an open casket and a public viewing . . . she was addressing the *world* . . . That was *her* way of putting people on notice.

(Abdul-Jabbar & Steinberg, 1996)

In the American imagination, Till's death now commonly receives a place alongside such other mythic moments as Rosa Parks refusing to settle for standing
on a Montgomery bus in December 1955—four months after Emmett's funeral.
Today, it is very common for both professional historians and regular American
citizens to acknowledge these two events of 1955 as the twin mechanisms that
jump-started the movement for civil rights, and Mamie's book echoes and aug-
ments that conception. American society's response to the death and public display
of Emmett Till, which was rooted in one mother's insistent stand exposing the
unjust hatred that killed her son, is one of the most important instances of continuing bonds provoking social change in American history. Like many parents

of deceased children, Mamie's conviction was that somehow Emmett's death could become meaningful, and that some redemption might come out of it. Her hope in this case was that Emmett Till's body would become a cultural shorthand for the horrendous treatment of black Americans in the south—which, in fact, it did (Bush, 2013). Mamie's "sledgehammer" is an even more fitting image for the traumatic impact of the photographs of Emmett's body, because Mamie herself was ready and willing to pry the box open herself, with a hammer and chisel. One mother's fearless resolve helped to usher in a long period of national debate over crucial issues of civil rights. Her goal was that her son Emmett would positively affect her community and her nation—even after his seemingly pointless death.

Mamie's notion of the "sledgehammer of God" is consistent with the effects of grief as documented in scores of other sad tales, in which a parent works diligently to protect the dead child's legacy by bringing attention to the horror and injustice of their loss. Numerous, more recent examples of continuing bonds with a dead child have also changed America for the better: from the bereaved mothers Candy Lightner and Cindy Lamb, who formed MADD (Mothers Against Drunk Driving) after their daughters were either killed or maimed by drunk drivers; to Judy Shepard, who wrote about her son in *The Meaning of Matthew* after he was beaten to death for being homosexual; to former Senator and presidential candidate George McGovern, who wrote about the death of his adult daughter in the poignant memoir, *Terry: My Daughter's Life and Death Struggle with Alcoholism* (1997). Another demonstration of one parent's continuing bonds with a dead child is seen in the anti-imperialist critique of Andrew Bacevich, a retired colonel (U.S. Army). Bacevich, now retired as a professor of history at Boston University, speaks with the authority of one who has given more to military causes than most of us: his son was killed in combat in Iraq in 2007. Bacevich has spoken about his bond with his son as a motivating force in several interviews. His turn against some of America's imperialist tendencies is striking for at least two major reasons: 1. Bacevich is an insider, having risen to elite levels within the military; and 2. Bacevich speaks from a decidedly conservative political vantage point (and thus, he cannot be labeled as just another "tenured radical"). Already a strong critical voice against American militarism before his son's death, that loss only multiplied the rage of his ongoing crusade, and he has become one of the most outspoken critics ever since. Because of scholarship produced by the likes of Bacevich and others, more and more Americans are rethinking their views about America's imperial legacies. And his grand rethinking of American missions abroad, especially in the region he has called "the Greater Middle East," comes in the wake of one father's continuing bond with his dead son (see e.g. Bacevich, 2016).

Another particularly poignant example of how continuing bonds have been represented by writers can be seen in Shane Claiborne's underground classic memoir *Irresistible Revolution* (2006), a book replete with grief and sorrow, much of which is fueled by the loss of children, both here and abroad. Claiborne's prophetic burden is to awaken the North American church to its calling to care for the poor and to stand for social justice. But in effect, and most simply, Claiborne wants us to work harder at loving our neighbors—and in recognizing that every individual we encounter during the course of our days is a neighbor, formed in the image of God and thus worthy of love and esteem. In some of the most moving passages of the book, Claiborne narrates the story of Bud Welch, a bereaved father whose 23-year-old daughter Jennifer was killed in the Oklahoma City terror attack in 1995. In his own words,

> Three days after the bombing, as I watched Tim McVeigh being led out of the courthouse, I hoped someone in a high building with a rifle would shoot him dead. I wanted him to fry. In fact, I'd have killed him myself if I'd had the chance. Unable to deal with the pain of Julie's death, I started self- medicating with alcohol until eventually the hangovers were lasting all day.
>
> *(Claiborne, 2006)*

But soon enough, Welch remembered his dead daughter and her long-term commitment to issues of reconciliation and justice. His bond with his daughter convinced him that he had allowed himself to become motivated largely by hate and revenge, and he knew that he must find a way forward by drawing upon some of his daughter's most cherished values. Largely in memory of Jennifer's courageous championing of reconciliation, Welch bravely set up a meeting with the father of Timothy McVeigh, one of the men who plotted the bombing and was now on trial for his life. In 1998, after McVeigh had been sentenced to death for his crime, Welch met with Bill McVeigh, the father, and assured him that he held no ill will against him. In Claiborne's account, the meeting of Welch and McVeigh represents one father's attempt to live out a certain neighborly ethic that might bring honor to the legacy of his dead daughter. Afterwards, he saw redemptive fruit from the meeting: he was able "to look into the eyes of Timothy McVeigh, the murderer, and see the image of God . . . Bud is one who still believes in the scandal of grace" (Claiborne, 2006).

Finally, and especially compelling at the present moment in our culture, are the lingering bonds with a long and growing list of dead black male victims, whose unjust deaths at the hands of local police officers have been featured prominently in our media. Much like the horror of the murder of Emmett Till, scores of similar injustices have become firmly rooted in the American imagination, particularly since Ferguson hit the headlines in August 2014. And yet, as with Emmett's mother, a sense of the constructive possibilities of pain resonates deeply in our culture at the present time. Almost every day, one hears survivors describe their stubborn resistance to the idea that their child has "died in vain." Recently, President Obama, speaking in July 2016 at the memorial for the slain Dallas police officers, made similar remarks:

> my faith tells me that they did not die in vain. I believe our sorrow can make us a better country. I believe our righteous anger can be transformed into more justice and more peace. Weeping may endure for a night, but I'm convinced joy comes in the morning.
>
> *(Obama, 2016)*

Like his forefather Lincoln, Obama here appeals to the promise of scripture, in this case Psalm 30:5.

Just days later, at the Democratic National Convention in Philadelphia, an emotional highlight was the appearance of the bereaved mothers of deceased black males such as Trayvon Martin, Michael Brown, Eric Garner, and others, appealing to their listeners to do something productive in light of their sons' untimely deaths. Another powerful episode was the poignant appeal of the father of Capt. Humayun Khan, a Muslim American soldier who was killed, followed by the uproar started by the uncaring and inept comments of Donald Trump afterwards. The prominence of these moments speaks to the lingering power of the bonds with the dead child in the lives of their surviving parents—and to the general public's high esteem for the sheer hell experienced by those survivors. They all hope that their child's unspeakable death may somehow find constructive fruit, so that they will not have "died in vain."

The subjects of my book, similar to these contemporary examples, all testify to a kind of inspired steadfastness that should be a great consolation to us all, whether traumatized or not. Perhaps the most poignant element of my approach has been to show how the perception of the bond has often reshaped the culture itself. Certainly, a perception of continuing bonds in America has frequently been the motor of decisive progress and social change. In my own case, I've long considered my work to be, after all, one more example of how the continuing bonds with the dead can bear constructive and beneficial consequences—the "peaceable fruits of righteousness" (Hebrews 12)—in the lives of others. As I've argued in my book, even the most horrific traumas cannot kill all the music in the world; instead, hope can live on. And speaking for myself, I certainly believe that the bonds about which I've written and researched over many years are "real." And so I invite others to begin with an open heart and listening ears, and to take seriously the ontological claims of the survivors, by throwing open widely the floodgates of faith. Hunter's appeal resonates with the work of William James, who insisted that belief depends upon a will to believe, since there are some domains in which truths will be hidden from us unless we go at least halfway toward them. Perhaps, as Hunter writes, the bonds are "genuine and meaningful interactions between the living and the dead."

Many grieving parents believe just that about these interactions. In a similar manner do many bereaved parents embrace a real hope, just as Michael Brown's grieving mother Lezley McSpadden hopes: that our dead child did not "die in vain," and that even an untimely, unjust death might come to mean something for those of us left behind. As McSpadden said publicly in the aftermath of her son's death, "My son's life and death has a bigger purpose on it. He was too good for this wicked world, so God picked the rose too soon." McSpadden has now published a memoir about her ordeal, *Tell the Truth and Shame the Devil* (2016), and has started a foundation in her son's honor: the Michael O. D. Brown We Love Our Sons & Daughters Foundation, whose mission is to advocate for "justice, improving health, advancing education, and strengthening families." Her words echo the sentiments of countless survivors of parental grief before her: the

untimely deaths of children cannot extinguish the ongoing legacy of their lives—
as long as we remember them. And her works echo the memorable, consoling
promises of scripture as well: that we need not die in vain. Well done, Lezley.
Well done.

Note

1 I will refer to Emmett's mother as either Mamie or Mamie Till-Bradley. When her son
died, Mamie went by the name Mamie Bradley. Later she called herself Mamie Till-
Bradley; then later still Mamie Till-Mobley, so there is some confusion regarding what to
call her regularly.

References

Abdul-Jabbar, K., & Steinberg, A. (1996). *Black profiles in courage: A legacy of African American achievement*. New York, NY: William Morrow and Company.

Ali, M. (1975). *The greatest: My own story*. New York, NY: Random House.

Bacevich, A. (2016). *America's war for the greater Middle East: A military history*. New York, NY: Random House.

Bush, H. K. (2013). Continuing bonds and Emmett Till's mother. *Southern Quarterly, 50*, 9–27.

Bush, H. K. (2016). *Continuing bonds with the dead: Parental grief and nineteenth-century American authors*. Tuscaloosa, AL: University of Alabama Press.

Caruth, C. (1996). *Unclaimed experience: Trauma, narrative, and history*. Baltimore, MD: Johns Hopkins University Press.

Claiborne, S. (2006). *The irresistible revolution: Living as an ordinary radical*. Grand Rapids, MI: Zondervan.

Florian, V. (1989). Meaning and purpose in the life of bereaved parents whose son fell during active military service. *Omega, 20*, 912–102.

Jackson, J. L. (2003). Foreword. *Death of innocence: The story of the hate crime that changed America*. New York, NY: Random House.

McAdams, D. P. (2006). *The redemptive self: Stories American live by*. New York, NY: Oxford University Press.

Obama, B. (2016). Remarks by the President at memorial service for the fallen Dallas police officers. www.whitehouse.gov/the-press-office/2016/07/12/remarks-president-memorial-service-fallen-dallas-police-officers.

Sellers, C. (1990). *The river of no return: The autobiography of a black militant and the life and death of SNCC*. Jackson, MS: University Press of Mississippi.

Till-Mobley, M., & Benson, C. (2003). *Death of innocence: The story of the hate crime that changed America*. New York, NY: Random House.

Twain, M. (2010). *Autobiography of Mark Twain, Vol. 1*. Berkeley, CA: University of California Press.

Whitfield, S. J. (1991). *A death in the delta: The story of Emmett Till*. Baltimore, MD: Johns Hopkins University Press.

Yancey, P., & Brand, P. (1993). *The gift of pain*. Grand Rapids, MI: Zondervan.

SECTION II

Continuing Bonds and Clinical Contexts

Introduction

Continuing Bonds: New Understandings of Grief had significant clinical implications without even addressing clinical practice per se. Its message freed clinicians to allow, accept, and possibly even encourage ongoing relationships with the deceased instead of working toward the relinquishing of the bonds as the dominant model dictated. The years since the continuing bonds model was introduced have seen the development of novel approaches to the therapeutic use of continuing bonds in highly nuanced and sensitive ways.

SUBSECTION II.1

Innovations for Working with Continuing Bonds

The first subsection brings together some examples of innovative practices, and it also samples of the psychological research that makes some welcome clinically relevant contributions to the field.

Robert Neimeyer and An Hooghe's chapter contains the full-length transcript of a therapy session, interspersed with commentary, in which the reader is invited to look over the shoulder of a master therapist as he skillfully helps a client renew the bond with her deceased mother in ways that are helpful for her ongoing life. The reader can follow a fascinating and intensive dialogue that resounds with evolving metaphors which both capture previously unspoken embodied feelings and create a new life-affirming narrative for the client and her bond with her mother.

Lorraine Hedtke shows how continuing bonds work fits into narrative therapy. She illustrates her work with a resonating case study. "We are born, not as isolated individuals," she writes, "but as members of an interlocking community of stories and relationships." Hedtke demonstrates how the interwoven individual and communal narratives become an important resource for her client.

In another example of clinical practice, Phyllis Kosminsky elaborates an attachment-focused approach to continuing bonds. She demonstrates the importance of a differentiated stance that takes account of the different starting points clients come with such as different attachment styles that require bespoke therapeutic responses. For example, she describes in detail the difficult work of reconfiguring an insecure attachment in the direction of an adaptive continuing bond, so the client is "more able to call upon the deceased as a continuing source of comfort and security."

While the chapter by Samuel Ho and Ide Chan does not directly describe a specific clinical approach, it reports clinically relevant research illustrated with clinical case examples. Ho and Chan offer a balanced discussion of the binary conceptualization of externalized and internalized continuing bonds. They report that they were unable to find a simple distinction between internal and external bonds with regard to bereavement adjustment and argue for an individualized approach to therapeutic practice.

Lisa Gassin opens the door of grief therapy to an area that tends to be associated with positive psychology or religion, as she examines the relationship between forgiveness and continuing bonds. By bringing forgiveness into the work with bereaved clients, Gassin points to some promising new ways of extending the well-established idea of working with "unfinished business."

The last chapter in this subsection by Bobo Lau, Candy Fong, and Celia Chan then provides an interesting perspective on continuing bonds in a specific type of grief, that is pregnancy loss, as they describe a new Chinese framework to continuing bonds that is further elaborated in Chapter 20, namely the Value-Action-Sensation (VAS) framework, which could be useful in other cultural contexts too.

6

RECONSTRUCTING THE CONTINUING BOND

A Case Study in Grief Therapy

Robert A. Neimeyer and An Hooghe

Over two decades since publication of the pioneering work on mourners' continuing bonds to the deceased, contemporary bereavement theorists and practitioners have clearly embraced its relevance for grief therapy (Neimeyer, 2015). But just how does attention to the relationship between the client and the deceased help direct the subtle give-and-take of the counseling process, as it unfolds in the intimate crucible of therapeutic dialogue? Our intent in the present chapter is to address this question by closely examining an actual session of grief therapy conducted along meaning reconstruction lines (Neimeyer, 2016a). We will begin by sketching a few of the cardinal themes of this perspective before introducing the detailed case study that will scaffold the chapter.

Loss and the Reconstruction of Meaning

Viewed through a constructivist lens, a central process in grieving is the attempt to reaffirm or reconstruct a world of meaning that has been challenged by loss. This does not imply that all experiences of bereavement entail a search for meaning, however, as we need not search for that which was not lost in the first place. Thus, when an important figure in our lives dies what we deem to be an "appropriate" death, one that fits comfortably enough into the narrative we hold of how life is or should be, it may pose minimal challenges to the practical patterns, relational scaffolding, and world assumptions that undergird our existence. But when that death is sudden, horrific, premature, or violent, or deprives us of a central figure on whom our sense of identity and security depends, we may be launched into an agonizing search for meaning in the loss and in our lives in its aftermath. The result, when we are unable to find meaning in what has befallen us, can be a grief that is perturbing, preoccupying, and prolonged, and perhaps even life-threatening. To date, a great deal of evidence converges to support the outlines of this meaning reconstruction model (Neimeyer, 2016a).

In light of the growing evidence base for the role of meaning-making in bereavement, adaptation in its wake has been theorized to entail two forms of narrative activity (Neimeyer & Thompson, 2014). The first of these is the need to *process the event story of the death itself*, and its implications for our lives in its aftermath. Making sense of the event story is particularly important when the loss is horrific and tragic, calling for a trauma-informed approach to integrating the narrative of the dying. The second involves an effort to *access the back story of the relationship to the deceased*, to resolve unfinished business and restore a measure of attachment security. Because this typically requires experientially vivid engagement with memories and images of the deceased, therapeutic work to reorganize the continuing bond requires an attachment-informed approach to grief therapy. Either or both of these forms of narrative processing may be called for in a given case, giving rise to a great range of creative therapeutic techniques (Neimeyer, 2012b, 2016b).

The Present Case

Inge and Erik were a Flemish couple in their 40s living in Belgium with their two children, ages 4 and 7, when they sought relationship therapy at Context, the Center for Marital and Family Therapy at the University Hospital in Leuven. Both confessed to An Hooghe, their therapist, that they had grown apart over the 10 years of their relationship, a pattern linked to Inge's intense engagement in her work as an international business consultant. Across eight sessions of earnest efforts in couple's therapy, both spouses stated that they had increased their mutual understanding, felt closer, made behavioral changes in their lives to permit more time together, and recommitted to their relationship. But in the course of exploring significant family relationships with each partner, Inge reported to An that she had lost her mother when she was 17 years old, a disclosure that was accompanied by an immense wave of sadness and tears. Of course, Erik knew this, but he had never met her mother, and Inge rarely spoke of her. Over the course of the sessions all noticed that Inge's grief for her mother remained a very sad and vulnerable place for her, one that continued tearfully to take her breath away each time the conversation of therapy touched on it. As the marital therapy came to a successful conclusion, Inge therefore approached An with a request for additional individual sessions to work on her prolonged and preoccupying grief, feeling that it would be too difficult to do so with her husband present. Both partners readily consented to the plan, with the intention to then bring them back together and share the story once Inge herself had found words for a grief so deep and pervasive that it seemed to elude expression.

In the 10 sessions of grief therapy that followed, Inge remained very "stuck" in her grief, nearly unable to access memories of her childhood or of her time with her mother. Witnessing this striking disconnection from her own history, and Inge's visible suffering with each mention of her mother's death over

20 years before, An noted that "it was as if everything were put away in a very secure place, which made it possible for her to function in her job and daily life." Working very slowly and with great caution, the two gradually began to access some memories of Inge's mother, and as she became better able to "hold" them, invited Erik back in to share the story. It was at this point that Robert Neimeyer (Bob) visited Belgium to offer some days of professional training in grief therapy, opening the prospect of Inge having a single session of therapy with him to supplement An's efforts, in view of Inge's near-native proficiency in English. After discussing this possibility as a couple, Inge and Erik accepted the offer, choosing to have Inge meet with Bob individually but on camera, while Erik watched the session alongside An and 15 other therapists in another room, to relieve each of the partners of the immediate impulse to take care of or "rescue" the other. This then was the arrangement as Bob welcomed Inge and Erik, intentionally limiting the background provided him (learning only that she struggled with her grief following the death of her mother), so as to allow Inge to present the problem to him in her own terms, unconstrained by previous case conceptualization. By mutual agreement, Inge, Bob, Erik, An, and the reflecting team of other therapists would then meet in a circle immediately afterward to share respectful questions about the therapy process before returning the couple to An's care for additional processing of its implications. The text that follows represents a verbatim transcription of the filmed interview, interspersed with Bob's first-person reflections on the work, which centered strongly on re-accessing and reorganizing Inge's continuing bond with her mother. The chapter then concludes with a brief summary of the subsequent couple's session, offering a window on the consultation's impact.

The Loss of Balance

Therapist (T; speaking initially in Dutch):	Inge, dank je wel nog eens voor deze conversatie [Thank you once again for this conversation]. I'm eager to learn something of your experience, and I wonder if we might begin with just asking you what kind of hopes or expectations might you have about this hour, about how it might be useful for you?
Inge (I):	Uhm, I don't have a lot of expectations and I'm not sure what to expect, but one thing that would help me is to find other ways of thinking about, uhm, thinking about (long silence) your *place* in the world among people, when there's a change in configuration, like when you lose someone, how you come back into your *balance*.
T:	Yeah, yeah, because the loss of another throws us *off balance* (gestures with arms and torso like a tightrope walker), and we find ourselves having a hard time finding our footing in the world again, in the sense of a solid *place*. And the loss that you've had, I understand, is the loss of your mother?

75

(Client nods, and immediately struggles with tears.) And just with the mention of her name the feeling rises in you. (Client begins to cry.) Yeah (gently). So what is that feeling (gesturing with hand at the level of his torso, like a rising fountain), if you were to describe it in words that were even partially adequate to the experience . . . What would we call that, the feeling that comes now?

I: Uhm (sigh) . . . Being *overwhelmed* (T: Overwhelmed, yeah.). (Pause) And in a way reliving it a bit (crying).

T: Reliving it a bit. Reliving the experience of her dying?

I: (Nods yes, tearfully.)

T: So the overwhelming feeling is one of . . .?

I: Yeah. Just, uhm, the loss, the loss of balance, loss of, the whole way that you thought your universe was functioning. And to have that go, disappear and be changed, and feel that's out of your control.

In response to my invitation to articulate her expectations about how this hour might be helpful to her—a bid to foster client agency in co-constructing the therapy—Inge pauses, and then in a slightly self-distancing, second-person voice, seeks a way to make sense of her "place" in the world in the wake of loss, to recover a sense of "balance." Hearing these vocally emphasized *quality terms* that begin to shape an implicit metaphor of her existential position, I echo the significant phrasing, lightly performing the image to give it more embodied presence in the room. A simple mention of her loss evokes strong emotion and tears, as we seek a preliminary verbal handle for the feeling, and spontaneously elaborate Inge's position in a universe that loses balance and coherence in light of her mother's death.

The Center of the Universe

T: Yeah. It's a deeply, deeply unwelcome change in the structure of the world, and you're left trying to relearn that world and relearn yourself because both are changed in this experience. . . . What position did your mother have in this world, in this universe of your childhood and young adulthood?

I: I was 17 when she died. (T: 17.) And she'd been ill on and off for a long time. But when she died it was still a surprise, because we didn't talk a lot of those things and she was very much a pillar figure in our house. She was a very dominant person, but not in a bad way. But she was called "Mrs. Thatcher" in her workplace (T: Ah, Mrs. Thatcher, the Iron . . .) The Iron Lady! (smiling and slightly laughing). And she was, not in a bad way, but she got her way in everything, had control over everything, she *governed* everything. In a way, she knew exactly what she wanted, what to do . . . when to do that.

T: The structures were there, and she was the one who kind of helped build them and keep them in good order.

I: Right. And she did that for us children but she did that for other relatives, for my father. There wasn't a big balance there, so she was very much a governing person in every sense of the word.

T: So in a way she was almost like a center of gravity or something for this solar system of the family, right? (Client nods.) And it's almost like, how does the solar system reorganize when the sun is extinguished, right?

I: Right (long pause, crying silently).

Our exploration of her mother's "governing" position in the family leads Inge to offer an affectionate characterization of her as "Mrs. Thatcher," the United Kingdom's forceful Prime Minister during the 1980s, whose unbending political will inspired the moniker used by her admirers. With my suggestion of a modest extension of Inge's metaphor of her imbalanced universe following her mother's death, she moves into several moments of wordless weeping, leading ultimately to my gentle intervention.

Introducing the Loved One

T: I wonder if you would be comfortable doing something with me just a moment, and that is, I would invite you just to close your eyes with me for just a second (closing eyes as client follows). And allow us to concentrate our breathing . . . just to allow our lungs to fill and empty . . . fill and empty (speaking slowly, and opening eyes to follow client's nonverbal behavior), in a natural rhythm. Just feeling maybe with each breath just a little release of the overwhelming feeling, recognizing that it's always accessible . . . and that that feeling probably has something to tell us . . . and teach us about this woman who was your mother, and still is your mother, in an important sense. (Client opens eyes.) And as we sit here speaking to each other, and as we kind of invite her to join us for that conversation in the ways we can, our goal is mutually to learn something about who you are, what you need, but also about who she is and what she would need, in seeing her daughter now, carrying this grief. (Client nods, silently.) So I wonder, would you be willing or be able to introduce her a little more, this Iron Lady (client laughs) who is the governor, and the center of this kind of universe. What was her name?

I: Yvette. (T: Yvette.) Uhm, she worked always very hard and she herself was an accident. At the time when she was born that was a big deal. (T: Ah.) But she had felt and we felt as children that she felt as an unwanted person for a large part of her life. (T: Wow.) And so that was something. She read a lot of books about it. She never talked to us about it but we could sense that she had that feeling in respect of her own parents.

T: And a real effort, it seems, across a period of years to make sense of that? Or to say, "Who am I and where do I fit in?"

I: Yes, and to get appreciation from her parents, which never really was to her satisfaction, and that was very frustrating. And I think that's probably why she worked so hard. (T: Ah.) Because it was something she felt she needed to make up for. And so she was a kind of person who would make all her own vegetables in the garden, she made all of our clothes (T: Wow.). She worked as a teacher; she did a lot of things. Even the evening before she would go to the hospital, she would wash all her clothes, and she made sure all the food was in place and the laundry was done. She did it by hand, even if she was meant to be in the hospital the next day. So she was this kind of indestructible force (smiling).

In the presence of Inge's strongly disregulating and isolating grief, I begin with a nearly meditative moment of mindful breathing, matching her respiration, and gradually slowing it in synchrony with my own. As her strong emotion softens in response and she spontaneously re-engages me, I invite Inge to "introduce her loved one," to appreciatively conjure her mother for me to re-access a seemingly broken bond (Hedtke, 2012). What emerges is a proud but incipient narrative of her mother's relentless work ethic, rooted, Inge surmises, in her being an unplanned and unwanted child and her lifelong effort to compensate for that.

A Quest for Connection

T: Yeah, almost an indestructible force. And how strange that must have been for her as well for you to witness this force having to contend with the force of illness. (Client: Yeah.) A cancer of some sort?
I: Yes, for years. And there were times, all through my high school period, she was ill on and off. And there were times when I was young and I would go to the hospital to visit her and I *liked* those times because she would sit still and not work. And I could talk to her (laughs with therapist)! And she would talk to me and so we had that special time together. So there were times when her illness was not a *threat* in that way . . .
T: Was almost a *friend* in that way?
I: Yes. It was something that was there.
T: And it opened a space for a special kind of mother–daughter conversation that with all of her busyness would otherwise be hard to find.
I: Right. And there were other times or times when she got really ill, and she asked me to read to her. She had a book that was by Siegel, Bernie Siegel. She read a lot of books about self-healing with thoughts about positive thinking. And she was in a lot of pain, in the end she was in a lot of pain, because the cancer had spread. And we read to her, and it was books in English (laughs). And she would say, "Is it okay for you to read so long to me in English?" (T: Wow.) And so we would sit with her, sometimes reading . . .
T: So part of your remarkable English language competence was really born in the crucible of that connection with her and reading to her?
I: Probably.

T: Wow, so you were giving that to her as a kind of *gift*. But she also kind of gave that to *you* as kind of gift, that you bring forward to *me*, even.
I: (Smiling tearfully) She was an English teacher (tenderly).
T: Ahh. She was an *English* teacher (nodding).
I: So that's why they called her Mrs. Thatcher (smiling). English teacher with an iron hand! (Both laugh.)
T: How perfect that is! I'm sorry to say I'm not Ronald Reagan. I can't exactly be the counterpart in the story of relationships across the sea! But it's a fascinating thing to meet her in this way. If you could picture her to convey what she looked like physically, what would I see in a picture of her?

Echoing but qualifying Inge's description of her mother as an "almost" indestructible force, I subtly open the door to the event story of her dying, having already begun accessing the back story of her personhood. What emerges is surprising: the periods of her mother's illness were more friendly than threatening, slowing her mother's otherwise intense activity to permit a special sort of mother–daughter bond. Significantly, this involved long exchanges in English as Inge read to her mother during her treatment, consolidating Inge's language competence at the same moment it consolidated the relationship. It is a short inferential step to formulate this as a legacy gift from her mother, as well as a reciprocal gift given to an ailing parent from a loving child. Connecting these dots to our own exchange in this same language completes the circle, and continues the work of invoking her mother's presence as a third participant in the therapeutic triad.

Inviting Mom's Presence

I: I have pictures of her with me so I can show them!
T: Yes if you're willing to show her.
I: So I have a picture of her (shows the framed black-and-white photo).
T: Ah, yeah (enthusiastically).
I: She looks a bit Thatcher-like! (Both laugh.)
T: Now in this picture, right, where we see this sort of expression, almost like a slight smile, and the eyebrows are little arched, what do you see in this expression?
I: Uhm, her *strength*, I think (T: Yeah), because she was already fighting at this point, she was already ill. This photo is taken not long before, 6 months or so.
T: You wouldn't know that, would you? (Client begins to lay the photo flat on the small table between them, as the therapist gently takes the frame and lifts it to standing.) Could we place her here, because we're certainly inviting her to be with us in the conversation today (client assists in situating the framed picture), and, yeah, to maybe just lend us her sense of presence, lend *you* her sense of presence, as you do this difficult work of addressing the relationship and the pain that comes with her physical dying? (Client weeps, and therapist gently hands her a tissue.)
I: Thank you (wipes nose and eyes).

Making a literal "place" in the shared space of therapy for her mother, we position her as a potential support figure in Inge's therapy. Deeply moved, she accepts this positioning, as she acknowledges her grief.

A Frozen Grief

T: Yeah . . . What do you sense now that you need in the aftermath of her dying, all those years ago? There's something now about this, of course, that touches you so deeply. But what would help there, with that?

I: (Pause.) I have been wondering that for a long time too. Uhm, because it still feels like a very short time ago, to me at least. And it doesn't feel to me like the feeling changes between now and 5 years ago or 10 years ago. It stays too, uhm, *open*.

T: It stays too open. And when you say, "It doesn't feel like it changes, to me at least," is there a feeling that it *has* changed for others, even for others who knew her, or who know and love you, that somehow their grief or feeling about her dying has evolved in a different way?

I: Mainly I'm thinking in terms how it normally *should* be (T: Aha). You think that these things will pass a little bit, but I think my brother and sister, as far as I can tell, don't have the same feeling, I think, but I'm not sure they would share it with me. I'm not sure. I was wondering, it should be, it should be something I should be able to talk about now without being overwhelmed.

T: "*Should*" . . . Who would say this *should*? Is this an expectation voiced by people, or just present in the culture in some way, or . . .?

I: Yeah, I think (pause). Or maybe it's something that I would expect from *myself*, to think I should be able to move past.

T: So like, almost a part of you (raising right hand to represent that part) is saying, "Inge, you need to be able to move past this, you need to be able to speak of her without the tears." But there's another part (raising left hand) that is very tender and very hurt, very sad (client weeps, but maintains strong eye contact), that feels that the structure of the universe lost its balance, has shifted somehow. And *you* feel off balance.

I: It's *stayed* out of balance. (T: Stayed out of balance.) And I kind of assumed (pauses, weeping) that I would regain the balance, in some way, over time.

T: Yeah, that time would *heal* the wounds. (C: Yeah). We kind of have a cultural prescription about that, don't we? And it doesn't seem like that's happened for you.

In response to my attempt to discern the need implicit in Inge's grief, she immediately notes its "open," unchanging character as the years of her bereavement turn to decades. Probing gently for a possible contextual or familial discourse underpinning her expectation of her course of grieving, Inge suggests that her siblings are less haunted by the loss, and hints that she "should" be moving past it herself. I frame this compassionately as an inner dialogue in two voices, both to validate her own possible double positioning regarding her grieving, and to foster greater self-compassion rather than self-criticism.

The Loss of Safety in the Family

I: No. And the feeling I had had when she died was one that (long pause) . . . We didn't talk about this very much at home and so I think each of us had our own emotion and just took that and lived with it the best we could. So there wasn't a lot of conversation. I think the feeling that I had was that there was no . . . *safe place* anymore. There was no *protection* (T: No safe place.), because she had been kind of the pillar of our family.

T: The protector, the supporter, the structure of the family, and now it's like the pillar of the family has collapsed.

I: Right, and there was nothing that ever really substituted for that. So we just each stayed on the ground, each individually finding our way back.

T: So she was not only the pillar but also like the *floor* or *foundation* of the family, and each of you found your way of standing on that in relation to each other. (C nods.) But with the collapse of that floor, each of you was kind of lost in your own world. (C: Right.) I see. (Pause) And you said something about finding your way back. Have you as a family, this is a brother, a sister, a father too?

I: A father too, who also died in the meantime.

As we continue to explore the meaning of this loss for Inge and its implications for her life now, Inge underscores in vivid metaphor the collapse of the secure base once provided by her attachment to her mother, and the resulting fragmentation of the family in the aftermath of her death.

A Silent Story

T: And did the three of you find your way back to connect again (C shakes head no), or . . .?

I: Not really. (T: Not really.) I think we get along, we see each other, we took care of my father when he passed. But we never talk about the experience. And we never shared that.

T: So there's a lot that's unsaid. A lot of silent stories that live within you, and that have no audience in the world.

I: Right (nodding repeatedly).

T: Have you been able to seek out and find others who can hear the stories that your family could not? About your Mom, about her illness, about her dying, about life since that time?

I: I haven't, really. I spoke to some friends about it, to my husband a little bit but . . .

T: What kind of responses do you get?

I: What I expect . . . listening, people listening. But it's such an overwhelming . . . I think because it's such an overwhelming feeling, I'm trying not to let it loose (gestures outward with her hands).

T: Ah, I see. So partly to not to overwhelm them you kind of, hold it in? Or not to overwhelm yourself?

I: Not to overwhelm myself. And putting me and them in a position . . . It would be awkward, I wouldn't know how to get out of it.

T: Yeah, yeah, yeah. How are you feeling now, in just this moment with me? You clearly experience and express in your tears, your face, and your words, some of this emotion.

I: I think now it's okay, I'm not overwhelmed anymore, at this moment. Because I'm trying to describe it, uhm, as opposed to experience it. I'm trying to do my best to not sit in it. So I guess it's a little better.

Although the narration of loss naturally occurs on every level from the intimately individual to the intricately social, in Inge's case her grief has become a self-censored, silent story, one that finds no audience in the world of others. However, in this case experiential avoidance of the core pain of grief seems only to have prolonged vulnerability to it, estranging Inge from family members, from herself, and in some sense from her mother. What seems called for, then, is a safe and supportive exploration of this grief in the crucible of a trusting relationship, in a way that takes into account its substantially wordless nature.

Analogical Listening

T: Yeah. Let me ask you this and see of this makes sense to you, to see if it's worth doing, but with no attempt to press this. How would it be if we were to almost accept that invitation to try to describe it, some of how you carry this grief about your Mom, without having you be swallowed up in that? If we were to do a kind of inner scan and visualization of how you carry the grief (gesturing with a slow wave over his torso, with eyes closed), allow it to speak to you from a place close to but not within it (gesturing to suggest this proximity to an inner shape). Would that be a welcome thing to be able to give it words, but not to be overwhelmed (making a wave-like gesture washing toward client) by those words?

I: Yeah. I don't know if I would be able to do it but I would like to try it.

T: Would you?

I: I think it would help because it's just what I experience, not intentionally, but that's what I'm experiencing right now. I'm trying to make this useful, to describe it to you, as opposed to just being overwhelmed. I think when I'm talking to a friend I'm just more overwhelmed, but now I really want to try and explain it, and so I think that is a better way.

T: Right. So here's my invitation, a little bit like we did a few minutes ago, just kind of to allow ourselves (slowing voice and closing his eyes) to close our eyes, and enter this place of quiet breathing, just kind of allowing our chest to rise and fall in a naturally deep rhythm (opening eyes to track client's nonverbal signals), emptying fully, and filling fully. As we just try to clear a space, a space between and around us, to invite this feeling to come (pause) in a way that gives it perhaps form and voice. Kind of a respectful invitation to a visitor, without having the visitor move in permanently. And what I would invite, if this feels okay to you, with your eyes closed, is to just do a kind of scan (gestures with hand slowly raising and lowering in front of his torso) through your body, allowing your awareness to maybe turn in and down (gesturing with his hand to suggest this movement), and into the space of your body, your torso, or wherever it might be drawn, as you just ask yourself the question: "Where in me do I carry this grief for my mother now?" (pause) And just wait for it to speak, and you might gesture toward it (touches chest lightly with fingers) to show the place where you feel its presence.

I: (Sighs, wipes her eyes, and places hand on her belly while weeping softly.)

T: Yeah. Kind of in your abdomen, almost, a deep place within your body, right? Just kind of retaining the privacy of closed eyes (closes his own, with hand on his abdomen, as client then does the same), just ask yourself in this place (speaking very slowly), this physical location that holds the grief: if the grief had a form or a shape, what might it be?

I: (Pause) Something like a blotch, something very changeable and expandable (gestures in and out with fingers).

T: A blotch. Changeable and expandable (mimicking and enlarging client's gesture). And with your fingers you kind of make the shape of expansion and contraction?

I: Right.

T: Does that have a color to it, as you just attend to it? (Closes eyes, as client then does the same.) (Pause) If it had a color what might the color or colors be?

I: Something reddish and purplish.

T: Reddish and purplish. (Pause) Kind of a constant color or changing color?

I: Changing.

T: Changing. Describe that change for me. What would it be looking like, changing from and to?

I: Like waves.

T: Waves. Like waves in the sea or . . . (making wave-like gestures with his hand)?

I: That rise up and that calm down again.

T: Ah. Rising up and calming down. That's that kind of expansion and contraction (making these gestures with his hand). Is that a good word for it?

I: Yeah.

T: Yeah (closing eyes, as client then does same). Is there a feeling associated with that image, that rising up and calming down? A bodily feeling or an emotional feeling?

I: A tightness, a muscle tightness.

T: A muscle tightness, like in your abdomen? (C: Right.) Right, yeah. I wonder if you can focus your attention in those abdominal muscles now. And just tighten them almost like you're doing sit-ups or something, like an exercise. Can you feel the tightening?

I: Yes.

T: As you do does that shape or image or color change in any way?

I: (Pause) It is a little more stable (laughs).

T: More stable, less fluctuation.

I: Yeah.

T: And if you just release that muscle tension . . . with me for a moment, and maybe just take a deep abdominal, diaphragmatic kind of breath, what happens with the image then?

I: (Pause) It becomes a little more, how to say that, less of a (smiling, making smoothing motions with her hands) . . . more calmer, laid out, like it's lying down.

T: Oooh, like it's lying down (smiling).

I: Like instead of the waves, it's more . . .

T: Less a tumultuous (C: Right.) raising up and falling but more of a calming. Calmer waters?

I: Right (pause).

Responding to my invitation to cultivate an unhurried, internal awareness through the breath-focused procedures of analogical listening (Neimeyer, 2012a), Inge quickly feels and visualizes where she holds the pain—in a reddish purple blotch (almost like a bruise) sensed in her abdomen. As we explore its sensory qualities of a wave-like expansion and contraction, Inge accepts my encouragement to consciously exaggerate the latter tension, and finds (perhaps surprisingly) greater "stability" in doing so. Releasing the tension at my invitation, she then notices a "calming" or "lying down" of the feeling, suggesting that she has some control over her terms of engagement with it, making further exploration of her relation to the abdominally held grief sufficiently safe to be feasible.

An Internal Dialogue

T: That's interesting (whispered). Just placing your attention near but not in that kind of watery expansive place, not drowning in it, but just sort of standing on the shore, I wonder if you would be willing to listen to it? Listening to anything that has to tell you. If it had a voice how would it speak? What would its vocal quality be like? (Client sighs.) Do that again (blowing softly out, as client does the same). How do you imagine it would speak, with what kind of voice?

I: I can't imagine it having a voice.

T: How would it communicate what it has to tell us or teach us?

I: (Pause.) I see it more as something that is not something communicative, but more something that is there to deal with and *carry*.

T:	To deal with and carry.
I:	Rather than it being communicative or . . .
T:	Uh huh, uh huh . . . So I wonder if, from that place near it but not in it, I wonder if you can just try some words like these, and see if they feel true to you? And if not, change them to make them so. Something like, "I'm willing to carry you." (Long pause) How would you need to change those words to make them fit for you? (Client begins to cry.) What's the feeling that comes to you with that?
I (weeping):	I was going to say, "I'm having a hard time carrying you."
T:	I'm having a hard time carrying you.
I:	(Nods yes.)
T:	I'm having a hard time carrying you. Then use those words: "I'm having a hard time carrying you." Tell her or it or him what it is that is hard about that. (Long pause.) What would you say about the difficulty carrying that dark, expansive, and contractive, sometimes tranquil, and sometimes more turbulent space?
I:	(Long pause). I guess it's difficult to carry because I sometimes feel like it's too overwhelming, it's too much and that it swallows me. And it feels like it's something I have to stay ahead of.

As we search for a way to dialogue with the image, we learn that it is less "communicative" than it is something to "carry," though at great emotional cost. Even with repeated efforts to establish a safe nearness to the feeling to explore the relationship to it, Inge is easily swallowed by the sea of grief, and seems at risk of drowning in it. What seems required, then, is a greater degree of separation that would make exposure to the feeling possible, but at greater distance.

Externalizing the Felt Sense

T: Something you have to stay ahead of? What if you could speak those words directly to the kind of feeling? And I wonder if we were to offer that image a place here with us, but a place a little bit outside you, would that be okay? (T places a third empty chair facing C, forming a triangle.) So if we offer a kind of comfortable chair here where it can repose, so it doesn't have to be lodged in your abdomen in this moment, I wonder if you can just return to those words, speak them to this sensed feeling, right? (Gesturing with both hands toward the empty chair.) "Sometimes it's overwhelming to carry you." What would you say to it about that?

I: Sometimes it's overwhelming to carry you (weeping). And it seems like it is never getting easier. It seems that it should get easier over time. Or that I should get better. It feels that I always have to be on my toes to not let it swallow me.

T: Say this and see if it feels like it fits: "It's like I have to be vigilant, or guard myself in some way." What's the "staying on my toes" feeling? What would you say about that?

85

I: It's also this feeling that I lost my place and universe a little bit. And so I have no safe position from within to carry you.

T: So you have no safe position?

I: No position of strength.

T: No position of strength to carry you.

I: And I have to do my best all the time.

T: Yeah, yeah. What would that position of strength look like if it had a physical shape, or structure?

I: (Pause.) Something very upright, like a rectangle, something very square.

Speaking to the now externalized feeling, Inge voices the essence of her struggle: deprived of the secure base provided by her mother, she has "no safe position from within to carry [her grief]." Turning her inner gaze from the visualized pain to the strength needed to carry it, she sketches briefly what it would look like: upright and rectangular. The geometry of her language and gesture suggests the next move.

Standing up to the Feeling

T: Shall we stand? Let's stand up and see how that is. (T and C stand up, as C chuckles.) So here we are, kind of rectangular (standing almost at attention, like a soldier). So how does it feel relating to this same image (gesturing downward, toward chair)? Is it still a quiet form or is it more turbulent? What is it?

I: It's turbulent.

T: It's turbulent?

I: Yeah.

T: How does it feel to just regard it (gesturing toward it) from this position of standing up (lifting hands to body) to it? Is there a difference between that and the kind of sitting with it? (As T speaks the word "sitting," he slowly sits down again, and client follows.)

I: No, it feels the same. Whatever shape it has or whatever shape I have, it can overpower anything. (T: I see.) So that's why I try to contain it in a *box* (C forms box with hands at level of her abdomen) (T: Oh, contain it in a box.) to make sure it doesn't get out of certain boundaries.

T: Oh, I see. That's the kind of almost abdominal tightness (forms tight box with hands), that's the boxing up of this? (C: Yeah). (Pause) And if it kind of leaks out of the box or spills over (gesturing to suggest these actions) then it feels more overwhelming?

I: (Nods yes.)

Inner strength, it seems, is not enough: soon enough the grief leaks out or over the embodied box that contains it. Something more is needed.

Consulting with Mom

T: Who or what might help you carry that sense, that feeling?

I: I thought a lot about that, and I don't know. (Pause) I don't know (crying).

T: I wonder, if you were to meet your mother's eyes in this moment of clear pain, what might she have to tell you about how pain can be carried, from a position of strength? (Turns photo toward client, and gazes at mother) What message would she have for us about that?

I: I remember she would read to me from those books that she kept reading about thinking positive.

T: The Bernie Siegel kinds of books. (C: Right.) So what kind of model or message might she have for you?

I: She was a strong person, she would say that I should shut up and move on.

T: Shut up and move on?

I: Yeah, she would have just said that, "Deal with it."

T: And she was able to somehow do that even in the midst of her cancer? (Client nods.) Were there times that it was even too hard for her?

I: I think there were times that were hard for her, but she showed those very rarely.

T: She had that kind of strength to contain the turbulence, the pain, in her own way (C: Yeah, yeah) . . . not wanting you to see that. (Long pause as client gazes at mother). What difference does it make if any to invite her into this conversation about the pain, about the grief? To have this very inner grief, right, this kind of reddish, purplish, swimming, elastic kind of form (gesturing to suggest wavy, expanding, and contracting shape at level of his abdomen), and then to bring Mom's kind of structure, and centering, and strength (making a vertical, upright gesture at abdominal level, melding to circle, and then to two closed fists, in synchrony with each description) to bear on that?

I (crying): It's hard because she *caused* it.

T: Because she caused it? I see . . . So how does it make that hard that she caused it by dying?

I: So sometimes thinking about her is good and gives strength, but sometimes thinking about her causes a feeling to be more overwhelming. So thinking about her is not a *safe place*.

T: It's not a safe place, I see . . . So sometimes you need a little distance from her just as you need the distance from this feeling?

I: Yeah. I used to spend—I told someone who was surprised about that—up until about a year or two ago, I spoke with her almost daily. Not explicitly, not in spoken words, but in thoughts.

T: In your mind? Did you ever write those down? Like in a letter to her, or . . .?

I: No.

T: Did you ever sense her speaking back to you, and kind of making it into a dialogue rather than a monologue?

I: Sometimes, when things would happen . . . for example, today is her birthday (smiling).

T: Today is her birthday?

I: Today is her birthday! (T: Ahh [warmly]). And so I felt this was a very odd setting. And my second son was born on her birthday too. I remember I had a conversation with her at the time: "I don't want him to be born on Friday the 13th or on Sunday," because there was no doctor in the hospital, and so he was born on her birthday three days later. So there are ways, and these are probably in my mind, there are ways in which I sometimes feel like there is some part of a conversation.

T: Yeah, yeah. And when you feel that conversation like really including her and that she's responsive to it, what does that do to the kind of reddish, purplish . . .?

I: It calms it, it's a nice feeling, because it's a presence, I guess it's more I feel her presence rather than her absence.

T: You feel her presence rather than her absence.

I: (Nods yes.) And sometimes when I think about it I only feel her absence.

T: Yeah, so I'm wondering, would it feel right to offer your Mom this chair (pulling the chair in a little closer), instead of the grief. (C: Right.) We can allow the grief to go wherever it needs to go, whether it's back into you or to just take a place in the hall for now. (C smiles and chuckles: Right.) As we kind of invite your mother's presence there in that chair. I don't know if we should sing her Happy Birthday or not . . .

I: (laughing) Probably not!

T: Probably not, but we could wish her that in some way (Looking at mother's photo, which he has placed in the chair) . . . She looks like she's amused in this picture now to me, with that little smile.

I (smiling and   Right . . . yeah.
gazing at
the photo):

As we consider what would help Inge carry her grief, we turn naturally toward her original secure base: her mother, visibly present in the room in the form of her picture. However, initial barriers must be acknowledged and overcome—Mom's stern gruffness, and more significantly, perhaps, the fusion of memories of Mom with painful images of her dying. Seeking a way to soften, even a little playfully, into the relationship, and to begin to differentiate between the mother Inge still needs and the grief over her death, I shift grief out of the chair and invite Mom to occupy it. Inge's expectant gaze suggests that more steps toward renewing the bond are now feasible.

Renegotiating Attachment

T: You know one of the hard things about grief, I think, is that in some ways we're having to negotiate a change between losing what we had (reaching out with both hands toward the photo, as client returns gaze to it), and then attempting to have what we have we've lost (pulling hands inward, toward abdomen, as if taking the photo into himself, as client follows the gesture with her eyes), but without the material presence of the other to anchor and structure that (client nods). Almost like we have to find a way to take that secure base and structure (gesturing to suggest the upright structure), and find a place for it inside us (drawing the gesture in, covering his heart).

I: Yes . . . (spoken softly and evocatively).

T: So we can carry some of what we need with us (leans in, as if moving forward). (C: Yeah.) And sometimes hearing the voice of the other or inviting that voice is a part of that. It's like the echoes of the conversation remain accessible, right? Do you ever sense that yourself?

I: Yeah, yeah.

T: What would you hear her saying to you at those times?

I: Umm, for example, there are times that I hear her say things, when I'm traveling in foreign cities, and I would say: 'Look, Mom, where I am now', especially when I was younger and on my first trips for work and I could hear her say: 'Wow that's great!' (T: Ahh!) 'Like you're doing all this traveling and all of these things that I never got a chance to do.' (T: Ahh . . .) So those are conversations that were nice to have.

T: She would be sort of cheering you on, and really celebrating you living large.

I: Yeah, that's encouraging.

T: Encouraging. Like you're moving out into a bigger world was not an abandonment of her. She was in a way going right along with you, and commenting on the experiences too.

I (smiling): Right. Sometimes I do feel that, like when we are decorating our Christmas tree and I use all the old ornaments (shaping her hand into an ornament with a hook), and I show my kids and I see her and I put the music on that we had too, I put on those old records that she used to put on. And she made us decorate the tree together, even when we were older and didn't want to do that together. And now I'm doing this with my kids and then I sense that she would probably be looking on in some way.

T: Sure, sure. That's a lovely image. I mean, I have the sense of your being a *link* (holds up right hand) between her (reaching higher up), and these kids (reaching down, as if to the next generation), even to a point where they're being a little reluctant now, they're getting a little *big* for this (voice suggesting a joking tone). But it's part of the family culture (voice slowing, becoming serious) and you're transmitting in some way something precious and unique, probably stories of her with the little ornaments that you're hanging in the tree (forming hands and fingers into ornaments with hooks and attaching them to a "tree" before him). You're hanging a memory or connection.

I begin by sketching, in language and gestures, a brief rationale for our work: grieving is partly a matter of importing a portable secure base derived from our ongoing relationship to the deceased into our ongoing lives, at a heartfelt level. Inge strongly resonates with this, and produces two vivid examples, in the form of her proud inner conversations with Mom as she began living large in the world, fulfilling her mother's dreams, and the sweet commemoration of mother, her music, and her stories during the holidays. Each ornament hung with her children on the tree is a link to Mom, as Inge is herself a link in a transgenerational story.

Holding the Feeling

I: Yeah. So there are things that *most* of the time, I should say, when I'm thinking of her it makes me positive. It's more the feeling that comes when I don't invite it to (wipes eye).
T: Ah, yeah, yeah (glancing up thoughtfully and shaking head slowly). So sometimes those feelings will come uninvited. And of course even if they're born of love, they carry strong feelings of loss. And I wonder if at those times it would be possible to find ways to invite Mom's presence alongside them, almost to help you *carry* them, you know (extends open hands, as if carrying something). (Client nods.) When you describe this kind of box (makes box shape with hands at the level of his abdomen) that you kind of contain the feelings in, what did you say it is made of?
I: I don't know, something metal or very strong.
T: Like iron?
I: Yeah!
T: And what did you call her?
I: Oh! The Iron Lady!
T: The Iron Lady. Maybe she's in a very good position to help you with this. Maybe she specializes in some of the strength that you now need as you carry this feeling and share it with others who are willing to stand in it, for even a short time. It needn't be something you're alone with.
I: Yeah (nods).

As she begins rewriting the terms of attachment to Mom, Inge confesses a problem: the invited memories may bring joy, but the uninvited ones can still bring pain. I then weave back to the metaphor of finding help carrying the grief, and associate to the container Inge and I co-constructed earlier: it, like Mom, is strong as iron. Completing this surprising connection, Inge brightens, and I feel a rush of emotion and admiration for Inge and the deep reconstruction of relation she is opening to after decades of impasse.

Re-engaging with Mom

T (spoken emotionally):	And that can be a loving gift that you allow your mother to give you, still, right? (Pause while client cries and nods, choked with emotion.) Do you have any mementos of her that you keep close to you?
I:	I have a lot of things; I have her jewelry, I have her diaries, that I have not read. I started to read but I thought they were too personal and not meant for her children (laughs) so after reading a little bit . . .
T (jokingly):	Maybe some stories that we're not ready to hear! (Both laugh.)
I:	So I have a lot of things of her. I put her *engagement ring* on (pointing to it, proudly). I never put it on but I thought today . . .
T:	Can I see? (Inge begins to take the ring off.) No, leave it on . . . it's quite beautiful (leaning in, touching it appreciatively).
I:	So today I put it on because I thought . . .
T:	Yeah, it's a large diamond, right? And is it surrounded by other stones, or is that a beautiful setting?
I:	I think it's just a setting. And I never carried it. It's just in a box in my bathroom.
T:	An *engagement* ring. And you *are* still engaged with her, aren't you? You're engaging with her right now.
I:	Right.
T (spoken with emotion):	And this is a kind of present she gave you. (Pause, as client cries softly and nods.) The *present* of *presence*. And she *is* here with us in a way. In this moment and this action. (Long pause, as client nods, gazes at the ring and exhales audibly.) Maybe this spontaneous action on your part, right (handing client a tissue to replace the one she has used), bringing this ring and wearing it as you have— it's almost like an intuitive recognition that this is what you need a little more of. It's not her *absence* but her *presence*, invited in this concrete way. And you bring her here to be with me (looking and gesturing to mother's photo in the chair), you invite others to hear the story. You kind of listen and look, for opportunities to speak something of the beauty and the sadness of her life to those who are willing to hear the story. And there *are* some others (client nods, looking at therapist intently), if we seek them out carefully.

91

In deep and substantially shared emotion, Inge and I discover in her impromptu decision to wear her mother's engagement ring for the first time on this, her birthday, a remarkable linking object that helps cement their "re-engagement" with one another, after decades of disconnection. This "present of presence," given originally by mother to daughter and reciprocated by Inge's proudly wearing the ring to her session with me, now fully invokes Mom's presence in our therapy, and more importantly, in Inge's ongoing life. Reorienting in my remarks to this broader social world—with Erik in particular watching with An and others in another room—I suggest that she has already taken strong steps toward the reopening of her mother's story to appreciative others, hinting at a social as well as personal reconstruction of the meaning of their shared lives in a way that calls forward her mother's presence.

Closing Reflections

T (Continuing emotionally): As we come into our final minutes of this session, Inge, I just want to acknowledge that I'm touched by your story. I'm touched by the love that you carry beyond the grave, giving it a place in you as you carry it with you through a life that continues to be touched by her absence but also by her strength (client nods). And it feels like an offering to her that you don't only reserve for her birthday. But in some important way she's with you year round (client cries and smiles). (Pause.) And I wonder if you have any thoughts or questions or concerns for me in these last minutes of our session, to anything we have spoken about, or where you would like to go with this?

I: I think I have realized through hearing this that I have tried to keep *her* in a box and keep the *feeling* very much in a box. But for me (spoken slowly, reflectively), I would feel better not putting it in a box, but having her help me through it.

T (summarizing, emotion in voice): "Maybe I would feel better not putting her in a box, but having her help me through it." I don't think anyone could say it any better than that (both teary).

I: Cause I saw it as a negative thing, and maybe it's not a negative thing.

T: Maybe it's not a negative thing, right? Maybe that kind of silent sea can also become something other than just a threatening space, like it could become something *not* negative?

I: Yeah (nodding). And I have had this feeling when she died, because I was so close to her, I think, that I was somewhat *uninvited* after her life.

T: That you were *uninvited* after her life?

I (weeping):	That there was something there that I knew I had to do my best to still be . . .
T:	Like *she* was requiring that of you, or . . .?
I:	No, that she had been a *safe* place and with her gone I would have to fend for myself and prove my own worth without a safe place . . .
T:	Just as she did.
I:	Right.
T:	Just as she did. To work hard to prove your worth? (Client nods yes.) But you also phrase that in the past tense, almost with an implication that maybe it doesn't have to *stay* that way? Maybe there's a *different* way to find security or . . .?
I (nodding):	I realized, when I was younger I thought I would just feel better once I had worked hard and earned a spot. And then I realized because I turned 40 this year, and I thought this feeling hasn't really changed, so it's not about getting better at things, because I could get better and better in many things but the feeling is not going to change.
T:	Maybe this is a lesson of her life? (Client nods repeatedly.) And so what would be (spoken slowly) needed then, rather than more hard work? Is there a second message of her life that would give us a hint about that? Another way?
I:	(Long pause) I don't know.
T:	. . . There *seemed* to be something, right, that you glimpsed, in that idea of not just having to grimly carry it yourself in this contained fashion, but having her help you with it (client nods). It seemed almost as if that would be a shared weight to carry. I was just trying to imagine ways of inviting her in. Maybe this (gesturing to suggest the ring), the ring of *engagement*, is a way of inviting her in. But maybe there are other ways too?
I:	Right (nodding), right.

Summarizing the key themes of the session, and validating Inge's impressive if incipient reconstruction of her relationship with her mother, I invite her thoughts on where she is now. She responds with the articulation of new awareness: she has struggled for decades to box up both her grief and her mother, creating a prolonged, complicated grief that has changed minimally in 23 years. Her solution to this grief and the loss of the "safe place" her mother provided was, by identification with Mom, unremitting hard work to "prove" herself and earn a place in the world. Now, however, she realizes that no amount of success can achieve this, and she glimpses the radical possibility that inviting her mother's greater presence in her life might help restore the strength and safety she requires. In our closing minutes, we add further fuel to this bright flame of possibility.

Future Steps

T: What would be some? I guess you're inviting her in, in this conversation, right, with me. (Client: Yes.) This is one step. Would there be another step in the same direction?

I (pause): That's hard to say. Because it's been such a long time and the world where I am in now is very different.

T: Yeah. The world has changed and you're still trying to learn it. But it seems like you're also still trying to find a world that is safe for your *mother*, right?

I: Yes.

T: How would it be to keep your mother's stories *alive*, in this world? And who might join you sometimes, in that? Just like at the Christmas tree. But not having to wait for Kerstfeest [Christmas] to do it, right?

I: Yeah (laughs). My family, my children. It's hard with them because I feel I have to do my best.

T: Sure. But maybe the definition of what is the *best* can be (gesturing fluidly with hands) flexible, and not quite so . . . (gesturing to form the box), you know?

I: Yeah.

T (looking up and nodding slowly): I had an idea . . . that your Mom kept a journal, she obviously wrote about things that were personal and important and emotional to her. And my guess is that *you* are personal and important and emotional for her. And I wonder if in the way that you might have the conversations with Mom and maybe can even imagine writing a letter to Mom, if you could imagine *her* writing a letter back to *you*, right? (Picking up pad and pen.) What would she say? And did she call you Inge?

I: Yes.

T: And so if you would write a "Dear Mom" letter, what would the "Dear Inge" letter look like? (Pause.) It might be something to experiment with, to almost give her your pen (extending pen toward client) and your hand (pantomiming writing). Because I take it you *do* hold her inside of you (gestures toward heart) in some ways. She's with you in a lot of ways (gesturing to suggest engagement ring). And maybe she could have some voice. (Client: Yeah, yeah.) That could be her birthday gift. (Client nodding repeatedly: Yeah, yeah.) A birthday letter to Inge. Now are you currently seeing a therapist?

I: I saw An, I'm seeing An, so yes.

T: Yeah, you're seeing An. So I wonder if we were to, if I were help to share this crazy idea with An about a kind of correspondence with Mom, just as something to try out to invite her in a bit more, would that be of interest to you?

I:	Yeah.
T:	You think you could do that?
I:	Yeah (nodding repeatedly).
T:	So what I'll do, I'll look for a couple of moments to talk with An and just share this and brainstorm with her, and then maybe you and she could just try it out and see how it is for you, with no obligation to continue with it.
I:	Yeah. That's a nice idea, yeah.
T:	It's a nice idea. Well, you're a nice daughter (client laughs softly, moved). And I think you are giving her the gift of your love *still*, on this birthday. (Client maintains strong eye contact through tears, as therapist leans in and shakes her hand firmly.) Thank you so much.

The session concludes with tears not of grief, but of hope, with the prospect that Mom's stories might find broader circulation in the world, and that a daughter's outreach to a mother she still needs might be imaginatively reciprocated with the assistance of her therapist. A handshake concludes a session that honors not only the day of her mother's birth, but also a day that symbolizes the re-birth of their relationship in continuing love.

Therapeutic Postscript

Viewing the live session by video feed in another room, An later noted that "Erik (and I) cried most of the session, being grateful to witness this from a distance, and to hear many of Inge's stories about her mother (which, as he said afterwards, he had never heard before)." In her summary of their next marital therapy appointment a few days later, An conveyed a cascade of changes that had followed my session with Inge: her spontaneous accessing and sharing of many stories about her mother with her husband and children; her recognition that she "had captured her mother in a box of sadness" for nearly two dozen years, so that she could not access memories of her without risking overwhelming grief; her ability since the session to separate her image of her mother from the grief, providing an uncontaminated form of bonding; and her realization that re-engaging with Mom represented a kind of relational gift that each continued to give the other. Equally profound were the systemic shifts that rippled out from these psychological insights. At a couples level, both Inge and Erik were able to allow Inge to express and explore her grief without either "rescuing" the other as a function of the unique structure of the session, to which Erik was simply an observer. And at a broader family level, Inge began to recognize the profound importance mothers have for their children, something with which she had previously been struggling as she questioned her role in the family. In summary, the session seemed to have triggered a reconstruction of meaning and feeling across all three relationships, leaving Inge more intimately connected to her husband and her children, as well as her mother.

Conclusion

The advent of contemporary scholarship concerning the continuing bond, amply documented in the present volume, has made clinical as well as conceptual contributions to many approaches to grief therapy. In this chapter we have explored this contribution in the context of a model of grieving as meaning reconstruction (Neimeyer, 2016a), which helps the client to identify, symbolize, articulate, and re-negotiate a world of passionate meanings that have been challenged by loss. In particular, we have emphasized here the high degree of tailoring and improvisation of interventions characteristic of responsive psychotherapy of any kind, which are particularly close to the heart of constructivist practice. In this view, the conversation of therapy unfolds as a collaborative co-construction, as the therapist "leads from one step behind" to deepen and direct the client's engagement with implicit questions, significant emotion, and experiential impasses that arise in the course of grieving. The result commonly is the generation of a series of "innovative moments" in the process of therapy, in which client and therapist alike discover fresh meaning in the form of novel reflections, actions, and emerging reconceptualization of the "dominant narrative" of the client's prolonged and intense mourning (Alves, Mendes, Gonçalves, & Neimeyer, 2012). As illustrated in the work with Inge, when the therapist is sufficiently attuned to the growing edge of the client's meaning-making, the outcome can be a rapid reconstruction of how the client holds her grief, and equally importantly, how she holds the relationship to the deceased.

Given the prominence of cognitive behavioral formulations in contemporary psychotherapy, it could be tempting to construe such meaning reconstruction in highly cognitive terms, viewing therapy as a process of testing and revising the client's misinterpretations or dysfunctional beliefs in the context of bereavement. But without denying the utility of this perspective, we find our approach to grief work to bear greater similarity to emotion-focused, humanistic, and narrative therapies, all of which share a constructivist or social constructionist epistemology. Like these kindred models, meaning reconstruction encourages the client to "follow the affect trail" to identify the client's implicit *need* and *readiness* to address it in each conversational turn of therapy. Therapeutic conversation itself is understood as a nuanced engagement with meaning only partially conveyed in explicit language, and at least equally resident in the language of gesture, expression, and embodiment on the part of both participants. Less evident in a typescript than in video recording, even spoken language is taken as a multidimensional resource, conveying meaning in the prosodic rhythms and emphases of speech and in poetic and metaphoric exchanges as much as in denotative descriptions or directions. Like two jazz musicians or improvisational actors, therapist and client each respond to the "offer" of the other in a way that moves therapy artfully in directions that neither could have predicted.

Finally, although our focus on a session of individual therapy risks suggesting that we view therapy, and indeed grieving itself, as a highly individualized, psychological process, in fact we strongly believe that *all grief therapy is family therapy in absentia* (Hooghe & Neimeyer, 2012). This proposition holds on at least two levels. Most obviously, just as a continuing bonds perspective implies, grief therapy is inherently about the *relationship* between the living and the dead, so that therapy sessions like the one with Inge conjure and use the presence of the deceased as a key component in treatment. But equally importantly, work done in even the most private of therapies carries active implications for the client's field of significant others, changing conversations, realigning relationships, and inviting integration of the event story of the loss or the backstory of the bond with the deceased into the family's shared narrative. In Inge's case this was deliberately orchestrated in collaboration with her and her husband, Erik, who viewed the session in another room, thereby offering the couple both a desired buffer and bridge at the same moment. The subsequent processing of the experience in couples therapy and in their family life completed the circle, and stimulated the ongoing performance of change initiated in the individual consultation. Therapists fostering reconstruction of meaning with a given client therefore require attunement to relevant family, social, and cultural discourses that both support and constrain these efforts, and that are subtly or substantially altered by them in turn.

In summary, grief therapy informed by a conceptualization of the continuing bond consists of far more than bereavement support for troubling feelings in the wake of loss—although it is that, too. More fundamentally, such therapy seeks to surmount complications entailed in pervasive and prolonged grieving by helping mourners with (a) processing the sometimes tragic story of the death, while also (b) accessing the back story of their relationship to the deceased, resolving issues in it, and often restoring a measure of attachment security that was shattered by loss. We hope the illustration of this process in the re-engagement of Inge with her mother helps de-mystify this dimension of grief therapy for those colleagues who join us in this work, whatever their theoretical orientation.

Author's Note

An expanded version of this chapter appears in R. A. Neimeyer (Ed.) (2018). *Techniques of grief therapy: Before and after the death.* New York, NY: Routledge.

References

Alves, D., Mendes, I., Gonçalves, M., & Neimeyer, R. A. (2012). Innovative moments in grief therapy: Reconstructing meaning following perinatal death. *Death Studies, 36,* 785–818.

Hedtke, L. (2012). Introducing the deceased. In R. A. Neimeyer (Ed.), *Techniques of grief therapy: Creative practices for counseling the bereaved* (pp. 253–255). New York, NY: Routledge.

Hooghe, A., & Neimeyer, R. A. (2012). Family resilience in the wake of loss: A meaning-oriented contribution. In D. Becvar (Ed.), *Handbook of family resilience.* New York, NY: Springer.

Neimeyer, R. A. (2012a). Analogical listening. In R. A. Neimeyer (Ed.), *Techniques of grief therapy: Creative practices for counseling the bereaved* (pp. 55–58). New York, NY: Routledge.

Neimeyer, R. A. (Ed.). (2012b). *Techniques of grief therapy: Creative practices for counseling the bereaved*. New York, NY: Routledge.

Neimeyer, R. A. (2015). Treating complicated bereavement: The development of grief therapy. In J. Stillion & T. Attig (Eds), *Death, dying and bereavement* (pp. 307–320). New York, NY: Springer.

Neimeyer, R. A. (2016a). Meaning reconstruction in the wake of loss: Evolution of a research program. *Behaviour Change*. doi: 10.1017/bec.2016.4.

Neimeyer, R. A. (Ed.). (2016b). *Techniques of grief therapy: Assessment and intervention*. New York, NY: Routledge.

Neimeyer, R. A., & Thompson, B. E. (2014). Meaning making and the art of grief therapy. In B. E. Thompson & R. A. Neimeyer (Eds), *Grief and the expressive arts: Practices for creating meaning* (pp. 3–13). New York, NY: Routledge.

7

REMEMBERING RELATIONS ACROSS THE YEARS AND THE MILES

Lorraine Hedtke

"Re-membering practices" highlight, extend, and celebrate the continuation of a bond. The therapeutic challenge is not just to discover a continuing bond as if it is already a perfectly formed, empirical fact, but to find ways to work with it, to knead it, shape it, and use it to open new conversations. This chapter showcases one such conversation, by way of illustration, where the stories, values, and connections to a deceased grandmother are woven into the stories of the living as one weaves threads into a tapestry. In the process, future resources and a form of a new relationship with those who have passed are generated.

Bronwyn Davies (1991) said, "We speak ourselves into existence." The concept of continuing bonds helps us hear our clients speaking and maintaining their precious connection long after a person has died. The assumptions embedded in the practice of building continued bonds between the living and dead take on particular import in this conversational form. Practitioners can take up a "future-forming orientation" (Gergen, 2015) to their work. Conversations between the living and the dead extend beyond simple discovery or confirmation of a bond that exists, but craft a connection that endures. This future-forming orientation is what Freedman and Combs (1996) mean by: "We ask questions to generate experience" (p. 113), thus breathing life into a posthumous relationship through the shared construction.

Continuing Bonds (1996) invited practitioners to take a step back from grief psychology's conventional ideas of stages or tasks that lead toward relinquishing the bond with the deceased. Specifically, the text addressed various kinds of suffering in which the continuation of relationship eased the pain of grief and provided many examples rooted in folk psychology (Bruner, 1990). The innovative readings did not, however, propose a practice. The concept of a bond continuing between the living and the dead, rather than being automatically severed by death, is a necessary, but not sufficient, assumption for the building of a conversation based on the practice of re-membering. The assumptions embedded in continuing bonds questions are designed to uphold relational legacies and give shape to future stories of living wherein a bond is intentionally crafted. Practice evidence confirms clients feel better when love, stories, and relationship are affirmed.

The publication of *Continuing Bonds* contributed to the shifting tide of grief psychology, and, in fact, many would suggest that this book created the wave. The constructions of grief in psychology and medicine during the preceding century have informed the whole of grief psychology to this day (Freud, 1957/1917; Kübler-Ross, 1969, and so on) by insisting upon severing ties. To free the ego again demanded an endpoint to relationship between the living and the dead (Freud, 1957/1917). While helpful for some, these models severely limited personal agency for others by squeezing their responses into an individual model of personal insight that curtailed relational and creative responses to death and grief. Cultural practices and thoughts promoted by *Continuing Bonds* challenged the dominant, Westernized version of the correct way to live with grief. It opened the gate to a culturally responsive model of bereavement, one that did not prescribe decathected versions, such as acceptance, letting go, and moving on.

The concept of continuing bonds is a critique of grief theories that prescribed stages and tasks that end in acquiescing to a life without the deceased. In this crisis of ideas emerged competing concepts, both about relaxing the insistence on a rigid model of grief counseling and models that curtailed the beauty of a sustainable and comforting posthumous relationship. Some of these practices, represented in other chapters of this book, have given rise to measurement tools to quantify the quality, timeliness, and potential benefits and risks of a continued bond. The evaluative step of assessing a bond can take away agency from the bereaved. The controversial aspect of measuring bonds is that it omits the data implicit in narrative form. That is, it omits the data in which holding close the memories of connection diminishes concern about doing grief incorrectly.

The new era of grief psychology affirmed love and the importance of meaning, thus ushering in a changed understanding and new vocabularies for praxis. Questions about whether a healthy bereavement is predicated on a tidy goodbye were raised (Hedtke & Winslade, 2004, 2017). Rather than focusing exclusively on the bereaved person and their internal experience of loss, a re-membering conversation assumes that the relationship does not have to go to the grave with the deceased's body but continues in at least a narrative form. It follows, therefore, that there is no need to say goodbye to or let go of all aspects of the relationship. There are many places where the relationship lives on, albeit in new forms, in both ordinary daily events and in larger life purposes.

A New Practice

The idea of continuing bonds stimulates a new form of practice that potentially produces a significant resource for the bereaved person who is facing the ongoing challenges of living or provides a source of comfort in the face of loss. We are born not as isolated individuals, but as members of an interlocking community of stories and relationships. When we die, our stories can become a rich source of comfort to those who live on. A re-membering conversation values the bond implicit in these stories. This new focus perhaps offers not only a sense of continuity but also the possibility of a renewed relationship with those no longer living. Stepping away from individual and pathologized versions of grief shifts practice toward a relational experience where culture and ritual support the continuing connections and, in fact, the forming of new contours of life.

The question remains, however, about how to craft such a conversation. One fruitful method is narrative counseling. Michael White's (1989) seminal article, *Saying Hullo Again*, introduces a narrative practice where the dead continue to matter and stands against the tide of modernism's insistence on letting go. This chapter showcases the narrative counseling practice of a relational model of grief by actively enlisting the posthumous voice, shared values, and meanings of the deceased. Sustainable bonds become the guiding principle to help and comfort those who are living with grief. This model does not measure the amount of a bond or dictate when a bond should be reinvested, but lets the story guide the quality and timing of this relationship. In this approach, the stories of the deceased provide the architectural design of a new home where identity can reside. The excerpts from a conversation below illustrate an aesthetic response to grief, one that captures the moments of historical beauty and crafts a future relationship (Hedtke & Winslade, 2017).

Re-membering (with the intentional hyphen) refers to the renewal of membership. Barbara Myerhoff (1982) said, "'re-membering' distinguishes between the active re-investing in a life and passive, wistful remembering. It suggests that a person's memory, stories and importance can be reintroduced in one's 'membered club of life'" (White, 1997, p. 22). This metaphor dramatically shifts how the dead might continue to play a vital role in the ongoing lives of the living. The dead can "advise" on matters of importance and "speak" on identity projects that can continue a life's purpose or a newly discovered meaning that is relationally inclusive. The dead can be introduced to new members of a club of life and have their legacy interwoven with the stories of the living

The question remains: how do we construct a bridge that transcends death? Re-membering conversations require the careful, intentional generation of a relationship, sometimes through uncharted territory with reflexive pauses. The following excerpts illustrate a re-membering conversation where an ongoing relationship between the living and the dead develops between a grandmother, her granddaughter, and their family members.

Introductions

I spoke with Siobhan the week following her maternal grandmother's death. She explained that her grandmother was 102 years old when she died in Taiwan. Her grandmother had immigrated to Taiwan from China with her husband and first-born child approximately seventy years earlier. Siobhan was raised in America with limited knowledge of her ancestral language.

The counselor starts by asking the bereaved person to "introduce" the deceased. If someone were still alive, we would expect this social courtesy of introduction. If the bond is continuing, then it still makes sense for such an introduction to take place. The introduction (Hedtke, 2012) sets the stage for unfolding a very different kind of grief conversation. The introduction establishes what is particularly unique about this person and about this relationship between the bereaved and the deceased. The introduction has two purposes. First, it makes visible the life of the person who has died, rather than just rehearsing the oft-repeated story of their death. Second, it alerts the counselor to troubled aspects of the relationship that might require a more nuanced re-membering conversation. The simple inquiry, "Can you introduce the person who has died?" constructs a platform for a different kind of bereavement conversation not focused on individual loss.

Lorraine: What did you call her?

Siobhan: I just called her grandmother, or grandma. It's kind of a funny thing, because I don't know Chinese very well, she doesn't know English very well.

L: I'm curious a little bit about her, about what kind of life she had.

S: It's interesting, because I've learned about her slowly over time. She was a very cultured woman. We'd probably refer to her as kind of, high society. In Chinese culture, the mark of someone who is very socially capable is impeccable manners—someone who knows how to be in a crowd and how to attend to people in a way that you should if you're of her status. But also someone who was able to get as much education as a female could have gotten of her generation. So she also learned art, and music, and dancing.

L: So tell me about your contact with her over the years. Did you go to Taiwan to see her when you were young?

S: Uh hum, yeah, we kind of regularly either went there or she and my grandfather came here.

Highlighting the Meaning of the Bond

In the first minutes of the conversation, there are already many possibilities for where the conversation might recognize and strengthen a strong posthumous bond. The story of the passing, or the internal psychological working of Siobhan's grief, is not the starting point. Instead, the focus is on a relational welcoming between Siobhan and her grandmother. Through a few simple questions, her grandmother's life, rather than her death, becomes visible in conversation.

Unlike conventional bereavement practice, re-membering conversation does not silence the dead by ignoring their presence in our lives. Nor does it favor recognition of their absence through encouraging "acceptance," "letting go," and "moving on." Speaking about a person in the past tense or writing letters of goodbye may plummet the bereaved into the abyss of grief. Conventional grief counseling practices invisibilize the existing love and force the dead into somewhere beyond the veil. Re-membering conversations recognize that we do not stop loving, or being entangled with, a person, simply because they are dead. We can use the practice of introduction to layer meaning into the ongoing relational bond.

L: What do you think it meant to your grandmother to be around her grand-daughter?

S: I think she was happy we were able to do it. Because my mother did the thing you actually weren't really supposed to do. She came to the U.S. and she stayed. So this was a way for my grandmother to be able to see her and still have a relationship with her grandchildren. So I think she was quite happy to have that.

L: For your mom, what do you think it meant for her, that she got to experience her mother being a grandmother to you?

S: I would imagine that was very unexpected for her. When my mother was growing up, because her family had achieved more wealth, it was common to have a nanny. When my mother saw her mother interacting with us, it was the first time she had seen her mother as a mother. Because her mother was actually the one teaching me and my sister how to cook. So you know, there's also a cultural heritage being passed on.

L: Your mom gained a new appreciation in watching her mother take that role with you?

S: I think so, yes.

L: What was it like for you to be schooled by your grandmother in Chinese life and Chinese culture?

The conversation shifts after the introductory questions and highlights the character of the deceased person. Questions in the above excerpt address the meaning of Siobhan's relationship with her grandmother when she was alive. Her answers punctuate the significance of the bond between them. The questions invite Siobhan to speculate on the relational meaning from her grandmother's and her mother's points of view. Her answers are not blind speculation. She has absorbed over time what it might mean to her grandmother and mother. Moreover, Siobhan is invited for this first time to voice her grandmother's thoughts and to locate them in a cultural context.

These questions look simple enough, but they are deceptively powerful in their construction of relationship. Responding to them might update meanings that have been important in the past or unearth long lost meanings and purposes that the bereaved might elect to take up on behalf of his or her deceased loved one. For example, Siobhan tells of what it might have been like for two generations of mothers to be witness to one another's parenting styles. Siobhan, a mother herself, might draw inspiration from this in how she parents her children.

While this is the start of the conversation, we are already discovering how Siobhan could act as a caretaker of her grandmother's stories and where she might find a community of witnesses for her grandmother's role in Siobhan's future life. We collectively create our stories rather than own them as individuals. There are many who can speak to the life of the deceased and give voice to a dead person's stories, their values. They can also act as witnesses to what remains as vital. The reverse is true as well. Stories die out over time, when they are not continued, and thus diminish the life of the deceased person. Bonds do not continue automatically, nor are they static. They require tending. Counseling conversations farm current and historical bonds for their usefulness. Re-membering facilitates shifts in the past story of relationship and points out what might become a source of comfort. It might include finding others who can strengthen the bond as it continues.

L: Since you have been a grown-up, how has your relationship with your grandma changed?

S: Oh gosh. It's changed in two ways. One that's probably stronger and one that is more difficult. The stronger one is that, as I've gotten older and been able to learn and make sense of what all this is, I have a tremendous appreciation for what she would have had to do. The more difficult part [that has changed the relationship] is that the last couple of years she could not communicate. So that's also created something there that's tough to navigate that changed the relationship.

L: How, over the last couple of years when she couldn't communicate, did you send messages to her?

S: There came a point where, if you've ever lived with someone who is terminally ill, I guess that point where you're always kind of waiting for the phone call. But then at some point you have to figure out, well how you are going to let your life continue on, because you never know when it's going to happen. So, for the last few years, that's kind of what my family and I have done. We were sort of waiting for the phone call, but it's like, we still have to make plans, you still have to just, kind of, go on. So I didn't do any literal communication, because I was always kind of waiting to actually be there.

L: During this time, for her, what do you think she would appreciate about how you held that space of both waiting and moving forward?

S: I think she would have appreciated the fact that we were paying attention. This is what I'd like to think.

L: What do you think she would have wanted you, Siobhan, to be paying attention to?

S: I think that she was, it sounds a bit ironic, but that she was alive. I don't mean that in the literal sense. Not that she's in the bed and she's alive—but that she had a life. You know that we could notice that she was a vibrant person who wasn't just a figurehead, but had something to really offer everyone around her.

L: So that period of waiting, that she would hold some place of feeling pleased? Is that right? Or are those my words and not yours?

S: I'm actually thinking about . . . I think she would have been pleased. I suspect she may have been surprised (laughs).

Listening to the Voice of the Deceased

Bonds shift and change over time when people are living and continue to do so after people die. Relationships are not monolithic. They are more like a kaleidoscope of colors and textures. Re-membering conversations invite the bereaved person to affirm what is important to them and highlight where the bond is sustaining and supportive. The challenges of living with death nearby become a resource for story. Siobhan is trying to make sense of something difficult. The thread of waiting refers to a commitment that could easily be overlooked, if we were not willing to hear the bond that it reveals. We hear the posthumous voice of Siobhan's grandmother speaking about her preferences for the meaning that lives in the waiting. What emerges is that her grandmother's life matters more than her death. The counselor's questions fold and unfold meanings between the living and the dead. Thus, the practice of re-membering also inquires into complexities of relationship and how they become a part of the fabric of the newly forming story Siobhan will craft. Re-membering is the affirmation that we matter.

The waiting she speaks of could become an identity project for Siobhan. She can fold the newly discovered story into her life as a resource for living. Her love for her grandmother is worth holding on to. It is a story that asks of Siobhan to reflect upon what was vital in the moments of waiting and hold these as moments as precious. Re-membering is what happens in the bond between a living person and a dead person, but it is more than this. It also seeks out others to become keepers of the deceased's stories. These others become the audience for the telling of stories so that they can continue. Siobhan offers an opening to the inclusion of such other members in her grandmother's club of life as we continue the conversation.

L: Really, why surprised?

S: Because I don't know how many people thought of her like that.

L: If the others who knew her, were all here, talking with us—the care workers, and your cousins who live in Taiwan—what stories do you think would stand out that they would tell about who this woman was?

S: I suspect people would tell stories about the ways that she was caring of other people. And I think in ways that are kind of unexpected.

L: Is there an example of what you're speaking about?

S: Well, one that I do know . . . Her care worker would have been in her twenties and spoke limited Mandarin, which is what my grandmother speaks. So my grandmother taught her Mandarin.

L: So what would this woman say about her?

S: I think she'd offer a lot of appreciation, because my grandmother did things like that. My grandmother made sure she was very well looked after.

L: Would these values that you are speaking of, about how your grandmother was with others, be something that your grandmother would have held dear?

S: I think, I think she valued a genuine regard for people. I think she actually valued just an inherent worth of people, I think that's what she's trying to communicate.

Siobhan is reminding us that our stories are not only our own. Our stories live in a community of stories with many people holding a thread until it is woven into a larger tapestry. Such threads are obvious in the varied textures that construct the continuing bond Siobhan describes. Revealing them brings the bonds from the past into the present. The tapestry of Siobhan's grandmother's life does not need to unravel with her death, nor does it need to be put away into a storage chest in the attic. It can become a life-sustaining work of art, given the right questions. Siobhan can also pick up on her grandmother's caring for her community, if she is invited to do so. The account of this caring thus travels through time from Siobhan's grandmother's past and becomes a thread that may be woven into Siobhan's future. The conversation continues and takes us to another new thread in Siobhan's story.

L: So how do you suspect she held onto that over the years, that belief in valuing another person?

S: That's a good question actually, because it would have been tough. I am not sure, because I think she would be a bit rare, not just for her generation, but also for her family. I think she may have stood outside some. She probably was considered a bit different.

L: Are there places where her differences resonate with you in any particular ways?

S: Well it's funny, because I'm thinking about this as we're talking. Let's say yes. Because in the sense of being in that position where you're slightly off-centered from everyone else, that's definitely something I can relate to.

L: I don't know if this is right, but I get this image of someone who was refined and spunky at the same time?

S: I think so, yeah. She was no shrinking violet. She's not like that. She's not delicate.

L: She's not delicate, yes. But she's cultured. She can use those avenues as well.

Siobhan and I have spoken for only twenty-five minutes, but in this short time, we have found numerous openings into a relational world where her grandmother might continue to play a part. We have not spoken about her grandmother's actual death or how Siobhan was notified or Siobhan's internal state of grief, but instead have developed a sense of what her grandmother has meant, and will continue to mean to her. A continuing bond is developed through re-membering questions and also forms a trajectory that passes through the moment of death and continues into the future.

In our conversation Siobhan established a delicate, perhaps even fragile, strand between Siobhan and her grandmother. They both walk in the world as outsiders. Being different could lead some other people to feel isolated, but here it is not only a source of connection between granddaughter and grandmother, but an expression of caring. It could become a useful resource for Siobhan to call upon in future occasions where "off-center" had been unsettling and functions as a place of solidarity and pride. She can call upon her grandmother's legacy to underscore the value of being different. She could even ask for guidance in an imaginary conversation with her grandmother's posthumous voice. This possibility develops further some of Siobhan's identity projects, focusing on who Siobhan wants to become.

L: Do you find any similarities or characteristics that you share in common with your grandmother?
S: Yes. Well it's funny because on one side, it's still kind of ingrained in me from a Chinese point of view that you don't talk about yourself . . . You don't talk yourself up. And [if I were to speak of] some of the similarities I would be talking myself up a bit.
L: What would she say, that she would like to talk up about you?

There are elements of value in this small exchange worth elaborating. I inadvertently invited Siobhan into a culturally uncomfortable position wherein speaking about herself could seem boastful. Such a direct conversation could go against what she has come to value and therefore she might understandably hesitate. Asking her to voice answers from her grandmother's imagined voice, however, leads to a more comfortable conversation where Siobhan is a witness to what her grandmother valued. She thus takes up a reciprocal position in this relationship. Her dead grandmother serves as a reflexive witness to Siobhan's life, voicing what Siobhan is uncomfortable saying. Siobhan knows her grandmother's stories and voice well enough to enter into the imagined world (Bruner, 1986) where the questions allow the bond between them to seep from her virtual, private world to where it can be actualized in conversation.

L: What would she say, that she would like to talk up about you?
S: I hope she'd identify the spunky part.
L: If she could see all of your life examples, would she have a particular example that you would hope that she would say, that would let her know that you are a spunky, non-shrinking violet?
S: I hope she would notice or point out that I speak up. I say things, and not even attempting to be belligerent about it. And I think that's where the comparison with having a sense of her being elegant, cultured, kind of refined. So I hope that's what she'd notice. Somewhere in my adulthood I learned how to do that.
L: She would have an appreciation for your willingness to be bold, occasionally?
S: Uh hum, yeah.
L: Would she have an appreciation for how you make visible things that aren't sometimes wanting to be made visible?
S: I think so. Because that's kind of what I remember.
L: Like what? What can you tell that's going on?
S: You can tell that she's saying the thing that other people are annoyed with.
L: I see, I see. She's making visible an important truth?
S: Uh hum, yeah.

L: So this is a trait that ties you to her?

S: I think so in some ways.

L: Where would you like this trait, this shared trait, to go next in both of your lives?

This virtual bond between them is important for Siobhan and no longer only about Siobhan's individual life. Siobhan is charged with caring for her grandmother's values and characteristics in a shared appreciation for what this means. We have witnessed a significant moment, one that records a specific value of integrity traveling intergenerationally that has traversed the valley of death. Something quite new has taken shape by positioning her grandmother to speak on Siobhan's behalf. The subjunctive question of possibility ("What would she talk up about you?") changes the relationship from a focus only on the past tense to making her grandmother an active future inspirational force. It travels through the liminal zone of the subjunctive. This question makes it possible to turn the hypothetical into actuality. It could become foundational for Siobhan to voice her discomfort. She might feel her grandmother nudging her on in such moments. Or she might sense a swelling of pride when she speaks on matters of importance in ways that are polite and refined. More than an exchange in which a continuing bond is recognized, it is also the construction of an inspiration for the living. It calls up the deceased as an imagined witness to preferred behaviors and meaning.

Re-membering the Future

This conversation travels through time. The questions start in a reflexive past about her grandmother's actions, move into the present-day skills Siobhan shares with her grandmother, and finally set the stage for a future configuration of actions and meaning. Chronological time does not limit re-membering stories. Re-membering does not insist we live in the harsh light of the indicative present. Instead it allows us to dwell in what Bakhtin (1981) referred to as "great time." They can be blended with the future across an elastic time. In this sense, the past, the present, and the future form a continuous arc across experience, each accessible at will. Her grandmother's previous stories serve as model acts of resistance that Siobhan can use in her life, now and in the future. This theme of resistance is picked up in the next exchange.

L: I'm wondering about the resistance: how is it that you notice your grandmother using her gender in statements of resistance to the power that she was living with?

S: Uh hum, yes! Now I have to think about that, because that is a good question. The thing is, I'm having a hard time linking onto an example, but I want to say that has something to do with presence. That she maybe that's why the visibility thing starts to become a big deal. She was never . . . she could never be dismissed. Does that make sense? She was there, even if there may have been an attempt to quiet her, you knew she was in the room. So that's what presence is, it's not always verbal, but she had a way of being there.

L: Was that way, of being there, part of how she held her space?

S: I think so. Um, yeah. Yeah. Because my grandfather was not a domineering kind of man. But again just the atmosphere of who is supposed to be important would have said she's supposed to step aside. And I think that's the interesting part: she was able to follow customs but not to the point where she was a subjugated female.

Here Siobhan has articulated, perhaps falteringly, a half-thought about her grandmother's presence in relation to her grandfather and the world in general. Her grandmother resists domination, even when that was probable in the cultural practices of her day. The articulated half-thought becomes actualized fully in Siobhan's taxonomy. Through being spoken, what is valued becomes true. This differs from counseling practices designed to unearth hidden truths that have already been actualized in a person's psyche. In this sense, the dialogue constructs the continuing bond, not so much as an empirical fact, but as a virtual truth that is actualized (Deleuze & Guattari, 1994). Once spoken, the reclaimed values and stories function as an ongoing point of connection between Siobhan and her grandmother. The next exchange traces the impact of this connection on Siobhan's life as she moves forward with a sense of her grandmother's love as witness to her actions.

L: If she were a fly on the wall now, what would she hope that you would hold onto in that witnessing of her resistance?

S: I think, I think it would be the part about how there are many forms that resistance can take. That sometimes it's through a direct statement but there are lots of other subtle ways.

L: Is this right Siobhan? That she had many ways to perform resistance?

S: I think so.

L: And many opportunities to perform resistance?

S: Yes, Uh Mhm.

L: Again, when you think about that, in terms of how you raise your daughter, and who she is in the world, what would you hope she would hold onto in her life?

S: I think it's a very similar thing. I think what's interesting about my daughter is she's already figuring that one out. She's loads more clever than I was at eight.

L: She's breathing different air?

S: I think so. Because I have watched her be verbal, physical, subtle, manipulative [laughs]. I mean the whole range.

L: Would your daughter have as many forms of resistance, do you think, as your grandmother?

S: I think she does. I hope she keeps it, yeah.

L: So when you see her moving forward and growing up, do you have a sense of how you could help to have your grandmother's knowledge embedded in your daughter to practice those acts of resistance?

S: Are you asking me if there's a specific way I see that happening?

L: Is there a way that you could broker that for her?

S: Well I hope I am. When I think about that it's like, I can think about sharing of story, but I actually don't think it's just about the sharing of story. I think it's demeanor. It's through the doing. And also the allowance of the space. If someone's going to develop they have to have the space to do that.

L: Like cooking.

S: Yes. Cooking, I mean, experimenting, you know . . .

L: What kind of advice would your grandma give you about how to be the best possible mother to raise a girl who is skilled in the art of resistance?

S: I hope she says, "Keep doing what you're doing." I think she would give the advice of being patient and steadfast.

L: What's it like talking about her now?

S: It's a little hard for me to put into words, in truth. I mean I'm feeling something but it's . . . having the audience [listening to our conversation] makes it hard to put words to what I'm feeling. But um, I partly wanted to do this because I wanted some words. And I am excited about some of the things that I've found.

In our exchange, Siobhan's grandmother continues to become something other than just a dead person. She has been constituted as a living entity, if you will, who can reflect back to Siobhan the importance of a woman who resists the negative or silencing effects of patriarchal power. The grandmother bears witness to Siobhan's mothering skills by inspiring a future generation of women who are non-shrinking violets. This valuable legacy serves both Siobhan and her grandmother, and hopefully Siobhan's daughter in the coming years. These re-membered acts uphold something precious that did not die with her grandmother.

Re-membering may be seen as a salve for the pain that is magnified by the insistence on negating a life after death. It can ameliorate the pain that may be worsened by an insistence on the severing of ties, often experienced as cruel by those who grieve. Re-membering, then, is not only an act between the living and the deceased, but spills over into their communities. Re-membering bridges the past and present by grabbing the stories that had meaning in the past to form a future. Through reiterating these stories, we can respond to the pain that grief brings by anchoring connections to what remains and to what people hold dear. The bond does not need to die as long as re-membering continues. It forms a continued bond, although transformed into a new format, one that can take shape and be molded into a future where our loved ones' stories are introduced and become inspirational for a life that matters.

Siobhan's Comments

I shared this chapter with Siobhan to include her voice in the process and in a commitment to professional transparency. A principle of narrative counseling is to privilege the agency of those whose story is being discussed. Re-membering practices further position the deceased posthumously as a protagonist in the story. Additional folds create textured depth in the newly formed relationships between Siobhan and her grandmother, but also include Siobhan's mother who saw the recorded interview. This is her response.

> After witnessing the interview, my mother expressed gratitude at seeing her mother [Siobhan's grandmother] described in these ways. For the several years leading up to my grandmother's death, my mother had struggled with watching the person she knew disappear, as her body and mind lost function. The figure in the hospice bed had stopped being the mother she knew. The depiction that emerged from the interview brought the person back she felt she had lost; my mother could clearly see a vibrant, intelligent person again who meant a great deal to her. In my sharing the interview with her, my mother told me more stories about her mother I had not heard. She also gave me several artifacts, for example, paintings, jewelry, or clothing that were proud representations of her mother's abilities. I am now the keeper of these articles, and more stories, to one day pass them on to my daughter.

References

Bakhtin, M. (1981). *The dialogic imagination* (C. Emerson & M. Holquist, Trans.). Austin, TX: University of Texas Press.

Bruner, J. (1986). *Actual minds: Possible worlds.* Cambridge, MA: Harvard University Press.

Bruner, J. (1990). *Acts of meaning.* Cambridge, MA: Harvard University Press.

Davies, B. (1991). The concept of agency: A feminist poststructuralist analysis. *Social Analysis: The International Journal of Social and Cultural Practice, 30,* 42–53. Retrieved from www.jstor.org/stable/23164525.

Deleuze, G., & Guattari, F. (1994). *What is philosophy?* (H. Tomlinson & G. Burchell, Trans.). New York, NY: Columbia University Press.

Freedman, J., & Combs, G. (1996). *Narrative therapy: The social construction of preferred realities.* New York, NY: W.W. Norton & Company.

Freud, S. (1957). Mourning and melancholia. In J. Strachey (Ed. & Trans.), *The standard edition of the complete psychological works of Sigmund Freud* (Vol. 14, pp. 237–259). London, UK: Hogarth Press. (Original work published 1917.)

Gergen, K. (2015). From mirroring to world-making: Research as future forming. *Journal for the Theory of Social Behaviour, 45*(3), 287–310. doi 10.1111/jtsb.12075.

Hedtke, L. (2012). What's in an introduction? In R. A. Neimeyer (Ed.), *Techniques of grief therapy* (pp. 253–255). New York, NY: Routledge.

Hedtke, L., & Winslade, J. (2004). *Re-membering lives: Conversations with the dying and the bereaved.* Amityville, NY: Baywood.

Hedtke, L., & Winslade, J. (2017). *The crafting of grief: Constructing aesthetic responses to loss.* New York, NY: Routledge.

Kübler-Ross, E. (1969). *On death and dying.* New York, NY: Macmillan.

Myerhoff, B. (1982). Life history among the elderly: Performance, visibility and remembering. In J. Ruby (Ed.), *A crack in the mirror: Reflexive perspectives in anthropology* (pp. 99–117). Philadelphia, PA: University of Pennsylvania Press.

White, M. (1989). Saying hullo again. In M. White (Ed.), *Selected papers* (pp. 29–36). Adelaide, AU: Dulwich Centre Publications.

White, M. (1997). *Narratives of therapists' lives.* Adelaide, AU: Dulwich Centre Publications.

8

WORKING WITH CONTINUING BONDS FROM AN ATTACHMENT THEORETICAL PERSPECTIVE

Phyllis S. Kosminsky

Continuing Bonds: For Better or For Worse?

You tell me "she goes on." But my heart and body are crying out, come back, come back. Be a circle, touching my circle on the plane of Nature. But I know this is impossible. I know that the thing I want is exactly the thing I can never get.

(*C.S. Lewis,* A Grief Observed, *p. 24*)

In his classic and wrenching account of the days and weeks following the death of his wife Joy, Lewis captures the hopelessness of grief. It is the hopelessness of knowing that what was most precious – love, comfort, security – has been lost and cannot be reclaimed. From an attachment theoretical perspective, grief is just this: the loss of an attachment relationship and all that it provided. Over time, he is able to assemble, from the ashes of his grief, a sense of the love that opened his heart. The changes wrought in him by love are permanent, and so is his connection to the woman who was responsible for them. This is what the sense of a continuing bond can do. This is how an attachment relationship can continue to serve as a source of comfort and love even when the attachment figure has died.

Of course, not all connections to the deceased are a source of solace.

As many of the contributions to this volume attest, continuing bonds (CB) cannot be unilaterally described as having either a beneficial or a detrimental effect on the course of grief. Given the considerable variations in the quality of people's attachments to the deceased, we would be surprised if it were otherwise.

The question, then, is not *whether* CB are helpful or unhelpful in adaptation to loss, but rather *when* and *how* they are helpful or unhelpful. The purpose of this chapter is to illustrate the utility of attachment theory in identifying and strengthening bonds that promote healing and moderating the effect of those that do not.

Attachment as a Factor for CB

> In understanding an individual's response to a loss it is necessary to take into account not only the structure of that individual's personality but also the patterns of interaction in which he was engaging with the person now lost.
>
> *(Bowlby, 1980, p. 212)*

An Attachment Perspective on Connection and the Loss of Connection

As a newly minted psychiatrist, John Bowlby had the opportunity to observe young children who had been separated from their parents and who were being cared for in a variety of settings, including hospitals, schools, and war-time shelters. Although they received adequate physical care, these children were markedly distressed. Bowlby came to believe that this distress arose from the child's need not only for food and warmth, but for the care and attention of a *specific person* with whom they had a very particular bond. This belief seeded the development of Bowlby's *attachment theory*, the fundamental premise of which is that human beings are born with an *instinct to attach to their primary caregiver*. This instinct is served by what Bowlby described as the *attachment behavioral system*, a system designed to maintain or restore proximity to the caregiver. Under conditions of stress (hunger, discomfort), if the caregiver is not immediately available, children will exhibit a range of behaviors designed to gain their attention and restore proximity (Bowlby, 1980).

In the language of American psychologist Mary Main, these behaviors are guided by the child's *internal working models* – the expectations they have about the likely outcome of various strategies for restoring and maintaining proximity (Main, 2000). In short, based on how their caregivers respond, children formulate a set of assumptions that form the foundation of their understanding of people and relationships. That is: if I cry, will my caregiver respond? Will they be calm and comforting, or distressed, or angry? Should I cling to them and cry to keep them close by, or are they more likely to attend to me if I'm quiet?

Bowlby described two contrasting types of insecure attachment, the first an anxious pattern characterized by clinging and extreme distress upon separation, and the other characterized by a pronounced tendency toward self-sufficiency and relational avoidance. In an experimental environment designed to test Bowlby's theory (the "Strange Situation"), Main observed the behavioral responses of young children when they were separated from, and reunited with, their mothers, and confirmed Bowlby's categorization. In addition to secure, anxious, and avoidant attachment, which she classified as *organized* patterns because of their relative consistency, she identified a fourth category, *disorganized attachment*. Children in this category exhibited erratic and unusual attachment behavior, and seemed unable to decide whether to move toward, or away from, the caregiver when she returned after the brief separation. Disorganized attachment, Main found, was generally seen in children whose caregivers responded to their children's bids for attention in a manner that was inconsistent and intermittently frightening. Subsequent research has substantiated the link between abusive or neglectful parenting and disorganized attachment in children and in adults (Allen, 2013).

In the course of his career Bowlby came to focus on attachment and loss across the life cycle. He believed that early caregiving and the security of the child's relationship to the primary caregiver had a lasting influence on the functioning of an individual's attachment system and their response to separation and loss. Bowlby identified adult grief as a mirror of childhood separation distress and emphasized that it was a *normative response* to separation from the attachment figure. Bowlby was particularly interested in the difficulties in coping with loss that he observed in *insecurely attached* patients and identified several of what he described as *disordered patterns of mourning* that corresponded to different types of insecure attachment (Bowlby, 1980).

Research on CB: For Better or for Worse

The work of early attachment theorists did not explicitly address, but has implications for, the role of CB in bereavement, as demonstrated by CB theory and research. Unsurprisingly, given the role of attachment security in CB, individuals who enjoy a secure relationship with a living person are likely to benefit from the bond they maintain with that person after they have died. Conversely, someone whose anxious or avoidant orientation to attachment interferes with their ability to sustain healthy, growth-promoting relationships is at greater risk for having CB that are problematic (Field & Filanosky, 2010).

Insecure Attachment as a Factor in CB: Anxious Attachment

It seems likely that a critical factor in whether a continuing bond is adaptive is the degree to which the expression of the bond reflects the bereaved individual's recognition and incorporation of the death into his or her ongoing life. It is important to distinguish between continuing bond experiences that may reflect disbelief and avoidance of the death and those that acknowledge the reality of the death.

(Field & Filanosky, 2010)

The type of problematic CB described here can be understood as a byproduct of insecure attachment, and an anxious attachment in particular. The most profound expression of anxiety-driven denial of death is seen in individuals who continue to relate to the deceased as if they were still alive. This denial, and the elements of magical thinking that accompany it, are not unusual in early grief. However, the persistence of this pattern of engagement suggests an underlying emotional framework that cannot accommodate reality and that will inevitably lead to problems in living (Bowlby, 1980; Mikulincer & Shaver, 2013).

Insecure Attachment as a Factor in CB: Avoidant Attachment

In contrast to anxiously attached clients, avoidantly attached clients tend to minimize the effects of a loss and may appear to be coping with it effectively. However, recent studies suggest that this is not always a true or complete picture and argue against confusing avoidance with resilience. The suppression of emotion in avoidantly attached individuals can interfere with the resolution of difficult and contradictory feelings about the deceased, and the avoidant individual's tendency to minimize the value of social support, as well as the value of therapy, may impede the resolution of unfinished business with the deceased and contribute to the maintenance of an unhealthy CB (Field & Filanosky, 2010).

Disorganized Attachment and CB: The Impact of Early Abuse and Neglect

Bereaved individuals who were subject to early abuse or neglect are more likely than others to experience a range of problems in processing loss and may require specific interventions that address the impact of such trauma (Allen, 2013). Problems are particularly likely to arise in cases where it is the deceased who was abusive (Kosminsky & Jordan, 2016). The safe environment provided by a strong therapeutic bond, which is important in all grief therapy, is essential in work with these clients, who will need help constructing a coherent narrative of the relationship and the loss. Table 8.1, below, summarizes the complications in adaptation to bereavement that theory, research, and clinical experience suggest are associated with different types of insecure attachment. The assumptions underlying this presentation of complications in grief are based on the Dual Process Model of Bereavement (Stroebe & Schut, 1999). According to this model, adaptation to loss takes place through a process in which the bereaved's energy and attention "oscillate" between a focus on the loss and a focus on restoration, the latter referring to activities and relationships that are not directly related to the loss. Problems in adjustment thus reflect a breakdown in oscillation which limits the bereaved person's ability to balance attention to loss-related thoughts and feelings with attention to ongoing relationships and roles (Kosminsky & Jordan, 2016).

The principal areas of difficulty identified in Table 8.1 have to do with difficulties in managing emotion, beliefs about the self and others that interfere with adaptation to loss, and difficulties in what attachment theorists refer to as *mentalizing*: the capacity to understand one's own thoughts and behaviors and those of others (Allen, 2013). Emotion regulation difficulties are present in

Table 8.1 Attachment-related Complications in Bereavement

Attachment Orientation	Related Complications
Anxious	Dependency in relationship: intensity of loss-related emotions interferes with oscillation and integration of the loss; misappraisal of circumstances and self capacities sustains painful emotions but is consistent with attachment needs
Avoidant	Dismissive of attachment: ambivalence about the person and/or avoidance of feeling about them interferes with oscillation and integration of the loss; low value placed on social support may contribute to social isolation; suppression of emotion may contribute to emergence of physical symptoms
Disorganized	Difficulty tolerating and managing emotion and lack of mentalizing capacity interferes with processing intense and conflicting feelings related to the deceased and interferes with integration of the loss

(Adapted from Kosminsky & Jordan, 2016)

most individuals with insecure attachment, but manifest differently in people with anxious versus avoidant attachment orientations. Difficulties with mentalizing are most prominent in individuals with disorganized attachment styles whose early attachment experiences were punitive or neglectful (Allen, 2013). In addressing these difficulties, our goal in each case is to promote flexible attention to the loss and to restore the oscillation that characterizes normal grief (Stroebe & Schut, 1999). This goal is reflected in the following attachment-informed definition of grief therapy:

> Grief therapy is a concentrated form of empathically attuned and skill-fully applied social support, in which the therapist helps the bereaved person reregulate after a significant loss by serving as a transitional attachment figure. This includes addressing deficits in affect regulation and mentalizing related to both the loss at hand, and early neglect or trauma, as needed. In an environment that encourages exploration and growth, the bereavement therapist supports the bereaved in experiencing and tolerating feelings relating to grief, integrating new information and skills, and developing a new self-narrative that incorporates the impact of the loss. The goal of grief therapy is integration of the loss on a psychological and neurological level. Successful grief therapy encourages a state of flexible attention to the loss, and to the relationships, roles and experiences that are still available to the bereaved individual, in order that they may reengage in life, without relinquishing their attachment to the deceased.
>
> *(Kosminsky & Jordan, 2016, p. 100)*

The remainder of this chapter will illustrate the implications of an attachment-informed approach to grief therapy as it relates to CB.

Attachment Security and CB: Treatment Implications and Recommendations

Attachment orientation influences the choice of defensive strategies and is likewise reflected in the problems that arise from overuse of these strategies. Thus, interventions to support emotion regulation (and grief interventions on the whole) should address the specific difficulties of a bereaved client's attachment style.

As with all therapeutic interventions, decisions about approach and technique in bereavement work should be made based on the needs of the client. This being said, there are recognizable patterns of defensive strategies associated with certain attachment styles that can contribute to the nature of CB, and in turn adaptation to loss, and an awareness of these patterns can help guide treatment decisions.

Anxious Attachment and CB: Acknowledging the Reality of the Loss

Among the problems that have been associated with anxious attachment is the tendency of the anxiously attached bereaved individual to have difficulty accepting the reality of the loss, a difficulty reflected in the manner in which the bereaved maintains a bond with the deceased. Researchers who have pointed to the problems related to CB that do not acknowledge the death recommend that intervention address rumination and other cognitive processes that sustain painful emotions and interfere with the bereaved's access to positive memories. Some researchers differentiate between what they call "external bonds" maintained through attachment to objects and conversation with the deceased, and "internal bonds" that are fueled by memory, and that are believed to reflect a more realistic view of the nature of the relationship with the deceased – namely, that they are deceased. The following case example illustrates these problems, and this approach to intervention.

Rachel: They Promised Me They Would Never Leave

Rachel is a middle school science teacher in her early forties whose parents both died within two years of her seeking treatment. Apart from a few brief separations, Rachel lived her entire life under her parents' roof. In their absence, Rachel has remained very connected to her parents, greeting them every day when she comes home from work, telling them about her day, and avoiding after-school activities that would delay her arrival at home. She does not sit in the chair that was her father's, and does not allow visitors to sit in it, because it is his chair. Rachel's parents always promised her that they would never leave her. Consequently, along with her grief, Rachel feels hurt and angry with her parents for failing to keep their promise. After two years, she cannot bring herself to talk about them in the past tense, nor can she adjust her actions to recognize that they are gone.

My mother died a year and a half ago. She had the bigger of the bedrooms, and I'd like to move into it, but my dog sleeps with me, and she
never wanted a dog in that room.

(Kosminsky, 2007)

Rachel would like to invite some of her colleagues from school for dinner but
says that her parents did not like having "strangers" in their home. She would
like to visit a friend in another state, but feels her parents would not want her
traveling on her own.

Rachel's therapy consisted of a combination of individual and group work.
In their individual sessions, the clinician gently invited Rachel to consider her
parents' role in her life. Regular criticism from her father about her clothing,
hairstyles, and outside activities undermined any confidence she might have had
in her own judgment. Rachel felt terribly unsure of herself and thus was desperate
to maintain a bond with her parents, but the nature of the bond made it impossible for her to make decisions, and kept her from making changes in her life that
would open her up to new people and new experiences. Rachel was becoming
increasingly despondent at the thought of continuing to live in such a restricted
and fearful manner, but she was at a loss as to how to break the habits of a lifetime.

I like to pretend that they're sitting on the couch. At first, talking to
them made me feel better. But now I'm beginning to wonder if maybe
it isn't so good for me to talk to them so much. But I can't turn my
back on them.

(Kosminsky, 2007)

Rachel's CB with her parents was problematic in several respects, starting with
the fact that it was not grounded in an awareness that they were dead. Fueled by
a potent mixture of love, resentment, and guilt, her relationship with her parents
obstructed her path forward. Despite its problematic nature, the clinician recognized that if she preemptively challenged Rachel's view of her parents, there was
a good chance that Rachel would discontinue therapy.

The primary counterbalance to the risk of confrontation in these cases is the
warmth of the therapist and the security of the therapeutic bond. Only once
the client has come to feel that the therapist cares about them, believes in them,
and wants to help them is it possible to challenge the client's defenses without
therapeutic rupture; even then, it does not always end well. In Rachel's case,
the clinician began by encouraging Rachel to talk about her work as a teacher,
her feelings about her students, her accomplishments, and her dreams of a life
outside the walls of her childhood home. These conversations were intended
to foster Rachel's self-confidence, as well as to build trust. Only then did the
clinician introduce, in a gentle and measured manner, the idea that along with
wanting what was best for her, her parents had also wanted her with them for
their own sake. Wanting her to remain at home, they had (not deliberately, perhaps) imposed a rigid set of rules that had the effect of deepening her dependence

on them rather than helping her develop into a self-sufficient, confident adult. Rachel's immediate reaction to these suggestions was to defend her parents and to reject what she felt was a pernicious strategy on the part of the clinician.

> Why do you say these things to me? So that I can love them less?
>
> *(Kosminsky, 2007)*

Rachel returned the week after asking the question above, and picked up where she had left off.

> Last time was very painful. For a while afterward I felt that by making me remember the hurt you were taking my parents away from me, that somehow I had lost the last vestiges of them. But after a few days I started to feel better. I started to say to myself: you know, something has to change. When I think about letting go of my parents, I can't pretend it isn't frightening. But I see the value of moving past what I fear, and I will go forward.
>
> *(Kosminsky, 2007)*

An important adjunct to Rachel's individual sessions was her participation in a support group for adults grieving the loss of a parent. Having overcome some of her defensiveness about her relationship with her parents, Rachel was able to absorb the group member's insistence that she take that trip, move into that room, and otherwise take charge of life. She continued to honor her parents' memory, but also began to take pride in her own accomplishments. True to her word, she moved forward.

Emotion Regulation in the Insecurely Attached: A Foundation for Reconfiguration of the CB

The preceding discussion illustrates the essential role that the therapeutic relationship plays in grief work. With Rachel, whose difficulty in accepting the reality of her parents' death had much to do with the fear that she could not survive without them, the work required sensitivity to the client's need to maintain her defensive strategy of acting "as if" her parents were still present, and could be relied upon for companionship and guidance. The role of the clinician in this case was to provide an alternative source of support, while simultaneously encouraging her to recognize her own strengths. In this way, it was possible for Rachel to create a different kind of bond with her parents – one that did not require her to live as though they were still alive and in charge of her life.

To enable the bereaved client to make this kind of transition, a transition from an external to an internal bond, the defensive strategy that imposes and sustains this strategy must be addressed. Strategies for building affect tolerance are discussed at length elsewhere (Kosminsky & Jordan, 2016).

Positive Functions of CB in the Anxiously Attached

CB theory and research suggest that a CB with an attachment figure can provide some of the same benefits derived from the relationship when the person was alive. The mourner may, for example, continue to use the deceased as an important source of felt security and safe haven, particularly in times of distress. The deceased may also function as a secure base for exploration, as in cases where a widow is able to make changes in her life, buoyed by the knowledge that her husband would want her to go on with her life. In the following example, this sense of permission to move on came about over time.

Lisa: Bound by Fear and Loyalty

Lisa, a widow in her fifties, described her sixteen-year marriage to Al as an adventure of the kind not many people have a chance to experience. Al was a world-class sailor, and the couple spent the first nine years of their marriage traveling the world together. When they returned, they opened a seafood restaurant that became a great success. Sailing and running a restaurant were ventures that reflected Al's passions: they were less in line with Lisa's personality and interests, and joining him meant giving up her work as a drug and alcohol counselor. But she embraced the life Al offered, which to her mind was far more exciting than the life she was living. Two years after Al's death, Lisa was still running the restaurant, and felt that she owed it to her husband to keep it going, although she no longer wished to do so. A recovered alcoholic, Lisa also worried that if she continued to work in the restaurant she would be putting her sobriety at risk.

The bond Lisa maintained with Al was built on a combination of fear and loyalty. So much of her identity was about being Al's wife and partner; if she let go of that identity, who would she be? What would she do? She was sure that Al would want her to keep the restaurant going and she felt she could not abandon the business they had built together. In a real sense, the restaurant was not just a restaurant: it was stand-in for her husband, a living, breathing embodiment of her husband's life and loves. Walking away from it would be like walking away from her husband. But the longer she stayed, the more trapped she felt and the less confidant she was of her ability to create a life that was more authentically hers.

The Turning Point for Lisa: A Continuing Role for Al

When she began therapy, Lisa had settled into a narrative of her marriage and her husband in which her choice was to either honor or not honor her husband's wishes. This narrative assumed that Al's first love was the restaurant. Through a series of questions Lisa was guided toward a different narrative, and indeed a more accurate narrative, concerning the loves of his life, of which Lisa was unquestionably the most important. As she talked about her husband and their marriage,

Lisa's anxious rumination about what to do about the restaurant began to subside. In its place was a deep sadness and longing for this man who had been so intent on making life wonderful for her. He had set out on their trip not only because he loved to sail, but because he loved to be *with her* and wanted their life together to be extraordinary. She recalled the many things he had done to make her happy, and in so doing, began to consider that he would want her to do whatever she needed to do to be happy. Having arrived at this conclusion Lisa was able to use her ongoing bond with Al to help her figure out what she should do, and it was not long before she decided that she should sell the restaurant.

In tandem with the work involved in reimagining what Al would want her to do, Lisa needed to focus on identifying her own goals. As she began to plan for her future, Lisa continued to seek Al's guidance when making decisions, but now she had a new way of thinking about what that advice might be. She realized that the way to honor Al's memory was not to live *the life* he had lived, but to live *the way* he had lived.

> At first, with Al not there, I felt like "it's not my world anymore." Now I feel like my life can proceed, and that some of that feeling comes from Al, that he infused me with the confidence to know that you have to listen to what you feel inside, to know what you want – and then live it. That's the gift he gave me.
>
> *(Kosminsky, 2007)*

The cases presented provide a sample of strategies for addressing problems in CB that may be present in anxiously attached individuals who are faced with a significant loss. Referring back to Table 8.1, we note that these approaches are directed toward helping the client shift from an external to an internal bond, strengthen emotion regulation, and address cognitive distortions that contribute to rumination and sustain negative emotional states.

Avoidant Attachment and CB:
Adaptation vs. Suppression

Moving now to the question of how avoidant attachment influences CB, we begin by pointing out that as a practical matter, avoidantly attached individuals are less likely than those with an anxious attachment style to present themselves for help in the aftermath of loss, making it difficult for us to observe the course of their bereavement, including their use of CB (Allen, 2013). Additionally, Bonanno and others have argued that many of those who might be classified as avoidantly attached are, in fact, resilient – meaning that they are simply not as affected by grief as are others, even those whose grief is described as "normal." Based on his research, Bonanno concludes that these individuals, by virtue of their resilient nature, are not avoiding or "suppressing" their grief: they are simply subject to a far less prolonged and painful bereavement experience. This view of resilience has been challenged by recent research that cautions against confusing suppression with resilience and that suggests that avoidantly attached grievers face their own problems in adaptation to loss, including problems that arise from the nature of their CB with the deceased (Meier et. al., 2013).

Suppressed Feelings

The defensive strategies employed by bereaved adults who are avoidant in their attachment orientation have much in common with the behavior of avoidantly attached children as described by Bowlby, Main, and colleagues. These children were able to mimic the non-reactive style of someone not terribly affected by the absence of the attachment figure, and not terribly excited about their return. Having learned that a more expressive display would not be well received by their caregiver, they keep their feelings under tight wrap. We see these early efforts to manage emotion reflected in the words and faces of adult clients who deny feeling much of anything, who can't tell us what they feel, or who dismiss whatever feelings leak out when they are speaking of a deceased loved one.

Emotional expression is not a prerequisite for adaptation to loss, and there are indeed individuals for whom the absence of tears is a feature of their psychological makeup rather than a symptom of complicated grief. For others, avoidance is a fragile shell, likely to crack under the pressure of extreme stress (Mikulincer & Shaver, 2013). These are the people we tend to see in treatment. Their response to the opening question of "what brings you in" is often a disparaging description of the excessive emotionality of their response to loss and a self-critical assessment of their failure to "get over it." They often express considerable skepticism about the value of therapy which is, after all, a relationship – and relationships, in the experience of these individuals, are not a place to put one's confidence or a safe place to reveal one's feelings. This set of beliefs – about the value of emotion, about the trustworthiness of other people, about the possibility of having another person understand or help them – is associated with problems in adaptation to loss. When, as is often the case, these beliefs are rooted in, and sustained by, the bereaved person's bond with the deceased, work to resolve these problematic aspects of the CB must begin by establishing a therapeutic bond that will allow them to be identified and addressed.

Hannah

There's no point in crying. I just have to take care of business and go on.
(Kosminsky & Jordan, 2016)

Hannah's husband died after a long illness that had depleted her considerable reserves of emotional and physical strength. With her husband gone and her children grown, Hannah saw no purpose in her life. She avoided looking at the clinician, gave abrupt answers to her questions, and made every effort to avoid showing emotion, even when describing the horrific suffering her husband had endured and that she had had to witness. Over time, these behaviors were brought to Hannah's attention and the clinician suggested that the effort she was making to avoid her feelings was exhausting her, and also making it hard for her to have a sense of ongoing connection to her husband. Where, the clinician wondered aloud, had Hannah learned to manage her feelings by keeping them stuffed inside? The implication that this was something she had learned as a child was met with a brusque response: "Why is any of this important? This is not what I'm here to talk about." Some weeks later, the clinician again raised a question about how feelings were managed in her childhood family, and who comforted young Hannah when she was upset. Anticipating a repeat of her question about "why any of this is important," the clinician explained that we learn a lot about how to value our feelings from the way our parents respond to us as children when we're afraid or upset. We learn things like whether our feelings are worth paying attention to, or sharing with other people. Hannah's parents traveled a great deal, and they were not very involved with her in the brief periods when they were at home. The independent little girl Hannah remembered herself as being had grown into a woman who was determined not to need anyone's help. Seeing that Hannah was still listening, the clinician said:

> I think it's really important for you to think of yourself as independent, someone who doesn't need anyone else. So, it's a risk for you to feel your feelings. If you let yourself feel really sad, you might need someone to comfort you. And that's not something you want to have to do, because deep down you figure no one is going to comfort you.
>
> *(Kosminsky & Jordan, 2016)*

It is inevitable that in talking about how we guide clients toward reconfiguring their bonds with the deceased, we end up helping them redefine their relationships with themselves. In many cases this redefinition is about the meaning and value they attach to their emotions, and their sense of how prepared they are to deal with strong feelings. Simply put, insecure attachment, whether anxious or avoidant, is associated with difficulties in emotion regulation, and these difficulties can interfere with the creation of a potentially adaptive bond with the deceased.

In working with avoidantly attached clients, the clinician must be prepared for a negative response to any recommendation about "getting in touch with your feelings." In this, as in all therapeutic work, pacing is everything. We often use the metaphor of letting air into a house: we're not throwing open all the doors and windows; we're opening one window, and opening it just a bit at a time. We talk about what it might be like to relax one's defenses against emotions; we consider what effect it might have on our relationships with the people who are living and those who have passed on.

If clients continue to come, as Hannah did, they will often find themselves less avoidant and critical of their feelings, and more inclined to allow space for them to exist. They can be encouraged to notice their feelings during the week, and also to notice what they say to themselves about their emotions when they are aware of them. They can be instructed to practice letting go of judgments about what they feel. Techniques for promoting emotional awareness and acceptance can be introduced in session, and practiced by the client at home (Kosminsky & Jordan, 2016).

Clients who are not comfortable sharing their feelings in session can also be encouraged to keep a journal, which they may or may not decide to show to anyone else. Research suggests that people who are reluctant to talk about their feelings are the most likely to benefit from expressing their feelings in writing, particularly when they are provided with suggestions that encourage them to experience and record their emotions related to painful events (Lichtenthal & Neimeyer, 2012).

Disorganized Attachment and CB

Early abuse and neglect have been linked to problems with emotion regulation, and these problems are most likely to manifest under conditions of heightened stress. No matter how attuned and compassionate a therapist is, recalling early abuse is painful and frightening. Given that grief is also painful and frightening, it is not surprising that bereaved clients who experienced early abuse or neglect may become overwhelmed, emotionally numb, and even dissociated in session. This kind of response seems to be related both to a client's limited recall of painful events and his or her limited capacity to tolerate the affective arousal that remembering these events provokes.

Further complicating the (pre and post-death) relationships of these individuals is the fact that they are limited in their ability to make sense of the thoughts, feelings, and behavior of others; that is, they lack the ability to mentalize.

Restoring Mentalizing

Allen (2013) attributes mentalizing difficulties in adulthood to early neglect or abuse, describing such adverse treatment of the child as a *failure of mentalizing* on the part of the parent: the parent is not attuned to the child's internal state, cannot understand what the child may be feeling, and responds to expressions of need with anger, or not at all. The child feels unseen, invisible, and alone. Growing up with a parent who does not mentalize leads to a number of developmental deficits, including a lack of mentalizing capacity in the child, a breakdown in the ability to understand what other people are feeling, and an inability to recognize internal emotional cues. As clinicians, we are in a position to model mentalizing for our clients, and to help them develop this capacity.

When clients describe relationships that were hurtful to them, particularly relationships with caregivers, the question of forgiveness is often raised. In our experience, forgiveness is not always possible. In any case, our goal in helping clients make sense of the behavior of the deceased is not to encourage forgiveness, but to facilitate the loosening of a painful attachment, and to help them establish whatever distance between themselves and the deceased feels right for them.

Audrey

In many cases, clients who have difficulty making sense of what others are think-ing and feeling are people who have had few if any close relationships, and the relationships they do have tend to be marked by conflict. This was the case for Audrey, a 42-year-old woman whose father had died five years before she sought help. During that time Audrey had had a series of health crises, had lost her job, and was living with her mother, with whom she had frequent arguments. Audrey resented her mother's demands for her attention and what she saw as her mother's over-involvement in her life. The one long-term relationship in her life was con-stantly on the verge of falling apart. Audrey recognized that many of the problems in her relationships were caused by her anger, and that much of this anger was left over from childhood and early adulthood, when she and other members of her family were continually subject to her father's emotional cruelty. The clini-cian described mentalizing as a skill that might help her get along better with her mother and with other people in her life, and said that it might also help her man-age the toxic anger that she carried toward her father. In the following exchange the clinician models the skill of mentalizing.

"She thinks I can't make my own decisions! She still treats me like a child!"
(She doesn't see that you're capable of taking care of yourself.)
"No one in my family does! No one in my family knows me!"
(I know. And that's a bad feeling, an old, bad feeling.)
"It's my whole life, that feeling."
(Yes . . . you felt that way so much growing up, mostly because of your father, all the criticism, the accusations, the yelling. This reminds you of him, when what you're trying to do is to not think about him all the time.)
"When my mother talks to me that way it's like he never left, like he never died."

(Kosminsky & Jordan, 2016)

Later in this exchange the clinician suggested an alternative interpretation of her mother's demands for Audrey's attention: perhaps she was simply glad to have her company and was interested in what she was doing. Audrey replied:

Well, I don't know about that. But maybe. It has been kind of nice, not being alone. We usually sit together and eat dinner. And now that you mention it, last week she handed me some files to look at. And I was getting ready to leave and I thought, why is she doing that right now? But then she went into the kitchen to get her supper and brought it out to where I was standing and looking at the files, and I said, you know, these files are interesting. I want to look at them for a minute. Why don't we sit down and I'll look at them while you eat your dinner.
(That was kind of you.)

(Kosminsky & Jordan, 2016)

The clinician noted that in the course of talking about this conversation with her mother Audrey's voice had become softer and that her body seemed more relaxed. Bringing these changes to Audrey's attention, she suggested that Audrey might consider how she could make "softening" a goal. She could begin to work toward this goal by being conscious of how she held her body, how she breathed, and how she interpreted other people's words and actions. If she were able to shift toward a softer way of being with other people, she might find that she could have a different outlook on their intentions and behavior. She might also find that over time, these changes would help her in letting go of some of the anger that was binding her to her father.

> I guess I'm carrying a lot of anger around all the time. Maybe if I could be softer with other people and with myself I could let some of that go.
> *(Kosminsky & Jordan, 2016)*

Closing Thoughts on an Attachment-Informed Approach to Working with CB

We come back, finally, to Bowlby, who regarded a secure bond with the caregiver as an essential element in healthy development, the base that allows a child to explore the world. Attachment security is what allows the child to tolerate separation from the caregiver. Similarly, attachment security in adulthood has been identified as a factor in people's ability to manage their response to loss, and a factor in the nature of CB. A secure relationship leaves the bereaved individual better positioned to accept the reality of the loss and more able to call upon the deceased as a continuing source of comfort and security. Insecure attachment compromises this process, and creates a number of problems for the griever, including problems in the manner in which they maintain a CB with the deceased.

CB as a Metaphor

The desire to maintain a connection with a beloved person is easy to understand: the bereaved want to hold on, any way they can, to the person who has died. But despite this desire, not everyone embraces the idea of CB when it is introduced. Like C.S. Lewis, some clients will insist that no kind of CB will allay their suffering. In the end, isn't it impossible to have a bond with someone who is not with us? Can we be comforted by a connection that is, some would insist, metaphorical?

George Vaillant, in his classic explanation of the myriad defensive strategies that human beings mount in an effort to cope with painful realities that are beyond their control, offers a counter-argument, reminding us of the healing power of metaphor, and illustrating his point with passages from *The Little Prince* by Antoine St. Exupery (Vaillant, 1993). As he is about to depart for his home planet, the Prince, seeing that his new friend the Fox is terribly sad, declares that it would have been better if he had never come: in that case, the Fox would not be in pain. The Fox, however, sees things differently. Yes, he will miss the Prince, but he will be comforted by his memories. Every day, there will be reminders of the Prince, and these reminders, although they will make him a bit sad, will also draw his attention to things he might otherwise have missed. Before, the wheat fields meant nothing to the carnivorous Fox; now, the gold color of the wheat fields will remind him of the Prince's golden hair, and the Fox will "love to listen to the wind in the wheat" (p. 334). His life, in short, will not be impoverished by his having known the Prince; it will be enriched. The Fox will grieve, and he may worry about what has happened to his little friend, but his pain will not break him. "We forget," Vaillant writes, "that healthy grief hurts but does not make us ill. . . . It is never having anyone at all to love that cripples us" (p. 335).

Attachment security is the platform that allows us to draw comfort and a feeling of safety from those we love. The child who has a secure relationship with his caregiver can tolerate brief separation; the adult who has enjoyed a secure and loving relationship carries within him resources that help him cope with the pain of loss. Those who have loved us, and whom we have loved, do not entirely leave us. It is not their absence, but the presence of those who do not love us well, that lays the groundwork for problematic grief.

There are many ways to conceptualize CB and to understand their impact. We have outlined an approach that emphasizes attention to attachment orientation as a factor in the formation of relationships and the nature of CB. We hope that what we have shared here will be helpful to those working in the field and will ultimately benefit the bereaved people they serve.

Acknowledgments

The author wishes to thank John R. Jordan for his comments on this chapter and for his contributions to the ideas expressed herein.

References

Allen, J. G. (2013). *Restoring mentalizing in attachment relationships: Treating trauma with plain old therapy.* Arlington, VA: American Psychiatric Publishing.

Bonanno, G. A. (2004). Loss, trauma, and human resilience: Have we underestimated the human capacity to thrive after extremely adverse events? *American Psychologist, 59,* 20–28.

Bowlby, J. (1980). *Attachment and loss, Vol. III: Loss, sadness and depression.* New York, NY: Basic Books.

Field, N. P., & Filanosky, C. (2010). Continuing bonds, risk factors for complicated grief, and adjustment to bereavement. *Death Studies, 34,* 1–29.

Kosminsky. P. (2007). *Getting back to life when grief won't heal.* New York, NY: McGraw-Hill.

Kosminsky, P., & Jordan, J. (2016). *Attachment informed grief therapy: The clinician's guide to foundations and applications.* New York, NY: Routledge.

Lewis, C. S. (1961). *A grief observed.* New York, NY: Harper Collins.

Lichtenthal, W.G., & Neimeyer, R.A. (2012). Directed writing to facilitate meaning making. In R.A. Neimeyer (Ed.), *Techniques of Grief Therapy: Creative Practices for Counseling the Bereaved,* pp. 165-168. New York: Routledge.

Main, M. (2000). The organized categories of infant, child and adult attachment. *Journal of the American Psychoanalytic Association, 48*(4), 1055–1096.

Meier, A.M., Carr D.R., Currier, J.M., Neimeyer, R.A. (2013). Attachment anxiety and avoidance in coping with bereavement: Two studies. *Journal of Social and Clinical Psychology* 32:315-334.

Mikulincer, M., & Shaver, P. (2013). Attachment insecurities and disordered patterns of grief. In M. Stroebe (Ed.), *Complicated grief: Scientific foundations for health professionals.* New York, NY: Routledge.

Stroebe, M., & Schut, H. (1999). The dual process model of coping with bereavement: Rationale and description. *Death Studies, 23*(3), 197–224.

Vaillant, G. (1993). *The wisdom of the ego.* Cambridge, MA: Harvard University Press.

9

EXTERNALIZED AND INTERNALIZED CONTINUING BONDS IN UNDERSTANDING GRIEF

Samuel M.Y. Ho and Ide S.F. Chan

Introduction

Cheng was a 50-year-old woman who came to therapy because of depressive symptoms related to the loss of both her beloved parents in the past two years. She was single and had always lived with her parents. After the death of her parents, Cheng became depressed and lost the will to do almost everything, including her favorite hobby, craftwork. Hiding in her bedroom, she felt cold and lonely. During the therapy sessions, Cheng revealed that she sometimes felt as though her parents were sitting beside her while she was doing her craftwork at home. She admitted that this feeling helped her to maintain an ongoing relationship with her parents and she would not want such a relationship to go away.

Cheng's craving to maintain a continuing bond (CB) (Field, Gal-Oz, & Bonanno, 2003) with her parents is a common experience among the bereaved of all ages and cultures (Klass, Silverman, & Nickman, 1996; Shuchter & Zisook, 1993). Our interest in CBs dates back to our early studies on grief reactions (Ho, Chow, Chan, & Tsui, 2002) and death metaphors (Cheung & Ho, 2004; Cheung & Ho, 2006). In a study to establish an instrument to assess the grief reactions of Chinese bereaved individuals, we found that the item "I do not want to abandon him/her" obtained the highest score among both men and women (Ho et al., 2002). We noted that Chinese believe that the deceased have a continuous linkage with the family through ancestral worship and the tablet placed in the domestic altar (Moser, 1975). Families may continue to celebrate the birthdays and death anniversaries of their deceased ancestors (Chan & Mak, 2000). The feeling that the deceased family members are still "living" with the family may be important for the mental health of the bereaved family members (Tsang, 1996).

In another study exploring the use of metaphor to understand personal perceptions of death among Hong Kong Chinese, we asked college students to rate the extent to which 30 death metaphor items represented their personal meaning of death (Cheung & Ho, 2004). Examples of the items included (death is) "a cold lonely journey," "a thankful goodbye," and "separation from a loved one." We found that three of the 10 highest-scored items in this study ("A separation from a loved one," "A thankful goodbye," and "People crying around my bed") were "interpersonally oriented," which is consistent with the interdependent self-construal tendency commonly found among Asian people (Markus & Kitayama, 1991). In a later study, we collected "death drawings" (i.e., drawings representing a personal perception of death) from people in Hong Kong including healthcare professionals, university students, and community samples (Cheung & Ho, 2006). An example of such a drawing is provided in Figure 9.1. We concluded that the negative emotions shown in the drawings were usually concerned with the reactions of others significant to the deceased person. Most of these drawings showed the sorrow or grief of the people around the deceased person, which is consistent with our previous finding that Chinese people may be more "interpersonally" focused.

Figure 9.1 "Interpersonally oriented" Death Drawings: Mourning of significant other

At about the same time as we were conducting the above work, Field and his colleagues (2003) started to use the CB concept to describe the bereaved individual's ongoing inner relationship with the deceased person.[1] It is logical to expect a conceptual relationship between CBs and the interpersonally focused personal perception of death, although we were not aware of this linkage back in the early 2000s. In retrospect, our subsequent collaboration with Field on CB studies represented a continuation of our interest in the interpersonal dimension of grief and death perception. In this chapter, we discuss our findings related to CBs with a focus on the implications for grief therapy. We first discuss whether maintaining a CB is beneficial to adjustment after bereavement, in terms of psychological theory and from a Chinese cultural perspective. We then describe our findings on CBs among Chinese conjugally bereaved individuals. We discuss the clinical implications of our findings toward the end of this chapter.

The Continuing–Relinquishing Bonds Paradigm

Li lost his 12-year-old daughter from his first marriage because of cancer. He had just had a new baby in his second marriage. Li had kept his deceased daughter's possessions in the room that once belonged to her. Now he was struggling to renovate the room and turn it into his new baby's room because he still had the feeling that his daughter was living there. He said that his daughter would be angry with him if he changed anything in her room for the newborn baby.

Although it is commonly accepted that CBs represent an important phenomenon among the bereaved, whether a CB represents a maladaptive (i.e., more grief-related distress) or an adaptive (i.e., less grief-related distress) adjustment to bereavement remains an unresolved issue among researchers and clinicians. The issue of whether to continue or relinquish bonds is also referred to as the continuing–breaking bonds controversy (Stroebe & Schut, 2005).

The theoretical framework underpinning the relinquishing of bonds can be traced back to classical psychodynamic theory. In *Mourning and Melancholia*, Freud (1917) proposed that the major task of a bereaved person is to relinquish the tie to the deceased (de-catharsis) by withdrawing the emotional energy tied to the person and reinvesting it in new relationships. Under this classical psychodynamic framework, failure to break the tie with the deceased may lead to symptomatic adjustment. Lindemann (1944), who later wrote the seminal grief paper following the 1942 Cocoanut Grove fire in Boston, U.S. (Lindemann & Cobb, 1979), perpetuated the notion that the healthy resolution of grief involves confronting the reality of the loss and severing the emotional bonds with the deceased. Later theories also carry a strong notion of relinquishing bonds. The stage theory of grief proposed by Kubler-Ross (1970), which stresses the need to reorganize representations of the deceased to allow the bereaved to reengage in normal activities and social relationships, also carries a strong notion of relinquishment. Worden's (2009) task model of bereavement suggests that mental health practitioners should help the bereaved to withdraw their emotional energy from the deceased and reinvest it in new relationships. The importance of working through and relinquishing bonds from the deceased as a critical goal of bereavement adjustment is implied. Neimeyer, Baldwin, and Gillies (2006) conducted an empirical study of 506 undergraduate students with experience of bereavement using a meaning reconstruction framework to guide the study. They reported that among participants with low sense-making (measured by a single item "How much sense would you say you have made of the loss?"), stronger CBs were associated with more grief-related distress.

The above proposition to relinquish bonds is inconsistent with the practices of many cultures, notably the Japanese (Klass et al., 1996) and Chinese (Wittkowski, Ho, & Chan, 2011) cultures, to maintain a relationship with the deceased. For example, in a paper on the perception of death among the Chinese (Wittkowski et al., 2011), we wrote:

> The traditional Chinese belief system strongly emphasizes the accept-
> ance of life and death as well as harmonious interdependence among
> family members and others. Because of this emphasis, the prospect of
> the loss of the emotional bond to significant others by death may be
> especially threatening to Chinese people.

Because losing an emotional bond with a significant other (including the deceased's ancestors) can be threatening, many cultures have elaborate rituals and festivals (e.g., the Ching Ming Festival, or Tomb-Sweeping Day, in Chinese culture) to maintain a CB with the deceased, and such relationships can last for several generations. It is tempting to believe that cultural practices to maintain CBs should have beneficial effects on bereavement adjustment. Stroebe and Schut (2005) conducted a literature review on CBs and concluded that it is inconclusive whether maintaining or relinquishing a CB leads to better bereavement adjustment. The study by Neimeyer et al. (2006) mentioned earlier also suggests that CBs do not necessarily lead to better or worse adjustment to bereavement, and this depends on the extent and nature of meaning reconstruction related to the bereavement experience.

It is possible that there are different types of CB with different effects on bereavement adjustment. Besides, the review of Stroebe and Schut (2005) focused predominantly on Western cultures and may not be able to reflect the possible differential function of CB in Asian cultures.

Variants of CB

Chau had low confidence in herself and always relied on her husband to make major deci-
sions. After her husband's death, Chau was overwhelmed by the demands of daily life and
reported heightened anxiety when faced with every decision.

There are different ways to remember the deceased, such as reviewing the deceased's life story and identifying ceremonial opportunities for including the deceased in the life of the bereaved (Vickio, 1999), as well as rituals, the use of tangible objects, and continuing to experience the deceased's influence (Rando, 1993). Field et al. (2003) derived a scale to measure CBs and included items related to recovering memories, the maintenance of possessions, a sense of presence, identification with the deceased, the legacy of the deceased, the deceased as a standard, and reminiscence.

Other researchers have proposed that CBs can be both adaptive and maladaptive. Reisman (2001) proposed that adaptive forms of grief are characterized by higher-order abstract schemas, whereas maladaptive forms of grief are represented by lower-order concrete schemas. Higher-order schemas are usually flexible, and lower-order schemas are extremely resistant to change. Maintaining a permanent connection with the deceased at an abstract level does not interfere with adjustment and reality testing. In contrast, lower-order bonds resist correction from outside reality and often represent denial. Boerner and Heckhausen (2003) proposed that the process of adaptive adjustment should involve both relinquishing concrete love and maintaining abstract love. Consistent with this framework, Field et al. (1999) proposed that there are two general forms of CB: the maladaptive form involves hanging onto the deceased's possessions, whereas the adaptive form is expressed through evoking fond memories. Field (2006) further proposed that CB expressions that fail to recognize the distinction between present and past relationships and fail to acknowledge the permanence of the physical separation are likely to be maladaptive. For example, illusory and hallucinatory CB expressions of seeing the deceased constitute dissociate experiences that fail to appreciate the finality of the separation. This dissociative experience means that the separation continues to be experienced as a very distinct event without it being integrated into other information in memory. The loss becomes an event of great significance that can elicit strong emotions (Berntsen, 2001). The idea of using reality contact (i.e., an awareness that the CB with the deceased represents a past relationship and an acceptance of permanent physical separation with the deceased) to categorize CB could be considered as a precursor of the externalized–internalized CB paradigm, which is discussed in more detail in the next section.

Externalized and Internalized CB

Wong, a 51-year-old woman, became panicky when she learned that she urgently needed cardiac surgery. She revealed that her father was a heavy smoker and had died of lung cancer when she was 10 years old. Wong blamed her father for not taking good care of himself, leaving her to grow up without support and love. She admitted that she was still blaming her father for leaving her when she was very young. This feeling was still haunting her. She worried that she would die early like her father and this idea was related to her strong apprehension about the upcoming surgery.

The above discussion suggests that using a CB as a source of comfort and as a means to integrate the positive memory of the deceased into one's self-identity may be more adaptive. A CB involving hallucinatory or illusory experiences of the deceased and incorporating the negative memory of the deceased into one's self-identity may be maladaptive. Field and Filanosky (2010) made the above distinction explicit by proposing two types of CB: externalized and internalized. An externalized CB involves illusionary and hallucinatory experiences of the deceased. An internalized CB involves using the deceased as a secure base. Field and Filanosky (2010) developed a 47-item questionnaire to measure all possible variants of CB expression. A subsequent factor analysis resulted in a 16-item measure with two subscales: (1) the internalized CB subscale (10 items, accounting for 41% of the total variance) measures the bereaved individual's positive memories and the influence of the deceased (e.g., "I thought about the deceased as a role model whom I try to be like"); and (2) the externalized CB subscale (6 items, accounting for 11% of the total variance) measures the extent to which the individual lingers on the physical existence of the deceased (e.g., "I actually felt the deceased's physical touch"). Externalized CB was shown to be positively associated with violent death and responsibility for the death, whereas internalized CB was negatively associated with these risk factors and positively linked to personal growth.

We were intrigued by the idea of internalized and externalized CB, and their potential differential relations with grief adjustment. In collaboration with Field, we administered the 47-item CB questionnaire developed by Field and Filanosky (2010) to 71 Chinese conjugally bereaved individuals in Hong Kong (Ho, Chan, Ma, & Field, 2013). Similar to Field and Filanosky (2010), two subscales were identified: internalized CB (14 items) and externalized CB (5 items). Subsequent analyses showed that externalized CB had a significant positive correlation with grief symptoms ($r = .36$, $p < .01$). Somewhat to our surprise, internalized CB also showed a weak but significant positive correlation with grief symptoms ($r = .29$, $p < .05$). Supporting the relinquishing paradigm, a stronger reliance on either an internalized or externalized CB was associated with more severe grief symptoms after the loss of a loved one. Following the argument of Field and Filanosky (2010), the positive relationship between an internalized CB and grief symptoms might be an indicator of an extremely close relationship to the bereaved, thereby creating more difficulties in bereavement adjustment. Boelen, Stroebe, Schut, and Zijerveld (2006) reported that the use of fond memories (which is a common expression in internalized CB) was a stronger predictor of later grief than the use of the deceased's possessions.

It is possible that individual items in the internalized CB category may relate positively, negatively, or even insignificantly to grief symptoms, leading to an overall weak positive correlation. To investigate the "adaptiveness" of individual CB expression, we conducted partial correlations to examine the relationship between the mean score for each of the 19 CB items and the total grief symptom score in the previous study of Ho et al. (2013). As before, religion and mode of death were controlled as covariates in the partial correlation analyses. The results are shown for internalized CB items and externalized CB items, respectively. The severity of grief symptoms was measured by the Grief Reaction Assessment Form (Ho et al., 2002).

Only one item ("I thought about how the deceased would have enjoyed something I saw or did"), classified as an internalized continuing expression in both the Chinese CB scale (Ho et al., 2013) and the original CB scale of Field and Filanosky (2010), was positively correlated with grief symptoms ($r = .24$). Three of the five externalized CB items had a significant positive relationship with grief symptoms: "I had the feeling that the deceased was haunting me" ($r = .33$),

"I imagined that the deceased might suddenly appear as though still alive" (r = .30), and "Even if only momentarily, I have mistaken other people for the deceased" (r = .23). However, it should be noted that the relationships were weak for all items (coefficient r less than .4) (see Figures 9.2 and 9.3).

Clinical Implications and Conclusion

It is tempting to group CB expressions into categories, such as internalized and externalized, and suggest that different types of CB are related to different outcomes of bereavement adjustment. However, both our findings (Ho et al., 2013) and the earlier literature review by Stroebe and Schut (2005) suggest otherwise. There does not seem to be a simple one-on-one relationship between types of CBs and bereavement outcomes. Our research findings suggest that the specific expression of a CB, per se, has no (or at most a weak) significant relationship with bereavement adjustment. Ongoing connections between the bereaved individual and the deceased encompass a wide variety of behavior. The relationship between each form of CB expression and bereavement adjustment may vary across individuals, and the relationship may depend on many other factors. Root and Exline (2014), for instance, suggested that the effective use of a CB to cope with grief depended on whether the bereaved appraised the bond as positive or negative, the quality of the pre-death relationship, and the afterlife beliefs of the bereaved. Relatively recently, Stroebe, Schut, and Boerner (2010) proposed a theoretical

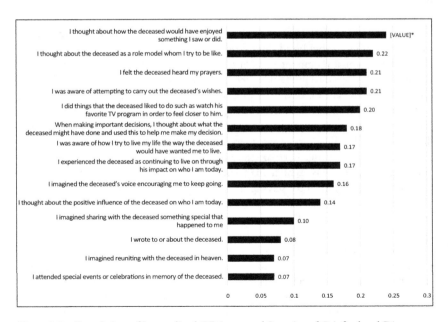

Figure 9.2 Correlation of Internalized CB Items and Severity of Grief-related Distress

*p < .05

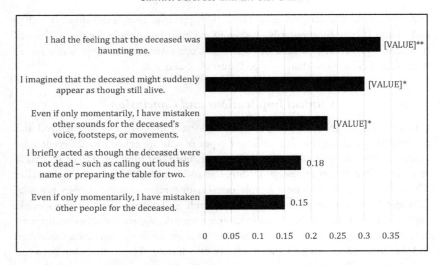

I had the feeling that the deceased was haunting me. [VALUE]**

I imagined that the deceased might suddenly appear as though still alive. [VALUE]*

Even if only momentarily, I have mistaken other sounds for the deceased's voice, footsteps, or movements. [VALUE]*

I briefly acted as though the deceased were not dead – such as calling out loud his name or preparing the table for two. 0.18

Even if only momentarily, I have mistaken other people for the deceased. 0.15

0   0.05   0.1   0.15   0.2   0.25   0.3   0.35

Figure 9.3 Correlation of Externalized CB Items and Severity of Grief-related Distress
**$p < .01$; *$p < .05$, ^$p = .05$

integrative model to guide judgment on the (mal)adaptiveness of continuing–relinquishing bonds. Similarly, cultural rituals to maintain (or relinquish) CBs may have other sociological and political values that may be unrelated to the psychological adjustment of bereavement.

As CBs have no direct relationship with bereavement adjustment, whether to maintain or relinquish a bond should depend on the unique situation of an individual. Professional judgment and consensus between the therapist and the client should be considered to guide intervention. Here, we describe how the therapist, Chan, the second author of this chapter, helped the four clients mentioned above.

Cheng was facilitated to recall the positive moments with her parents. She reported that one of the best moments was when she was in the sitting room doing craftwork while her parents were sitting beside her doing their own activities. From time to time, her parents would attend to her work and give some encouraging comments, which made her feel warm and supported. Using this picture, Cheng began to try staying in the sitting room to resume her craftwork. She revealed that she sensed a warm current flowing through her fingers, which became more dexterous. This was the first time she had been able to pick up her craft and started to enjoy her work again.

Li was guided to explore the change in his daughter from baby to pre-adolescence. He could tell how his daughter had changed through the years. He remembered how she started to share her toys with her younger brother at times, and shared her favorite stationery with her classmates. Li started to realize that his daughter had become more generous and accommodating before she passed away. He felt relieved after realizing this and decided to renovate the room for the new baby.

Chau was helped to recall what factors her husband would consider in a decision-making process. She learnt to draw on her husband's experience to help her cope with the demands of daily life in the future. She felt empowered and her anxiety was reduced.

Wong was helped to have a conversation with her father in an empty-chair exercise, in which she was able to express her anger and sadness over losing him. After working through her feelings, she showed gratitude toward her father for giving her a meaningful life. In the empty-chair exercise, she said goodbye to her father, who also encouraged her to be brave and confident before leaving. Afterwards, Wong used her father's encouraging statements from the empty chair to get through the cardiac surgery. She mentioned that her father no longer bothered her.

Acknowledgment

We would like to express our sincere gratitude to the late Dr. Nigel Field. Nigel left this world in December 2013. His departure is a great loss to us, both personally and professionally.

Note

1 It should be noted that in previous papers, Field and his colleagues used other labels (e.g., continuing attachment) to describe a related but not identical concept to CB (Field, Nichols, Holen, & Horowitz, 1999). Other researchers, notably Klass et al. (1996), used the term CB before Field et al.

References

Berntsen, D. (2001). Involuntary memories of emotional events: Do memories of traumas and extremely happy events differ? *Applied Cognitive Psychology*, *15*, S135–S158. doi: 10.1002/acp.838.

Boelen, P. A., Stroebe, M. S., Schut, H. A., & Zijerveld, A. M. (2006). Continuing bonds and grief: A prospective analysis. *Death Studies*, *30*(8), 767–776. doi: 10.1080/07481180600852936.

Boerner, K., & Heckhausen, J. (2003). To have and have not: Adaptive bereavement by transforming mental ties to the deceased. *Death Studies*, *27*(3), 199–226. doi: 10.1080/07481180302888.

Chan, C. L.-W., & Mak, J. M.-H. (2000). Benefits and drawbacks of Chinese rituals surrounding care for the dying. In R. Fielding & C. L.-W. Chan (Eds), *Psychosocial oncology and palliative care in Hong Kong. The first decade* (pp. 255–270). Hong Kong: Hong Kong University Press.

Cheung, W.-S., & Ho, S. M. Y. (2004). The use of death metaphors to understand personal meaning of death among Hong Kong Chinese undergraduates. *Death Studies*, *28*, 47–62.

Cheung, W.-S., & Ho, S. M. Y. (2006). Death metaphors in Chinese. In C. L. W. Chan & A. Y. M. Chow (Eds), *Death, dying and bereavement. A Hong Kong Chinese experience* (pp. 117–126). Hong Kong: Hong Kong University Press.

Field, N. P. (2006). Unresolved grief and continuing bonds: An attachment perspective. *Death Studies*, *30*(8), 739–756. doi: 10.1080/07481180600850518.

Field, N. P., & Filanosky, C. (2010). Continuing bonds, risk factors for complicated grief, and adjustment to bereavement. *Death Studies*, *34*(1), 1–29. doi: 10.1080/07481180903372269.

Field, N. P., Gal-Oz, E., & Bonanno, G. A. (2003). Continuing bonds and adjustment at 5 years after the death of a spouse. *Journal of Consulting & Clinical Psychology*, 71(1), 110–117.

Field, N. P., Nichols, C., Holen, A., & Horowitz, M. J. (1999). The relation of continuing attachment to adjustment in conjugal bereavement. *Journal of Consulting and Clinical Psychology*, 67(2), 212–218. doi: 10.1037/0022-006X.67.2.212.

Freud, S. (1917). Mourning and melancholia. In J. Rickman (Ed.), *A general selection from the works of Sigmund Freud* (pp. 124–140). New York, NY: Anchor Books.

Ho, S. M. Y., Chan, I. S., Ma, E. P., & Field, N. P. (2013). Continuing bonds, attachment style, and adjustment in the conjugal bereavement among Hong Kong Chinese. *Death Studies*, 37(3), 248–268. doi: 10.1080/07481187.2011.634086.

Ho, S. M. Y., Chow, A. Y. M., Chan, C. L.-W., & Tsui, Y. K. Y. (2002). The assessment of grief among Hong Kong Chinese: A preliminary report. *Death Studies*, 26, 91–98.

Klass, D., Silverman, P., & Nickman, S. L. (Eds). (1996). *Continuing bonds: New understandings of grief*. Washington, DC: Taylor & Francis.

Kubler-Ross, E. (1970). *On death and dying*. New York, NY: Macmillan.

Lindemann, E. (1944). Symptomatology and management of acute grief. *American Journal of Psychiatry*, 101, 1141–1148.

Lindemann, E., & Cobb, S. (1979). Neuropsychiatric observations after the Cocoanut Grove fire. In E. Lindemann & E. Lindemann (Eds), *Beyond grief: Studies in crisis intervention*. New York, NY: Aronson.

Markus, H. R., & Kitayama, S. (1991). Culture and the self: Implications for cognition, emotion, and motivation. *Psychological Review*, 98, 224–253.

Moser, M. J. (1975). Death in Chinese: A two-dimensional analysis. *Journal of Thanatology*, 3, 169–185.

Neimeyer, R. A., Baldwin, S. A., & Gillies, J. (2006). Continuing bonds and reconstructing meaning: Mitigating complications in bereavement. *Death Studies*, 30(8), 715–738. doi: 10.1080/07481180600848322.

Rando, T. A. (1993). *Treatment of complicated mourning*. Champaign, IL: Research Press.

Reisman, A. S. (2001). Death of a spouse: Illusory basic assumptions and continuation of bonds. *Death Studies*, 25, 445–460. doi: 10.1080/07481180126216.

Root, B. L., & Exline, J. J. (2014). The role of continuing bonds in coping with grief: Overview and future directions. *Death Studies*, 38(1–5), 1–8. doi: 10.1080/07481187.2012.712608.

Shuchter, S. R., & Zisook, S. (1993). The course of normal grief. In M. S. Stroebe, W. Stroebe, & R. O. Hansson (Eds), *Handbook of bereavement. Theory, research, and intervention* (pp. 23–43). Cambridge: Cambridge University Press.

Stroebe, M., & Schut, H. (2005). To continue or relinquish bonds: A review of consequences for the bereaved. *Death Studies*, 29, 477–494. doi: 10.1080/07481180590962659.

Stroebe, M., Schut, H., & Boerner, K. (2010). Continuing bonds in adaptation to bereavement: Toward theoretical integration. *Clinical Psychology Review*, 30(2), 259–268. doi: 10.1016/j.cpr.2009.11.007.

Tsang, W. H. (1996). Attitudes towards "life" and "death" in Chinese bereaved widows: Implications for bereavement work in Hong Kong. Unpublished MSW dissertation, the University of Hong Kong, Hong Kong.

Vickio, C. J. (1999). Together in spirit: Keeping our relationships alive when loved ones die. *Death Studies*, 23, 161–175. doi: 10.1080/074811899201127.

Wittkowski, J., Ho, S. M. Y., & Chan, W. C. H. (2011). Factor structure of the Multidimensional Orientation Toward Dying and Death Inventory among Hong Kong college students: A preliminary study. *Death Studies*, 35, 59–72.

Worden, J. W. (2009). *Grief counselling and grief therapy: A handbook for the mental health practitioner* (4th ed.). New York, NY: Springer.

10

FORGIVENESS AND CONTINUING BONDS

Elizabeth A. Gassin

Forgiveness and Continuing Bonds

From the perspective of the history of science, the study of forgiveness qualifies as but a child. Arguably, it was "born" only in the late 1980s with the publication of Enright, Santos, and Al-Mabuk (1989). In that paper, the authors provided evidence that reasoning about forgiveness progresses in a manner similar to Kohlbergian moral reasoning. Specifically, these authors found that across the first half of the lifespan, when asked to justify forgiving, people moved from an emphasis on reciprocity and/or social pressure as prerequisites for forgiveness to an understanding that it can be an unconditional expression of ethical principles such as generosity or even love. Since 1989, the field has grown and diversified greatly. We find evidence of that diversity in this chapter, in which I connect forgiveness studies to continuing bonds (CB) in various ways. For example, although many psychologists distinguish forgiveness and reconciliation, as we will see below, the forgiver usually hopes for restoration of a relationship. When the offender is already deceased, perhaps it is more accurate to say the forgiver opens herself to adaptive CB. In addition, we have initial evidence that CB can promote forgiveness, which in turn often provides mental health benefits. In this chapter we explore the concept of forgiveness, reasons to expect it is linked with bonds that reach beyond the grave, what the research suggests about this link, and how this information can be relevant for future research and applied work with bereaved individuals.

What Is Forgiveness and Why Might It Be Linked to CB?

We will first briefly explore the concept and research on forgiveness. What do we mean when we talk about forgiveness? This is a crucial and controversial question, and, as we will see, very tentative evidence suggests the answer affects how forgiveness and CB may be related. I will rely heavily though not exclusively on the work of Enright (e.g., Enright, 2012; Enright & Fitzgibbons, 2015). From Enright's perspective, interpersonal forgiveness occurs in the context of an unfair relational offense. The relationship may be enduring and close (e.g., spouses) or fleeting and non-intimate (e.g., a customer service representative). When an offense occurs, be it a spouse's sexual infidelity or rudeness in a business transaction, we experience varying degrees of hurt, anger, and shame. Forgiveness involves steps such as being honest about the offense and its impact on us, realizing that the impact must be addressed in a healthy fashion, and reframing (Knutson, Enright, & Garbers, 2008). This latter process, reframing, involves developing a greater understanding of the offender by exploring her background and the various factors influencing her behavior at the time of the offense. It can take a more philosophical nature as well, as the one who has been hurt realizes that the offender is still a person, and by virtue of this fact possesses worth (Enright & Fitzgibbons, 2015).

Theory and research suggest that almost universally, people engaging in the forgiveness process report decreases in negative thoughts, feelings, and behaviors vis-à-vis the offender. Respectively, this could include less condemnation of the offender, less anger, and less likelihood of seeking revenge. Some models and empirical investigations also note increases in positive thoughts (e.g., wishing the offender well), feelings (e.g., warmth and even love), and behaviors (e.g., being friendly) vis-à-vis the offender (Enright & Fitzgibbons, 2015). Authors of systematic reviews of the forgiveness literature regularly find that engaging in the process of extending interpersonal mercy to an offender offers a variety of mental health benefits (Baskin & Enright, 2004; Reik & Mania, 2012; Wade, Hoyt, Kidwell, & Worthington, 2014).

Defining forgiveness also includes distinguishing it from similar but distinct concepts. For example, it is important to note that reframing the offender does not mean excusing or justifying him, but seeing him in his wider context. In addition, psychologists usually distinguish between forgiveness and reconciliation, the latter being the actual restoration of a relationship. I will also refer to the concept of *pseudoforgiveness* in this chapter, which is akin to denial of the offense and/or its consequences (Enright & Fitzgibbons, 2015). For example, consider Joe, who has been verbally abused for months by a dating partner but simply shrugs his shoulders and says, "It doesn't bug me. I still have all the respect in the world for her." In such a case, we might suspect he is engaging in pseudoforgiveness. While a complete examination of the construct of forgiveness is beyond the scope of this chapter, readers are encouraged to consult Enright (2012; Enright & Fitzgibbons, 2015) or visit the International Forgiveness Institute (IFI) website at internationalforgiveness.com. Worthington is also a prolific creator of materials useful for academics (2005), human service professionals (2014), and laypersons (2001).

Why might there be a relationship between forgiveness and CB? We can attempt an answer to this question on both logical and empirical levels. Logically speaking, both concepts are relationally oriented. In fact, CB is basically defined as the presence of a relationship. Although forgiveness is not the same as maintaining a relationship with someone, it will affect the desire of one party to be in relationship with the other and the quality of that relationship. It seems reasonable to hypothesize that forgiveness may lead a person to be open to some forms of bonds that endure after a person's death. Given that forgiveness has been linked with mental health, presumably these would be adaptive forms of CB. Considering that some research (e.g., Field & Bonanno, 2001; Field, Gal-Oz, & Bonanno, 2003; Ho, Chan, Ma, & Field, 2013) has found CB to be connected to relational problems with the person who died, it is also plausible that non-forgiveness may be linked to a subset of CB experiences, presumably ones that are less adaptive in nature. Finally, in line with Parker's (2005) finding that bonds can help resolve "unfinished business" with the deceased, it may also be that CB contributes to survivors forgiving their deceased offenders.

Aside from our fledgling research program, there is little empirical work that directly assesses the connection between the two concepts of interest. However, related research suggests how and why the concepts might be connected through third variables. A strong candidate for such a third variable is attachment, or the type of relational pattern a person displays with others to whom he is very close (Mikulincer & Shaver, 2007). Rooted in physiology, attachment has cognitive, emotional, and behavioral aspects as well. When studying attachment, most researchers divide the concept into two dimensions: anxiety (desire for closeness but insecurity about partner reliability) and avoidance (discomfort with closeness). Evidence suggests that the most adaptive type of attachment is low in both anxiety and avoidance (Mikulincer & Shaver, 2007).

Several empirical projects relating attachment and CB have now been published. Many of these studies distinguish between two types of bonds: internalized (relying on mental representation of the deceased, such as considering his typical point of view when making a decision) and externalized (involving sensory experience of the deceased, such as hearing her voice) (Field & Filanosky, 2010). Although we cannot yet definitively answer if one form of bond is more adaptive, it is starting to look like internalized CB is healthier than externalized (e.g., Field & Filanosky, 2010; Scholtes & Browne, 2015). Ho et al. (2013) produced data demonstrating a significant, positive, moderate correlation between externalized CB and attachment anxiety, whereas neither attachment variable correlated with internalized CB. Currier, Irish, Neimeyer, and Foster's (2015) work found only that attachment avoidance was negatively related to reporting CB. Unfortunately, the CB measure used in Currier et al.'s study did not differentiate between internalized and externalized bonds. Finally, Yu, He, Xu, Wang, and Prigerson (2016) assessed similar constructs and found that attachment anxiety is significantly, positively, and moderately related to both internalized and externalized bonds, whereas attachment avoidance is significantly, negatively, and weakly related only to externalized CB.

It is difficult to draw clear conclusions from these studies, but given that high levels of attachment avoidance and/or anxiety are often associated with interpersonal conflict in close relationships (e.g., Feeney, 2016; Mikulincer & Shaver, 2007), it is reasonable to guess that the frequency and intensity of offenses in the relationships represented in these studies increases as attachment avoidance and/or anxiety increases. In addition, we know from forgiveness literature that those with insecure attachment styles tend to be less forgiving (e.g., Dwiwardani et al., 2014; Murphy, Laible, Augustine, & Robeson, 2015). In turn, this raises the possibility that anger and hurt from offenses are contributors to the presence and/or quality of CB among those with less adaptive attachment styles. Specifically, low levels of forgiveness may lead to either lack of CB or a form of CB that is maladaptive, as the offended party continues to struggle with anger and blame. The attachment–CB literature also points to the importance of controlling for attachment as we research the forgiveness–CB connection so that we are not confusing a lack of forgiveness with insecure attachment.

Research Directly Exploring the Forgiveness–CB Connection

Given that only recently have we begun asking about links between forgiveness and CB, it is not surprising that there is little research on it. In fact, as of this writing, a literature search in PsycINFO including the key phrases "forgiveness" and "continuing bonds" brings up only our work and a study by Suhail, Jamil, Oyebode, and Ajmal (2011). Suhail and colleagues reported results of interviews with survivors of a family death in Pakistan. Of the different types of CB they reported, one category – doing actions to benefit the deceased – was in part based on a theological conviction that such actions may obtain divine forgiveness for the deceased. These actions were typically religious rituals, such as reciting verses from the Koran. In this case, we have a situation where CB promotes forgiveness of the deceased. However, the forgiveness in question is not offered by the survivor. Instead, the survivor is using CB as a way to garner divine forgiveness for the deceased. The other studies reviewed here focus on how the survivor forgiving a deceased offender may or may not be related to CB experienced with that individual.

I and my colleagues have completed two quantitative studies on links between forgiveness and CB in cases where the decedent is also the offender. In both projects, our measure of forgiveness was the Enright Forgiveness Inventory (Enright & Rique, 2004), a measure that defines the construct as (a) absence of negative thoughts, feelings, and behaviors and (b) presence of positive thoughts, feelings, and behaviors directed at the offender. This creates subtests of different aspects of forgiveness: cognitive, affective, and behavioral, respectively. Gassin and Lengel (2014) reported two studies, the first of which was conducted before Field and Filanosky (2010) published their updated measure that differentiated between internalized and externalized CB. In the first study, after controlling for pseudoforgiveness and attachment, only affective forgiveness significantly predicted CB, measured with Field's early, generic CB assessment (Field et al., 2003). In the second study, which used the updated CB measure, most forms of forgiveness predicted internalized CB even after control variables were factored out. Affective forgiveness tended to predict higher internalized bonds scores more strongly than other forms of forgiveness. Forgiveness variables were not significantly related to externalized CB.

Gassin and Burton (2016) completed a replication and extension of the previous study, assessing how well both forgiveness and gratitude predicted the two forms of CB. In this project, the test of which forms of forgiveness related to CB was more conservative, as when testing the impact of one type of interpersonal mercy, the analyses controlled not only for pseudoforgiveness and attachment but also for the other forms of forgiveness. For example, when testing the relationship between cognitive forgiveness and CB, we made sure to factor out any overlap between cognitive forgiveness (on the one hand) and both affective and behavioral forgiveness (on the other). When all three forgiveness subscores and the gratitude score were considered as a group, they predicted stronger internalized bonds. Neither of these four scores individually was a significant predictor of internalized CB at traditional levels of statistical significance. However, affective forgiveness was marginally significant ($p < .10$), with a prediction coefficient almost twice as high as the next largest. None of the variables, either alone or together, predicted externalized CB.

While there is some consistency between these two studies, they are far from definitive. In some ways, they raise more questions than they answer. As noted above, some research suggests externalized bonds in particular are linked with poor adaption (e.g., Field & Filanosky, 2010; Ho et al., 2013). Research usually demonstrates a link between forgiveness and positive mental health, and therefore we might expect forgiveness to be negatively related to externalized bonds. Yet forgiveness shows little relationship with this type of CB. Perhaps this is in part because the meaning of externalized bonds changes as grief progresses: it is fairly ubiquitous in the early days of bereavement but – at least in our culture – may be experienced more by those with maladaptive forms of grief as the bereavement process continues (Field, 2008; Field, Gao, & Paderna, 2005). Therefore, an assessment of externalized CB at one point in time does not distinguish between the commonly experienced physical-sensory connections of early bereavement and the possibly problematic experience of them after much time has passed. Another possible confound is more conceptual in nature. In some cases, it may be that internalized and externalized CB are not as clearly distinct as the Field and Filanosky (2010) measure makes them out to be. For example, research on experiencing a sense of the deceased's presence shows such an encounter often has sensory as well as cognitive and emotional elements (Steffen & Coyle, 2010, 2011). It also may be in part because the reliability of the externalized CB scale in our studies has been relatively low ($\alpha = .58$ and .78, respectively) compared to other scales and measures used.

Another question remaining is that of causality. Although we structured our statistical analyses with forgiveness as a predictor, ultimately these analyses are correlational and say nothing about whether forgiveness leads to a certain type and/or frequency of CB or vice-versa. It is even possible they are both simply proxies for some other characteristic, such as positive coping mechanisms, and therefore are not at all causally related to one another. The assumption implied in the statistical analyses we did for these studies was that higher levels of forgiveness pave the way for a higher level of healthy CB, but as we will see below, it may well be that CB paves the way for more forgiveness.

Beyond these and other unanswered questions, there are also limitations to these studies, the main one being the homogeneity of the samples. They have been largely White women, and at least nominally Christian. This, of course, raises the question of how far beyond such a group we can generalize our findings.

We are beginning to incorporate qualitative research into our exploration of the forgiveness–CB connection, which we hope will bring more subtlety to our topic and perhaps contribute to solving some of the dilemmas noted in the previous paragraphs. As of this writing, interviews for the main study are ongoing, but we can share results from a small pilot study. In preparation for our larger study, I conducted semi-structured interviews of two individuals who reported both (a) an offense by someone close to them who is deceased and (b) working on forgiving that person for the offense. As is the case with our quantitative work, it seems to be mostly White, Christian women responding to efforts to recruit participants. Both persons interviewed in the pilot project were White women who identified as Christians. They both reported verbal and physical abuse by their fathers, who subsequently had died.

While the childhood stories of the two women involved in our qualitative pilot were similar and both reported working on forgiveness, their orientations toward CB and their understanding of its connection to forgiveness were quite distinct. Of course, the names and some details included in the following data have been altered to protect identities. Tia, who is currently in her early 30s and whose abusive father died when she was 10, noted that she has learned much more about her father's own difficult life since his death, resulting in compassion for and much less fear of him. Nonetheless, she reports struggling with symptoms of PTSD connected with the abuse and is aware of what triggers her experience of those symptoms. From her perspective, experiencing CB would put her at risk of exposure to those triggers. She explained:

> I think that for my own . . . mental health and safety, I think if there were connections that they would have done more harm than good. So like I guess subconsciously if there was (*sic*) connections that my subconscious ignored them because they saw it as a threat . . . I'm ok, I'm ok not having that connection . . . I would like to say I would like a connection but I honestly think it's the safest that I don't have one. I just don't want any triggers to happen.

Tia conceptualizes a lack of CB as a form of setting up a boundary for self-care. When asked about any connection between her forgiveness journey and the possibility of developing bonds with her deceased father, she reported seeing them as two independent processes that had no mutual influence.

The second pilot participant, Stephanie, is currently in her early 50s and lost her father just a few years ago. Despite his long history of abuse toward her when he was alive, Stephanie reported being very interested in maintaining CB with her father, even to the point of working with a medium to be able to converse with him. She reported seeking contact with him in part because of a lack of resolution of their conflict. Ultimately, Stephanie attributed the beginning of her forgiveness journey to the conversation with her father:

Stephanie:	He kept saying [through the medium] at the end of it that I need to forgive for – how did he word it with her . . . trying to think. Hmmm, I need to forgive so that he can move on . . . where he's at or something . . . So that kind of triggered it [forgiveness] too.
Interviewer:	Sure. Had you thought about forgiveness before you had had that experience?
Stephanie:	Not so much. I always felt like I was going to, you know, hold a grudge and be mad at him.

Stephanie reporting that a CB encounter prompted working on forgiveness was recently echoed by a young woman, Victoria, in one of the interviews we are currently conducting for the main portion of this study. She is working on forgiving her deceased father who struggled with addiction. Victoria mentioned that keeping some of her father's personal possessions around the house helps her to remember other aspects of his life and personality besides those involved in his offending behavior. She noted that reflecting on what these items told her about her father assists her in viewing him as more than just an offender and, in doing so, move closer toward forgiveness. For Victoria, CB serves as part of the reframing process, in which the forgiver sees the person who hurt her in a wider context.

Stephanie's experience with CB appears to be multifaceted. Not only did she report being in contact with her father through a medium, but she also noted that he occasionally appears in dreams, which she finds comforting. She also has a few of his personal effects. She remarked that she particularly enjoyed going through his bible: he had underlined some of his favorite passages, and reading them provides a sense of intimacy with him. Stephanie also understood hearing trains as a sign of her father's protection:

> he was an engineer for the railroad, so I hear train whistles and I always think he's around . . . watching over me.

While it is difficult to define precisely how Stephanie's experience with CB is related to her forgiveness process – she herself found it hard to identify the connections, despite acknowledging they exist – I can offer at least two hypotheses by comparing other aspects of her interview to Tia's. Whereas Tia had gathered quite a bit of information about her father and his background, Stephanie had not. Stephanie's interview is permeated with questions about why he behaved the way he did and frustration at a lack of information, so it may be that in part, her drive for CB is motivated by a desire for answers about and even from him.

This could serve as part of the reframing process in forgiveness, mentioned above, and if it serves that function, some forms of CB may even be seen as a catalyst to forgiveness.

Another difference between the two lies in their respective understanding of forgiveness. In response to the question, "How will you know when you've forgiven?", Tia responded that she will know when she experiences no anger about the abuse. Several minutes of our interview were taken up by Tia's expression of compassion for her father as a result of reframing. However, Tia ultimately did not see an interpersonal goal to forgiveness: its main signifier was a reduction in anger within her. When Stephanie was asked how she viewed forgiveness, she initially responded that it was "being at peace with yourself," and that forgiveness is "not for that person [the offender], it's for yourself." However, as our discussion about her conception of the forgiveness process moved on, she eventually noted that, "I honestly don't know if I can answer it . . . to how I know [if I've forgiven]." It may be that not only a lack of information about her father, but also confusion and openness about what forgiveness looks like contribute to Stephanie's greater desire for CB. Tia herself noted that her father's absence was one of the biggest obstacles to forgiving, as she was not able to converse with him about their respective lives. Through other relationships, church, counseling, and education, Tia was eventually able to reframe her father and understand what her forgiveness path would look like. Stephanie has not yet achieved that, which may heighten her desire to remain connected with her father.

Because our qualitative exploration of the forgiveness–CB connection is just beginning, these thoughts should be seen as extremely preliminary. Undoubtedly, even if continued data collection establishes that one link between forgiveness and CB is rooted in a desire for clarity about the offense and the nature of forgiveness, it is very likely that there will be other types of relationships as well. Drawing on Suhail et al. (2011), we can conceive of persons in some religious traditions maintaining CB via rituals, perhaps not only to call down God's mercy on the person but also to express their own forgiveness toward offenders. In other situations, healthy forms of CB may simply be the way a forgiver reconciles with the offender, if indeed he considers reconciliation an important goal. Finally, despite the preliminary nature of these suggestions, it seems fairly clear that the forgiveness–CB relationship moves in various directions. In fact, given our initial qualitative data, we probably have more evidence that CB leads to more thorough forgiveness, rather than forgiveness leading to more CB, which was how we conceptualized the relationship in our quantitative studies.

How Can We Use This Information?

I have discussed some of the many remaining research questions above, so in this section, I will focus on applied implications of this work. Although the research on the forgiveness–CB connection is in its infancy, several decades of investigation substantiate a cluster of negative interpersonal experiences – anger, blame, and insecure attachment – that are related to poor bereavement outcomes. Such negative interpersonal experiences almost certainly involve interpersonal offense. Given that experimental research, demonstrating cause and effect, shows that forgiveness-based interventions improve mental health (Baskin & Enright, 2004; Wade et al., 2014), in cases where interpersonal offense is impairing a survivor's bereavement process, forgiveness should be considered as an option for healing. Because forgiveness itself is sometimes conceptualized in relational terms, it may well mean that some change in CB will play a role in this process.

Our quantitative work shows that emotion-related aspects of forgiveness may be the most powerful correlates of what is likely the healthiest form of CB: those that are psychological, rather than exclusively physical, in nature. At minimum, affective forgiveness includes the reduction of negative emotions directed at the offender, like anger and resentment. Some forgiveness scholars argue it also includes an increase in positive emotions such as warmth and compassion (Enright & Fitzgibbons, 2015). However, emotional experience can be very hard to change simply by willing it to change. Therefore, mental health practitioners may find it more expedient to work specifically on cognitive and behavioral forgiveness first, as well as general emotion regulation strategies. Work on cognitive aspects of forgiveness might include emphasizing reframing and using cognitive-behavioral techniques such as thought substitution (e.g., substituting a positive thought for a negative thought about the offender). Behavioral forgiveness interventions could include practices such as committing oneself not to talk badly to others about the offender or completing religious rituals in his honor or for his benefit. CB may be helpful in these processes. For example, as we saw above, it seemed to promote reframing for some research participants. We may also find that healthy forms of CB increase as the person makes progress in forgiveness.

At least two cautions are in order. First, although the purpose of this chapter is to demonstrate possible connections between forgiveness and CB, we must realize these two experiences do not have to co-occur. A very important application of this observation is that regardless of what kind of CB (if any) that a client experiences, mental health professionals must realize that forgiveness is always a client's choice. Undertaking such a journey cannot be imposed on those we serve. Second, therapists and other practitioners should be sure that CB is not promoting or reflecting experiences that can be confused with forgiveness but may actually be hurtful for the client. For example, practitioners should be familiar with the concept of pseudoforgiveness and be sure a person is not seeking CB simply out of a desire to deny all negative feelings toward the offender and "prove" he is over the hurt. As mentioned above, research suggests that some forms of CB are linked with poor bereavement adjustment and compromised mental health. Logically it seems more likely unhealthy reactions that may masquerade as forgiveness would be linked to such forms of CB. Mental health professionals wishing to use forgiveness in their work with bereaved people should educate themselves on the concept and its assessment before using it. Toward this end, I have included resources for practitioners in the first major section of this chapter, above.

Conclusion

Research on the connection between forgiveness and CB has the potential to help answer various questions in the field of death, dying, and bereavement. This includes questions such as: Which forms of CB are adaptive and which are not? How do we help people suffering from complicated forms of grief, especially in those cases where the complications seem rooted in anger and hurt experienced because of the deceased's behavior? Much about the connection between these two concepts remains unclear, but the small body of work to date raises interesting questions for future research. It also very tentatively suggests some helpful approaches to helping those reeling from twin injuries to the heart: being hurt by a loved one and mourning that person's death.

References

Baskin, T. W., & Enright, R. D. (2004). Intervention studies on forgiveness: A meta-analysis. *Journal of Counseling and Development, 82*, 79–90.

Currier, J. M., Irish, J. E. F., Neimeyer, R. A., & Foster, J.D. (2015). Attachment, continuing bonds, and complicated grief following violent loss: Testing a moderated model. *Death Studies, 39*, 201–210.

Dwiwardani, C., Hill, P. C., Bollinger, R. A., Marks, L. A., Steele, J. R., Doolin, H. L., . . . Davis, D. E. (2014). Virtues develop from a secure base: Attachment and resilience as predictors of humility, gratitude, and forgiveness. *Journal of Psychology and Theology, 42*, 83–90.

Enright, R. D. (2012). *The forgiving life: A pathway to overcoming resentment and creating a legacy of love.* Washington, DC: American Psychological Association.

Enright, R. D., & Fitzgibbons, R. P. (2015). *Forgiveness therapy: An empirical guide for resolving anger and restoring hope.* Washington, DC: American Psychological Association.

Enright, R. D., & Rique, J. (2004). *The Enright Forgiveness Inventory instrument and scoring guide.* Menlo Park, CA: Mindgarden.

Enright, R. D., Santos, M., & Al-Mabuk, R. (1989). The adolescent as forgiver. *Journal of Adolescence, 12*, 95–110.

Feeney, J. A. (2016). Adult romantic attachment: Developments in the study of couple relationships. In J. Cassidy & P. R. Shaver (Eds), *Handbook of attachment: Theory, research, and clinical applications* (3rd ed.) (pp. 435–463). New York, NY: Guilford Press.

Field, N. P. (2008). Whether to relinquish or maintain a bond with the deceased. In M. S. Stroebe, R. O. Hansson, H. Schut, & W. Stroebe (Eds), *Handbook of bereavement research and practice: Advanced in theory and intervention* (pp. 113–132). Washington, DC: American Psychological Association.

Field, N. P., & Bonanno, G. A. (2001). The role of blame in adaption in the first 5 years following the death of a spouse. *American Behavioral Scientist, 44*, 764–781.

Field, N. P., & Filanosky, C. (2010). Continuing bonds, risk factors for complicated grief, and adjustment to bereavement. *Death Studies, 34*, 1–29.

Field, N. P., Gal-Oz, E., & Bonanno, G. A. (2003). Continuing bonds and adjustment at 5 years after the death of a spouse. *Journal of Consulting and Clinical Psychology, 71*, 110–117.

Field, N. P., Gao, B., & Paderna, L. (2005). Continuing bonds in bereavement: An attachment theory based perspective. *Death Studies, 29*, 277–299.

Gassin, E. A., & Burton, T. R. (2016). *Forgiveness, gratitude, and bereavement.* Manuscript submitted for publication.

Gassin, E. A., & Lengel, G. J. (2014). Let me hear of your mercy in the mourning: Forgiveness, grief, and continuing bonds. *Death Studies, 38,* 465–475.

Ho, S. M. Y., Chan, I. S. F., Ma, E. P. W., & Field, N. P. (2013). Continuing bonds, attachment style, and adjustment in the conjugal bereavement among Hong Kong Chinese. *Death Studies, 37,* 248–268.

Knutson, J., Enright, R., & Garbers, B. (2008). Validating the developmental pathway of forgiveness. *Journal of Counseling and Development, 86,* 193–199.

Mikulincer, M., & Shaver, P. R. (2007). *Attachment in adulthood: Structure, dynamics, and change* (1st ed.). New York, NY: Guilford.

Murphy, T. P., Laible, D. J., Augustine, M., & Robeson, L. (2015). Attachment's links with adolescents' social emotions: The roles of negative emotionality and emotion regulation. *Journal of Genetic Psychology, 176,* 315–329.

Parker, J. S. (2005). Extraordinary experiences of the bereaved and adaptive outcomes of grief. *Omega, 51,* 257–283.

Reik, B. M., & Mania, E. W. (2012). The antecedents and consequences of interpersonal forgiveness: A meta-analytic review. *Personal Relationships, 19,* 304–325.

Scholtes, D., & Browne, M. (2015). Internalized and externalized continuing bonds in bereaved parents: Their relationship with grief intensity and personal growth. *Death Studies, 39,* 75–83.

Steffen, E., & Coyle, A. (2010). Can "sense of presence" experiences in bereavement be conceptualized as spiritual phenomena? *Mental Health, Religion, & Culture, 13,* 273–291.

Steffen, E., & Coyle, A. (2011). Sense of presence experiences and meaning making in bereavement: A qualitative analysis. *Death Studies, 35,* 579–609.

Suhail, K., Jamil, N., Oyebode, J., & Ajmal, M. A. (2011). Continuing bonds in bereaved Pakistani Muslims: Effects of culture and religion. *Death Studies, 35,* 22–41.

Wade, N. G., Hoyt, W. T., Kidwell, J. E. M., & Worthington, E. L. (2014). Efficacy of psychotherapeutic interventions to promote forgiveness: A meta-analysis. *Journal of Consulting and Clinical Psychology, 82,* 154–170.

Worthington, E. L. (2001). *Five steps to forgiveness: The art and science of forgiving.* New York, NY: Crown.

Worthington, E. L. (Ed.). (2005). *Handbook of forgiveness.* New York, NY: Routledge.

Worthington, E. L. (2014). *Forgiveness and reconciliation: Theory and application.* New York, NY: Routledge.

Yu, W., He, L., Xu, W., Wang, J., & Prigerson, H. G. (2016). How do attachment dimensions affect bereavement adjustment? A mediation model of continuing bonds. *Psychiatry Research, 238,* 93–99.

11

REACHING THE UNSPOKEN GRIEF
Continuing Parental Bonds During Pregnancy Loss

Bobo H.P. Lau, Candy H.C. Fong, and Celia H.Y. Chan

Introduction

In Chinese culture, a child is known to bear the bones and flesh of their biological parents (親生骨肉, *Qinsheng-gurou*). Pregnancy loss therefore means loss of an important piece of the bereaved couple's future as well as the sense of control, assumption of fairness, anticipated uplifting moments, personal and relational goals, opportunities for personal transcendence, and social standing. For some women pregnancy loss seems as if her body has "failed her", leaving her doubting whether her body is still a safe place to nurture a new life. Even though the loss happens at the neonatal phase, people other than the bereaved couple often fail to appreciate its impact. Unlike grieving for an adult or a child, the social sharing of grief is often precluded, and the bereaved couple is left on their own to heal (Lang et al., 2011).

Chinese culture duly acknowledges the possibility of pregnancy loss and the vulnerability of a fetus or newborn child. Cultural taboos are widely practiced by expecting parents to avoid such unfortunate incidents. Although continuing the bloodline of a family through reproduction is a filial obligation, the grief of bereaved parents experiencing pregnancy loss is often silenced, unrecognized, and belittled. Using a Value-Action-Sensation (VAS) model of continuing bonds (CB), we will illustrate how establishing a healthy CB helps bereaved couples to make meaning out of their dire experience and reorganize their lives after loss. We postulate that the experience of seeing and holding the deceased child, keeping memorial objects related to the child, philanthropic actions, and journaling the grief experience can foster healthy CB, and assist bereaved couples to transcend the abysmal experience into a precious lesson of life.

The Impact of Pregnancy Loss

Perinatal loss covers miscarriage, still-birth, and neonatal deaths. In Hong Kong, miscarriage is defined as spontaneous termination of a pregnancy or early loss of fetal tissue before 28 complete gestational weeks. Perinatal mortality includes both late fetal and early neonatal mortality (mortality up to 1 week after delivery). The rates of late fetal mortality and perinatal mortality were 2.5 and 3.1 per 1,000 live births respectively (Hospital Authority, 2016). There have been calls for recognizing earlier pregnancy losses as perinatal loss, such as those that happen before 12 weeks of gestation, in view of the advances in ultrasonography and other pregnancy testing techniques which entail the development of earlier parental bonds.

Pregnancy loss can be a wrenching experience for couples. The loss of the pregnancy may be discovered during a routine check-up or ultrasonography that show no vital signs, or it can happen spontaneously with sudden heavy bleeding or pain. The loss may also happen post-delivery as the baby dies shortly thereafter. The common initial reactions in all those circumstances may include shock, horror, confusion, disbelief, and despair. Concurrent to contemplating what has just happened, the couples face a multitude of medical procedures (especially those who have not yet delivered) and tough decisions (e.g., disposal of the fetus/burial, how to explain to family members). The loss is often a sudden one that leaves little time for processing anticipatory grief or facilitating farewell. In stark contrast to most losses, such as death from chronic diseases, joy and excitement from assuming a viable pregnancy often precedes the loss as the fetal condition is often unbeknownst to the expecting parents. Compared to mothers of live births, women who had a perinatal loss had nearly 4-fold higher odds for depression and 7-fold higher odds for posttraumatic stress disorder (Gold, Irving, Boggs, & Sen, 2016). About half of the women experience clinical depression within several weeks after miscarriage in Western countries (Garel et al., 1992). Similar psychiatric morbidity is less prevalent (10–12%) in Hong Kong (Lee et al., 1997). A significant proportion of men experienced heightened depressive mood after miscarriage but the distress was less enduring compared to women (Kong et al., 2010). Self-blame, guilt, and shame are also common among bereaved couples with pregnancy loss (Keefe-Cooperman, 2004–5). Morally, the couple, especially the mother, may accuse themselves of not being able to protect the baby from harm.

Pregnancy loss may strain familial relationships, especially when the family members grieve secretly in their own ways and without socially desirable recognition. Often, while women are grieving expressively for the loss of the pregnancy and managing their significant doubts due to their "reproductive failure", men play a supporting role in protecting their partners from further emotional injury and suppress their grief reactions. The unexpressed emotional distress may be interpreted as coldness and indifference and may engender distancing and eventually the dissolution of the relationship (Gold, Sen, & Hayward, 2010).

Pregnancy Loss as an Ambiguous Loss

Pregnancy loss is often ambiguous and disenfranchised (Lang et al., 2011). This is particularly true among early loss that preceded any visible signs of pregnancy. For the bereaved couple, the bonding may have begun much earlier than the birth of the child. The invisible bond with a future child may begin at the time of the couple's consensus to have a baby, the sexual intercourse, the conception, the verification of pregnancy, or the slightest physical symptoms in early gestation (e.g., sickness, dizziness). For outsiders, the "living proof" of the fetus may come only from the couple disclosing the pregnancy or noticing the physical changes of the expecting mother. The ambiguity of the loss stems from the scant valida-tion from social surroundings regarding the life of the fetus. In other words, if the couple were not to disclose the pregnancy, they and their doctors would be the only persons who know of the existence of the unborn human being. The ambiguity, as Pauline Boss put it, comes from the combination of physical absence with psychological presence (1999), and is aggravated by the complex and arcane procedure of determining the unviability of the pregnancy, the anomic process of delivering and handling the remains of the dead fetus, and being unsure about whether and how to share the grief socially.

While society commends pregnant women as the bearers of new lives, parental grief because of pregnancy loss has been largely unrecognized and marginalized (Lang et al., 2011). Differences in the understanding of who has been lost may arise within and outside the couple. While the couple may perceive the loss as a loss of future, a baby, "daddy's girl", "mommy's sweetheart", or "the precious gift from God", in the worst cases the loss may be reduced to the disappearance of fetal tissue or "a group of cells" by insensitive outsiders. The possibility of a future pregnancy also disenfranchises the grief. Some well-intentioned but insensitive comments may include "You are still young and can try again next time", "It is meant to be something good for you and your child", "Your child must be too sick to live", "You should take good care of yourself for the next one". For out-siders, the lost child might be replaceable by his/her healthier siblings. However, for the parents, each child is different. Also, the pregnancy experience is often reduced to a merely "mechanistic" reproductive process, and the psychological intimacy between the couple and the lost child is undervalued. Couples are often advised not to grieve extensively but to take good care of themselves for the next round. The grief has to give way to preparing oneself for the next attempt.

Pregnancy Loss in the Chinese Context

Chinese culture duly recognizes the possibility of fetal malformation and pregnancy loss, as reflected by the multitude of antenatal taboos practiced for preventing mis-carriage or giving birth to a child with unfavorable physical (e.g., skin problems, cleft, slow growth, perceived ugliness) and psychological (e.g., naughty) traits (Lee et al., 2009). According to the tradition, the pregnancy is not to be disclosed until after the third month of gestation, or else the fetus may "feel upset" and miscarriage may happen. Such taboos could be associated with the higher prevalence of pregnancy loss during the first trimester compared to the second or third. Some of the taboos appear to have roots in traditional Chinese medicine. For instance, eating snake or drinking herbal tea or cold drinks may disturb the internal balance of *qi* (energy) and may induce miscarriage. However, most are neither empirically verified nor theoretically substantiated, and are merely born out of analogies or age-old customs. For example, spreading glue in the apartment of the expecting parents is prohibited as the fetus will have his/her ears stick to the head (perceived as an ugly facial feature). Because the word "mutton" is in the Chinese expression for epilepsy, eating mutton is thought to lead to epilepsy in the future child. The teeth of a rabbit and the jumpiness of a frog figuratively resemble cleft palates and the behavior of a naughty child. Thus, rabbit and frog meat are prohibited. Many expecting mothers experience stress and feel that their freedom is relinquished by adhering to these taboos. The adherence to these unverified practices may also instigate tensions and arguments between the couple and their in-laws or older family members, and may in turn create heavy psychological distress for the expecting parents.

These unsubstantiated and prohibitive antenatal taboos may turn pregnancy from a joyful time for bonding with the unborn child into an anxiety-provoking process of mere reproduction. First, the practice of concealment precludes social support for miscarrying couples. It is hard to break the news of pregnancy and its loss all at the same time to others. Instead of emphasizing the intimate and reciprocal relationship between the mother and the new life in her womb, the taboos tend also to reduce the mother's role to that of a vessel containing the family bloodline. Furthermore, by stressing what she should not do, society may perceive the pregnant woman as more vulnerable than she is. In the name of protecting the baby, the mother's personal ambition and freedom are often relinquished. Nonetheless, the list of proscriptions hold the woman almost single-handedly accountable for any "failure". In most cases, pregnancy loss is idiopathic. Instead of seeing the loss as an accident for which even the doctors can hardly tell who is responsible, these restrictive taboos could reinforce fault-finding in the mother and make her a scapegoat for this haphazard, unfortunate event.

Although the prevalence of clinical depression after pregnancy loss has been found to be lower than in other cultures (Lee et al., 1997), the loss may bring about intense feelings of guilt and shame in Chinese women, especially those who perceive adherence to the antenatal taboos as important and attribute the loss to their own misbehavior. Consequently, the grief is disenfranchised as the unfortunate event is thought to be the failure of the mother. The grief is marginalized, and the impact on the bereaved couple is belittled. A great pressure is put on the couple to recover from their pain, restore their healthy and pregnancy-facilitating routines (e.g., drinking nutritious soups, taking Chinese medicine, avoiding intense exercises and attire that leaves the legs bare), and get on with the next trial. The Chinese expression for attempting to give birth to the next child is literally translated as "*chasing* for the next one". The bereaved couple is expected to get back on the "running track" as soon as possible. Pregnancy loss is hardly thought of as a loss that is worth grieving, and instead is seen as a failure to achieve.

In contrast to the elaborate funeral rituals for adults who have passed away, there is no specific death- or funeral-related ritual for pregnancy loss or the loss of an infant. Instead, ghostly tales about the souls of lost fetuses haunting the mothers or the couples are popular in the traditional culture. In these haunted cases, Daoist priests or Buddhist monks are often called upon to conduct religious rituals to pacify these disturbed, juvenile souls. The tie between the juvenile soul and the bereaved couple has to be properly severed by religious rituals, so that the juvenile soul can reincarnate and the bereaved couples can have their peace of mind restored. Such tales are particularly common around abortions. The hurtful assumption behind this could be that the mother or the couple has done something sinful to an unborn life. This assumption hardly squares with the corpus of scientific evidence related to most cases of pregnancy loss (Yan, 2003), and could significantly add to the pain of grieving couples.

Continuing Bonds in Parental Grief

Although traditional Chinese culture emphasizes severing and tying up the loose ends of the bond between the bereaved couple and the deceased child, increasingly the international literature on psychosocial care for parental grief is witnessing the benefits of facilitating a healthy continuation of the parental bond. The landmark study of Klass (1993) on CB was begun with members of a parental grief peer support group, the Compassionate Friends, highlighting the realness and purpose of the inner representations of the deceased children to the couples. The couples of the study found solace in retaining an elaborate bond between themselves and the inner representation of their deceased children through linking objects, religious devotion, and memories. Rather than throwing away the objects that contain the memories between the parents and the deceased children, these objects were dearly kept and used to keep the deceased children alive in the psychological and even social world of the parents. The deceased children were also reconnected to their parents on religious occasions or in parents' memories. The deceased children never vanished from the parents' daily activities and remained an active source of influence to their parents' lives. Instead of severing the bonds with the deceased children or diminishing the intimacy of their parental bond, parents relied on the vivid inner representation of their deceased children to heal. Using the analogy of amputation, the parents believe that the loss will remain visible and tangible in their lives forever, just as a lost limb would not grow back or be replaceable by a prosthetic one. However, the wound will heal, and the loss can be readjusted and integrated into their future lives. Keeping their deceased children alive in the social world appears to help parents integrate the loss in their life journeys (Davies, 2004). By recognizing and finding adaptive meaning from the loss, the parents may be able to reconcile the heart-wrenching conflict between the preponderance of their offspring in their life journey and their premature departure.

However, not all kinds of CB with deceased children are adaptive. Field et al. (2005) hypothesized that adaptive CB expressions may involve emphasizing the lost fetus or infant is safe in heaven. Analyzing the memory book for bereaved couples at the Overbrook Hospital in the U.S., Cadge and colleagues (Cadge, Fox, & Lin, 2016) found that bereaved couples took solace from constructing a vivid identity for their children (e.g., calling them by their names), connecting them to the family heritage (e.g., pointing out physical resemblances to their grandparents), believing that their children are in the good hands of God or their ancestors (e.g., knowing that their children are playing happily with angels and being taken care of by their deceased grandparents), and perceiving a continued relationship with these children in heaven (e.g., asking the deceased child to watch over living siblings). However, maladaptive CB may involve imagining the deceased child blaming the parents for not protecting them from harm or death (Field et al., 2005), or yearning for a concrete externalized connection which is no longer possible. While the adaptive form of CB gives strength to the parents to reintegrate the loss into their life journey and move forward with new perspectives about life and death, the maladaptive form may indicate stagnation and unresolved grief.

Establishing Continuing Bonds in Pregnancy Loss

The concept of CB has been rooted in Eastern culture, brought to attention in the bereavement field by Klass et al. (1996). To provide a comprehensive understanding of CB in the Chinese context, an exploratory study with Hong Kong Chinese bereaved persons was conducted, and a Value-Action-Sensation (VAS) framework has been proposed. The framework underscores some culturally specific ways which help Chinese bereaved persons to maintain meaningful bonds with the deceased. For example, it is important for the bereaved to feel that they have lived out and passed on the wisdom, value, and learning from the deceased, which symbolize the continuous spiritual existence of the deceased in family life. There are also rituals and actions performed by the bereaved to fulfill filial obligations to care for the post-death life of the deceased. Sensory CB experiences are commonly interpreted as evidence for relational affirmation from the deceased. The VAS aspects are interactively linked with one another: dreaming of a deceased family member triggers reminiscence and memories, and may initiate actions to visit gravesites and provide offerings, or to remember the teaching from the deceased.

Klass (1993) noted that some clinical situations involving CB with the deceased child could be complicated, with pregnancy loss being one such example. The loss is often ambiguous. The couple's bond with the deceased children is often incongruent with the expectations from their familial and social contexts and not well recognized. While family and friends may not regard the deceased fetus or infant as a child, the couple may already have bonded with the fetus or infant, including the entire set of accompanying expectations and hopes. CB may help legitimize and concretize the loss. CB may also assist couples to reintegrate the short presence of such an important family member as well as the unfortunate loss into their life journey by allocating a designated place to the deceased child in the psychological and social world of the family.

Sensational Experience

CB can be in the form of sensational experience, serving as proof for the once-existing human life and the parent–child bond. This can be in the form of visualizing and touching the babies (O'Leary & Warland, 2013). It is common for bereaved persons to have extensive concern over the physical remains of the deceased (Chan et al., 2005), especially for parent–child dyads (Schwarz, Fatzinger, & Meier, 2004). Couples often need time, space, and privacy to be with the deceased babies. Opportunities to see or hold the baby should be offered as a choice on multiple occasions, interspersed with anticipatory guidance (Capitulo, 2005). The physical bodies remain the meaningful symbolic representation of the baby and the parent–child bond, and it is consoling for couples if the clinical staff treat the fetus in respectful and humane ways. This is particularly true for many still-births and neonatal deaths involving physical malformations. It is important for the clinical staff to wash the baby and present him or her to the couple in a decorated basket or crib. The baby can be clothed in baby clothes, blankets, a sleep sack, laced handkerchiefs, or baptismal clothes, with the malformations covered up. Head malformation, which is common among still-births, can be covered with a newborn cap. The use of baby powder may further help the couple remember the sweet scent of their baby. The nurse may ask if the couple had prepared any accessories for the baby (e.g., baby ring, bracelets) and offer them to help put this on. In one local case, the physical malformation was so extensive that the nurse decided to cover almost the whole baby, leaving only the well-formed feet exposed, and placed the baby in a tiny baby basket to present to the couple. The couple understood the good intention of the nurse and the critical condition of their baby, and remarked that their baby had the most beautiful feet they had ever seen. Ensuring the baby's body is in good condition can be an important act of kindness which helps the bereaved couples find some sweet moments in their bitter loss.

Some couples may long to see and hold their deceased babies, while others may be reluctant to do so, especially immediately after the loss or if the baby is too tiny or suffers from extensive malformations. Physically touching a dead body is also a taboo in Chinese culture, as it is believed to bring bad luck and ill health. Thus, the couple's decision on whether to see or hold their baby during their stay in the hospital should be respected. Alternatively, family and individual portraits can be offered when the couple visit their baby. Photographs of the babies together with name tags, crib cards, or other memorial objects deemed appropriate should be kept, for instance, in memory boxes in the hospital. In our team's experience, couples who were reluctant to see and hold their babies may come back to retrieve the picture of their babies several years later. Apart from the physical body, memorial objects related to the baby can also facilitate the conversion from an ambiguous loss to a healthy CB. Such objects can be a lock of hair, photographs, ultrasonic pictures, identification bands, crib cards, baptism certificates, baby's rings, bracelets, birthstone charms, stuffed animals, plaster hand/footprints, clothing (e.g., baby gowns, sleepers, shirts), and blankets. They help to concretize the bonding between the couples and the deceased fetus or infant, and legitimize the grief (Gensch & Midland, 2000).

Riches and Dawson (1998) documented how the parents of a pair of twins who were miscarried at 20 weeks of gestation used photographs, locks of hair, name tags, and markers in the cemetery to reassert their parenthood. The mother in the case expressed that she fully recognized how the miscarriage might mean that it would be hard for them to be parents again. Therefore, they decided to savor their 20 weeks of parental experience and celebrate the short lives of their twins by taking family portraits with their very tiny babies, keeping whatever objects that could be proofs of their existence, and journaling the grieving process. The authors remarked that the artifacts helped to reassert the couple as parents, recognize the loss as something profound, and legitimize their grief. The dissonance between physical absence and psychological presence marginalizes the loss and complicates the grieving process. Parents may feel confused and unable to describe what they have lost and are grieving. The sensational experience with artifacts can create memories in consoling bereaved couples who encounter pregnancy loss through enriching the parental bond with more "substances" to remember and to be continued.

Actions and Rituals

Actions and rituals can also be transformative to parents. After returning home, the parents may be faced with the decision of whether to dispose of the clothes, blankets, and other items they had prepared for their baby. This could be a particularly hard time as they must confront the harsh reality head-on that their baby has died. The disposal may signify that their efforts in preparing for the arrival of the baby have been in vain. One action parents can perform, as suggested by Capitulo (2005), is making a quilt out of the clothes and blankets that once belonged to their deceased baby. The process of quilting can be psychologically soothing and symbolize a transformation of the loss for the bereaved couples.

Sometimes actions and rituals can carry special values and meanings for both the bereaved couples and the deceased babies. For instance, bereaved couples may consider donating the everyday items prepared for their babies (e.g., unused milk bottles, diaper packs, body wash and shampoo, wash cloths) or money to a charity on behalf of the unborn child. Such acts of kindness do not only acknowledge the existence of the child in the social world. Many Chinese bereaved couples believe that the charitable acts would ensure a good afterlife and smooth reincarnation of their babies. Planting trees and growing flowers can be another way for parents to honor the deceased children (Gensch & Midland, 2000). The life of the babies is symbolically represented by the trees and flowers, and parents can continue to care for and love their babies through growing them.

Value and Life Lessons Learned

Journaling the experience of grief may help consolidate the life lessons inspired by the child and the loss, and could be conducive to establishing a healthy CB with the child. Some bereaved couples find the loss experience, albeit abysmal at first, transformative. In a local qualitative study, Lee and colleagues (Lee, Choi, Chan, Chan, & Ng, 2009) documented a number of gains for couples who had experienced an unsuccessful IVF treatment, which included a sense of humility, more intimate marital and familial relationships, and spiritual growth. The process of journaling may soothe emotions, consolidate thoughts, and crystalize life lessons. Kersting and colleagues (2013) found that a 5-week, self-administered, internet-based intervention, which required bereaved couples who have experienced pregnancy loss to write down their feelings and perceptions of the loss, reflect upon their guilty feelings, challenge their dysfunctional intrusive thoughts, and establish a coping plan for the future, was effective in reducing posttraumatic stress, prolonged grief, depression, and anxiety at the 3-month and 12-month follow-ups.

In summary, CB may help bereaved couples to concretize their loss and make sense of their abysmal experience. Sensory CB through artifacts such as photographs, ultrasound pictures, locks of hair, and name tags provide living proof of the deceased child. They can reassert the loss of a precious life and give permission to the bereaved couple to grieve. Rituals and actions such as growing a tree or flowers, or philanthropy, can symbolize the continuity of the bonding between the bereaved couple and the deceased child. The possibility of forgetting their deceased children terrifies many bereaved couples (O'Leary & Warland, 2013). These rituals and actions can help reassure the bereaved couples that their children will live on in their psychological and social worlds. Journaling the grief experience can help remind bereaved couples of the strength they relied on for working through their grief and the valuable life lessons their deceased child has taught them.

Conclusion

Pregnancy loss is a common but invisible event. The grief over the loss of an unborn child is often unrecognized due to the concealment of early pregnancy and the lack of validation of the unborn child as a "complete" or "real" human being. However, the impact of the loss is heightened as the grief is disenfranchised and marginalized. Continuing the bond between bereaved couples and their deceased children can help concretize the loss and give permission to the parents to grieve and make sense of this abysmal life event. The use of artifacts such as photographs, ultrasound pictures, and crib cards can help to prove the existence of the deceased child and signal the loss as something profound. Planting flowers/trees and documenting the grief experience in a journal can remind bereaved couples of this preponderant life event, their strengths to transcend the loss, and the valuable lessons imparted by their deceased child.

References

Boss, P. G. (1999). *Ambiguous loss: Learning to live with unresolved grief.* Cambridge, MA: Harvard University Press.

Cadge, W., Fox, N., & Lin, Q. (2016). "Watch over us sweet angels": How loved ones remember babies in a hospital memory book. *Omega, 73,* 287–307.

Capitulo, K. L. (2005). Evidence for healing interventions with perinatal bereavement. *MCN: American Journal of Maternal Child Nursing, 30,* 389–396.

Chan, C. L. W., Chow, A. Y. M., Ho, S. M. Y., Tsui, Y. K. Y., Tin, A. F., Koo, B. W. K., & Koo, E. W. K. (2005). The experience of Chinese bereaved persons: A preliminary study of meaning making and continuing bonds. *Death Studies, 29,* 923–947.

Davies, R. (2004). New understandings on parental grief: A literature review. *Journal of Advanced Nursing, 46,* 506–513.

Field, N. P., Gao, B., & Paderna, L. (2005). Continuing bonds in bereavement: An attachment theory based perspective. *Death Studies, 29,* 277–299.

Garel, M., Blondel, B., Lelong, N., Papin, C., Bonenfant, S., & Kaminski, M. (1992). Depressive reactions after miscarriage. *Contraception, Fertility, Sexuality, 20,* 75–81.

Gensch, B. K., & Midland, D. (2000). When a baby dies: A standard of care. *Illness, Crisis & Loss, 8,* 286–295.

Gold, K. J., Irving, L., Boggs, M. E., & Sen, A. (2016). Depression and posttraumatic stress symptoms after perinatal loss in a population-based sample. *Journal of Women's Health, 25,* 263–269.

Gold, K. J., Sen, A., & Hayward, R. A. (2010). Marriage and cohabitation outcomes after pregnancy loss. *Pediatrics, 125,* 1202–1207.

Hospital Authority. (2016). *Health facts of Hong Kong.* Hong Kong: Hospital Authority.

Keefe-Cooperman, K. (2004–5). A comparison of grief as related to miscarriage and termination for fetal abnormality. *Omega, 50,* 281–300.

Kersting, A., Dolemeyer, R., Steinig, J., Walter, F., Kroker, K, Baust, K., & Wagner, B. (2013). Brief internet-based intervention reduces posttraumatic stress and prolonged grief in parents after the loss of a child during pregnancy: A randomized controlled trial. *Psychotherapy and Psychosomatics, 82,* 372–381.

Klass, D. (1993). Solace and immortality: Bereaved couples' continuing bond with their children. *Death Studies, 17,* 343–368.

Klass, D., Silverman, P., & Nickman, S. (Eds). (1996). *Continuing bonds: New understandings of grief.* Washington, DC: American Psychological Association Press.

Kong, G. W. S., Chung, T. K. H., Lai, B. P. Y., & Lok, I. H. (2010). Gender comparison of psychological reaction after miscarriage: A 1-year longitudinal study. *BJOG: An International Journal of Obstetrics & Gynaecology, 117,* 1211–1219.

Lang, A., Fleiszer, A. R., Duhamel, F., Sword, W., Gilbert, K. R., & Corsini-Munt, S. (2011). Perinatal loss and parental grief: The challenges of ambiguity and disenfranchised grief. *Omega, 63,* 183–196.

Lee, D. T. S., Ngai, I. S. L., Ng, M. M. T., Lok, I. H., Yip, A. S. K., & Chung, T. K. H. (2009). Antenatal taboos among Chinese women in Hong Kong. *Midwifery, 23,* 104–113.

Lee, D. T. S., Wong, C. K., Cheung, L. P., Leung, H. C. M., Haines, C. J., & Chung, T. K. H. (1997). Psychiatric morbidity following miscarriage: A prevalence study of Chinese women in Hong Kong. *Journal of Affective Disorders, 43,* 63–68.

Lee, G. L., Choi, W. H. H., Chan, C. H. Y., Chan, C. L. W., & Ng, E. H. Y. (2009). Life after unsuccessful IVF treatment in an assisted reproduction unit: A qualitative analysis of gains through loss among Chinese persons in Hong Kong. *Human Reproduction, 24,* 1920–1929.

O'Leary, J., & Warland, J. (2013). Untold stories of infant loss: The importance of contact with the baby for bereaved couples. *Journal of Family Nursing, 19,* 324–347.

Schwarz, B., Fatzinger, C., & Meier, P. P. (2004). Rush specialkare keepsakes: Families celebrating the NICU journey. *American Journal of Maternal/Child Nursing, 29,* 354–361.

Riches, G., & Dawson, P. (1998). Lost children, living memories: The role of photographs in processes of grief and adjustment among bereaved parent. *Death Studies, 22,* 121–140.

Yan, C. M. (2003). Management of miscarriage in general practice. *Hong Kong Practitioner, 25,* 367–372.

Specific Perspectives for Working with Sense of Presence

Common yet controversial experiences in continuing bonds are the "sense of presence" or "after-death communication." These "extraordinary" or "anomalous" experiences have a central place within the continuing bonds perspective, but when it comes to clinical attitudes to such phenomena, we quickly encounter different versions of Freud's pathologizing stance toward such experiences as "wishful hallucinatory psychosis."

Jacqueline Hayes and Edith Steffen explore different forms these experiences can take. Rather than categorize them as hallucinatory or imagined, as benign or pathological, they take as their starting point the clients' perspectives on whether the experiences are welcome or unwelcome. How the client regards the experiences then determines how the experiences can be worked with in a therapeutic context.

Julia Beischel, Chad Mosher, and Mark Boccuzzi make the controversial argument that we should take medium consultations more seriously as therapeutic alternatives or complements to traditional psychotherapies. The authors provide evidence for the benefit of medium readings and after-death communications for the bereaved and argue for connecting such practices with conventional clinical approaches to maximize the potential benefits for the client.

The two chapters in this Subsection are in a sense a transition to the next Section that asks whether or how continuing bonds can be real or true. What are clinicians to do when they choose to neither ignore the experiences nor explain them away?

12

WORKING WITH WELCOME AND UNWELCOME PRESENCE IN GRIEF

Jacqueline Hayes and Edith Maria Steffen

"Hallucinations", "illusions", "awareness", "continuing bonds" – the phenomena that are the focus of this chapter have come under varied descriptions (see Table 12.1). Some invoke a medical framework of understanding – others suggest spiritual, others still relational connections. Acknowledging that every term evokes a landscape of associated concepts and relevancies, we have used the terms "sense of presence" (Steffen & Coyle, 2011) and "experiences of continued presence" (Hayes & Leudar, 2016) in our own doctoral work to align with the phenomenal qualities of the experience. Here, we join forces and use the term "sense of presence" to refer to voices and visions of the deceased, smells and feelings of touch relating to the deceased, as well as the "feeling of presence" or "impression of the presence" (first reported by James, 1890, p. 322) that many report that seems at times to be independent of the five senses. The experiences are not only relationally vivid and meaningful, but such is their cultural embeddedness that the socio-cultural environment may even change the frequency at which they are reported; in Anglo-European studies the proportion of the bereaved reporting experiences of presence has been in the range of 40–60% (Rees, 1971; Castelnovo, Cavallotti, Gambini, & D'Agostino, 2015) – a study of widows in Japan, however, put this figure at 90% (Yamamoto, Okonogi, Iwasaki, & Yoshimura, 1969).

Table 12.1 A Selection of Descriptions Used to Denote "sense of presence" Experiences

after-death communication	continued presence	illusion
anomalous experience	extraordinary experience	imaginal relationship with the deceased
apparitional experience	grief hallucination	sense of presence
continued encounter	ideonecrophany	spiritual connection

Empirical work has documented a variety of consequences that sense of presence may have. In Rees' (1971) survey of widows, respondents were given the option of indicating whether the experiences had been "helpful", "unpleasant", or "neither helpful nor unpleasant". The majority (69%) reported they were helpful – just 5.9% unhelpful, but around a quarter (25.5%) responded that they were "neither" – suggesting a complex picture. In Tyson-Rawson's (1996) study of father-bereaved young women, a distinction was made between "welcome presence" and "intrusive presence", with 70% of the reported experiences falling into the former and 30% into the latter category.[1] Elsewhere in the literature, benefits for the bereaved are largely reported including less loneliness (Glick, Weiss, & Parkes, 1974), more restful sleep, mitigation of loss (Parkes, 1972), comfort (Parker, 2005), providing guidance and encouragement for the bereaved (Conant, 1996), and as having the potential for leading to spiritual and personal growth (Steffen & Coyle, 2011). They have also been thought instrumental in helping to resolve any "unfinished business" the bereaved has with the deceased (Klass, 1992; Klass, Silverman, & Nickman, 1996), from conflict before the death to belatedly saying goodbye. However, sense of presence has also been associated with loss of reality and pathological grief processes (Baegthe, 2002; Field & Filanosky, 2010; Kersting, 2004).

A recent empirical paper sought to identify the consequences of what the authors termed "experiences of continued presence" in personal accounts (Hayes & Leudar, 2016). The authors identified a range of functions: helpful presence in assisting the bereaved with a current problem; helpful presence in resolving unfinished business with the deceased; saying goodbye; a feeling of absence; continuing fraught relationships; and unclassified (ambiguous). In all cases, the consequences were intelligible in light of the bereaved's relationship with the deceased. The authors argued that it is important to not be caught between the polarities of pathology versus positivity when accounting for these phenomena, as both positions are reductionist of the varied consequences that sense of presence can have for even one bereaved person. Furthermore, the impact and consequences of sense of presence change over time and in new here-and-now situations. This interdependence of consequences with context and relational meaning indicates the potential for talking therapies – which work on meaning change in a relational context – to help the bereaved make sense of what is happening and transform consequences that are unwelcome. However, talking about such experiences in the context of grief therapy or counseling may not only be difficult for clients, but practitioners may feel unprepared and may unwittingly exacerbate distress and confusion. A study by Taylor (2005) into the counseling experiences of bereaved clients who had sensed the presence of the deceased showed that 80% of the interviewed clients were dissatisfied with their counselors' responses, as they did not feel understood or felt dismissed.

The current chapter is therefore about working with both the "welcome" and "unwelcome" presences in the lives of the bereaved, as well as those ambivalently present in between. It considers how as practitioners we may go about helping those with sense of presence to make sense of what is happening, and to change the impact of hostile sense of presence. But first, we consider how we may respond as practitioners to presence that is welcome and healing.

The Challenge of Working with Welcome Presence

Anna[2] is a client who lost her husband a year ago in a fatal car accident. One day she starts the session with a beaming smile: "He came to me again yesterday. I really felt him. He put his arms round me and told me everything was okay. He told me that he cannot come to me as often now because of where he is and that it is getting harder for him to come through, but he assured me that he will always be looking down on me . . . So like him – he's got to make sure I'm okay!"

As indicated above, the majority of sense of presence experiences are viewed as largely pleasant and helpful by those who perceive them. A sense of "welcome presence" is more common, and over the past few decades evidence has been consistently growing that can reassure practitioners and clients with regard to the salutary effects of most sense of presence experiences (cf. Steffen & Coyle, 2012, for an overview). In much of the bereavement literature there is consensus that these experiences are no longer viewed as automatically indicating "pathological grief" (e.g., Datson & Marwit, 1997; Sanger, 2009), with some notable exceptions (e.g., Field & Filanosky, 2010). New grief therapy techniques draw on experiential connections with the deceased that appear to normalize and validate sense of presence and invite contact, even if only at a symbolic or imaginary level (e.g., Armstrong, 2012; Krawchuk, 2012). Sense of presence experiences can form the starting point for an exploration of the continuing bond with the deceased. They can be a gateway toward accessing "the back story" of the relationship (Neimeyer, 2016) which can be therapeutically supported with specific techniques such as letter-writing and dialoguing with the deceased. The bereaved person can be encouraged to reflect on which aspects of the deceased loved one and which aspects of the relationship seem to be particularly significant in these encounters and how these meanings and messages can be taken forward into the bereaved person's ongoing life. When exploring the loss of the loved one, bereaved clients will often grieve not only the person who died but also the part within them that has been connected with the deceased and which may be experienced as lost and unavailable too. Through making sense of sense of presence experiences, the bereaved person may, however, come to view that part of the self as perhaps not entirely lost, for example a mother feeling that she will remain a mother to the child who died, albeit with a reconfigured sense of what this means and requiring different ways in which this reconstructed identity can find expression.

One might assume that working with welcome presence thus offers many therapeutic opportunities and should not nowadays be marred with associations of pathology. As therapists and counselors we may simply enjoy the privilege of walking alongside our bereaved clients and supporting them in drawing on these experiences as beneficial resources on their grief journeys. However, it may not be so straightforward. While the stigma associated with sense of presence in bereavement has become loosened, the reality status of the experiences remains controversial. The fact that a sense of veridicality is often part and parcel of this phenomenon is often discredited. What clients are reporting are experiences that, at least in Western contexts, clash with dominant understandings of what is real and what is not. These experiences present ontological challenges to how dominant scientific paradigms distinguish between life and death, self and other, inner and outer, material and spiritual, and so forth. Clients may report positive and welcome experiences of having sensed the presence of the deceased, and they have often not spoken about these experiences with others for fear of not being believed or being ridiculed. How therapists respond when such experiences are disclosed is therefore of great sensitivity. Taylor's (2005) research indicates that many practitioners may avoid the topic. Deflection was one of the most frequently observed responses of counselors when clients raised the issue. Open non-acceptance and being told that they needed to come to terms with reality was another frequent response, as well as not being shown any response at all. In some instances, clients felt so unsure about their counselors' attitude that they avoided talking about the experiences altogether. This highlights the necessity for practitioners to reflect on their own beliefs and assumptions with regard to sense of presence experiences and to ask themselves if their own convictions might get in the way. As Tedeschi and Calhoun made explicit (2006, p. 111):

> When clinicians venture into this territory with bereaved persons, they should be willing to hear about all sorts of experiences that might seem alien to them, including encounters with ghosts, discussions about mediums who communicate with the dead, a variety of assumptions about the afterlife, and a host of spiritual or religious views that may prove uncomfortable for some clinicians.

Affirming the Client's Perspective

Advice for practitioners that can be found in the existing literature on sense of presence includes the need to listen, to offer respect, empathy, acceptance, normalization, reassurance, and validation of the client's experience, to explore the meanings these experiences have for the individual, and to be willing and (culturally) competent to explore spiritual and religious implications (Steffen & Coyle, 2012). This guidance may not sound strange or radical to most therapists; however, when it is applied to experiences with a controversial reality status, and when faced with a client who insists on the actuality of the phenomenon, it may be more challenging for some practitioners to work within the client's belief system. What should be avoided is a stance of partial empathy in which the therapist empathizes with the beneficial consequences the client may experience as a result of the experience but dismisses (whether openly or secretly) it in terms of its veridicality. Partial empathy may risk a further alienation for a client who already feels stigmatized. Instead, what may be more helpful here is to adopt an affirmative stance (Steffen, Wilde, & Cooper, in press). Can we take a leap of faith and believe in our client's relational and/or spiritual reality? This seemingly radical suggestion is nothing but an extension of a basic premise for working with any client: we are trying to understand our clients from within, entering the client's frame of reference and becoming a co-inhabitant of their world. For some, this may not be difficult, as ontological flexibility may come more naturally. The idea here is to move beyond narrow definitions of concepts such as "belief" or "truth" or "reality". Rather than aiming for cognitive agreement with factual statements about material reality, we may seek to carefully enter our clients' relational and/ or spiritual reality as an embodied other who has been invited to share in their subjective experience. While we may not actually be able to share in the client's "experiential knowledge" (Scrutton, this volume) of the presence of their deceased, we may still be able to approach the client's experiences and sense-making with an attitude of ontological openness or flexibility; for example, Hunter (this volume) describes this as deeply engaging with experience without putting up barriers that protect the dominant worldview. We can become a participant rather than merely a witness.

Companions on the Journey

> As Anna explored the meanings of her sense of presence experiences in therapy, she said: "I can't talk about this to anyone! My children think I am crazy, and at church, they tell me that the dead are with God and that it could be the Devil fooling me when my husband comes to speak with me! But I know it is him! I know it is him!"

From this place of ontological openness and flexibility that enables us to fully engage with and participate in our clients' experiences, we are then in a position to become complete "companions on the journey through grief's unfamiliar territory" (Tedeschi & Calhoun, 2006, p. 112), helping our clients explore the meanings of experienced presence. This is likely to include not only the implications of the experience for the continuing bond with the deceased and any changes to the bereaved person's sense of self in the light of this ongoing and changing relationship, but also implications for the person's assumptive world more generally, their personal stance toward life and death, spirituality and religion, as well as challenges for their wider socio-cultural narratives and frameworks. While experiences of welcome presence tend to be associated with feelings of comfort and a confirmation of the continuing bond with the deceased, personal and/or spiritual growth appears to require prolonged meaning-making efforts due to the lack of readily available socially sanctioned conceptual frameworks within which these experiences can be made sense of, at least in most Western contexts (Steffen & Coyle, 2010).

Clients may face a number of challenges as a result of their cherished experiences. They may struggle to find support and understanding from their nearest and dearest, from their networks and support systems, their wider communities and religious and cultural affiliations. In addition to the opposition often encountered in the outside world, many clients find that the experiences also clash with their own personal belief system, for example a client who does not believe in an afterlife but finds that they believe the experience of sensing the deceased was real. The therapist or counselor may be the only person who can accompany the client in working through these dilemmas, disruptions, and crises of meaning, and the associated personal and social implications. Here it is vital for therapists not to be held back by their own rigid beliefs. They need to be respectful of the client's existing beliefs while, where relevant, creating space for confusion and ambivalence about what the experiences mean, and for "meaning protest" (Elliott, Watson, Goldman, & Greenberg, 2004). Tedeschi and Calhoun (2006) have observed that clients tend to adjust their beliefs so as to comfortably accommodate the continuing bond with the deceased. In some instances, however, the meaning-making journey may not reach a happy resolution, yet being able to hold seemingly conflicting views with a sense of assumptive humility can also be an outcome of such shared meaning exploration, pointing to the possibility of achieving greater wisdom and post-traumatic growth in the process.

> Anna engaged in a long search through the Bible, finding passages that seemed to support her in her grief and that did not deny her experience. She brought these readings to therapy and reflected on what they meant to her. While she did not find her church community more accepting of the phenomena, she experienced less of a conflict between her experiences and her faith as a result. This strengthened her in her belief in the ongoing presence of her deceased husband, and she felt she did not need her children's approval of this any longer, although she continued to feel sad that they were unable to share her experiences and what they meant to her. At the end of the therapy she fed back that what had made the greatest difference to her was to be somewhere where she was being believed.

Encountering Unwelcome Presence

Just as an experience of presence can be a source of healing, it may also carry a destructive potential. A presence may be unwelcome for many reasons. It may be that a sense of presence, in its very vividness, brings a loved one back to life to the extent that they have to be lost again, and grieved. This may occur particularly often in the early days and months of a bereavement and has been called a "feeling of absence" (Hayes & Leudar, 2016). In therapeutic terms, these may be seen as "opportunities" (albeit stark, and unwanted) to connect with the new reality, how it is different from the old one, and the change that has occurred – in short, situations where doing what we so often in the profession call "grief work" is forced upon the bereaved. In a therapeutic space of sufficient holding and containment, these moments of the rawest grief may be recognized and met in their saturation of personal meaning for the client. Such moments may hold within them other clues. Why did the deceased appear then? Why did they do or say what they did? What does this do for the bereaved? Perhaps this foregrounding of grief, in some, reflects a prior denial or pushing away of pain – a dwelling in a "restoration orientation" which is ended abruptly by the moment of presence and following sense of absence. Maybe it is grief's version of banging at the door, demanding not to be ignored. The feeling of absence is unwelcome insofar as it feels like raw grief – *it is* raw grief.

Perhaps the moment of presence distracts the bereaved from the routine business of life, with which they are trying to continue – plunging them into an unbearable longing from which it becomes hard to have the public identity of "getting on with it" which is required by so many around the person. It may be common for the presence to happen when trying to complete a particularly difficult task – "why does X always pop up like this: when I'm trying to fill out my tax return?/ on Monday morning?/ just before Aunt Y visits?", and so forth. This is why context is so important when we are thinking about consequences of experiences of presence (Hayes & Leudar, 2016) – they may be such a vivid foregrounding of what was had, and what was lost, and these reminders can feel somewhat untimely. They encapsulate the paradox of grief – the presence in absence; the absence in presence. This bittersweetness may account for Dewi Rees' 25% who were not able to tick the "helpful" or "unpleasant" boxes (Rees, 1971).

Some presences, furthermore, continue a particularly fraught relationship – or the most hostile and "unresolved" elements of a relationship. In Hayes' doctoral research into this subject, this type of function tended to be manifested in the form of hearing a voice, although further empirical investigation is needed to substantiate this observation as a general feature of experiences of unwelcome presence. Julie's story illustrates an intense example of unwelcome presence. Prior to the interview extract that follows, Julie had been talking about hearing her mother's voice calling her name, which had started a few weeks after her mother's death, after Julie had returned from a holiday:

Extract 1

452. Julie: that went on, .hh:::=hh:: ((sighs)) I'm trying to think of how long
453. (3.0)
454. I don't know, for a while anyway
455. JH: right
456. Julie: erm, then she started calling me names like, "Slag" [and "Slut"]
457. JH: [right]
458. Julie: and "Whore"
459. JH: right
460. Julie: and telling me I wasn't fit to live
461. JH: right
462. Julie: "take all your tablets"

For Julie, this was her mother speaking to her. She did not see it as a hallucination, or as a part of herself. Instead she made sense of it as a continued rejection, and provided biographical details to make this intelligible:

Extract 2

346. Julie: My father (.) had (.) a mistress
347. JH: mm:
348. Julie: I pieced that together long after
349. JH: right
350. Julie: erm, and he named me after my, after his mistress,
351. JH: right
352. Julie: Julietta,
353. JH: right
354. Julie: but he said I had to be called Etta, which I absolutely hate
355. JH: Okay
356. Julie: and my mum never gave up calling me Etta.
357. JH: right
358. Julie: I took Julie

The voice, when it summons her now, uses this name "Etta", identifying her with her mother's rival. This is a continuation, as her mother had always used this name, rather than her preferred name, "Julie". One of the very first things Julie said in her interview, before giving any details of the voice, was that she had always felt rejected by her mother:

Extract 3

147. JH: Just talk for as long as you want
148. Julie: yeah
149.   (1.0)
150. JH: so, er (.) when you're ready
151. Julie: Yeah
152. JH: go for it
153. Julie: hm
154.   (9.0)
155.   I never had a fantastic relationship with my mum
156. JH: Right
157. Julie: erm ((clears throat))
158.   (3.0)
159.   she was always more for my older brother, I've two older [brothers]
160. JH: [Right]
161. Julie: one's in Australia, one's in this country [the oldest]
162. JH: [Right]
163. Julie: one [and]

170

164. JH: [Yeah]
165. Julie: she was (.) always for him (.) [erm]
166. JH: [Okay] okay (.) for the oldest one?
167. Julie: Yeah, yeah. He was her
168.   (1.0)
169.   her son

Julie characterized herself as an unwanted child from an unwanted time – she was herself an unwelcome presence, a reminder of loss. The function of the presence seemed to be to crystallize the previously unspoken hostile elements of the relationship in stark, abusive language. And the consequences of this for Julie? She starts to believe that her mother may be right – perhaps she is unworthy of life, perhaps she should take the tablets she's been prescribed all at once.

However, it is not inevitable that someone feels this way when hearing an undermining voice. The biographical contextualization – or in other words, the elements of life and relationship history that give the presence intelligibility – may be different. This difference is instructive for therapeutic work. Matt was 14 when his father killed himself and blamed him in his suicide note. Matt hears his father since, insulting him and undermining his plans of action. However, the consequences are different for him. He considers the message, but does not align with it. Instead, he uses it as a source of motivation. For example, when the voice tells him he's a failure and won't be able to achieve a difficult task, Matt considers whether this is accurate – is it likely he can achieve it? He then uses this opportunity to prove his father wrong – and in effect the voice becomes an (unwanted) source of motivation.

We became curious as to why some people with hostile presences could transform these consequences, while others became trampled by them. There were no differences in the "reality status" afforded the presence – whether it was seen as the person communicating directly, or as part of self. There was no difference in the pragmatic elements of the language the voice used – insults, destructive commands, summons. But one difference we did notice was that those who mitigated the destructive potential of these continuing presences had an explanation for the motivations for the deceased. Matt, for example, explained that his father was extremely threatened by him, and was motivated by jealousy. He called him an "intrinsically unreasonable person". The voice he hears now, it is clear to him, is fueled by jealousy. This explanation seemed to allow Matt to dismiss the undermining presence as motivated by jealousy, and not a true reflection of his own abilities. Others had similar explanations – one woman who heard her husband's insults explained that "he was a very angry man". For Julie, and others like her that experienced the unwanted presence as personally destructive, it seemed that one thing that was missing was an answer to the question "Why is this happening?/Why do they hate me?" – and that this gap was filled by a growing sense of self-doubt and a deeper,

171

more monologic internalization of the message.[3] Julie suggested that her voice was a continuation of the rejection and hostility she felt – but what she did not seem to have was an explanation for her mother's rejection in the first place that was satisfactory to her, and that provided Julie with a way of not conflating herself with the rival. Somehow, for her mother (and, by implication, her father), Julie symbolized the rival within the family structure – this is encapsulated in the name the voice uses.

By using these examples of unwelcome presence, we are not meaning to suggest that all presences are like Julie's, or Matt's. However, what they demonstrate is that the way the presence is made sense of, and the biographical details that the presences pertain to, are important to examine in therapeutic work, and are a route for change. Therapist and client may work together on the biographical source of meaning, or the here-and-now response, to change the consequences of the presence. Returning to Julie's case for an example, the voice that insults her identifies her with the division in the family, and commands her to kill herself: how much does Julie's sense of her own agency align with this voice? What parts of her agree, and why? What parts disagree? What is her attitude to her own sexuality? To her father having an affair? What was it like growing up in the crossfire between her mother and father? To symbolize the discord, her mother's pain and envy?

Unwelcome presences are richly informative; portals into psychologically embedded relational realities.

If thinking about the historical relationship with the deceased is too overwhelming for the client as a starting point, in what ways can the here-and-now response of the client to the unwelcome presence be different to enable a less monologic internalization of destructive messages? Can the message be considered, and then engaged with critically, as with Matt's response to his father's voice? Is there any worth in what is said? What might the voice even be trying to highlight, or protect one from, in this situation? There is certainly evidence that those that engage with the meaning of voices, considering their worth or value, cope better (Leudar, Thomas, McNally, & Glinski, 1997; Davies, Thomas, & Leudar, 1999) – a dialogic relationship is created.

These kinds of conversations may occur naturally in the course of an empathic and holding therapeutic space, with an open and willing therapist, and are best done at the pace and level of tolerance of the client. However, there are particular techniques that may also facilitate dialogue with the unwelcome presence – such as the empty-chair exercise in emotion-focused/gestalt therapies (cf. Elliott et al., 2004), or writing letters to the deceased. With the former, it is probably wise to exercise caution with some clients who may find bringing the deceased "back to life" in the room too overwhelming or intolerable at a particular point in time. In addition, much may be achieved without even putting the unwelcome presence center stage; in practice we have seen destructive voices gradually disappear as the concerns they raise are examined through the means of the client's own agency – as the concerns are played with, and ultimately owned.

Therapeutic Principles for Working with Presence

We conclude by drawing together some therapeutic principles for working with presence in bereavement.

1 *Assessing the impact of the presence.* "Welcome" presence experiences can not only give comfort and hope, in therapy they can stimulate the exploration and development of the continuing bond with the deceased, invite conversations with the deceased in a variety of forms, they can be drawn on to restore and reconstruct parts of the identity of the bereaved that have been tied up with the deceased, and they can generally be mined as resources for moving forward in life *with* the deceased. It is important to respect clients' own perspectives on the reality status of these experiences – including those clients who dismiss the experiences as hallucinatory, or see them as a part of self – and also accompany them in any spiritual or religious quests that may ensue.

2 *Paying careful attention to how the client contextualizes their interactions with the deceased.* These can provide clues to the unresolved conflicts with the other and to unresolved ways of viewing self that may be fueling an unwelcome presence.

3 *Providing opportunities for working on the meaning of the relationship.* What concerns do the bereaved have about their relationship to the deceased? These may be questions like: Why did they behave the way they did when they were alive? Why I am hearing this now? If the presence is crystallizing an element of the relationship, what was the rest of the relationship like? Why is this "figure" emerging from the "ground"? This may allow the relationship with the deceased to become more nuanced again. In terms of continuing bonds, perhaps the more sticky/glue-like elements of this bond will become loosened, allowing a relationship of greater fluidity.

4 *Providing opportunities for exploring different ways of being in the relationship in the here-and-now.* This includes considering questions such as: Why might the presence appear in this situation, in this manner? The client and therapist might work out together what a range of responses might be, and the client may try out new ways of responding.

Notes

1 This is notably different from the results of Rees' (1971) survey, and this could be for many reasons – including that this study was conducted 25 years later. But one hunch of the authors is that this greater reporting of unwelcome presence in the Tyson-Rawson study is due to the nature of the bond – father–daughter as opposed to spousal. We might guess that the spousal relationships are less likely to be fraught as those that were very hostile in nature would be more likely to divorce before one of the pair dies. In addition, if we view self as largely socially constituted, children are more likely to hear their parents due to their important role in regulating action developmentally. More research is needed to investigate if certain types of familial bonds are more likely to lead to hostile continuing relationships.

2 "Anna" is a composite case, drawn from the stories of a number of clients and research participants.

3 The term monologic internalization is used in an attempt to distinguish between those destructive messages that are not considered and evaluated for their worth (and are internalized directly as a view of self), and those that are. The latter could be termed a dialogic internalization – the undermining message is internalized but can be argued with and does not become a "final" way of viewing self.

References

Armstrong, C. (2012). Envisioning connection through guided imagery. In R. A. Neimeyer (Ed.), *Techniques of grief therapy: Creative practices for counseling the bereaved* (pp. 256–258). New York, NY: Routledge.

Baegthe, C. (2002). Grief hallucinations: True or pseudo? Serious or not? *Psychopathology, 35,* 296–302.

Castelnovo, A., Cavallotti, S. Gambini., O., & D'Agostino, A. (2015). Post-bereavement hallucinatory experiences: A critical overview of population and clinical studies. *Journal of Affective Disorders, 186,* 266–274.

Conant, R. D. (1996). Memories of the life and death of a spouse: The role of images and sense of presence in grief. In D. Klass, P. R. Silverman, & S. L. Nickman (Eds), *Continuing bonds: New understandings of grief* (pp. 179–196). Washington, DC: Taylor & Francis.

Datson, S. L., & Marwit, S. J. (1997). Personality constructs and perceived presence of deceased loved ones. *Death Studies, 21,* 131–146.

Davies, P., Thomas, P., & Leudar, I. (1999). Dialogical engagement with voices: A single case study. *British Journal of Medical Psychology, 72*(2), 179–187.

Elliott, R., Watson, J. C., Goldman, R. N., & Greenberg, L. S. (2004). *Learning emotion-focused therapy: The process-experiential approach to change.* Washington, DC: American Psychological Association.

Field, N. P., & Filanosky, C. (2010). Continuing bonds, risk factors for complicated grief, and adjustment to bereavement. *Death Studies, 34,* 1–29. doi:10.1080=07481180903372269.

Glick, I. O., Weiss, R. S., & Parkes, C. M. (1974). *The first year of bereavement.* New York, NY: Wiley.

Hayes, J., & Leudar, I. (2016). Experiences of presence: On the practical consequences of hallucinations in bereavement. *Psychology and Psychotherapy: Theory, Research and Practice, 89*(2), 194–210.

James, W. (1890). *The principles of psychology* (Vol. 2). New York, NY: Dover Publications.

Kersting, A. (2004). The psychodynamics of grief hallucinations: A psychopathological phenomenon of normal and pathological grief. *Psychopathology, 37,* 50–51.

Klass, D. (1992). The inner representation of the dead child and the worldviews of bereaved parents. *Omega, 26*(4), 255–272.

Klass, D., Silverman, P. R., & Nickman, S. L. (Eds). (1996). *Continuing bonds: New understandings of grief.* London: Taylor & Francis.

Krawchuk, L. (2012). Body imagery for sustaining connections. In R. A. Neimeyer (Ed.), *Techniques of grief therapy: Creative practices for counseling the bereaved* (pp. 70–72). New York, NY: Routledge.

Leudar, I., Thomas, P., McNally, D., & Glinski, A. (1997). What voices can do with words: Pragmatics of verbal hallucinations. *Psychological Medicine, 27*(4), 885–898.

Neimeyer, R. A. (2016). Meaning reconstruction in the wake of loss: Evolution of a research program. *Behaviour Change,* published online 07.04.2016.

Parker, J. S. (2005). Extraordinary experiences of the bereaved and adaptive outcomes of grief. *Omega, 51,* 257–283.

Parkes, C. M. (1972). *Bereavement.* London: Penguin.

Rees, D. (1971). The hallucinations of widowhood. *British Medical Journal, 4,* 37–41.

Sanger, M. (2009). When clients sense the presence of loved ones who have died. *Omega, 59,* 69–89.

Steffen, E., & Coyle, A. (2010). Can "sense of presence" experiences in bereavement be conceptualised as spiritual phenomena? *Mental Health, Religion & Culture, 13*, 273–291.

Steffen, E., & Coyle, A. (2011). Sense of presence experiences and meaning-making in bereavement: A qualitative analysis. *Death Studies, 35*, 579–609.

Steffen, E., & Coyle, A. (2012). "Sense of presence" experiences in bereavement and their relationship with mental health: A critical examination of a continuing controversy. In C. Murray (Ed.), *Mental health and anomalous experience* (pp. 33–56). Hauppage, NY: Nova Science Publishers.

Steffen, E., Wilde, D., & Cooper, C. (2018). Affirming the positive in anomalous experiences: A challenge to dominant accounts of reality, life and death. In N. J. L. Brown, T. Lomas, T., & F. J. Eiroá-Orosa (Eds), *The Routledge international handbook of critical positive psychology* (pp. 227–244). London: Routledge.

Taylor, S. F. (2005). Between the idea and the reality: A study of the counseling experience of bereaved people who sense the presence of the deceased. *Counselling and Psychotherapy Research, 5*, 53–61.

Tedeschi, R. G., & Calhoun, L. G. (2006). Time of change? The spiritual challenges of bereavement and loss. *Omega, 53*, 105–116.

Tyson-Rawson, K. (1996). Relationship and heritage: Manifestations of ongoing attachment following father death. In D. Klass, P. R. Silverman, & S. L. Nickman (Eds), *Continuing bonds: New understandings of grief* (pp. 125–145). Bristol: Taylor & Francis.

Yamamoto, J., Okonogi, K., Iwasaki, T., & Yoshimura, S. (1969). Mourning in Japan. *American Journal of Psychiatry, 125*, 1660–1665.

13

THE POTENTIAL THERAPEUTIC EFFICACY OF ASSISTED AFTER-DEATH COMMUNICATION

Julie Beischel, Chad Mosher,
and Mark Boccuzzi

Many grieving individuals choose to receive readings about the deceased from psychic mediums. A Google (November, 2016) search of the phrase "medium readings" garnered nearly 38 million results. The psychic services industry in the United States (including mediumship) is currently valued at $2.0 billion (IBIS World, 2015).

With the widespread use of this self-prescribed "treatment," it would be beneficial for healthcare providers, counselors, caregivers, social workers, mental health professionals, chaplains, grief workers, palliative and hospice care professionals, volunteers, and other supportive individuals to be aware of the basics regarding the relationship between mediumship readings and grief to best serve the bereaved population. This is especially relevant within a continuing bonds perspective. Previous researchers have made similar suggestions regarding phenomena analogous to receiving a reading about the deceased from a medium, that is, spontaneous experiences of communication with the deceased by the bereaved. For example, Sormanti and August (1997) noted that, "In the context of mental health work, the need for carefully constructed definitions of spirituality not linked to any particular psychological, religious, or cultural belief system is evident" (p. 461).

Several authors have also emphasized that the primary issue regarding the experiences of the bereaved is not whether they reflect actual communication with the deceased, but rather how the experience can be used to aid in coping with the loss (e.g., Drewry, 2003; Klugman, 2006; LaGrand, 2005; Parker, 2005). In their work, Nowatzki and Grant Kalischuk (2009) assume "that encounters with the dead have been defined as real and important by those who experienced them, are real in their consequences and, therefore, are a reality to be studied" (p. 93).

We suggest that a similar unbiased awareness regarding assisted after-death experiences gained during readings with psychic mediums—one based on current research rather than historical stereotypes or popular culture depictions—would be equally helpful in clinical settings. Our intention is that the information contained herein provides a basis for willing professionals from various backgrounds to begin to understand the phenomenon of mediumship and its potentially therapeutic relationship to grief.

Grief and Treatment Options

A discrepancy exists between the potentially serious risks of complicated grief (e.g., Stroebe, Schut, & Stroebe, 2007) and the presence of effective treatments that may be offered to the grieving. Despite its widespread acceptance and use, the effectiveness of traditional grief counseling interventions is suspect (e.g., Schut, Stroebe, van den Bout, & Terheggen, 2001). Outcome studies have yielded mixed results regarding the effectiveness of grief therapy ranging from positive, neutral, and negative outcomes to the therapeutic process and have been hampered by numerous methodological issues including lack of control groups and improper participant assignment procedures (reviewed in Schut et al., 2001).

Larson and Hoyt (2007) pointed to the popular yet pessimistic consensus within the grief and bereavement literature that grief counseling was at best ineffective and at worst harmful to clients seeking help. Similarly, in a previous meta-analysis of the literature regarding psychotherapeutic interventions for the bereaved, Currier, Neimeyer, and Berman (2008) reviewed 61 outcome studies. Their findings revealed a "discouraging picture for bereavement interventions" (p. 656) which they found added "little to no benefit beyond the participants' existing resources and the passage of time" (p. 657).

In addition, pharmaceutical antidepressants are often ineffective for acute grief responses due to the extended time it takes for them to reach full efficacy. Besides the lack of strongly established findings regarding psychopharmacologic treatments, it is ill-advised to provide potentially lethal quantities of medications to those in the midst of a grief response (Worden, 1991). Taken as a whole, the tools the mental health community has to offer the bereaved for recovery from acute experiences of grief are limited.

Alternative Experiences and Interventions

In contrast to psychotherapeutic and pharmaceutical therapies, non-traditional interventions and experiences have repeatedly demonstrated positive, sometimes dramatic impacts on bereaved individuals. These include both spontaneous and induced phenomena. Though these types of after-death experiences have been described with words like "paranormal" and "extraordinary" or even associated with delusion and psychopathology, the reality is that spontaneous experiences of after-death communication (ADC) are quite common. Nearly a third of American adults believe that "people can hear from or communicate mentally with someone who has died" (Newport & Strausberg, 2001). People "from all walks of life have experienced the extraordinary when mourning" (LaGrand, 2005, p. 6), and 35–97% of grieving individuals experience the deceased in some way after the death (Klugman, 2006). ADCs are "universal in nature; that is, they occur in all socioeconomic and religious groups, types of death, and at various times after the death" (Houck, 2005, p. 124). They "occur along a continuum of intensity and emotional impact" (Drewry, 2003, p. 75) and are "common, natural, non-pathological, mostly beneficial and comforting, helpful in facilitating the grieving process, and sometimes extraordinarily spiritually healing to a bereaved individual" (p. 75).

These ADCs include a wide variety of experiences for the bereaved including sensing the presence of the deceased; visual, olfactory, tactile, and auditory (voices or sounds) phenomena; conversations; powerful dreams; hearing meaningfully timed songs on the radio or music associated with the deceased; messages from objects; lost-things-found; communication through electric devices (e.g., flickering lights); natural phenomena; symbolic messages; synchronicities; and other unusual incidents or unexplainable phenomena (reviewed in Beischel, Mosher, & Boccuzzi, 2014–15). ADCs seem to be a natural part of the grieving process (e.g., Klugman, 2006; LaGrand, 2005).

Several researchers have investigated the effects of ADCs on the grieving processes (reviewed in Krippner, 2006). Parker (2005) found that ADCs fulfill "specific grief, bereavement, and/or other needs for individuals such as consolation, comfort, reassurance, and encouragement" (p. 272) and "facilitate a sense of psychological well-being" (p. 277). LaGrand (2005) noted that ADCs "spawn personal and/or spiritual growth, reduce existential fear, and generate new perspectives and purpose in life through the questions they suggest and the obvious answers provided" (p. 9).

Unfortunately, not all clinicians accept reports of ADCs. In a study of the counseling experiences of bereaved people who sense the presence of the deceased, Taylor (2005) found that 62% of participants had "totally unsatisfactory" experiences (p. 60). They "all described feeling unaccepted, abnormal, not understood, unable to connect to counselors, and that they had received no empathy" (p. 60).

In general, ADCs maintain the bond and develop new, meaningful relationships between the bereaved and the deceased (e.g., Klugman, 2006; Walliss, 2001). In addition to spontaneous experiences, it appears that induced after-death experiences also positively affect the resolution of grief. Through the use of eye-movement desensitization and reprocessing (EMDR) techniques in his clinical practice of treating patients with post-traumatic stress disorder, Allan L. Botkin (2000) observed that patients were reporting spontaneous ADCs during the EMDR sessions and discovered that a particular sequence of psychotherapeutic events could be used to induce the experience in any patient. In the initial 83 patients for whom Botkin attempted the ADC induction, 81 (98%)

achieved an ADC, which he defined as "any perceived sensory contact with the deceased" (p. 198), and of that subset, 96% reported "full resolution of grief following the ADC" (p. 198). Botkin also discovered in the hundreds of cases he has observed, that "the difference in subjects' prior belief systems is of little consequence" (p. 199).

The second well-documented method for the induction of after-death experiences is a mirror-gazing procedure developed by Raymond Moody (1992) which he called a Psychomanteum. Participation in the Psychomanteum process involves spending time in a "dimly lit room in which a sitter gazes with open eyes into a mirror, with the intention of contacting a deceased individual" (Hastings et al., 2002, p. 212). A study from 2002 investigated the phenomena, experiences, and effects on bereavement of 27 Psychomanteum participants. The participants reported a variety of experiences including physical sensations, external phenomena in the room, imagery that appeared in the mirror, sense of presence, communications and dialogue, and auditory, visual, and olfactory phenomena (Hastings et al., 2002). It was discovered that people reporting contact as part of their experience showed significant self-reported changes in needing to improve the relationship and needing to communicate as well as in the feelings of grief and loss. Even those participants who did not experience contact reported significant improvements in feelings of grief and sadness and the need to communicate (Hastings et al., 2002). As a whole, participants also reported significant alterations in unresolved feelings, missing the person, and feelings of grief, loss, sadness, guilt, and fear (Hastings et al., 2002).

This extensive body of research demonstrating the positive effects of spontaneous and induced ADCs on the bereaved implies a potential for similar effects after assisted ADCs during readings with psychic mediums.

Psychic Mediums

We use the term *medium* to describe an individual who experiences regular communication with the deceased. A *psychic* regularly experiences information about or from people, events, places, or times unknown to him/her. It is often said that all mediums are psychic but not all psychics are mediums. (The term *psychic medium* is often used to simply differentiate this type of medium from other uses of the word.) Anyone can have mediumistic and/or psychic experiences and the terms medium and psychic are used specifically to describe people who have those experiences regularly, reliably, and often "on-demand."

During the mediumship process, the medium conveys messages from deceased people or animals to those who survive them (called sitters) during an event (called a reading). The sitter's experience of hearing from the deceased during a mediumship reading is termed an *assisted ADC*.

Although mediumship has recently received increased media attention, it is "ancient and ubiquitous across cultures" (Hunter & Luke, 2014, p. 9) and has been scientifically investigated since the late 19th century (e.g., Carter, 2012). Modern research (reviewed in Beischel & Zingrone, 2015) has used qualitative and quantitative methods to examine mediums' practices, experiences, training, use of language, psychology, neurophysiology, and societal impact as well as the historical and anthropological roots of mediumship all over the world.

Contemporary mediumship research also includes proof-focused studies of the accuracy of the readings mediums provide under controlled laboratory conditions (e.g., Beischel, Boccuzzi, Biuso, & Rock, 2015). This line of research has demonstrated that certain mediums are able to report accurate and specific information about the deceased using a research protocol (Beischel, 2007) that eliminates fraud, cold reading of sitters' body language and other clues, and similar "sensory" explanations for the source of their information.

At the Windbridge Institute, we have been conducting research since 2008 with a team of mediums whose abilities have been demonstrated under these controlled conditions. This allows us to study the phenomenon with participants who are able to effectively and repeatedly provide information about the deceased during various research protocols. These mediums have been screened, tested, trained, and certified to serve specifically in research studies and as part of the research team.

Each certified medium agrees to standards of conduct that include: being drug- and violence-free, consuming minimal or no alcohol at least 12 hours prior to a research reading, demonstrating confidentiality of readings, and not doing readings outside of those specifically requested (i.e., not offering unsolicited readings). Though we can only report on our experiences with the certified mediums on our team, they are potentially representative of the larger population of secular American mediums in their histories, practices, experiences, and beliefs.

Most certified mediums report that during the non-research readings from their own practices, they prefer receiving as little information as possible from sitters. (During research, they receive no access to or information about sitters prior to readings and no feedback from any sensory source during readings.) Because the mediumship process appears to be an intuitive rather than an analytical task, visual and verbal information can engage the medium's brain to make assessments and judgments about the sitter and disrupt the mediumship process. This is why some mediums prefer phone readings and why some mediums close their eyes during in-person readings. Mediums have very little control over who communicates and what information is conveyed during readings; their experience is that the right deceased individuals find them and not *vice versa*. Sitters should be aware of this to create accurate expectations prior to readings (e.g., Beischel, 2013).

In our experience, there are three types of information that are reported most often during mediumship readings. The first is information identifying the deceased. This can include descriptions of the person when s/he was living such as his/her physical appearance (e.g., hair and eye color, height, build, unique scars or birthmarks, and typical clothing preferences), personality characteristics, other deceased people or animals with him/her, and favorite activities, foods, events, places, etc. The purpose of this information seems to be for identification of the deceased so the sitter feels confident that the information is coming from the "right" person.

The second type is information about events in the sitter's life that have occurred since the death. A medium may convey statements such as "She saw the photo album you put together," "He likes the color you painted the kitchen," or "He walked you down the aisle." The purpose of this information seems to be providing evidence for the sitters that the deceased continue to observe and participate in their lives.

The third type of information is messages specifically for the sitters. LaGrand (2005) found that spontaneous ADCs may give advice, be inspirational or supportive, or let the bereaved know the deceased are still involved in their lives. The information reported in mediumship readings appears to be similar. This can include simple messages like "I love you" and messages seemingly intended to alleviate guilt or sorrow such as "There was nothing you could have done to prevent my death" or "I didn't feel any pain." Messages can also offer advice (e.g., "You should sell the house"), reprimand (e.g., "Why hasn't my headstone been installed yet?"), or encourage (e.g., "It's time to start dating again"). Sitters can choose to heed or ignore advice or direction from the deceased just as they would comments from any well-meaning friend or family member. Walliss (2001) described the relationship between the living and the dead as "in many ways a continuation of the lived one, with the deceased offering support and advice which the living can then either act on or not" (p. 142).

The collection of information reported during mediumship readings assists sitters in recognizing that their bonds with the deceased continue.

The Intersection of Grief, Continuing Bonds, Assisted ADCs, and Clinical Practice

The continuing bonds model of grief may include experiences in which contact with the deceased occurs (e.g., Klugman, 2006). Field, Gao, and Paderna (2005) found that continuing bonds with the deceased may "represent a transition from a corporeal attachment to a spiritual attachment" (p. 295).

Silverman and Nickman (1996) said that when new models of grief arise, "our culture develops new rituals of helping to match the new model" and individuals acquire 'folk remedies' to match their lived experiences" (p. 354). Though readings from psychic mediums may currently be one of these "folk remedies," the effects of mediumship readings on bereavement are not clearly understood. Numerous anecdotal reports exist regarding the positive and profound effects a reading with a psychic medium can have on the bereaved. For example, one participant in our early mediumship research reported, "After the devastating loss of two sons, mediumship has proven to me that we survive the death of our bodies, and has made my life not only bearable but worthwhile again." The profound effects a reading with a medium may have on the bereaved warrant a serious look at this phenomenon, particularly within the continuing bonds paradigm.

A reading may be more accessible to individuals who may experience fear associated with the idea of a personal after-death contact that occurs unexpectedly (e.g., with spontaneous ADCs) or through induction (e.g., with the EMDR or Psychomanteum methods). The concept of the deceased being once-removed from the individual and the medium serving as the go-between for the deceased's messages may be more palatable to some. In addition, it has been demonstrated that both "extremely positive" and "extremely negative" experiences during spontaneous ADCs are "related to poor adaptation and lack of coping with bereavement" (Lindström, 1995, p. 19). Thus, a more controlled environment during which contact can be experienced may have more positive effects on the bereaved.

Additionally, a reading with a medium may be preferred in cases in which an individual longs for contact but has not experienced it. Because mediums focus on the discarnate rather than the sitter, they "may have something to offer mourners denied them by those bereavement counsellors who focus on the client's feelings" (Walter, 2008, p. 50). A medium may also serve as a like-minded participant without disparaging, disbelieving, or ridiculing the experiences or worldviews of the bereaved—a risk that exists when speaking about or sharing ADC experiences with others.

Mediums' readings also involve potential disadvantages that should be acknowledged. In situations which induce communication with the deceased (including Botkin's EMDR method and the use of a Psychomanteum), a trained facilitator participates in the process or is actually present during the experience; this is not necessarily the case for a mediumship reading. Previous research has demonstrated that mediums' experiences of communication may include alterations in some aspects of their phenomenology including volitional control, self-awareness, and memory (Rock & Beischel, 2008). Thus, mediums may not be in a psychological position to facilitate the reading experience for the bereaved sitter; their role, instead, is simply to convey what they experience regarding the deceased to the sitter. Follow-up visits with a qualified facilitator may be necessary for some sitters.

Exploratory Study

In one pilot study (Beischel et al., 2014–15), data were collected via an anonymous, online survey to investigate individuals' recollections of their experiences of grief to assess the potential therapeutic benefit of assisted ADCs in the treatment of grief. Participants were asked to retrospectively rate their levels of grief before and after a mediumship reading: no grief; a very low level; a somewhat low but manageable level; a somewhat high level; and a very high, almost unbearable level of grief. The responses were assigned numerical values from zero to four, respectively. Data are reported as mean ± standard error of the mean.

A total of 83 participants completed the survey in full and reported a mean level of grief of 3.13 ± 0.10 (higher than "somewhat high") before a reading and 1.96 ± 0.11 (lower than "somewhat low") after a reading ($\Delta = 1.17$). Because of the methodological limitations of the survey data collected (described below), statistical analyses could not be completed on these data. This finding is congruent with previous research into the effects of ADCs on grief considering, as discussed above, that the messages received during assisted ADCs during mediumship readings are similar to those received during spontaneous ADCs.

Representative Participant Comments

Perhaps most indicative of the potential therapeutic benefits of assisted ADCs in the treatment of grief were the participants' responses to a final open-ended survey question: "Do you have any other comments about your grief that you would like to share with the investigators?"

The following representative comments were provided regarding the effects of a mediumship reading on the experience of grief:

> Before my reading with [the medium], I still had a low level of grief . . . that I accepted as the loss that will always be there. After the reading, I felt as though that "weight" was lifted and I had a different definition of my relationship with my mom that was more special than I could ever expect.
>
> When I am approached by my loved one that has passed, I am much more accepting of her presence and look forward to the joy instead of the pain . . . I wish I had had the reading 16 years ago!
>
> I believe going to a good medium is an untapped resource for faster grief management.
>
> [The medium] helped me manage the grief that has been with me for more than 20 years.

In addition, several participants provided negative feedback regarding their experiences with a mental health professional:

> For me, the various grief support groups were not the answer.
>
> I only went to a grief counselor for four sessions. I did not continue because I didn't feel that she was helping me either way.
>
> When my first counselor negated the reading I had with a medium, I switched to someone who understood and supported "my new reality" and therefore received much more constructive help with my grief.

We feel the last comment above is very important in demonstrating the potential of clients to seek out and employ counselors accepting of and knowledgeable regarding mediumship readings and supports the need for new training modalities for counselors (described below).

Several participants also specifically commented on the importance of the combination of the two interventions—mediumship readings and work with a mental health professional—on their recovery:

I can't begin to express how helpful my readings have been in my healing journey. I know that I personally needed to go through counseling as well. However, the level of healing was accelerated by getting readings.

The medium reached my heart, the social worker my mind.

It is important to note that the data from this study were collected for the purpose of determining if this line of inquiry warranted further study and they should not be viewed as demonstrative of an effect. The participants were self-selected to include individuals who already held a belief that a mediumship reading could be helpful and were, therefore, predisposed to finding the experience beneficial. The participants' reports of their experiences of grief were retrospective. However, it seems probable that these positive findings, even considering these limitations and the exploratory nature of the study, could be extrapolated to at least a portion of the population actively receiving mediumship readings as a "folk remedy" for their grief.

Conclusions

Although grief is experienced across cultures and is ubiquitous to the human experience, complicated grief can have detrimental effects on mental and/or physical health and wellness. Traditional grief counseling approaches, with a focus on the client's acceptance of separation and integration of loss, may be ineffective. Conversely, therapeutic approaches that incorporate a continuing bonds perspective exhibit positive results for the bereaved.

Methods of healing from grief outside of a therapeutic scenario include the bereaved experiencing communication with the deceased. Both spontaneous and induced ADCs have been repeatedly demonstrated to diminish or even entirely alleviate grief. Other bereaved individuals seek out assisted ADCs through readings with psychic mediums, and anecdotal reports and initial survey data posit the positive effects of this practice. These trends warrant further study into the benefits of assisted ADCs during personal mediumship readings from credentialed mediums i.e., mediums whose abilities have been tested by an independent third party that does not stand to gain (e.g., financially) from the certification.

Future Directions

With objective research on this topic, investigators and counselors may be able—at the very least—to offer suggestions to the large population of individuals choosing to receive mediumship readings and—ideally—to become part of the decision-making process and follow-up. We suggest a scenario in which credentialed mediums work together with licensed professionals in addressing the acute grief experiences of the bereaved who may benefit from readings. This cross-collaboration will require research assessing who may benefit most from mediumship readings—and for whom it might be detrimental—regarding factors including, for example, the gender and age of the sitters and the deceased, time since the death, type of death, psychological and personality characteristics of the sitter, level of adaptation to bereavement, etc.

As a first step in discerning who might and might not benefit from readings, we have designed a randomized clinical trial called the Bereavement And Mediumship (or BAM) Study using a standard randomization scheme, waiting list control group, group assignment method, quantitative grief instrument, and statistical analysis to examine the impact of a reading on the grieving. Support for the completion of this study has been acquired through crowd-funding and a grant from the William H. Donner Foundation. Only with controlled research such as the BAM Study can the grief community effectively determine if receiving mediumship readings is helpful, harmful, or neither for different of the bereaved.

With the results from this, similar, and subsequent research, an effective collaboration can develop between clinicians and mediums that will best serve the bereaved population. The role of the mediums will be to assist sitters who may benefit in beginning work with mental health professionals. Likewise, the role of the mental health professional will be to suggest readings to select individuals and to assist them in integrating the information provided by mediums into their lives. Though individual mental health professionals may be including mediumship readings in the suggestions they offer to their clients (as we have heard anecdotally), an organized dialogue and list of agreed-upon standard practices is only in its infancy (see, for example, the work of the American Center for the Integration of Spiritually Transformative Experiences, www.aciste.org). Furthermore, this collaboration should include an open dialogue between researchers and those directly interacting with the bereaved: the mental health professionals and mediums. The experiences of those groups regarding the effects of readings on the bereaved are invaluable.

This collaboration between mental health professionals and mediums will require training for both halves. The training of mental health professionals may include information about the basics of mediumship processes, including the topics of ethics and reading styles discussed above as well as general error rates and where to find reputable, certified, or credentialed mediums and how to best prepare for a reading (Beischel, 2013). Mediums should be provided with information gained from research regarding which sitters may require further work with a mental health professional after a reading. In addition, a list of licensed mental health professionals trained regarding mediumship processes should be distributed to credentialed mediums for the purpose of sharing with their clients. This is particularly important considering that a large portion of mediums provide phone readings to sitters who may be in other states or countries which may make establishing local relationships with mental health professionals somewhat ineffective.

We believe this scenario is a necessary and practical solution to the increasing use of mediumship readings by the general public and the limited demonstrable efficacy of traditional grief therapy. We are currently working on bringing it to fruition through controlled research and training material development.

References

Beischel, J. (2007). Contemporary methods used in laboratory-based mediumship research. *Journal of Parapsychology, 71*, 37–68.

Beischel, J. (2013). *Meaningful messages: Making the most of your mediumship reading.* Retrieved from www.amazon.com/dp/B00FE910V0.

Beischel, J., Boccuzzi, M., Biuso, M., & Rock, A. J. (2015). Anomalous information reception by research mediums under blinded conditions II: Replication and extension. *EXPLORE: The Journal of Science & Healing, 11*(2), 136–142. doi: 10.1016/j.explore. 2015.01.001.

Beischel, J., Mosher, C., & Boccuzzi, M. (2014–2015). The possible effects on bereavement of assisted after-death communication during readings with psychic mediums: A continuing bonds perspective. *Omega, 70*(2), 169–194. doi: 10.2190/OM.70.2.b.

Beischel, J., & Zingrone, N. (2015). Mental mediumship. In E. Cardeña, J. Palmer, & D. Marcusson-Clavertz (Eds), *Parapsychology: A handbook for the 21st century* (pp. 301–313). Jefferson, NC: McFarland.

Botkin, A. L. (2000). The induction of after-death communications utilizing eye-movement desensitization and reprocessing: A new discovery. *Journal of Near-Death Studies, 18*, 181–209.

Carter, C. (2012). *Science and the afterlife experience: Evidence for the immortality of consciousness.* Rochester, VT: Inner Traditions.

Currier, J. M., Neimeyer, R. A., & Berman, J. S. (2008). The effectiveness of psycho-therapeutic interventions for bereaved persons: A comprehensive quantitative review. *Psychological Bulletin, 134*, 648–661.

Drewry, M. D. J. (2003). Purported after-death communication and its role in the recovery of bereaved individuals: A phenomenological study. *Proceedings of the annual conference of the Academy of Religion and Psychical Research,* 74–87.

Field, N. P., Gao, B., & Paderna, L. (2005). Continuing bonds in bereavement: An attachment theory based perspective. *Death Studies, 29*, 277–299.

Hastings, A., Ferguson, E., Hutton, M., Goldman, A., Braud, W., Greene, E., et al. (2002). Psychomanteum research: Experiences and effects on bereavement. *Omega, 45*, 211–228.

Houck, J. A. (2005). The universal, multiple, and exclusive experiences of after-death communication. *Journal of Near-Death Studies, 24*, 117–127.

Hunter, J., & Luke, D. (Eds). (2014). *Talking with the spirits: Ethnographies from between the worlds.* Brisbane, Australia: Daily Grail Publishing.

IBIS World. (2015). *Psychic services market research report.* Retrieved on November 3, 2016, from www.ibisworld.com/industry/psychic-services.html.

Klugman, C. M. (2006). Dead men talking: Evidence of post death contact and continuing bonds. *Omega, 53*, 249–262.

Krippner, S. (2006). Getting through the grief: After-death communication experiences and their effects on experients. In L. Storm & M. A. Thalbourne (Eds), *The survival of human consciousness: Essays on the possibility of life after death* (pp. 174–193). Jefferson, NC: MacFarland & Company, Inc.

LaGrand, L. E. (2005). The nature and therapeutic implications of the extraordinary experiences of the bereaved. *Journal of Near-Death Studies, 24*, 3–20.

Larson, D. G., & Hoyt, W. T. (2007). What has become of grief counseling? An evaluation of the empirical foundations of the new pessimism. *Professional Psychology: Research and Practice, 38*, 347–355.

Lindström, T. C. (1995). Experiencing the presence of the dead: Discrepancies in "the sensing experience" and their psychological concomitants. *Omega, 31*, 11–21.

Moody, R. (1992). Family reunions: Visionary encounters with the departed in a modern-day psychomanteum. *Journal of Near-Death Studies, 11*, 83–121.

Newport, F., & Strausberg, M. (2001). *Americans' belief in psychic and paranormal phenomena is up over last decade: Belief in psychic healing and extrasensory perception top the list.* Retrieved on November 3, 2016, from www.gallup.com/poll/4483/americans-belief-psychic-paranormal-phenomena-over-last-decade.aspx.

Nowatzki, N. R., & Grant Kalischuk, R. (2009). Post-death encounters: Grieving, mourning, and healing. *Omega, 59,* 91–111.

Parker, J. S. (2005). Extraordinary experiences of the bereaved and adaptive outcomes of grief. *Omega, 51,* 257–283.

Rock, A. J., & Beischel, J. (2008). Quantitative analysis of mediums' conscious experiences during a discarnate reading versus a control task: A pilot study. *Australian Journal of Parapsychology, 8,* 157–179.

Schut, H., Stroebe, M. S., van den Bout, J., & Terheggen, M. (2001). The efficacy of bereavement interventions: Determining who benefits. In M. S. Stroebe, R. O. Hansson, W. Stroebe, & H. Schut (Eds), *Handbook of bereavement research: Consequences, coping, and care* (pp. 705–737). Washington, DC: American Psychological Association.

Silverman, P. R., & Nickman, S. L. (1996). Concluding thoughts. In D. Klass, P. R. Silverman, & S. L. Nickman (Eds), *Continuing bonds: New understandings of grief* (pp. 349–355). Washington, DC: Taylor & Francis.

Sormanti, M., & August, J. (1997). Parental bereavement: Spiritual connections with deceased children. *American Journal of Orthopsychiatry, 67,* 460–469.

Stroebe, M., Schut, H., & Stroebe, W. (2007). Health outcomes of bereavement. *Lancet, 370,* 1960–1973.

Taylor, S. F. (2005). Between the idea and the reality: A study of the counseling experiences of bereaved people who sense the presence of the deceased. *Counseling and Psychotherapy Research, 5,* 53–61.

Walliss, J. (2001). Continuing bonds: Relationships between the living and the dead within contemporary Spiritualism. *Mortality, 6,* 127–145.

Walter, T. (2008). Mourners and mediums. *Bereavement Care, 27,* 47–50.

Worden, J. W. (1991). *Grief counseling and grief therapy: A handbook for the mental health practitioner* (2nd ed.). New York, NY: Springer Publishing Company.

SECTION III

The Truth Status and Reality Status of Continuing Bonds

Introduction

We noted in the book's Introduction that when continuing bonds are regarded as normal in bereavement, we cannot dodge questions about the reality or truth in what bereaved people experience in their interactions with those who have died. The issue of the ontological status of the dead is, we noted, a theme running through many of the chapters in the book. In this Section we have three chapters that take on the ontological issue directly.

Jack Hunter describes three standard approaches to the paranormal in social science that have remained fairly constant in the history of social science. First, reductionism that accounts for the experiences in terms of some other dynamic; second, avoiding the reality question by describing the social or psychological value of the belief; and third, bracketing – that is, setting aside the reality question and focusing only on the experiencer's interpretation. The second and third seem to be the default positions in the contemporary study of continuing bonds. Finally, Hunter proposes a very interesting position that he calls ontological flooding. Rather than simply suspending disbelief, ontological flooding encourages us to consider a wide range of explanations. Reality, he says, does not play by our rules.

Callum Cooper examines the question of the reality of post-death encounters from a parapsychological perspective, looking into the so-called survival hypothesis. Cooper carefully evaluates the arguments and empirical evidence for both sides of the survival question, drawing on a range of theorists and researchers as well as illustrating the points with interesting case material, and he is able to show – in a scientifically grounded way – that the possibility of the reality of post-death encounters cannot be ruled out at this point, but neither can it be proven.

Anastasia Scrutton says there are different kinds of knowledge. We might think, for example, that knowing someone is different from knowing about someone. Scrutton looks closely at the rituals in which so much of grief is experienced and expressed in all cultures. She shows how ritual facilitates an experiential kind of knowing that goes deeper than mere factual knowledge or belief. She says that "because they are bodily, rituals can provide people with a more embedded and recalcitrant form of cognition than the more superficial forms provided by propositional means."

14

ONTOLOGICAL FLOODING AND CONTINUING BONDS

Jack Hunter

There are three fairly standard approaches in the social scientific investigation of the so-called "paranormal," a term which I take as referring to any phenomenon that seems to exceed or challenge the limitations of *current* scientific understanding (Kripal, 2014, pp. 243–4). These approaches include: 1) a reductionist approach, where the paranormal is explained away in terms of pathology, misunderstanding, cognitive illusion, and so on; 2) the social facts approach, in which questions about reality are sidestepped in favour of exploring the social value and function of paranormal *beliefs*; and 3) the phenomenological bracketing approach, which completely brackets out the question of reality, arguing that the "reality of the paranormal" is not a problem that social scientists are suitably equipped to resolve (or even need to resolve), and focuses purely on how the paranormal is experienced and interpreted by the experiencer. These approaches very often go hand in hand; the bracketing approach frees up the researcher to get on with investigating the social reality of the phenomenon, which might then be reductively explained in terms of cognitive factors, for example. Nevertheless, each of these approaches does move us gradually closer to a more holistic view of the complexity of paranormal experience, but none of the individual explanations is completely adequate for the task. What seems to be needed, then, is an approach that is open to further possibilities – an approach that embraces the idea that there might be more going on than the dominant explanatory paradigms if the social sciences can account for (Howard, 2013; Hunter, 2015a).

In this chapter I would like to explore the potential for a fourth way, which I have tentatively called "ontological flooding," as a possible route towards overcoming some of the drawbacks associated with these approaches. My interests are, therefore, *ontological* – I am interested in questions of reality, of how we know what is real, how best to engage with that reality (no matter how weird). Before I explain more precisely what I mean by the term ontological flooding, however,

I think it would be useful to give some examples of the above-mentioned dominant approaches in action, to highlight some of their limitations and my reasons for striving to develop a new approach. This chapter will provide a sort of history of social scientific approaches to the transpersonal, religious and paranormal, and will conclude with a brief discussion of possible applications of ontological flooding for social research and bereavement counselling, and especially – in the context of the theme of this book – for continuing bonds researchers and experiencers. Let us begin.

Reductionist Approaches

Perhaps the clearest examples of reductionist approaches are those that seek to pathologise and cognitivise anomalous experiences. Each of these approaches attempts to explain anomalous experience by collapsing it down to a single causal factor – either some form of psychological or physiological pathology, or to the action and misunderstanding of innate cognitive (mental) processes. A good example of an early pioneer of this approach is Sir Edward Burnett Tylor (1832–1917), one of the founding fathers of the discipline of anthropology and key populariser of the concept of *animism* (Harvey, 2005, pp. 7–9). Tylor was interested in explaining the widespread belief in spirits found in disparate cultures around the world – from the traditional beliefs of Australian Aboriginal people to the spirit beliefs of the Zulus, and the craze for Spiritualism that was sweeping through European society in his day (Stocking, 1975).

Tylor's explanation for the seemingly pan-human *belief* in spirits rested on two key assumptions: first, that there is evidence in human cultures of evolutionary stages of "intellectual development," with "primitive" cultures at one extreme, and Victorian rationalism at the other; and second, that so-called "primitive" peoples were unable to distinguish between fantasy, hallucination and "reality" owing to their ignorance of rational and scientific principles. His explanation for the origin of the belief in spirits, therefore, goes something like this:

> The idea of the soul which is held by uncultured races, and is the foundation of their religion, is not difficult for us to understand, if we can fancy ourselves in their place, ignorant of the very rudiments of science, and trying to get at the meaning of life by what the senses seem to tell them.
>
> *(Tylor, 1930, p. 87)*

Tylor goes on to suggest that, with a lack of scientific understanding, "primitive" peoples misunderstood their encounters with human figures in dreams as interactions with non-physical beings, *erroneously* concluding that their visionary experiences were "real" experiences relating to objective "realities." In essence, what Tylor is suggesting is that the belief in spiritual beings (and so also the afterlife, spirit world, etc.) arises from failing to grasp the notion that dreams and hallucinations are *not* "real," that they are illusory, and that with sufficient intellectual development this *ought to* become clear and obvious. Along with later secularisation theorists, as well as certain new atheists, Tylor would suggest that with increasing popular awareness of scientific principles and theories we should expect to see a decline in supernatural and religious beliefs – in other words, we *should* learn to know better so we can "break free from the vice of religion" (Dawkins, 2006, p. 28).

The more recent approaches of the cognitive sciences of religion can also be understood as diverging branches of Tylor's reductionist tradition. Pascal Boyer's book *Religion Explained* (2001), for example, concludes that religion can be explained purely

> in terms of systems that are in all human minds and do all sorts of precious and interesting work, but were not really designed to produce religious concepts or behaviours . . . religion is portrayed here as a mere consequence or side-effect of having the brains we have.
>
> *(Boyer, 2001, pp. 378–9)*

Admittedly, Boyer isn't saying here that religion is a *simple* phenomenon that can be easily explained; rather, what he is suggesting is that religion is the result of a "variety of underlying processes" (p. 379). Nevertheless, Boyer *is* implying that religion can be explained in terms of basic cognitive processes responsible for such mundane (though essential) things as attention, making sense of other minds, detecting agents in the environment, and so on. In Boyer's view, it is through a combination of otherwise normal cognitive processes that religion ultimately emerges – through misunderstanding and misinterpreting these processes as evidence of something else (spirits, gods, telepathy, etc.). In the words of materialist philosopher Gilbert Ryle (1900–76), supernatural belief is the result of a "category mistake" (Ryle, 1949).

Reductionist approaches, therefore, seek to explain complex human experiences in terms of relatively simple underlying causes. They may be useful in pinpointing specific correlations, for example between certain kinds of experiences and certain cognitive or physiological processes, but they very often fail to provide a satisfying account of the bigger picture – how these simple processes relate to the holistic first-person experience, which often includes other elements that do not fit into such a simplistic model. We can, for example, detect the areas of the brain that are activated and deactivated during psychedelic experiences (see, for example, Carhart-Harris et al., 2016), but without any accompanying first-person narrative this data gives us very little insight into the actual experience of the psychonaut themselves. Such research also gives very little insight, for instance, into the nature and meaning of entity encounters under the influence of psychedelics (Strassman, 2001; Luke, 2011). The same problem might also arise in conducting continuing bonds research, where in attempting to find a neat explanation for the experience of continuing bonds with the deceased (e.g., it is all just hallucination), we reduce the experience down into categories, concepts and processes that ultimately lose sight of the overarching complexity of the phenomenon – its *gestalt*. This clearly isn't good enough.

Social Facts and Functions

The social facts approach takes the work of the pioneering sociologist Emile Durkheim (1858–1917) as its starting point. Durkheim argued that there are certain things in social life that seem to have an independent existence beyond our subjectivity – social things that have the *appearance* of objectivity because we are born into a particular social context, and because they are presented to us as real throughout our lifetimes – things like our social roles as brothers, sisters, partners, and spouses, the fact that we use money to quantify our trading of goods and to pay our debts, or the taken-for-grantedness of God's existence in religious cultures. Durkheim writes:

> Here, then, are ways of acting, thinking, and feeling that present the noteworthy property of existing outside the individual consciousness. These types of conduct or thought are not only external to the individual but are, moreover, endowed with coercive power, by virtue of which they impose themselves upon him, independent of his individual will.
>
> *(Durkheim, 1982, p. 2)*

By avoiding the question of whether these "social facts" have any kind of reality in themselves, Durkheim was able to focus on what interested him most – what these social facts actually *do* in society, or how they *function*. This is the basic starting point of Durkheim's functionalist view of society. He is not interested in whether, for example, God exists, but rather is interested in the *function* the "belief in God" (a social fact) performs for a given society – usually the function is to maintain social cohesion. Later theorists also focused on the function of social facts for the individual psychology of members of a particular society. The anthropologist Bronislaw Malinowski (1884–1942), for example, interpreted magic and religion as performing psychological functions for the members of a social group in times of stress and uncertainty. Gardening magic on the Trobriand Islands, for example, serves the function of alleviating the stress associated with worrying about how well the crops will grow (Malinowski, 1974, p. 79). Malinowski is not concerned with whether magic is *real* or not, only with the function that the social fact of the belief performs:

> Both magic and religion arise and function in situations of emotion and stress: crises of life, lacunae in important pursuits, death and initiation into tribal mysteries, unhappy love and unsatisfied hate. Both magic and religion open up escapes from such situations and such impasses as offer no empirical way out except by ritual and belief in the domain of the supernatural.
>
> *(Malinowski, 1974, p. 87)*

This "social facts" approach, then, can only take us so far in understanding the continuing bonds that might exist between the bereaved and their deceased loved ones. It penetrates only so far as explaining what the "belief in a continuing bond" does for the believer, but falls short of a complete account. Yes, undoubtedly continuing bonds with the deceased can have a positive impact on the emotional well-being of the deceased (its psychological function in Malinowski's terms), but might there not also be something more going on? What about the apparent depth and complexity of the experience, and the little details that give experiencers the sense that their experience is *more* than a simple hallucination, more than an illusion – that it is *real*? Moreover, what is it about such experiences that gives them their special character – what makes them different from everyday experiences? The experiencer does not describe their own experience of continuing bonds in terms of social facts performing psychological functions. They describe them as real, deeply emotional interactions with their loved ones (Klass, 2006). There is clearly a disconnect here between the explanation (the social or psychological function of *belief*) and the experience itself, which is often actually the foundation of the belief (see Hufford, 1982).

Phenomenological Bracketing

Phenomenology emerged in direct response to the ever-increasing abstraction of Western philosophy in the late nineteenth and early twentieth centuries, which seemed to have become too distanced from direct lived experience in the world. The term itself is derived from the Greek *phainómenon*, referring to "that which appears," or "immediate perception," and *lógos*, meaning discourse and study. Phenomenology is, therefore, the "study of what appears to our immediate perception," our first-person consciousness. It was formally developed by the German philosopher Edmund Husserl (1858–1938), who wrote of it in his book *Ideas* (1931). A key concept in Husserl's phenomenology is what he called *epoche*, or *bracketing*, a process of observing our subjective experience without preconceptions – without questioning the "reality" of our sensory experiences, or asking whether there is an actual "thing-out-there" that corresponds to a particular experience we are having (Tufford & Newman, 2010).

Bracketing helps to focus in on first-person conscious experience in itself. Phenomenologists want to know what the experience itself is like, how it was experienced by the experiencer and how it affects them as it is happening. All of this can be achieved without questioning the "reality" of that which is experienced – that is, whether, for example, the experience of a continuing bond corresponds to an "actual" relationship between the living and the deceased. We can treat the experience itself as data without having to ask if it is real or not. To a certain extent it doesn't matter – the experience *is* the experience, it is the data and we don't need to know if it correlates objectively with anything. From this perspective, there is no need to ask if it is real or not. However, I think these are precisely the questions most people are interested in, questions about the "reality" of such things, and the phenomenological method as employed in the social sciences tends to avoid such questions.

Writing on the use of bracketing in social scientific investigations of magic, anthropologist Jeremy Northcote (2004) explains how bracketing, when put into practice in the field, often serves to reinforce the dominant explanatory framework of the social sciences (usually a form of reductionist functionalism). In practice, unfortunately, bracketing actually puts up barriers around certain kinds of questions (e.g. are spirits *real?*), so that the researcher can focus on more important questions such as, for example, what the belief in spirits *does* in a particular society, or for a specific individual. These questions are permitted in the academy, because they do not challenge the dominant explanatory models of the social sciences (which preclude the existence of spirits), while questions of ontology (what really exists) are bracketed out, and put to one side, because their implications appear to go beyond the materialist framework that is currently employed in mainstream academia. I do not think this is the way Husserl intended his bracketing methodology to be used, but it very often is in the social sciences (see Hunter, 2015a, b).

So, phenomenological bracketing takes us a significant step closer to where we want to be – into the very midst of the experience itself – but it pulls back, very slightly admittedly, at the last second. It is, nevertheless, a vital springboard to propel us one step further down the rabbit hole.

Ontological Flooding

Phenomenological, or ontological, bracketing often unwittingly perpetuates the standard models we have so far discussed by ignoring (bracketing out) the ontological questions that anomalous experiences seem to throw up – are they evidence of "something beyond our current models" going on? Understood from this perspective, the bracketing process can be seen as analogous to erecting flood gates designed to hold back the tides of what the collector of anomalies Charles Fort (1874–1932) called "damned facts" (Fort, 2008; Hunter, 2016a) – those unusual events and experiences that seem to challenge our dominant explanatory models – floodgates that enable us to believe we have some kind of solid explanation for what "all of this" is about. The approach I would like to put forward here is essentially an inversion of ontological bracketing – removing the flood barriers and letting the damned facts flow. In Fort's words, we would have:

> A procession of the damned. By the damned I mean the excluded. We shall have a procession of data that Science has excluded. Battalions of the accursed, captained by pallid data that I have exhumed, will march . . . The power that has said to all these things that they are damned is Dogmatic Science. But they'll March.
>
> *(Fort, 2008, p. 3)*

So, while bracketing in the social sciences tends to reinforce the standard models (beginning from a point of certainty that science has already made good progress in describing and explaining what is *really real* – as well as what is *not real*), flooding should begin from a point of uncertainty – we simply don't know everything about the universe – there are no barriers to ontological possibility. Cultural relativity and postmodernism suggest that there is no single cosmology or philosophical position that can claim a monopoly on truth (Lyotard, 2005), and as such it seems reasonable to put all models on an equally questionable footing – as equally plausible and equally implausible simultaneously. Through adopting such a framework, it is possible to engage deeply with experience without putting up barriers to protect the dominant worldview, because there really isn't one! The essence of this approach, then, becomes a form of open-minded *participation* and *engagement* (Hunter, 2016b). This is more than simply suspending our disbelief, which does little to actually embrace alternative ontological possibilities, and is really just another form of bracketing. Ontological flooding is the opening up of what neuroscientist David Eagleman has called a "possibility space," or what Charles Fort called a state of "intermediatism":

> like a purgatory, all that is commonly called "existence," which we call Intermediateness, is quasi-existence, neither real nor unreal, but the expression of attempt to become real.
>
> *(Fort, 2008, p. 15)*

It is through such an intermediate lens that we can begin to move towards greater participation with the anomalous, and a more *empathetic* understanding of the experiential life-worlds of our informants – we must be open to the *possibility* that what they tell us is true and real. To illustrate the benefits of such an ontologically open, participatory and engaged approach in illuminating the anomalous, I will now turn to the experience of anthropologist Edith Turner (1921–2016) during her research into the *Ihamba* healing ceremony of the Ndembu in Zambia. Edie had observed the ritual once before, years earlier, with her late husband Victor Turner (1920–83), but it was only when she fully *participated* – bodily and emotionally – in the ritual herself that she finally began to understand it. It was through this participation that she achieved what she called a "breakthrough" experience. She writes:

> And just then, through my tears, the central figure swayed deeply: all leaned forward, this was indeed going to be it. I realized along with them that the barriers were breaking – just as I let go in tears. Something that wanted to be born was now going to be born . . . I felt the spiritual motion, a tangible feeling of breakthrough going through the whole group . . . Suddenly Meru raised her arm, stretched out in liberation, and I *saw* with my own eyes a giant thing emerging out of the flesh of her back . . . I was amazed – delighted. I still laugh with glee at the realization of having seen it . . . We were all just one in triumph.
>
> *(Turner, 1998, p. 149)*

Edie's "breakthrough" experience ultimately led her to a new understanding of religion and ritual, an experiential understanding that induced her to call on other anthropologists to learn to "see what the Natives see" (Turner, 1993, p. 11). In other words, we are encouraged to dismantle our ontological floodgates, and open ourselves up to experience – not just our own, but also the experiences of our informants – to take them seriously. Moreover, the flooding approach encourages us to take the complexity of such experiences seriously, and to consider multiple perspectives simultaneously, rather than attempting an explanation in terms of a single explanatory framework. For example, continuing bonds may very well per-form vital psychological functions for the bereaved, they might very well rely on innate cognitive processes to be experienced and interpreted, and they are *certainly* socially real, but might they not also relate to some form of independent ontologi-cal reality – might there not be "something more" going on? For Edith Turner, witnessing the extraction of the Ihamba spirit was a validation of Ndembu ritual and belief, and it required her full participation for this to become clear – she had to let down her barriers so she could finally *see* and *understand* what her informants had been telling her all along:

> again and again anthropologists witness spirit rituals, and again and again some indigenous exegete tries to explain that spirits are present . . . and the anthropologist proceeds to interpret them differently.
>
> *(Turner, 1993, p. 11)*

Conclusions

So, what are the potential implications of a participatory, engaged and onto-logically flooded approach to continuing bonds research? First, for counsellors helping the bereaved experiencing continuing bonds with the deceased (whether through visions, dreams, apparitions or more subtle feelings and experiences), an ontologically flooded perspective might assist in overcoming some of the nega-tive associations of the prevailing paradigms, and allow therapists to engage with the experiences of the bereaved not as "simple" hallucinations, category mistakes, cognitive illusions, or social facts, but as genuine and meaningful interactions between the living and the deceased. Rather than simply suspending disbelief, ontological flooding encourages us to consider a wide range of interacting expla-nations, including the possibility that there are *real* interactions between the living and the dead. Indeed, there is a lot of very interesting research being done in contemporary parapsychology that offers some evidence in support of the exist-ence of spirits as a contributing factor (see, for example, the work of Beischel et al. in this anthology). An ontologically flooded perspective would require that this kind of evidence also be taken into account, while the standard approaches would normally ignore it.

For the bereaved themselves, an ontologically flooded, participatory approach may provide a new means of dealing with the fear that the experience of con-tinuing bonds is an indication of mental or physical pathology. It is an alternative framework for interpreting such experiences, open to a wide range of possi-bilities regarding the ultimate ontology underlying these enigmatic experiences.

In other words, we do not automatically have to jump to a reductionist conclusion, or a functionalist conclusion, or a psychological conclusion (even if they *do* play their own roles). Furthermore, the ontologically flooded perspective, grounded as it is in the discourse of social and cultural anthropology, demonstrates that such experiences are not by any stretch of the imagination isolated or abnormal. In the cross-cultural context, for example, communication with ancestors, the deceased and discarnate entities is actually relatively common throughout human cultures (Hunter & Luke, 2014), and non-Western explanatory models may be of benefit to the experiencer in interpreting and understanding their own continuing bonds with the deceased.

To conclude, the ideas presented here are intended as a springboard for further engagement with continuing bonds, rather than as a definitive statement. The purpose of this chapter is to encourage researchers to explore a wide range of possibilities in their investigations, and not to feel limited in their conclusions by the theoretical models that currently dominate scholarly discourse. There may be more going on. Reality doesn't play by our rules.

References

Boyer, P. (2001). *Religion explained: The human instincts that fashion gods, spirits and ancestors.* London: William Heinemann.

Carhart-Harris, R. L. et al. (2016). Neural correlates of the LSD experience revealed by multimodal neuroimaging. *PNAS, 113*(17), 4853–4858.

Dawkins, R. (2006). *The god delusion.* London: Transworld.

Durkheim, E. (1982). *The rules of sociological method, and selected texts on sociology and method.* London: Macmillan.

Fort, C. (2008). *The book of the damned: The collected works of Charles Fort.* New York, NY: Jeremy P. Tarcher.

Harvey, G. (2005). *Animism: Respecting the living world.* London: C. Hurst & Co.

Howard, A. J. (2013). Beyond belief: Ethnography, the supernatural and hegemonic discourse. *Practical Matters, 6,* 4–25.

Hufford, D. J. (1982). *The terror that comes in the night: An experience-centred study of supernatural assault traditions.* Philadelphia, PA: University of Pennsylvania Press.

Hunter, J. (2015a). "Between realness and unrealness": Anthropology, parapsychology and the ontology of non-ordinary realities. *Diskus: Journal of the British Association for the Study of Religion, 17*(2), 4–20.

Hunter, J. (2015b). "Spirits are the problem": Anthropology and conceptualising spiritual beings. *Journal for the Study of Religious Experience, 1*(1), 76–86.

Hunter, J. (2016a). *Damned facts: Fortean essays on religion, folklore and the paranormal.* Paphos, Cyprus: Aporetic Press.

Hunter, J. (2016b). Engaging the anomalous: Reflections from the anthropology of the paranormal. *European Journal of Psychotherapy and Counselling, 18*(2), 170–178.

Hunter, J., & Luke, D. (2014). *Talking with the spirits: Ethnographies from between the worlds.* Brisbane: Daily Grail.

Husserl, E. (1931). *Ideas.* London: Routledge.

Klass, D. (2006). Continuing conversation about continuing bonds. *Death Studies, 30*(9), 843–858.

Kripal, J. J. (2014). *Comparing religions: Coming to terms.* Oxford: Wiley Blackwell.

Luke, D. (2011). Discarnate entities and dimethyltryptamine (DMT): Psychopharmacology, phenomenology and ontology. *Journal of the Society for Psychical Research, 75*(902), 26.

Jack Hunter

Jack Hunter

Jack Hunter

Jack Hunter

Jack Hunter

15

CONSIDERING ANOMALOUS EVENTS DURING BEREAVEMENT AS EVIDENCE FOR SURVIVAL

Callum E. Cooper

Chapter Overview

It has been noted that experiences of perceived interaction with the dead are common for the bereaved. Surveys have reported that around 50–60% of individuals will report that they have had such an experience following a significant death. These reports are spontaneous by their very nature and can involve a variety of experiences, from sensing the presence of the dead, to dreaming about them, seeing apparitions in the waking state, witnessing poltergeist-type phenomena, and others. Even so, it is acknowledged that instances of alleged reincarnation where a young child may relay information from a deceased individual have been noted, and sought phenomena such as sittings with mediums and therapy-induced experiences suggestive of interaction with the dead could produce information pertaining to survival. However, this chapter will focus purely on spontaneous anomalous experiences occurring following loss.

The question remains: What are the ontological roots of such experiences? Mainstream opinions have conceptualized such reports as purely pathological and typical by-products of a grieving mind. However, is there a case for something more at work? To answer this, we not only need to understand the psychology of bereavement, but indeed the parapsychology of bereavement as well. This chapter will consider the place of anomalous bereavement experiences in the debate of "consciousness and its survival beyond bodily death" (AKA, the survival hypothesis), and what evidence exists from such events which may add weight to the debate and goes beyond current conventional understanding.

Introduction

Anomalous experiences can be defined as experiences in which the *abilities* a person claims to have, or *experiences* they have, may appear to be non-ordinary to the person having the experience or any witnesses present (see Smith, 2010, p.1) – or to the culture in which they operate. Where conventional explanations don't appear to account for the observed phenomenon, we may speak of the experience as being anomalous in the sense that the processes involved do not seem to be explainable via current scientific paradigms. As the research develops, it is hoped that understanding of such processes should become clear and commonplace within science. Yet, as this chapter shall demonstrate, the features of such experiences – to date – have already been studied in great depth. Anomalous experiences could involve precognitive visions or telepathic dreams, or the witnessing of apparitions, poltergeist-type phenomena and a variety of sensory experiences, such as sensing the presence of people who are not physically present. Therefore, in anomalous bereavement experiences, experients typically report a diversity of spontaneous sensory phenomena which they may interpret as interaction and/or communication with significant people who have died. This could include the sense of presence experience, through to hearing the deceased, smelling fragrances associated with the deceased (e.g., perfume or tobacco), feeling their touch, dreaming about them, movements and manipulations of objects associated with them, through to the witnessing of apparitions (see Cooper, Roe, & Mitchell, 2015). The extent to which these experiences actually provide evidence for the survival of consciousness and human personality beyond death is still highly debatable. Even so, we shall discuss some of the key thoughts on the survival hypothesis within this chapter. Before entering this discussion, some brief consideration will be given to understanding how common such phenomena are among the bereaved, and how well established the research into such matters has become within the social sciences. Thus, it will be demonstrated that parapsychology is firmly engrained within the social scientific community, especially where clinically oriented parapsychology matters are concerned (Steffen, Wilde, & Cooper, in press).

Anomalous experiences during a time of loss are common events. During the early work of the Society for Psychical Research (est. 1882), a study was conducted to understand the typical features and frequency of anomalous experiences which occurred for the bereaved. Edmund Gurney and Frederic Myers (1889) extracted 211 accounts from the extensive and highly detailed book *Phantasms of the Living* (see Gurney, Myers, & Podmore, 1886), where it appeared that anomalous events sometimes occurred following loss. Using an early form of a content analysis, common themes of such experiences and frequencies of their occurrence began to emerge from the accounts. Of these cases, 134 spontaneous anomalous experiences were reported to have occurred within the hour of death, and 29 between 1 and 12 hours after death (post-mortem apparitions beyond this time were excluded from *Phantasms of the Living*) (see Figure 15.1). The researchers commented:

[T]he recognised apparitions decrease rapidly in the few days after death, then more slowly; and after about a year's time they become so sporadic that we can no longer include them in a steadily descending line.

(Gurney with Myers, 1889, p. 427)

Gurney and Myers were aware that the experience of encountering sensory stimuli associated with that of deceased friends and relatives was common. They were also very aware of many common ill-informed explanations for such experiences, such as "the person was drunk or delusional at the time" or "emotionally excited, and perhaps misinterpreted sights or sounds of an objective kind." They noted that:

A very little careful study of the subject will, however, show that all these hypotheses must be rejected; that the witness may be in good health, and in no exceptional state of nervousness or excitement, and that what he sees or hears may still be of purely subjective origin – the projection of his own brain.

(pp. 403–4)

Their study suggested that there is argument for the hallucination to not be purely subjective if: 1) additional people present also saw the apparition, or 2) the apparition conveyed information only known by the deceased and not by the experient, but is later confirmed to be correct. Many books on bereavement

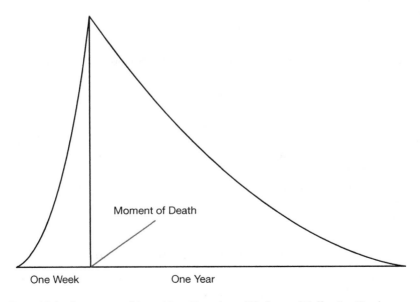

Figure 15.1 Frequency of Apparitions Experienced Before and Following Death (Gurney with Myers, 1889, p. 427)

throughout this time simply passed such experiences off as pure side effects of grief, and in the *Complete Psychological Works of Sigmund Freud* (25 volumes) such experiences were simply dismissed in three lines as "psychotic hallucinations" (see Rees, 2000, p. 83).

It could be argued that it wasn't until eight decades later with the publication of a longitudinal study conducted as part of a medical doctorate by Rees (1971) that the experiences began to be taken seriously in the "mainstream." The study published in the *British Medical Journal* was entitled "The hallucinations of widowhood." The term "hallucination" was used very loosely, referring to anomalous sensory experiences ranging from a sense of presence, through to: smells, touch, voices, and full visual apparitions of the dead. The participant sample was collected in an area of mid–Wales including 227 widows and 66 widowers, all of whom were interviewed to determine the extent of their experiences during widowhood/bereavement. Upon analysing the data, it was found that the sense of presence of the dead was among the most common of experiences occurring in around 39.2% of cases, while around 13–14% of cases reported visual and auditory hallucinations. In 11% of cases, the bereaved claimed to have not only experienced the presence of the dead, but also conversed with them and interacted.

The study by Rees (1971) demonstrated not only the commonality of such experiences, but also how beneficial these experiences often are to the bereaved, offering comfort and therapeutic values. Figures of between 50% and 60% of the bereaved reporting such phenomena have remained consistent over time (e.g., Burton, 1982; Castelnovo, Cavallotti, Gambini, & D'Agostino, 2015). The research has created a noticeable chain reaction of various study replications and alternative approaches, to understand in greater depth the therapeutic aid such experiences can bring (Krippner, 2006). In current research, attention has been given to the cognition of hope, and how individuals who report such experiences increase in personal health and well-being due to obtaining a greater personal sense of hope for personal life goals and for survival beyond death (Cooper, 2016a). Clinical parapsychology has been a key focus of research into anomalous experiences during bereavement since the publication by Rees (1971); that is, in terms of what *impact* such experience have on our health and well-being, rather than investigating their ontology (e.g., Cooper, 2016; Kramer, Bauer, & Hövelmann, 2012; Roxburgh & Evenden, 2016). With this in mind, let us now give some attention to this matter and consider what aspects of anomalous experiences following personal loss could possibly constitute "evidence" for survival of human personality beyond bodily death.

Cases of Potential Evidence for Survival

For cases of spontaneous anomalous experience during bereavement to become of interest to theorists and researchers of survival, we would expect there to be key features of the experience which would suggest something more than a subjective nature and perhaps purely illusory creation (created either consciously or unconsciously due to loss and longing for the deceased's return) – this is in accordance with the conclusions made by Gurney and Myers (1889). Even though there is a large amount of literature and research, documenting and discussing accounts of anomalous phenomena suggesting survival (to cite but a few: Baird, 1944; Berger, 1988; Betty, 2016; Fontana, 2005; Gurney, Myers, & Podmore, 1886; McAdams & Bayless, 1981; Myers, 1903; Robertson, 2013; Rogo, 1986; Thomas, 1929), the case for survival as a whole is far too extensive to discuss in any depth or fair summary in a single book chapter (as previously noted by Gauld, 2005). However, here we are specifically concerned with cases suggesting survival during a period that could be considered bereavement for the experient, which are arguably limited within the available literature against other cases suggestive of survival (e.g., experiences prior to the knowledge of loss, mediumship, reincarnation events).

We know that such accounts exist on record, and are reported to occur, but it requires a good deal of searching to identify such cases. This is for two reasons: first, survival-type phenomena cover a range of experiences, and are not just limited to experiences of the bereaved, and second, if these experiences are not reported by experients to the appropriate people and organizations, they never become committed to record and are lost. Some have questioned this as a decline effect in the phenomenon itself (e.g., Gauld, 2010). I would go further to argue that it is due to a failure in reporting, which was highly favourable a hundred years ago as psychical research literature demonstrates, and in the early work of the Parapsychology Laboratory at Duke University (see Horn, 2009; Weiner & Haight, 1986). This is partly caused by issues of the media's negative portrayal of parapsychology and the wider public knowing little about who the professional and reliable researchers are, and how to contact them to report their experiences and have them professionally investigated (see Thomas & Cooper, 2016; Winsper, Parsons, & O'Keeffe, 2008). This matter is also closely linked with other professional sciences/scientists knowing little of the research evidence from parapsychology (and openly not wanting to, in some cases), and yet publicly dismissing it out of hand based on personal biases (Fontana, 2007). This is not a credible scientific attitude, and thus is a poor and unjust approach to science, grossly misleading their audiences. Even so, let us consider some noteworthy cases suggestive of survival that are on public record.

Following Rees (1971), Julian Burton was the next person to complete a doctoral study on the commonality of anomalous experience in bereavement and their characteristics (Burton, 1980). He began this academic attempt to understand such reports after he had such an experience regarding of his own mother, who had died seven months prior to the episode. It was recalled as follows:

> I had always felt a strong bond between us but by September most of us in the family had returned to our routines, reconciled to her death. One evening that September my wife and I were entertaining relatives. I was in the kitchen cutting a pineapple when I heard what I thought were my wife's footsteps behind me to the right. I turned to ask the whereabouts

of a bowl but realized that she had crossed to the left outside of my field of vision. I turned in that direction to repeat my question *and saw my mother standing there.*

(Burton, 1982, p. 65)

Burton said his mother's apparition looked 10 years younger than she appeared when she died and was in good health; however, she was wearing a detailed pale-blue gown which he had never seen before. He continued:

> "Ma!" I exclaimed. She smiled – and then dissolved. She did not disap-pear; she dissolved. I let out a great sigh and felt as if a heavy weight had been lifted from me, a weight I had not even felt until then.

(ibid)

The next morning Burton related his experience to his sister who, he said, became upset, not because of the occurrence he described, but largely because she had not had such an experience herself. However, she believed Burton's account because two weeks before their mother's death, she had taken their mother shopping, and recalled their mother having tried on a pale-blue gown that matched Burton's description. (Their mother didn't buy the gown because the price was too high.) Burton's experience confirmed survival of death for both siblings, and established a form of continued bond for Burton, stating that "The experience had a pro-found effect on me; it encouraged me to make a major change in my life" (p. 68). This major change is what pushed Burton back into education to take on a PhD at the age of 42, to understand more about such experiences in the wider population.

Baird (1944) compiled an important collection of cases suggestive of survival encompassing eleven different forms of parapsychological phenomena. Within this, apparitions of the dead were discussed with some falling within the category of "bereavement-type phenomena." Interestingly, in the majority of experiences, as noted previously in this chapter, the cases involved witnessing an apparition of a deceased person before the experient knew that person to be dead. And yet, the time of the experience coincided with the time of death and veridical information was received by the experient. Even so, below is a classic example from Baird's compilation of the apparition occurring sometime following conscious awareness of the loss. It was originally reported in the *Proceedings of the Society for Psychical Research* (volume 5), and is summarized here from Baird's (1944) presentation:

> In 1867, my older sister, a young lady of eighteen years, died suddenly of cholera in St. Louis, Mo. My attachment for her was very strong, and the blow a severe one to me. A year or so after her death the writer became a commercial traveller, and it was in 1876, while on one of my western trips, that the event occurred.
>
> I had "drummed" the city of St. Joseph, Mo., and had gone to my room at the Pacific House to send in my orders, which were unusu-ally large ones, so that I was in a very happy frame of mind indeed.

My thoughts, of course, were about these orders, knowing how pleased my house would be at my success. I had not been thinking of my late sister, or in any manner reflecting on the past. The hour was high noon, and the sun was shining cheerfully into my room. While busily smoking a cigar and writing out my orders, I suddenly became conscious that someone was sitting on my left with one arm resting on the table. Quick as a flash I turned and distinctly saw the form of my dead sister, and for a brief second or so looked her squarely in the face; and so sure was I that it was she, that I sprang forward in delight, calling her by name, and as I did so the apparition instantly vanished. Naturally, I was startled and dumbfounded, almost doubting my senses; but with the cigar in my mouth, and pen in hand, with the ink still moist on my letter, I satisfied myself that I had not been dreaming and was wide awake. I was near enough to touch her, had it been a physical possibility, and noted her features, expression, and details of dress, etc. She appeared as if alive. Her eyes looked kindly and perfectly naturally into mine. Her skin was so lifelike that I could see the glow or moisture on its surface, and, on the whole, there was no change in her appearance otherwise than when alive.

Now comes the most remarkable *confirmation* of my statement, which cannot be doubted by those who know what I state actually occurred. This visitation, or whatever you may call it, so impressed me that I took the next train home, and in the presence of my parents, and others, I related what had occurred. My father, a man of rare good sense and very practical, was inclined to ridicule me, as he saw how earnestly I believed what I had stated; but he too, was amazed when later on I told them of a bright red line or *scratch* on the right hand side of my sister's face, which I distinctly had seen. When I mentioned this my mother rose trembling to her feet and nearly fainted away, and as soon as she sufficiently recovered her self-possession, with tears streaming down her face she exclaimed that I had indeed seen my sister, as no living mortal but herself was aware of the scratch, which she had accidently made while doing some little act of kindness after my sister's death. She said she well remembered how pained she was to think that she should have unintentionally marred the features of her dead daughter and, unknown to all, how she had carefully obliterated all traces of the slight scratch with the aid of powder, etc., and that she had never mentioned it to a human being from that day to this. In proof, neither my father nor any of our family had detected it and positively were unaware of the incident, yet *I saw the scratch as bright as if just made.*

(quoted by Baird, 1944, pp. 64–5)

Taking these cases into consideration, and reflecting on my own work with the bereaved who reported spontaneous experiences following loss (Cooper, 2016a), some similar features which could meet the criteria of "possible evidence for survival" do appear present in contemporary cases. To briefly discuss one such incident, the fact of multiple witnesses involved makes the case most intriguing. One participant in my research – a nurse of many years' experience especially with the terminally ill – witnessed the passing of her own husband while sitting by his hospital bed. Jane [pseudonym] reported that her mobile phone immediately began acting irregularly and would not work, which she personally found most peculiar in light of what had just happened. During her husband's illness, he had said that if he did survive beyond death, that he would give her a sign. In the week that followed, a number of unusual events happened in Jane's life, especially around the home. A number of electrical disturbances occurred including the electric car windows playing up and not closing, which held personal meaning for Jane (due to discussions and experiences Jane had had with her husband regarding the car before he passed), and sense of presence experiences were encountered (see Wright, 1998, for similar examples of this phenomenon). At the funeral, which took place within two weeks of her husband's passing, Jane reported the following event during interview:

> My brother-in-law and his girlfriend sat down at the table with their drinks and they put the girlfriend's drink right on the inside of the table, and the drink proceeded to be pushed off the table and fell on the floor, and the actual glass landed up, it didn't fall it landed actually on the actual base . . . the drink spilt but the glass didn't smash.
> *(Cooper, 2017; see Appendix for interviewee profiles)*

Jane reported that she did not personally witness this incident, but it was witnessed by her brother-in-law, his girlfriend, and seven other witnesses close by. She immediately went to see what all the commotion was about and was told straight away of what had happened. Her brother-in-law was reportedly lost for how to explain what had been seen, and subsequently became more open minded to the possibility of life after death. The table had been covered with a table cloth, and so the glass could not naturally have slid against the table due to any possible condensation or spillage from the glass. Jane also noted that she had not reported her anomalous experiences prior to that day to anyone. The event at the wake was witnessed by nine people in total, and confirmed for her that these occurrences were objective and signs of her husband's survival from which she gained great comfort.

Thoughts on the Reality of Survival

It has been argued by Gauld (2005) that what exactly would constitute evidence for survival of death is by no means clear or agreed upon. Some people are too quick to jump to conclusions of evidence for survival from experiences (and in bereavement events that is understandable on the part of the bereaved), while for other people, no amount of empirical findings would personally convince them of survival. Even though Gurney and Myers (1889) argued that either *veridical information* or *multiple witnesses* should be involved to begin to constitute a possible case for survival, extensive debate within parapsychology since that time has cast some doubt over these two features and their potential for providing concrete evidence for survival.

Burton (1982) commented at the end of his study that "It is certainly interesting, in this regard, that when a person has been contacted, he knows exactly what has happened. He needs no formal 'proof' that he has had a valid experience" (p. 73). From a scientific point of view, we require more than this personal interpretation to persuade us of survival being a possibility. It would seem, however, as pointed out by Gurney (with Myers, 1889), that if we apply simple investigation to such common experiences of the bereaved, we can discover the elements of the experience which would suggest survival of death. It is simply a case of considering all avenues of conventional explanations and cautiously applying Occam's razor (Martínez-Taboas, 1983; Romer, 1996) to identify the conventional explanations that would apply to the experience that is being perceived as survival. In other words, we would accept the fewest assumptions required as possible to explain the phenomena.

Murphy (1943) proposed the notion of active and passive telepathy against the problem of survival evidence. In short, he stated that if there are apparently no conventional explanations for the phenomena encountered, then we must assume that some form of extra sensory-perception (ESP) is responsible. However, who activates this ESP becomes another question. For example, are the deceased communicating with the living via such means, or is the experience generated by some living agent projecting hallucinations and information about the deceased via some form of ESP? This could even account for instances of multiple witnesses to an apparitional encounter, where one witness has unconsciously created the hallucinatory imagery for everyone else to bear witness via a telepathic process (see Rao, 1986).

Where conventional explanations do not appear to account for the phenomena witnessed, Occam's razor would still lead us to question the presence of ESP, but to support this assumption would strongly suggest that the experience is more likely the creation of a living mind than that of the deceased communicating with the living through telepathic means. The only objection Murphy (1943) could place to this assumption is that we must ask ourselves who instigated the experience? If a bereaved individual is actively thinking about the deceased, then it is most likely *they* who generated the experience through some form of cognitive process not yet fully understood. However, if the experient was engaged in a particular task, or conversation with other people, etc., and not actively thinking about the deceased (though there is the possibility of them unconsciously ruminating about the deceased), the possible explanations for such experiences would lead to several possible conclusions, which still leaves some scope for the reality of survival – as none of the conclusions could be empirically confirmed through scientific means, or indeed disproven. This simply emphasizes the difficulties involved in researching and understanding phenomena that by their very nature occur spontaneously, and leaving almost entirely nothing but anecdotal evidence.

Trying to determine what generated the experience currently remains almost impossible to assess; as John Palmer has argued in such cases, "the demonstration of psi says nothing directly about the source of the psi – in particular whether it was a discarnate entity" (see Cooper, 2012, p. 171). In more recent decades, this debate has grown in popularity through the "Super-psi hypothesis" (Braude, 1992) and what William Roll termed "the catch-22 of survival" (Roll, 1980). Essentially, we are faced with the problem that once conventional explanations are suitably ruled out, it becomes difficult to separate instances of ESP (or other forms of psi) from survival. Further to that, ESP could be responsible for the interpretation of survival within a given experience, and by following Occam's razor, it would appear on the surface more likely to assume that the experience was generated by the living than by the surviving consciousness of the deceased. John Randall proposed that we need to work harder on trying to develop a method for separating one from the other, if indeed that is at all possible (see Cooper, 2012, p. 167). Further to this debate, Storm (2006) discussed "radical survivalism" in relation to rethinking all survival-type experiences. He argued that since knowledge itself cannot be destroyed, consciousness is somehow able to dip into this pool from time to time and obtain knowledge which experients would assume was known only by the deceased. This debate in itself could be considered an extension of the super-psi hypothesis, but takes into account Jungian theory (Jung, 1960) and modern psychological thought on consciousness research in light of parapsychology (Braude, 2003; Thalbourne, 2004).

When we survey the wide array of arguments for survival (e.g., Coly & McMahon, 1993; Gauld, 1977; Storm & Thalbourne, 2006), there do appear to be instances where we have to make greater steps/assumptions through Occam's razor to assume ESP is responsible for the interpretation of survival if we are to accept the experience was generated on the part of the living. For example, in the case of the bereaved who witness phenomena attributed to the deceased, their conscious knowledge of personal loss and the symptoms of mourning have been argued as responsible for creating the events (e.g., Baker, 1996). However, survival becomes more of a greater possible conclusion when the experient does not discover until after the anomalous event that the person they envisioned was dead at the time of that experience. Such a case would not constitute a bereavement encounter, given that the experient has no conscious knowledge of being in loss. Therefore, if we consider survival evidence presented only within the context of bereavement, further conventional psychological explanations begin to pile up and move the possibility of survival further away. These explanations could especially include misinterpretation of events and false memory, which are the typical sceptical assumptions we may first investigate.

Sudduth (2016) has presented a detailed philosophical critique of the typical arguments in favour of survival. In short, he concluded that in many accounts argued as evidence for survival, it *might* be the case that these are genuine examples of survival; however, when examining them against *classical arguments*, they do not appear to constitute evidence for survival at all, or at least not *good* evidence.

Cases can be discovered to have pitfalls against the existing classical theories for survival which lead to alternative explanations, and can often fall within the remit of currently understood paradigms. Sudduth concludes that a good empirical argument for survival is not impossible, but we do not currently possess one, based on the kinds of research data presently available. This would further emphasize John Randall's point (see Cooper, 2012, p. 167) and that of Storm (2006), in that now is the time to refine what we know about evidence we label as survival and develop a better experimental system for assessing the data and what would truly constitute survival without room for alternative explanations. It is perhaps the case that the more we begin to understand about consciousness itself, the more likely this process of refining the assessment for survival is to become.

Conclusion

In this chapter, the commonality and general features of spontaneous anomalous experiences during a time of bereavement have been briefly defined and outlined. From there, examples of experiences suggestive of survival of death were also discussed, namely being instances of *veridical information* being received during the experience from the perceived deceased, or *multiple witnesses* to the event. In very briefly considering some of the key thoughts on survival, it is evident that what would truly constitute empirical evidence for survival is neither clear nor agreed upon throughout scientific inquiry into such events. Although the two demands put forth have been demonstrated in many cases, with no apparent conventional explanations for their occurrence, there is still room in some cases for alternative theoretical assumptions to account for the phenomenon. Therefore, it is possible that spontaneous anomalous experiences during bereavement can be instances of the surviving personality of the deceased, contacting a bereaved living individual. How we go about objectively demonstrating this is still beyond the realms of current scientific understanding, and stands shoulder to shoulder with the hard problem of consciousness.

References

Baird, A. T. (Ed.). (1944). *One hundred cases for survival after death*. New York, NY: Bernard Ackerman.

Baker, R. A. (1996). *Hidden memories: Voices and visions from within*. New York, NY: Prometheus Books.

Berger, A. S. (1988). *Evidence of life after death: A casebook for the tough-minded*. Springfield, IL: Charles C. Thomas Pub.

Betty, S. (2016). *When did you ever become less by dying? Afterlife: The evidence*. Hove: White Crow Books.

Braude, S. E. (1992). Survival or super-psi? *Journal of Scientific Exploration, 6*, 127–144.

Braude, S. E. (2003). *Immortal remains: The evidence for life after death*. New York, NY: Rowman and Littlefield.

Burton, J. (1980). *Survivors' subjective experiences of the deceased*. Unpublished doctoral thesis, International College, Los Angeles, CA.

Burton, J. (1982). Contact with the dead: A common experience? *Fate, 35*(4), 65–73.

Castelnovo, A., Cavallotti, S., Gambini, O., & D'Agostino, A. (2015). Post-bereavement hallucinatory experiences: A critical overview of population and clinical studies. *Journal of Affective Disorders, 186,* 266–274.

Coly, L., & McMahon, J. D. S. (Eds) (1993). *Parapsychology and thanatology: Proceedings of an international conference.* New York, NY: Parapsychology Foundation.

Cooper, C. E. (2012). *Telephone calls from the dead: A revised look at the phenomenon thirty years on.* Old Portsmouth, UK: Tricorn Books.

Cooper, C. E. (2016). The therapeutic nature of anomalous events: A union of positive psychology and parapsychology. In M.D. Smith, & P. Worth (Eds), *2nd applied positive psychology symposium: Proceedings of presented papers* (pp. 98–107). High Wycombe, UK: Bucks New University.

Cooper, C. E. (2017) *Spontaneous post-death experiences and the cognition of hope: An examination of bereavement and recovery.* Unpublished doctoral thesis, University of Northampton, Northampton, UK.

Cooper, C. E., Roe, C. A., & Mitchell, G. (2015). Anomalous experiences and the bereavement process. In T. Cattoi & C. Moreman (Eds), *Death, dying and mysticism: The ecstasy of the end* (pp. 117–131). New York, NY: Palgrave Macmillan.

Fontana, D. (2005). *Is there an afterlife? A comprehensive overview of the evidence.* Blue Ridge Summit, PA: O-Books.

Fontana, D. (2007). Why the opposition to evidence for survival? *Network Review, 93,* 3–6.

Gauld, A. (1977). Discarnate survival. In B. B. Wolman (Ed.), *Handbook of parapsychology* (pp. 577–630). New York, NY: Van Nostrand Reinhold Co.

Gauld, A. (2005). Survival. In J. Henry (Ed.), *Parapsychology: Research on exceptional experiences* (pp. 215–223). London: Routledge.

Gauld, A. (2010). Reflections. *Mindfield, 2*(1), 6–7.

Gurney, E., with Myers, F. W. H. (1889). On apparitions occurring soon after death. *Proceedings of the Society for Psychical Research, 5,* 403–485.

Gurney, E., Myers, F. W. H., & Podmore, F. (1886). *Phantasms of the living* (2 vols.). London: Trübner.

Horn, S. (2009). *Unbelievable.* New York, NY: HarperCollins.

Jung, C. G. (1960). *The structure and dynamics of the psyche.* Princeton, NJ: Princeton University Press.

Kramer, W. H., Bauer, E., & Hövelmann, G. H. (Eds). (2012). *Perspectives of clinical parapsychology.* Bunnik: Stichting Het Johan Borgman Fonds.

Krippner, S. (2006). Getting through the grief: After-death communication experiences and their effects on experients. In L. Storm & M. A. Thalbourne (Eds), *The survival of human consciousness* (pp. 174–193). London: McFarland & Co.

Martínez-Taboas, A. (1983). Uses and abuses of Occam's razor in parapsychology. *Journal of the Society for Psychical Research, 52,* 128–132.

McAdams, E. E., & Bayless, R. (1981). *The case for life after death: Parapsychologists look at the evidence.* Chicago, IL: Nelson-Hall.

Murphy, G. (1943). Spontaneous telepathy and the problem of survival. *Journal of Parapsychology, 7,* 50–60.

Myers, F. W. H. (1903). *Human personality and its survival of bodily death* (2 vols.). London: Longmans & Co.

Rao, K. R. (1986). L. E. Rhine on psi and its place. In K. R. Rao (Ed.), *Case studies in parapsychology in honor of Dr. Louisa E. Rhine* (pp. 52–62). Jefferson, NC: McFarland & Co.

Rees, W. D. (1971). The hallucinations of widowhood. *British Medical Journal, 4,* 37–41.

Rees, W. D. (2000). The bereaved and the dead. *Christian Parapsychologist, 14*(3), 81–86.

Robertson, T. J. (2013). *Things you can do when you're dead: True accounts of after death communication.* Guildford: White Crow Books.

Rogo, D. S. (1986). *Life after death: The case for survival of bodily death.* London: Guild.

Roll, W. G. (1980). The catch 22 of survival research. *Journal of the Academy of Religion and Psychical Research, 3*, 23–24.

Romer, C. (1996). The poverty theory: Notes on the investigation of spontaneous cases. *Journal of the Society for Psychical Research, 62*, 161–163.

Roxburgh, E., & Evenden, R. (2016). "They daren't tell people": Therapists' experiences of working with clients who report anomalous experiences. *European Journal of Psychotherapy & Counselling, 18*(2), 123–141.

Smith, M. D. (2010). Preface. In M. D. Smith (Ed.), *Anomalous experiences: Essays from parapsychological and psychological perspectives* (pp. 1–4). Jefferson, NC: McFarland.

Steffen, E., Wilde, D., & Cooper, C. E. (in press). Affirming the positive in anomalous experiences: A challenge to dominant accounts of reality, life and death. In N. J. L. Brown, T. Lomas, & F. J. Eiroá (Eds), *International handbook of critical positive psychology: A synthesis for social change*. London: Routledge.

Storm, L. (2006). A solution: Radical survivalism. In L. Storm & M. A. Thalbourne (Eds), *The survival of human consciousness: Essays on the possibility of life after death* (pp. 285–300). Jefferson, NC: McFarland.

Storm, L., & Thalbourne, M.A. (Eds). (2006). *The survival of human consciousness: Essays on the possibility of life after death*. Jefferson, NC: McFarland.

Sudduth, M. (2016). *A philosophical critique of empirical arguments for post-mortem survival*. New York, NY: Palgrave.

Thalbourne, M. A. (2004). *The common thread between ESP and PK*. New York, NY: Parapsychology Foundation.

Thomas, J. F. (1929). *Case studies bearing upon survival*. Boston, MA: Boston Society for Psychic Research.

Thomas, K., & Cooper, C. E. (2016). *Investigation of viewer opinions on the use of "science" in paranormal reality television shows*. Paper presented at the 40th International Conference of the Society for Psychical Research, University of Leeds, Leeds, UK.

Weiner, D. H., & Haight, J. (1986). Charting hidden channels: Louisa E. Rhine's case collection project. In K. R. Rao (Ed.), *Case studies in parapsychology in honor of Dr. Louisa E. Rhine* (pp. 14–30). Jefferson, NC: McFarland & Co.

Winsper, A. R., Parsons, S. T., & O'Keeffe, C. J. (2008). *Have the lunatics taken over the (haunted) asylum?* Paper presented at the 32nd International Conference of the Society for Psychical Research held jointly with the Parapsychological Association, University of Winchester, Winchester, UK.

Wright, S. H. (1998). Experiences of spontaneous psychokinesis after bereavement. *Journal of the Society for Psychical Research, 62*, 385–395.

16

GRIEF, RITUAL AND EXPERIENTIAL KNOWLEDGE

A Philosophical Perspective

Anastasia Philippa Scrutton

Introduction

Rituals are significant for continuing bonds theory. The decline of rituals during World War I was partly responsible for the shift towards prescriptively short periods of grief, and the emphasis on severing bonds. Conversely, ancestor rituals were influential in the move back towards the idea that continuing bonds with the dead can be healthy and even beneficial (Steffen & Coyle, 2012). Self-help grief literature often advises people to create their own rituals, frequently in ways that involve continuing bonds, and empirical studies suggest that rituals are an effective way of alleviating painful elements of grief (Norton & Gino, forthcoming). Because of the decline of rituals, modern western societies are sometimes regarded as having insufficient therapeutic resources for grievers. Continuing bonds theory responds by turning to other cultures for wisdom that includes ritual when helping people respond to grief, and pointing to new rituals that are emerging informally within western society.

Despite the importance of rituals to continuing bonds theory, rituals are under-theorised in continuing bonds literature. This chapter will explore some reasons why rituals are important and powerful, contributing to our understanding of therapeutic practices for responding to grief. To set the scene for this, I will outline the rituals of two very different communities – those of Shona people in Zimbabwe and of Pagans in the United Kingdom – pointing to ways in which these might be seen to respond to features of grief highlighted by continuing bonds theory. Truth claims (formal doctrines and informal statements about the nature of reality) are often taken to be the most important and powerful aspects of religion and related phenomena, but I am interested in the ways in which the ritual aspect of religions and of human life more generally are important and powerful in distinctive ways. In particular, as I will argue, rituals are distinctively important and powerful because they are diachronic and narratival. As a result, they provide experiential knowledge or understanding of the view of reality that truth claims (for example, about the continued existence of the deceased) express more thinly. Furthermore, rituals are typically narratives that are sensorily rich, and so they enable the imaginative conceptualisation of perceived realities. In addition, because they are bodily, rituals can provide people with a more embedded and recalcitrant form of cognition than the more superficial forms provided by propositional means. Experiential and bodily forms of cognition are relevant when considering grief, because bereaved people undergo significant changes in their views of reality and relationships to it. In grief, this can include gaining a sense of the intelligibility of the deceased person's absence, and yet of their continued felt presence, and of a continuing but changing relationship with them. Ritual's relational character also contributes to its power and importance, because it enables grief to be shared and makes it a qualitatively different experience. At the end of the chapter, I will point to some of the implications of the account of ritual I have given for how we respond to grief in practice.

At the heart of this chapter is the idea that, while much talk of cognition is to do with asserting facts about the world that we can articulate in propositions (for example, the proposition "the earth goes round the sun"), not all cognition is of this propositional sort. Some cognition is experiential rather than propositional, such as knowledge of what it is like to see colours or what it is like to feel pain. This kind of cognition is experiential because it is acquired by having experience (e.g. of seeing colours or feeling pain). Furthermore, it can *only* be gained through experience – we would not really know what seeing colours or feeling pain is like purely from someone else's description of these things. The idea that I put forward in this paper is that experiential cognition is at the heart of ritual's power and importance. Because ritual is experiential, narratival, bodily and sensorily rich, it provides us with experiential cognition, which goes beyond the propositional cognition offered by truth claims. This makes ritual relevant for grief, because grief involves not only changes in propositional cognition (for example, "the person I love has died", "the world is now a different place", "my relationship with the person I loved who has died continues but is changed", "my relationship with others around me continues but is changed"). Grief also involves seeking and struggling to experience these things as true. Ritual's ability to provide experiential cognition is therefore relevant to grief, because it is a significant way in which people come to experience these and other elements of grief as real.

Rituals and Continuing Bonds: Two Case Studies

Shona Bereavement Rituals in Zimbabwe

Among the Shona people of Zimbabwe, there are around seven kinds of ritual that follow a person's death, which begin at the moment of their death and are spread over a number of years. Washing the body, mourning and comforting the family, burial and honouring the deceased person all take place within a few days of the person's death. Outside the times at which the rituals take place the grave is not visited because it is believed that the deceased person must be tired and need time to rest and should not be troubled too much (Mwandayi, 2011, p. 212). Around two weeks after the person's death there is a ritual of purification, the purpose of which is to "cool" any ire being felt by the spirit.

The "kurova guva" ritual takes place between one and two years after the person's death and has as its purpose the reintegration of the dead person into the family as an ancestor. Correspondingly, as Canisius Mwandayi says, "Grief, desire, even other things that may have been obstacles between the living and the dead are supposed to be brought to an end by this feast" (Mwandayi, 2011, p. 218). Prior to the ritual, the spirit wanders the earth, and if the kurova guva ritual is not performed, the spirit may sulk because the world has not shown proper respect or concern for them (Mwandayi, 2011). At the start of the kurova guva ritual, the entire community gathers and a small pot of beer is offered to the ancestors, informing them of the ceremony. A formal address is made to the spirit of the deceased person, telling them that this is their cleansing beer. Once this formal element of the beginning of the ritual is at an end, people drink beer and dance to music in honour of the deceased. The next day, the beer-offering is carried in a procession and is poured over the grave. Formal address is made to the deceased person to "come home". What happens after this differs among the various Shona people. Among the Valley Korekore, a pathway is made from the grave to the family home. There is singing, and the personal belongings of the deceased are distributed.

Following the kurova guva, the deceased person is treated as one of the ancestors who protects the family, and is honoured approximately annually at doro raanasekuru (or "beer of the ancestor") ritual. The Shona say that "once dead one is good", and ancestors are generally regarded as benevolent and protective presences. In cases where the deceased person was a significant moral failure, however, the kurova guva is not undertaken, and so they are not regarded as among the family ancestors (Mwandayi, 2011). Despite the fact that the ancestor is generally held to be good, they may nevertheless sometimes fail to protect the family adequately. In this case, the formal address to the ancestor at the doro raanasekuru is accompanied by reprimands and complaints (Mwandayi, 2011). Once these grievances have been aired, people clap and dance and drink beer in honour of the ancestor. In some circumstances the ancestor may also be regarded as angry and as having withdrawn their protection: in these kinds of cases there is also an appeasing ritual. The rituals of appeasement vary widely, and tend to depend upon the relationship between the victims and ancestor, the crime that may have provoked the ancestor's anger, and the nature of the misfortune that has befallen the family (Mwandayi, 2011).

Pagan Samhain

Paganism is a new religious movement that includes Druidry, Wicca, Shamanism and other groups, which take as their inspiration traditions of the past such as pre-Christian Saxons, Norse and Celts. The feast of Samhain (pronounced SOW-in) is thought by some to have its roots in pre-Christian Celtic religion and is celebrated at the same time as the Christian and secular festival of Halloween. In addition to being a time of harvest, Samhain is regarded as a liminal time when the boundary between this world and the other world can more easily be crossed, and a common saying in Paganism is that Samhain is the time at which "the veil between the worlds is thin". Many Pagans will do something to mark Samhain such as put out food for the dead or light candles for them, and some describe it as a time when people who have a "talent" for sensing the presence of the dead actively seek to contact departed loved ones.

Some Druid Pagans observe Samhain at a ritual in Avebury in Wiltshire, one of the most sacred Pagan sites. At 11pm on Samhain Eve, the community gather at the Red Lion pub and walk the avenue of stones that links Avebury town to the Sanctuary. The ritual begins about midnight, with the Keeper of the Stones beginning by "calling the quarters": turning to the four directions of the compass and welcoming the spirits associated with that direction. This is a typical way for any Druid ritual to begin and it is a way of setting the sacred space for the ritual to be done. The Keeper will then explain that Samhain is the time of year when the spirits of people who have died that year pass from our world to the "Summerlands" – a place of afterlife peace which the living are still able to connect to when invoking the ancestors. Druids commonly believe that while people die throughout the year, at Samhain they are gathered together and pass to the Summerlands together. Following the calling of the quarters everyone takes an apple from a bucket, and dedicates it to someone they know who has died. Sometimes the dedication is for a recent death, and sometimes it is for someone who is remembered every year. Following the dedications, people disperse, with a small group going back to the Keeper's cottage in the village where they hold a vigil over the apples for the remainder of the night, which takes place amid much drinking and joking. At dawn, the Keeper goes on his own to Swallowhead Spring, the source of the River Kennet – at this point, the Keeper will drop the apples as a symbol of life "renewed and recycled" (Wildcroft, personal correspondence, 9 November 2015).

Kurova Guva, Samhain and Continuing Bonds

How might these rituals relate to grief? Central to continuing bonds theory is the idea that in grief people often look for ways to continue to relate to the deceased. Furthermore, finding a way to continue to relate to the deceased can be and often is a healthy aspect of grief. As Phyllis Silverman puts it, "the bereaved maintain a link with the deceased that leads to the construction of a new relationship with him or her . . . Many mourners struggle with their need to find a place for the deceased in their lives" (Silverman, nd). Rituals such as the kurova guva and Samhain seem to make space for a continuing relationship with the deceased, rather than demanding that people sever ties with them for their grief to be healthy. In the case of the kurova guva, the deceased person returns to the family home; as an ancestor rather than a living family member his or her relationship with the living continues but is significantly changed. Samhain enables both a "letting go", though not a "breaking" of bonds, with the deceased, and the possibility of reunion with them at particular times in future years.

A second way in which these rituals are to do with grief relates to the fact that, as continuing bonds theory recognises, healthy grief is often lengthy and recurrent, and may even recur throughout a person's life, rather than being the swift process some psychologists have posited. Furthermore, grief can involve positive and life-enriching as well as negative hedonic experiences (Rosenblatt, 1996). Relatedly, grief is best understood as an experience through which people need support rather than a problem to be solved or an illness to be cured (Davies, 2002). Shona and Pagan rituals make space for a much longer period of bereavement than has often been regarded as healthy within western psychological and psychiatric literature, and for joyful as well as sorrowful experiences within it.

So far, (hopefully) so good – but on the points just mentioned we might substitute "doctrines" (or "truth claims" or "statements about reality") for "rituals", and make much the same points about how some religious traditions facilitate continuing bonds and make space for lengthy and recurrent grief. In what follows, I will explore some of the reasons why rituals in particular are important and powerful, and thus lend support to the continuing bonds intuitions that rituals are indeed significant and worth attending to in the context of grief.

Ritual

Ritual and Experiential Knowledge

One area of scholarship in which ritual is significantly theorised is Pagan Studies, since ritual is generally more important for Pagans than are doctrines or formal religious tenets, and since Pagan Studies scholars engage (as scholars and often also as practitioners) with Pagan understandings of ritual (see Ezzy, 2014). By emphasising ritual, some Pagans perceive themselves as challenging the preference for the intellective, non-physical and non-emotional that has often been found in western (and especially post-Enlightenment) culture. Thus, Douglas Ezzy argues that it is precisely the emphasis on the experiential, somatic and relational that draws many people to Paganism (Ezzy, 2014). Taking as a case study the erotic festival Faunalia, Ezzy describes the experience of one Pagan, an ex-Catholic, who finds that "While she stopped believing in the burning fires of Hell, it was only after her ritual work [at Faunalia] that the fires of Hell 'didn't feel real'" (Ezzy, 2014, p. 11). In Ezzy's words, through the ritual she moved from simply "knowing cognitively" that having sexual desire would not cause her to go to hell, to having her feelings about herself transformed in a deeper way (Ezzy, 2014, pp. 14–15). Therefore, symbols and rituals should not be understood only in terms of the cognitive, but also in terms of the experiential, emotional, aesthetic, somatic and relational – and to regard these as secondary is to miss aspects that are essential to ritual's power and importance (Ezzy, 2014).

Ezzy is surely right when he highlights the power of the experiential, somatic and relational in ritual and indicates that it affects people in ways that go deeper than is possible solely through assent to propositions. To use Ezzy's own example, solely assenting to the proposition "sexual desire will not cause me to go to Hell" might not transform a person's feelings about themselves as effectively as attending a Faunalia ritual, precisely because in the ritual the idea is experienced as true. At the same time, I argue that one important amendment is needed to Ezzy's analysis. Ezzy's account is problematic in that Ezzy in fact affirms a dualistic (intellective vs. bodily and affective) worldview by separating the experiential, emotional, somatic and so on from the cognitive. This is not only (as I interpret him) contrary to Ezzy's aims, but it also fails to be true to lived reality by overlooking the existence of experiential knowledge, with which emotions and the body have a particularly strong relationship. Recognising the existence of experiential knowledge can help us to make sense of the power and importance of the experiential and somatic elements of ritual in a way in which we cannot do if we regard experience, emotions, etc. as an amorphous, non-cognitive "other".

Experiential knowledge is knowledge that can only be known through experience and that is not reducible to propositions. That there is this kind of knowledge can be shown by the following thought experiment. Imagine a neuroscientist, Mary, who has researched everything about colour perception but has been confined for the entirety of her life in a black-and-white room so that she has never seen colour. If she were released from the black-and-white room into a world with colour, we would say that when she saw colour for the first time, Mary learned something new about colour and about perception of it – something inexpressible via propositions and inaccessible until she had had experience of it (Jackson, 1982). We might say that Mary had moved from having solely propositional knowledge of colour perception to having experiential knowledge of it: a particular kind of knowledge which can be gained by having experience of it and through no other means. Therefore, there is a kind of knowledge that is experiential, that is distinct from propositional knowledge, and for which propositional knowledge cannot be a substitute.

Of central importance here is that experiential knowledge is knowledge. As such, it is genuinely cognitive. To exclude experiential knowledge from the realm of the cognitive, for example by classing it as something else, is to adopt both the dualist's way of carving up human nature and, implicitly, even the prioritisation of propositional and "text book" forms of knowledge by classing these alone as knowledge and as cognitive.[1] When we recognise that experiential knowledge is genuinely cognitive, we can see that the transformation of deeper feelings that the person attending the Faunalia ritual reports is (like Mary's perception of colour) not an additional and separate thing from "knowing cognitively", but is a crucial – and infungible – element of it.

Experiential Knowledge and Narrative

Because it provides experiential cognition, ritual is distinct from the more propositional elements of religion articulated through truth claims (e.g. doctrines). In part, this is because ritual is narratival and narrative is particularly well equipped to provide us with experiential cognition. As narratives, rituals involve imaginative construals of (real or fictional) events that become more alive to us by virtue of our lived experience of them. Thus, for example, the Christian eucharist is a narrative about remembering or participating in the death of Jesus as a sacrifice for the sins of the world, and it involves other narratives within it, such as the story of the Last Supper conveyed in the Synoptic Gospels. The Samhain ritual is a narrative in some way about letting go of and in some way being in contact with the deceased, and it also involves a narrative about their journey to the Summerlands and continued existence there. The Shona rituals include a narrative about the journey of the deceased person, beginning from the time of their death when they are regarded as shocked and upset by their departure from the world of the living, to being reintegrated as one of the family ancestors. Thus rituals have the potential to bridge the gap between assenting to propositions such as that "Jesus suffered and died for us" or "the veil between the worlds is thin" or "the deceased person will return as one of the family ancestors", and having a more complete form of understanding or experiential cognition of what these things actually mean.

A related aspect of the fact that ritual is narratival is worth drawing attention to, despite being rather basic. This is that rituals, as narratival, are diachronic: rather than being instantaneous, they take place over a period of time. Time matters, because it gives us the possibility of having a richer kind of experience of something, and this contributes significantly and infungibly to our understanding of it. If we read a plot summary of a novel, even if it maintained the main elements of the story in compressed form we would be left with something far thinner and less powerful than if we immersed ourselves in the novel itself. By the same token, doctrines – often derived from religious practices rather than the reverse – are often compressed versions of what religious people think; they do not themselves give us adequate understanding of a person's religious worldview or what their faith entails. That rituals take place over time, as well as being narratival in the sense of telling a story, furthers our ability to see how rituals contribute to experiential knowledge and understanding.

The Senses and Imagination

Rituals are distinct from at least some other kinds of narrative (for example, novels) because rituals are often particularly sensorially rich. In keeping with the idea of narrative given above, anthropologists have sometimes understood healing rituals, in which we might include at least some bereavement rituals, in terms of Claude Lévi-Strauss' idea that in ritual an affliction is mapped onto a mythic landscape, and that healing occurs through the metaphorical journey from ritual to health, which causes changes in attention, cognition and experience (Lévi-Strauss, 1967). Rather than implying that the mythic landscape is necessarily fictional or false, "myths" in Anthropology are the cultural lenses through which we all interpret our experiences. "Metaphor" refers to thinking of one thing in terms of another – this might include not only words but also images. Thus, Bruce Kapferer argues that "the efficacy of much ritual is founded in its aesthetics", since rituals dramatize the journey from darkness and affliction to goodness and harmony in diverse sensory ways (Kapferer, 2006, p. 129). Cremating someone who has died and sprinkling their ashes in a special place, digging a path from the grave to the family home and letting go of a dedicated apple in a sacred space are sensorially rich metaphors of the deceased person's and the bereaved people's transitions, enabling the imaginative conceptualisation of particular narratives about what has happened, in a way that is more powerful than non-sensorily rich narratives are able to do. The involvement of the senses, through its ability to stimulate the imagination, is a further respect in which rituals contribute to distinctively experiential forms of cognition.

Bodily Ritual and Bodily Knowing

Discussion of the involvement of the senses in ritual highlights the fact that rituals frequently involve bodily activity in ways that assenting to religious doctrines (while requiring a physical brain) typically do not. Reflection on knowing how to play a musical instrument, ride a bicycle, or perform a dance suggests that distinctively bodily forms of cognition are one kind of experiential knowledge. For example, knowing how to play a musical instrument is both bodily and experiential, and is distinct from having propositional knowledge about how a musical instrument is played. If I read and perfectly understood and remembered a manual on how to play the flute but had never played it, I could not pick up a flute and begin to play it fluently. Might the idea of distinctively bodily forms of knowledge help our understanding of the importance and power of ritual?

Elsewhere, ritual has received attention not primarily in terms of distinctively bodily understanding and memory, but, rather, distinctively bodily forms of learning. Kevin Schilbrack argues that religious practices such as lighting candles (or, we might add, digging a path from a grave, or returning an apple to the earth) may be cognitive prosthetics or props, enabling us to investigate relevant aspects of reality – perhaps in these cases, to do with illumination and enlightenment, the return of the deceased to the family home, or the naturalness of death and the emergence of new life (Schilbrack, 2014). From an early age we gain our understanding of reality from our bodily engagement with the world, reflected in spatial metaphors such as "progressing in our career", "growing apart from a friend" and "getting sidetracked" from our tasks. In similar vein, Schilbrack argues, religious rituals and symbols can lead to the formation of abstract concepts which have the potential to correspond to propositional forms of knowledge.

This seems right to me. However, I think we might add to this that rituals and symbols might not only be a basis for abstract philosophical reflection, but also for bodily cognition that we might associate more with experiential knowledge and understanding than with the propositional cognition we associate with doctrines and religious tenets. This is perhaps why rituals are significant and potent not only for normally intellectual adults who might engage in abstract thinking about the nature of the world, but also for small children and adults with intellectual disabilities whose abstract cognition is undeveloped but whose bodily cognition is not. While understood in terms of the psychic unconscious rather than bodily cognition, this resonates with Jung's idea that symbols are powerful because they open up a psychic level that is primordial. We can explain some of this potency with reference to the interplay between past and present in bodily memory. As Thomas Fuchs puts it,

> In body memory, the situations and actions of the past are, as it were, all fused together without any of them standing out individually. . . . Body memory does not take one back to the past, but conveys an implicit effectiveness of the past in the present.
>
> *(Fuchs, n.d., p. 91)*

In a ritual involving lighting a candle, for example, we remember and bring with us in a general, unconscious and bodily way past examples of lighting candles, their meanings in those contexts and the people who were with us at the time. In this way, bodily rituals can act as cognitive prosthetics for or means of gaining distinctively bodily cognition such as body memories. Body memory is an especially powerful kind of cognition because it is typically deeply embedded and recalcitrant (Fuchs, n.d.). Thus, practices such as rituals that create and draw on body memory are particularly powerful aspects of human experience.

Relationality and Emotional-Cognitive Off-Loading

So far, I have looked at the ways in which rituals involve narratives, the senses, and the body to make sense of their power and importance, arguing that they stimulate the imagination and provide us with experiential forms of cognition that are distinct from and cannot be substituted by the propositional aspects of religion. In so doing, I have agreed with Ezzy (2014) that an account of ritual ought to have the experiential, emotional, sensory, and somatic as its centre, while arguing that these things are not separate from cognition but distinctive, infungible aspects of it. Ezzy's account also includes a focus on the relational within ritual, and it is to the relational in the context of grief and ritual that I will now turn.

In grief theory, bereaved people are sometimes described as engaged in "grief work" (Lindemann, 1944). This is generally understood in individualistic terms, but I suggest we might understand the very diverse processes people undergo following grief in more relational or collective ways. Consider Max Scheler's account of a couple's grief over the death of their child:

> Two parents stand beside the dead body of a beloved child. They feel in common the "same" sorrow, the "same" anguish. It is not as if A feels this sorrow and B feels it also, and moreover that they both know they are feeling it. No, it is a *feeling-in-common*. A's sorrow is in no way an "external" matter for B here, as it is e.g. for their friend, C, who joins them and commiserates "with them" or "upon their sorrow". On the

contrary, they feel it together, in the sense that they feel and experience in common, not only the same value-situation, but also the same keenness of emotion in regard to it. The sorrow, as value content, and the grief, as characterizing the functional relation thereto, are here *one and identical.*

(Scheler, 1954, p. 12f.)

According to Scheler, there is a sense in which an emotional state such as grief can be collective or shared which does not mean simply that it is the sum total of the parents' individual grief. Whether or not we want to subscribe to Scheler's stronger claim that these parents might feel precisely the same sorrow as one another, what is important in Scheler's account for our purposes is that the fact that the parents' grief is shared is an essential feature of their grief: it is one of the things that defines the quality of their grief such that, if it were not shared, their grief would have a very different phenomenal quality. The sharedness of their grief is not an additional property of it but something absolutely fundamental to it.

Responding to the case Scheler describes, Joel Krueger argues that sharing grief may be possible for the parents precisely because they have shared memories and stories, and had shared hopes about their child – they have a "diachronic narrative intimacy" comprising "an indefinite number of shared experiences, memories, and associations that define internal history unique to every family" (Krueger, 2015, p. 271). In addition to this diachronic dimension, there is also synchronic intimacy between them – they stand together, and, we might suppose, they will hold one another, weep together, and observe and respond to one another's bodily reactions (Krueger, 2015). In this case, their responses are therefore bound up with one another – and even integrated – in both synchronic and diachronic ways (Krueger, 2015). We might regard this as a kind of mutual (cognitive-emotional) "off-loading" because, rather than experiencing isolation and undertaking the "work" of grief alone, the parents are supported by one another, and their shared emotion intensifies their feelings of mutual understanding and connection.

The idea of shared grief enabled by synchronic and diachronic intimacy, and the way in which this may support people in the context of grief, is suggestive for our understanding of ritual. Rituals may help us share grief and even (if Scheler's stronger claim is correct) form collective kinds of grief, in which memories and stories about the person who has died can come together in a way that ensures that mourners do not undertake the emotional work of grief on their own. In other words, if grief can be shared partly as the result of synchronic and diachronic intimacy, then ritual may (by virtue of bringing about these things) be an instrument for the sharing of grief. While we might apply the idea of collective emotions to other kinds of ritual and other kinds of emotion, it is perhaps particularly important in the context of grief, because alienation and isolation are often significant features of grief. In bereavement rituals, synchronic intimacy is often created through the sharing of memories, bodily postures, and the temporal structure of the ritual accompanied by sensory stimulation (for example, music) during which different emotional states are encouraged at various times.

Because of the importance of diachronic intimacy for shared grief, shared grief and thus cognitive-emotional off-loading within or because of rituals is likely to be found especially within close-knit communities, whose shared experiences and memories and whose intimacy with one another make such off-loading possible. If this is right, then the relational and collective nature of ritual can be thought to contribute significantly to ritual's importance and power, in this case because it alters the experience of grief.

Practical Implications

What are the practical implications of this account of ritual? Grief therapy includes advice to people to create their own rituals, often in ways that resonate with emphases in continuing bonds theory. For example, one fairly typical self-help grief website advises people to create their own rituals, for example by lighting a candle at dinner time to represent sharing a meal with the deceased person, creating a special mix of music that reminds the bereaved person of them, visiting their burial site, or planting a tree in their honour (Helbert, 2011). Following some empirical studies in psychology, these therapeutic approaches tend to attribute the effectiveness of ritual to its capacity to provide people with a sense of control. Furthermore, they suggest, an extremely broad range of ritual activities might be effective in accomplishing this goal, some even indicating that the kind of ritual undertaken is completely irrelevant, provided that a ritual is undertaken (Vitelli, 2014; see Norton & Gino, forthcoming).

My account of ritual does not negate all of this advice, but it does suggest some rather different emphases. In particular, it suggests that ritual is important and powerful for reasons that are not only to do with regaining feelings of control. Rituals can also (for example) provide experiential understanding of the continuing relationship with the deceased that some formal religious doctrines seek to articulate. In addition, rituals can provide a means for creating shared grief, so that the quality of the grief becomes something different than the grief would be were the "grief work" undertaken by an individual alone. Implicit in these points is that the purpose of grief work and grief therapy might not be primarily to do with lessening feelings of grief and "getting over it", but, rather, with finding ways of integrating the death of the person into our lives. If my account of ritual is persuasive, then different rituals are not interchangeable and the form they take is important. Rituals that are diachronic and narratival, sensorily rich, and bodily and highly relational are likely to be powerful and important in ways in which rituals that are not these things are not.

Conclusion

There are many things that could be said about ritual, and about ritual in the context of grief. In this chapter, I have drawn attention to the experiential, narratival, sensory and somatic aspects of ritual. Because these aspects are distinctively cognitive, ritual can make a distinctive contribution to people's understanding of the world, including, in grief, their understanding of the changed and changing relationship with the person who has died. Furthermore, through the relational aspects of ritual, grief work need not be undertaken individually, and the experience of grief can become something different to what it would be were the person to experience it alone. This is significant for continuing bonds theory, supporting the continuing bonds intuition that ritual is important, and for therapeutic practice, suggesting that rituals that are narratival, diachronic, relational, bodily, and sensorially rich have a distinctive value and power.

Acknowledgements

A large number of people read or heard versions of this chapter and commented helpfully on aspects of it. It is not possible to mention everyone here, but particular thanks go to Jenny Uzzell, Theo Wildcroft, Matthew Ratcliffe, Benedict Smith, Joel Krueger, Mark Wynn, Emma Tomalin, Graham Harvey, Mikel Burley, Nick Wiltsher, Dennis Klass, and Edith Steffen.

Note

1 This presupposes that we attach a positive value to knowing and to cognition; however, this seems uncontroversial so I don't argue for it here.

References

Davies, D. (2002). *Death, rituals and belief* (2nd ed.). New York, NY: Continuum.

Ezzy, D. (2014). Reassembling religious symbols: The pagan god Baphomet. *Religion.* DOI: 10.1080/0048721X.2014.949898.

Fuchs, T. (Nd). Body memory and the unconscious. Available at www.klinikum. uniheidelberg.de/fileadmin/zpm/psychatrie/fuchs/Body_memory_Unconsious.pdf. Accessed 21 December 2015.

Gibson, J. (2003). Between truth and triviality. *British Journal of Aesthetics, 43*(3), 224–237.

Helbert, K. (2011). Creating rituals to move through grief. Available at www.goodtherapy. org/blog/creating-rituals-to-move-through-grief. Accessed 31 March 2016.

Jackson, F. (1982). Epiphenomenal qualia. *Philosophical Quarterly, 32*, 127–136.

Kapferer, B. (2006). Sorcery and the beautiful: A discourse on the aesthetics of ritual. In B. Kapferer & A. Hobart (Eds), *Aesthetics in performance: Formations of symbolic construction and experience*. New York, NY: Berghahn.

Klass, D., Silverman, P. R., & Nickman, S. L. (Eds). (1996). *Continuing bonds: New understandings of grief*. New York, NY: Routledge.

Krueger, J. (2015). The affective "we": Self-regulation and shared emotions. In T. Szanto & D. Moran (Eds), *The phenomenology of sociality: Discovering the "we"*. New York, NY; London: Routledge.

Lévi-Strauss, C. (1967). The effectiveness of symbols. In *Structural anthropology*. New York, NY: Basic Books.

Lindemann, E. (1944). Symptomology and management of acute grief. *American Journal of Psychiatry, 101*, 141–148.

Mwandayi, C. (2011). *Death and after-life rituals in the eyes of the Shona: Dialogue with Shona customs in the quest for authentic inculturation*. Bamberg, Germany: University of Bamberg Press.

Norton, M., & Gino, F. (Forthcoming). Rituals alleviate grieving for loved ones, lovers and lotteries. *Journal of Experimental Psychology*. Available at https://dash.harvard.edu/bitstream/handle/1/10683152/norton%20gino_rituals-and-grief.pdf?sequence=1. Accessed 31 March 2016.

Rosenblatt, P. C. (1996). Grief that does not end. In D. Klass, P. R. Silverman, & S. L. Nickman (Eds), *Continuing bonds: New understandings of grief*. London: Taylor & Francis.

Scheler, M. (1954). *The nature of sympathy* (Trans. P. Heath). London: Routledge and Kegan Paul.

Schilbrack, K. (2014). *Philosophy and the study of religions: A manifesto*. Chichester, Sussex: Wiley-Blackwell.

Silverman, P. R. (n.d). Continuing bonds. *Encyclopedia of death dying*. Available at www.deathreference.com/Ce-Da/Continuing-Bonds.html. Accessed 21 January 2016.

Steffen, E., & Coyle, A. (2012). "Sense of the presence" experiences in bereavement and their relationship to mental health: A critical examination of a continuing controversy. In C. Murray (Ed.), *Mental health and anomalous experience* (pp. 33–56). New York, NY: Nova Science Publishers.

Vitelli, R. (2014). Can rituals help us deal with grief? *Psychology Today*. Available at www.psychologytoday.com/blog/media-spotlight/201403/can-rituals-help-us-deal-grief. Accessed 5 July 2016.

SECTION IV

Continuing Bonds in Cultural Contexts

Introduction

Culture is a theme running through many chapters in this book. One way to deal with culture is to do studies of individual cultures or comparisons of two or three cultures. The assumption behind that method is that if we have an account of lots of cultures, then the patterns will be self-evident. We see the question as more complex than that. In this Section the authors explore how individuals interact with cultural narratives, how the grief narratives for particular deaths are created, how the bonds create social solidarity as well as personal identity, how different cultural contexts force us to rethink the descriptions formulated in Western contexts, and how not all continuing bonds are with the deceased.

Continuing Bonds' Complex Roles in Cultures

Christine Valentine describes the same dynamic in two cultures, Japan and Britain. The two have different models of identity, interdependency in Japan, individual autonomy in Britain. She says both post-industrial cultures provide multiple scripts for restructuring identity after a significant death. In both cultures, she says, bereaved people choose, combine, and adapt the scripts to fit their particular circumstances.

Continuing bonds also play significant roles in the creation of the narratives that communities shape to deal with particular deaths. Michael Robert Dennis and Adrianne Kunkel examine the literature of grief: eulogies, elegies, grief self-help books, grief accounts, and self-disclosures in research on grief. They describe writers and speakers remembering the dead, speaking for and to the dead, and searching for larger meanings as they use their personal search for meaning to articulate narratives on which others could scaffold theirs.

Renata MacDougal applies the idea of continuing bonds to some of humankind's oldest written texts, cuneiform tablets from the ancient Near East. The long-standing explanation of nineteenth and twentieth-century archeologists was that certain rituals were to placate hostile spirits of dead family members so they did not harm the living. Continuing bonds, of course, reflect our own culture, not the culture of those archeologists. With a continuing bonds lens, MacDougal finds the rituals maintain the dead as members of the family and thus promote social identity and solidarity.

The chapter by Candy Fong and Amy Chow reports research that points toward the complexity of continuing bonds within Chinese cultural contexts. They extend the idea of internalized and externalized bonds, and report qualitative research that charts the specific Chinese meanings of continuing bonds. They develop a new framework, the Value-Action-Sensation (VAS) model, that provides a structure for different forms of continuing bonds in a Chinese context

Hani Henry, William Stiles, and Mia Biran say the continuing bonds model helps us understand the experience of people who migrate from one culture to another, whether to escape violence or for better economic opportunities. Migrants lose shared values, traditions, social status, familiar patterns, and even the sense of self that is in their native language. "Like people mourning the loss of a loved one, immigrants preserve some inner representation of their native culture, history, and emotional ties to help them manage the challenges of immigration."

17

IDENTITY AND CONTINUING BONDS IN CROSS-CULTURAL PERSPECTIVE

Britain and Japan

Christine Valentine

Introduction

Adopting a cultural perspective, this chapter explores how responses to death and loss, particularly how people continue their relationships with those who have died, shed light on identity, agency, and social participation. By looking across cultures at an experience that threatens identity and continuity (Parkes, 1988), a broader, more in-depth, complex, and nuanced picture of continuing bonds emerges. Focusing on societies with contrasting models of identity, the chapter considers the implications of an emphasis on individualism in Britain and inter-dependency in Japan for recovering identity in each context. It asks, "How do people use available cultural scripts to make sense of 'unusual' experiences, such as those breaching the boundaries between the living and the dead?"

Drawing on qualitative interviews with British and Japanese mourners, the chapter illustrates the importance of continuing bonds with deceased loved ones for recovering identity. In focusing on two post-industrial societies with dif-fering understandings of identity, it examines the implications of individualism in Britain and interdependency in Japan for regaining a sense of self. By study-ing how mourners articulated their experiences in both contexts, this chapter exposes the limitations of both individualism and interdependency in capturing these. Specifically, it identifies how an emphasis on autonomy in Britain does not fully capture mourners' experiences of continuing relationships, while, in Japan, prioritizing the interdependence of the living, dying, and dead may pose problems for mourners bereaved through suicide. At the same time the chapter illustrates people's creative agency in adapting cultural scripts to accommodate such experiences, repair identities, and continue bonds.

As noted by Seale (1998), contemporary, late capitalist, consumerist societies provide multiple scripts for understanding and managing death and loss, for example official or expert discourse, media representations, conventional wisdom, and common-sense understandings. These scripts are not determinative but rather "raw materials that are strategically (though not always consciously) used in particular situations" (1998, p. 68). Studying how people choose from among cultural scripts, creatively combining and adapting these to deal with their particular and personal circumstance, illuminates the diversity within and between cultures, and how cultures overlap in complex and subtle ways.

The following cross-cultural comparison analyzes data from two successive interview studies, the first conducted in Britain and the second in Japan. Twenty-five bereaved individuals, 14 women and 11 men, aged 17 to 63, were interviewed in Bath, England, from 2004 to 2006; and 17 bereaved individuals, 13 women and four men, aged 29 to 63 in Tokyo, from 2007 to 2008.[1] In both studies interviewing was open-ended and conversational, allowing experiences of continuing bonds to emerge voluntarily. The following analyses draw on sub-samples of the two data-sets, interviews being purposively selected to best represent how individuals use available cultural scripts to convey "unusual" experiences, which may be harder to articulate.

Continuing Bonds in Britain

Studies of bereaved Westerners have evidenced the varied ways in which mourners relate to their dead and the dead maintain presence and influence in the lives of the living (Hallam & Hockey, 2001; Klass, Silverman, & Nickman, 1996; Unruh, 1983; Valentine, 2008; Walter, 1999). In Britain, where religious belief and practice have increasingly diversified (Davie, 2000), the idiosyncratic nature of these relationships may in part reflect a lack of grounding in shared traditional religious or cultural structures. Rather, they demonstrate a culture of individualism that respects diversity in how people mourn and remember their dead. Allowing scope for individual self-expression, this approach is reflected in increasing numbers of self-styled funerals (Davie, 2000). These "mixed economy" funerals celebrate the deceased's life and encourage mourners to make their own, frequently secular, contributions often within an essentially Christian framework.

The absence of a shared tradition of continuing bonds was evident in the British interviews. Mourners often conveyed embarrassment, or sought to justify their continuing bond with the deceased, wondering if they ought to have "moved on" or "got over it" by now, according to popular psychological discourse. Some disclosed that they rarely talked with others about such feelings and expressed surprise at the strength of their attachment to their dead that became apparent during the interview. The reported experiences of nine mourners, five women and four men, are analyzed using three themes that capture how the dead retained identity, presence, and agency by virtue of their relationships with the living: mutual affirmation; contact initiated by the dead; and contact as double-edged.

Individual Narratives

Mutual Affirmation

In keeping with the cultural emphasis on personal autonomy, individual choice, and self-determination, interviewees represented relationships with dead loved ones as mutually affirming. Interweaving individualism with ideas about inter-dependence and relatedness, they recounted experiences that validated both the relationship itself as well as the identities of both parties. For Anik,[2] aged 19, of Asian roots and Sikh faith, his own and his sister's continuing bond with their deceased father enabled them to "rise above" family discord that threatened the occasion that was dedicated to the scattering of his father's ashes, their efforts being a source of mutual pride:

> in India my mum was squabbling with my aunt from Canada and my brother was squabbling with me and my sister and my aunt and I thought, this is supposed to be time for my dad, you shouldn't be squabbling . . . and I felt proud of myself and my sister because we were making such an effort – and we thought, dad's looking down at us and probably thinking you're doing well guys, like you're making me proud.

Stephen, in his late 30s, acknowledged the pleasure his father would have taken in his studies, having been an academic himself. Drawing on supernatural ideas, he further conveyed the mutually affirming nature of their continuing bond, his father having "mysteriously" intervened to help him locate a particular book he needed for his studies.

> there's one book that I've been chasing around for quite a long time to do with my thesis . . . it's been out of print for a while and you know I've always thought to myself it would be really good if I could get hold of my own copy of it. Walked into the LSE bookshop . . . went to the second hand book section and there was one second hand copy. So basically it was . . . ooh did my father sort of mysteriously have that put on the shelf for me because he would know that would be a book that I was really really after?

Brian, in his 30s, described his mutually affirming bond with his grandmother in terms of her "supernatural" powers of seeing and knowing. Thus she was able to "see into'" and appreciate how her grandson's demeanor at her funeral demon-strated his ongoing affection for her.

I've no doubt she was watching her own funeral and from that point of view she knows how much I loved her and felt for her 'cos just by the way I acted at the funeral.

Contact Initiated by the Dead

Some mourners used supernatural ideas to represent continuing bonds as initiated not only by the living but also by the dead. Thus contact could be experienced via the senses, such as seeing, hearing, or being physically touched by the deceased person. In these cases mourners would often question their experiences in light of more "rational" or "common-sense" understandings that viewed such experiences as imaginary. In recalling these, mourners negotiated competing discourses of scientific rationality and supernaturalism, sometimes switching between the two. Their recollections demonstrated how, in contrast to rational attempts to explain such experiences away, supernaturalism provided a language that enabled mourners to assert their reality and power (Bennett & Bennett, 2000).

Elisabeth, aged 50, was convinced of the "reality" of her deceased husband's physical and verbal contact, finding this both reassuring and comforting. At the same time, she questioned the experience in light of the common-sense view that she had imagined it.

> I'll swear it was him . . . I felt a tap on my shoulder – I was asleep and he said it's alright love it's only me but everything's fine. And I swear to this day that I wasn't dreaming . . . I didn't know whether it was my imagination or not but I'm sure it wasn't – I thought well perhaps he's telling me it's ok you know get on with life and don't worry.

Sandra, aged 17, in sensing her deceased friend's presence, understood this as his way of supporting and comforting her early on in her grief. Religious and spiritual ideas about the soul's continuing existence beyond the physical realm enabled her to make sense and convey the impact of her experience. Yet, like Elisabeth, she also reverted to a more common-sense perspective, which explained the experience away.

> I felt like he was there with me. He hadn't left yet so I had him for a little bit longer. I kind of felt . . . that his soul wasn't gonna be around forever but I kind of felt he hadn't just gone, just totally disappeared . . . and sometimes it sounds really loony and I'll think am I making this up – did my mind just construct something because it helped?

For Pat, aged 40, the transformative impact of sensing her deceased aunt's presence served to validate its reality regardless of any rational attempts to explain it away.

> and then I just lost it and started crying . . . and I felt a hand on my back which was what she used to do when I'd leave . . . kind of gently

stroke . . . and I heard it will be ok – and things just kind of came to – all the rage and rawness . . . just like a deflated balloon. I don't know if I've conjured her up – it doesn't really matter – it works.

Contact as Double-Edged

In addition to providing mutual support and validation, experiences of the deceased's presence could be double-edged. While to some extent comforting and affirming, such presence could also be a poignant reminder of the person's absence, presence and absence being closely intertwined. Mourners negotiated this paradox using images of physical wounding and loss of bodily integrity to capture the experience of absence, with Adrian, aged 40, conveying how integral his father had been to his sense of identity.

> It's as though I have to live without my arms or something like that . . . but I can't put a finger on it because it's not visible . . . I have to try and learn to live without this vital – you know like my sight or something because that's how integral my dad was.

For Lynne, in her 50s, her mother's death left her with a wound that would never fully heal, yet would always remind her of their continuing bond:

> there's certain bits of you which they never actually quite heal over . . . in a way I'd rather feel that – it's sort of paying tribute to her . . . I'm not going to forget about her.

The body could also be experienced as a site of continuing presence through the sense of incorporating the deceased person within or as part of the self. For Stephen, embodying his father meant more than "being like" or "taking after" him, being experienced as his father living on inside him.

> There's almost a feeling that in some sense he lives on through me not just in a genetic way but a more personality way because we do things that are frequently quite similar and I might be doing or saying something and then suddenly think to myself, that's what my father used to do . . . so you almost feel as though the person's still living inside you.

Tania, in her 40s, felt comforted and affirmed by the sense that her mother was more a part of her in death.

> I kind of feel she's more part of me now – and what I like is the realization of just how much I'm like my mum . . . I get a lot of comfort from that.

These extracts capture the limitations of identity as discrete, bounded, and autonomous in making sense of loss. They illustrate how mourners negotiated competing discourses in attempting to validate experiences that defied more common-sense, rational forms of knowing. Such negotiation reflects how contemporary, late capitalist societies provide multiple scripts from which individuals may draw, adapting, revising, combining, and switching between or rejecting these according to individual and personal circumstances (Long, 2004). In Japan, similarly characterized by late capitalism, in spite of strong pressures for social conformity I found similar negotiations between personal and social imperatives, though in contrast to Western individualism, identity is relational. With interdependence and mutual obligation in continuing bonds being long-established and culturally sanctioned, mourners are less likely to feel obliged to justify or question the validity of such experiences. Yet mutuality too had its limitations, particularly in making sense of "bad" deaths.

Continuing Bonds in Japan

In contemporary Japan, as in Britain, the way people die and mourn is shaped by a system of medicalized dying, commercialized mourning, and various forms of bereavement care services. The institutions involved promote ideas linked to bio-medicine, consumerism, and human rights, such as patient/client autonomy, awareness, control, and self-responsibility, through open disclosure, personal involvement, and choice (Seale, 2000). These ideas reflect a Western, particularly Anglophone model of identity, which prioritizes personal autonomy, freedom of choice, and self-determination. However, in Japan they are understood and negotiated in a context where interdependence predominates, identity defined by one's role in the group rather than personal priorities (Tsuji, 2005). Relationships based on reciprocity, gratitude, and loyalty find expression in receiving and returning favors. Self-assertion and pursuing one's own goals, so valued in Western, particularly Anglophone societies, tend to be viewed as selfish and arrogant. Rather the individual's relationship to the wider community is based on conformity to the group and sensitivity to the needs of others so as to foster and maintain harmonious relationships (Ohnuki-Tierney, 1994).

Cultivating sensitivity to others is particularly important with those who are dying, family care-givers being expected to provide not only physical, but also emotional and psychological care. Creating a harmonious atmosphere to protect the dying person from distress and boost their spirits is a priority, in some cases keeping the person from their terminal condition. Being present at the moment of death assumes particular importance, both for affirming familial solidarity and witnessing the person's dying demeanor. Evidence of having fulfilled care-giving obligations is sought from the person's "peaceful face" in death as embodying dignity in dying and gratitude to carers (Long, 2004).

Following a death, bereaved families typically engage in a series of collective and domestic Buddhist rites, known as *sosen sūhai* or ancestor veneration to support the deceased's smooth passage to the afterlife and eventually ancestorhood (Valentine, 2010). These rites encompass funeral, cremation, and memorial services, grave visits, and home altar rituals designed to reinforce and perpetuate continuing bonds between the living and the dead. These bonds are linked to the kinship ties of the traditional extended household or *ie* system that underpinned a predominantly agrarian society. This system accorded ancestorhood special veneration, depending not on individual merit but on the family's continuing loyalty and devotion after death (Smith, 1974). Continuing bonds are an expression of family solidarity and continuity that transcends the life–death boundary. Defined by reciprocity and mutual dependency, the living provide care and comfort for the dead who in turn look out for the living.

Because of increasing urbanization, the *ie* system has largely given way to smaller family units and relationships of choice; people's lives and values having become increasingly secular, individual, and private. Yet the obligation to provide care and comfort to the spirits of those who have died and ensuring they remain connected to their families and the wider social world persists. However, fulfilling such obligations may pose difficulties for those bereaved by bad deaths, such as suicide, accidents, or murder, which may involve dying alone and away from home. Being sudden, unanticipated, premature, and violent, these deaths are believed to produce unsettled, unhappy, and potentially dangerous spirits, who may threaten the harmony and well-being of their families. These deaths may attract stigma to surviving loved ones who are considered to have failed in the care-giving obligations that would have ensured both the deceased person's well-being and a harmonious post-mortem bond.

Individual Narratives

From the sample of 17 Japanese mourners, three individuals, two women, and one man were bereaved as a result of suicide. Momoka, in her 20s, recalled her shock and disbelief on discovering that her best friend had thrown herself in front of a train, having spoken to her on the phone earlier that day. Kioshi, in his 30s, recalled how his sister, who was living in Paris and being treated in hospital for depression, came to throw herself out of her 16th-floor apartment window. Mieka, in her 40s, recounted how her younger brother, recently separated from his wife, threw himself over the railings on the 12th floor of an apartment block.

In trying to make sense of these deaths, which called into question their sense of integrity and reason to go on living, these three mourners interwove ideas associated with the ancestral tradition and day-to-day socialization with more contemporary medical, psychological, and spiritual understandings. In a culture of social conformity, they took a variety of positions on these ideas. Their narratives are analyzed using four themes that capture their responses to the death and the rituals that followed, the meanings they gave to the deceased's motives, and how they found a reason for going on living: the person's suffering face in death; traditional beliefs and practices; psychological explanations; and "experiences of difference."

The Person's Suffering Face in Death

Each of the three mourners remembered the deceased's face in death as embodying a suffering and wounded identity. Momoka reflected on how hard it must have been for her friend to take such a step; Kioshi recalled how his sister's face belied her pain; while Mieka was unprepared for the damage to her brother's face.

> When I saw her face at the funeral, because she jumped in front of a train there was blood between her teeth — she must have been very hurt and maybe deciding to commit suicide itself must have been very hard for her . . . she was so much loved by friends and she had a boyfriend. And looking around at all the people at the funeral I thought why couldn't any of us help her at all?
>
> *(Momoka)*

> It was difficult because she looked as though she was in pain — it wasn't as if she'd found peace — she had a very painful expression.
>
> *(Kioshi)*

> He had a very prominent nose but it was all buried in his head and it was very shocking and distressing to see him . . . and how much his face had deteriorated.
>
> *(Mieka)*

As indicated, suicide deaths are traditionally believed to produce unsettled, unhappy, and vengeful spirits who must be ritually pacified to prevent them threatening the harmony and well-being of their families. However, these three mourners were more concerned about how unsettled and unhappy the deceased had been in life. For Momoko and Kioshi, what threatened their harmony and well-being was having failed to read the signs that might have prevented the deaths. Reflecting on their telephone conversation, Momoka wondered if she had failed to appreciate the extent of her friend's loneliness:

> and I felt so guilty not coming to school when she called me. Probably she was in that room by herself — and it was raining and probably she felt even more lonely.

Kioshi reproached himself for failing to appreciate how depressed his sister had been.

> I think I should have taken a leave of absence from work and gone to Paris to be with my sister. But it's too late . . . but I have regrets that I should have gone and helped her.

Mieka reflected on feeling powerless in being the only one who seemed aware of her brother's struggle with bouts of depression, which she felt his wife did not take seriously.

> I was concerned that he should go to the hospital and have a proper consultation . . . But his wife was the kind of person who took all these things quite lightly and it was as though I was the only person who could see what might be coming.

Traditional Beliefs and Practices

Most Japanese people feel obliged to opt for a traditional Buddhist-style funeral, a typically lavish, ostentatious, highly formalized, and costly send-off, designed to affirm the deceased, not so much as an individual, but as part of a whole social network. The open coffin provides an opportunity for others to witness the deceased's peaceful face as evidence of the family having performed their duty. Suicide deaths may thus present a problem for social viewing, as Mieka explained, the violent nature of her brother's death having considerable impact on the funeral arrangements:

> you have a wake, then the funeral and then the cremation. But in my brother's case the body was so deteriorated that we didn't have a wake . . . we did the cremation first . . . and normally people say goodbye from a little window in the coffin, but in my brother's case they said the face was so badly damaged that we couldn't do this. So the fact that I couldn't say goodbye properly at the cremation was upsetting.

Kioshi's and his immediate family's decision to hold a more private ceremony at home reflected their sense of shame, the difficulty of accepting how his sister had died, and his father's aversion to religion.

> We asked the Buddhist priest to come to the house to do a ceremony. My father is really against religion . . . he has a view that it's all meaningless, so that's why we didn't do anything big. Also it was very shameful – and very difficult to accept, so that's why we didn't tell other family members what had happened.

In contrast, stigma was not apparent in the way Momoka's friend was mourned, her body placed in an open coffin, covered with flowers, at a traditional Buddhist funeral. Momoka, however, experienced the occasion as "really traumatic" with lasting impact in the way it affected her experience of a more recent funeral.

> Well, last week, one of our older scholars died and it all flashed back . . . I asked a friend from school to go with me and in fact it affected me very strongly . . . And also the coffin, when I saw the face in the coffin her face flashed back to me.

Psychological Explanations

In attempting to understand the suffering entailed in these deaths, the three mourners turned to psychology. For Momoka and Kioshi, this involved piecing together what they knew of the person's life to try to make sense of a death that seemed to belie the life lived:

> we would talk and laugh – she had a lot of humor – and a lot of friends – she even had a boyfriend. She wasn't really a person that anyone would expect to commit suicide. She was like a cheerful person and she died in the 3rd year of university and I saw her the day before she died, before she jumped in front of the train after school.
>
> *(Momoka)*

> She liked to study – she went to University in New York, did a Masters in Paris, she had two other degrees. I think she was capable of anything that she really wanted.
>
> *(Kioshi)*

However, Momoka had since discovered more about her friend's life that prompted her to revise her initial assessment, concluding that both she and close others had failed to appreciate her friend's suffering.

> She was brought up in New York and her father is a bank manager and very wealthy and her sister goes to the same university and is really smart . . . But my friend had her tongue pierced and . . . her parents didn't like her smoking. I also heard that her first experience of sex was with somebody she didn't know . . . a much older business man. So I think her self-esteem was very low . . . I feel so guilty because I didn't know any of this.

For Kioshi, a medical explanation in terms of depressive illness made some sense as having triggered his sister's suicide, though still leaving him to figure out why she was depressed in the first place. Nor did it absolve Kioshi of guilt and regret for failing to provide the help that might have prevented his sister from taking such a drastic step.

> At the time it was very difficult to understand what a mental illness is, that it was a disease – and now it's too late, but I have regrets that I should have helped her more.

Mieka, however, felt burdened by her prior knowledge of her brother's vulnerability. Though her expressed interest in psychology enabled her to read the signs, being unable to convince his wife left her unable to act on her concerns.

My brother from very young was able to see spirits so I thought this might have been some kind of mental problem. He kept repeating, even in front of his family, that he wanted to die and I felt a strong sense of crisis. I'd read a book on how to tell if people are suicidal – they spend lots of money, or have affairs and that's exactly what he did.

Experiencing Difference

In articulating how failing to prevent the death had undermined their sense of self and their relationship with the deceased, mourners also conveyed how they came to realize that they were also different and separate from the person. For Mieka and Momoka this entailed an encounter with their own suicidal impulses. Mieka recalled wanting to join her brother, yet being stopped by recalling his children's voices, these giving her a reason to go on living.

> I had this strong feeling that I wanted to die and follow him. Then when I visited his children in the flat on the 5th floor, I rang the bell and the little girl answered . . . I could hear the other two in the background. Then when I went up in the lift, instead of getting out on the 5th floor I got out on the 12th and tried to jump off the building like my brother did. But suddenly the children's voices came back to me and that stopped me jumping.

Reminding herself that her brother had still gone ahead in spite of having seen his youngest son "face to face just before he jumped," Mieka differentiated herself from her brother. She sought counseling support as a safety net for her suicidal impulses, talking about her loss eventually giving way to her preferred medium of craft work. Indeed she found herself making numerous collages that came to represent a process of healing and recovering her relationship with her brother and with herself.

> I felt if I do nothing about this feeling it would be very dangerous. So I started to see a counselor . . . and that really saved my life. But after a while I was so tired of talking, so because I like doing craft work I started making collages about six months after my brother's death. I wanted to try and connect with my brother and . . . heal my sadness.

In addition to counseling, Mieka drew on more traditional understandings to explain how her collage making enabled her to go on living.

> In Japan people say that after you commit suicide you will be locked in the dark, so by making collages I tried to lighten the darkness where my brother is and also to help his spirit. And I was in the darkness too so I needed some light for myself to save myself.

241

In her efforts to heal herself and her brother, she recognized that she had also nurtured a talent that subsequently enabled her to make collages for others.

> After this it has been mainly for other people – before this I did it for myself and for my own feelings and now I find it surprising that I now do it for other people.

Momoka too recalled how in attempting to follow her friend, she came to both understand her better and discover that she was separate from her.

> I took these pills and drank a lot . . . and had this feeling that I was apart from everybody, like you're going to a place you do not know and it was like a very lonely feeling and I started shaking. So I called my friend and – talk to me, I need to hear your voice. And my friend was shocked – and when she walked into my room she came over and slapped me. She said, don't you die by yourself. What am I going to do? Think about me. Then I realized what I was doing and I thought I have to live. But I also realized how my friend who committed suicide was probably feeling, like you're falling into a bottomless place.

Momoka's experience prompted her to visit a psychic healer who told her that her friend's suicide was not planned but impulsive and that she was no longer suffering. Though unable to take this on as a certainty, it offered an alternative version of events that raised questions about her friend's suffering and Momoka's responsibility for that suffering.

> After talking to the psychic healer I felt a certain distance from my friend. I still think of her, but hearing that it wasn't planned but an impulsive thing and that she's . . . no longer suffering, has brought me some relief. I don't really believe the power of psychic healing but it's like a possibility. So I began to think maybe I couldn't help, even though I knew she was depressed. But the feelings go back and forth, maybe I could have helped her?

Kioshi's solution to unbearable grief was to throw himself into his work. Yet when visiting the place where his sister had died, he suffered a series of panic attacks, causing him to identify with and better understand his sister's predicament. He also realized how the different ways they manifested their suffering affected how others responded to them.

> An anxiety attack is really hell and there's nothing you can do about it. That's when I thought, god this is what my sister went through. I couldn't imagine it until it happened to me – that's when I felt my sister's pain . . . I thought what's family for if you can't be there for your

family members, even if the situation is difficult? When I had my panic attack both my aunt and my mother were there for me, but my sister had nobody – partly due to her aggressive behavior.

Kioshi eventually learned to master his panic attacks with the help of counseling and various alternative self-help therapies. Failing to find relief for his guilt from traditional Buddhist practices or familial relationships based on harmonious interdependence, Kioshi converted to Catholicism. Interweaving religious and psychological ideas, Kioshi described how by putting his faith in a superior being he was able to contemplate letting go of his guilt and regret.

I felt my suffering and pain was too strong for any human being to understand and I had to rely on God . . . what I now realize is that I need to let go of all the guilt and regret.

These recollections illustrate the limitations of relational identity, particularly where the sense of separateness becomes crucial to survival – both physical and psycho-social – without the deceased.

Conclusion

In both contexts, mourners' experiences were shaped by dominant cultural understandings of identity, agency, and the individual's relationship to the wider socio-cultural environment. In Britain, where this relationship is based on personal autonomy and self-responsibility, more intersubjective experiences of identity were still evident in how mourners articulated continuing bonds, whether initiated by the living or the dead. Indeed relationships between the vulnerable living and disembodied dead offered mutual support, affirmation, and empowerment. In capturing such experiences, mourners drew on supernatural, including religious and spiritual, ideas to assert their reality and power. In sensing the deceased's presence, they would switch from supernaturalism to a more rational, common-sense position that questioned the "validity" of such experiences. Presence could evoke absence and a consequent painful sense of loss of integrity, mourners relying on images of embodiment as either painful experiences of physical wounding or positive reminders of continuing presence.

In Japan, where the individual's relationship to society is defined by interdependency and mutual obligation, mourners bereaved by suicide struggled to recover identities and continuing bonds that were spoiled by feelings of guilt and failure. Yet a sense of shared vulnerability with their dead evoked previously unacknowledged difference and separateness. Using medical, psychological, and spiritual ideas, they redefined relationships to enable them to go on living without the deceased. Mieka, in pursuing her interest in craft work, improvised a personal ritual through which she recovered her relationship with both her brother and herself, as well as discovering a unique talent. Momoka found an alternative explanation of events that created sufficient distance from which to be able to live with her friend's memory. Kioshi, by putting himself in the hands of a superior being, was able to consider the possibility of relinquishing his guilt and regret, having been unable to do so via traditional Buddhist forms or familial relationships based on harmonious interdependence.

The culture-specific nature of these experiences is apparent in how British mourners described their continuing bonds as diverse, idiosyncratic, and improvised, while Japanese mourners were grounded in a shared tradition of mutual obligation and harmonious interdependency across the life–death boundary. Both British and Japanese mourners showed how the lack of resonance between dominant norms and individual grief both challenged and engaged their personal resources in repairing identities and continuing bonds. In both contexts, the role of the person's creativity in adapting culture-specific beliefs and practices to accommodate personal circumstances was evident. Mourners' recollections conveyed the complex, ambiguous, and shifting ways that individuals interpret and negotiate cultural scripts to accommodate the pressures and contingencies of daily living. Such pressures and contingencies, being considerably magnified for those suffering bereavement, may be obscured by more generalized social categories and dominant cultural scripts. The reported experiences of how individual mourners from different socio-cultural contexts maintain continuing bonds with their dead may therefore provide an important source of data for further illuminating issues of identity, agency, and social participation.

Notes

1 Though based on small, purposive, and non-representative samples, these data provide a range of experiences and understandings that reflect common cultural themes and the diversity of responses beyond these samples.
2 Pseudonyms are used to protect interviewees' confidentiality.

References

Bennett, G., & Bennett, K. (2000). The presence of the dead: An empirical study. *Mortality, 5*(2), 139–157.
Davie, G. (2000). Religion in modern Britain: Changing sociological assumptions. *Sociology, 34*(1), 113–128.
Hallam, E., & Hockey, J. (2001). *Death, memory and material culture*. Oxford: Berg.
Klass, D., Silverman, P. R., & Nickman, S. L. (Eds). (1996). *Continuing bonds: New understandings of grief*. London, Philadelphia, PA: Taylor and Francis.
Long, S. (2004). Cultural scripts for a good death in Japan and the United States: Similarities and differences. *Social Science and Medicine, 58*(5), 913–928.
Ohnuki-Tierney, E. (1994). Brain death and organ transplantation: Cultural bases of medical technology. *Current Anthropology, 35*(3), 233–254.
Parkes, C. (1988). Bereavement as a psycho-social transition: Processes of adaption to change. *Journal of Social Issues, 44*(3), 53–65.
Seale, C. (1998). *Constructing death*. Cambridge: Cambridge University Press.
Seale, C. (2000). Changing patterns of death and dying. *Social Science and Medicine, 51*(6), 917–930.

Smith, R. J. (1974). *Ancestor worship in contemporary Japan*. Stanford, CA: Stanford University Press.

Tsuji, Yohko (2005). Mortuary rituals in Japan: The hegemony of tradition and the motivation of individuals. *Ethos, 34*(3), 391–443.

Unruh, D. (1983) Death and personal history: Strategies of identity preservation. *Social Problems, 30*(3), 340–351.

Valentine, C. (2008). *Bereavement narratives: Continuing bonds in the 21st Century*. New York, NY, London: Routledge.

Valentine. C. (2010). The role of the ancestral tradition in bereavement in contemporary Japanese society. *Mortality, 15*(4), 275–294.

Walter, T. (1999). *On bereavement: The culture of grief*. Maidenhead, Philadelphia, PA: Open University Press.

18

EVOLVING ROLES IN RESEARCH EXPLORING COMMUNICATION ABOUT GRIEF

Meaning Making and Continuing Bonds

Michael Robert Dennis and Adrianne Kunkel

Season 2 of the podcasting sensation, *Serial*, is an investigation of the strange case of Army Private Bowe Bergdahl. In episode 11, "Present for Duty," Andy and Sondra Andrews, informed for five years that their son, Darryn, a Second Lieutenant, had been killed by a rocket-propelled grenade on a mission to arrest a Talibani in Afghanistan, learn that he actually lost his life while searching for the AWOL Bergdahl. Mrs. Andrews recalled, "You know, we'd kind of fit the story into our life. We had, uh, talked about it. And now all of that was gone. We had a whole new story to get used to" ("Serial Transcript Episode 11: Present for Duty"; https://serialpodcast.org/season-two/11/present-for-duty/transcript). The experience of the Andrews family illustrates the roles of meaning making and communication about death and grief in the evolution of relationships with the deceased.

Motivated by our own experiences of loss, we began to merge our respective areas of interest, health communication, and interpersonal social support, in an effort to inform the discipline of grief scholarship. The resulting program of qualitative analyses has taken us on a two-decade journey across a wide range of different types of grief-related expression as we spotlight the relationship between grief-related psychology and communication. In doing so, our understanding of the association of continuing bonds, the making of meaning, and other valuable constructs has grown deeper and wider. In the sections that follow, we describe the most relevant findings from our interpretation of texts such as eulogies, elegies, grief self-help books, a genre we labeled "grief accounts," and self-disclosures about grief generated in social science experiments.

Eulogies: Expressions of Honor and Support at Funerals and Memorial Services

Eulogies are speeches delivered at funerals and memorial services that are crafted to positively affect the audience of mourners' evaluations of the deceased while also providing consolation to them. Kunkel and Dennis (2003) operated from the assumption that the memorialization aspects of eulogies are self-evident; eulogizers frequently (re)create impressions of the deceased as generous, brave, loving, and a host of other positive qualities, while also describing their note-worthy accomplishments. Indicators of the eulogistic obligation to soothe the grief-stricken audience have been less widespread and directions for doing so even more limited.

We decided to apply psychological constructs of coping and communicative strategies of interpersonal comforting to our analysis of contemporary eulogies. Our resulting framework of elements found commonly in eulogies instructs both their creation (and criticism) and includes: (a) establishment of credibility to eulogize; (b) praise for the deceased; (c) self-disclosure of emotion; (d) prescriptions for problem-focused coping in the form of suggested actions; and (e) promotion of emotion-focused coping forms of positive reappraisal (e.g., reference to after-life, appreciation of time(s) spent with the deceased) (Kunkel & Dennis, 2003). In subsequent investigations, we determined that specific subsets of eulogies, such as those provided for heroic figures by American presidents (Dennis & Kunkel, 2004), and for presidents by presidents (Dennis, Ridder, & Kunkel, 2006), feature elements of the framework but also varieties on the themes and rhetorical devices such as fostering common ground and unity. We believe that we have exposed how eulogies function to portray particular experiences of grief in its early stages, as well as narratives that depict and direct social, cultural, and personal meanings of bereavement.

In this chapter, however, we would like to expand on the final construct first discovered by Kunkel and Dennis (2003, pp. 7–8):

> (f) affirmation of vivid past relationships (e.g., notation of the deceased's flaws and revelation of private insights/relationships regarding the deceased) and continued interactive bonds (e.g., addressing the deceased and referring to the deceased in the present tense) with the deceased.

In early versions of the 2003 article, we devised a less-than-compelling ration-ale for our surprising discovery that eulogizers occasionally spoke directly to the deceased and sometimes portrayed their unique knowledge of them, includ-ing their secrets or even shortcomings. Thankfully, the Editor of *Death Studies*, Dr. Robert Neimeyer, introduced us to the burgeoning literature recognizing the utility of preserving and reshaping, rather than severing, valuable relationships and bonds with lost loved ones. We were then inclined to argue that audiences are encouraged to model the behavior of eulogizers in recalling distinct properties of the deceased, marking vivid relationships with them, and continuing interaction with them.

An example of affirming the real qualities of the deceased, sometimes in unflattering ways, is embodied in the words of Mae Negrino's granddaughter who eulogized her with, "Everyone in the family has a memory of the time Mae commented on their clothes, their weight or their choice in mates. Some would call her outspoken. Others would call her blunt" (Kunkel & Dennis, 2003, p. 15). Another comes from President Bill Clinton who revealed personal experiences with Richard Nixon: "For the past year, even in the final weeks of his life, he gave me his wise counsel, especially with regard to Russia" (Dennis et al., 2006, p. 341). Similarly, Noa Ben-Artzi Filosof divulged experiences with her grandfather, the assassinated Prime Minister of Israel, Yitzhak Rabin, that only she and other family members would know: "the caress of your warm, soft hands and the warm embrace that was just for us" (Kunkel & Dennis, 2003, p. 15). Earl Charles Spencer's expression of gratitude toward his sister, Princess Diana of Wales, is evidence that eulogizers may show how interaction with the dead can be maintained even in their wordly absences: "Today is our chance to say thank you for the way you brightened our lives even though God granted you but half a life" (Dennis & Kunkel, 2004, p. 711).

These observations marked our initial encounters with continuing bonds manifested in a distinct type of communication centered on the expression of grief. More nuanced interpretation of the phenomenon emerged as we expanded our scrutiny beyond the eulogy to other genres such as the elegy.

Elegies: Poetry About the Dead

Elegy is poetry that regards longing and mourning, while often featuring lamentation, melancholia, and idealization of the deceased. The elegy is noteworthy for its frequent provision of meaning associated with loss, consolation for writers and readers, and considerations of life and mortality. The representations in elegy range from "visions of bright and glorious afterlife for the deceased to gruesome description of a body during or after death" (Dennis, 2009, p. 401). Its tropes, such as the invocation of pastoral imagery, derive from origins in ancient Arabic and Greek societies. Renowned poets such as Ovid, Geoffrey Chaucer, John Donne, Percy Bysshe Shelley, Alfred Tennyson, and Ralph Waldo Emerson have contributed to the elegiac tradition.

Elegists may affirm relationships with the deceased by way of revealing attachments to them as "my cub, my kid, my nestling, my suckling, my colt" (Meehan, 2001, p. 274), by unveiling their frailties such as daughters fighting to ignore their departed mother's assertions (Rich, 2001), or by describing them vividly such as "big-boned and hardy handsome" (Hopkins, 2001, p. 284) or with "soft, indefinite-coloured hair" (Millay, 2001, p. 286). Bonds are continued as the deceased sit in God's house in comfort (Larkin, 2001), watch us on their heavenly television sets (Gunn, 2001, p. 141), and look for their shoes so as to "rise, like waves out of the hot fields" (Akers, 2001, p. 146).

Self-Help Books and Grief Accounts: Survivor Literature

Whereas eulogies and elegies are longstanding traditional expressive responses to grief, others are relatively more recent. In fact, as we observed trends in coping with grief (e.g., reconstruction of meaning, continuation of bonds with the deceased) in related scholarly literature and in our own analyses, we wondered whether print media were instructive in contemporary ways of bereavement.

An examination of grief-related self-help books (Dennis, 2012) indicated that they may be. Samples of books written to help survivors deal with their grief were drawn from the eras of pre-1990, the 1990s, and post-1999 and analyzed for indicators of meaning made about the loss, for emphasis of attachment with, instead of detachment from, the deceased, and for acknowledgment of varied ways of grieving rather than reliance on prescribed stages. The pre-1990 sample featured many instances of formulaic grieving, such as staying determined and learning to let go. Also, though, examples of survivors redefining identity and goals were evident as readers were urged to seek insight and pursue cognitive restructuring. The self-help books published from 1990 to 1999 largely refrained from providing formulas or prescriptions, focusing instead on "continuing bonds, relations, interactions, and representations of the deceased loved one" (Dennis, 2012, p. 407), as well as reconstruction of meanings.

Finally, self-help books since 1999 have tended to embrace finding "ways to sustain our love in separation" with the deceased while also learning to "welcome them back into our lives even though we are apart" (Attig, 2000, pp. 26–7). Stimulation of meaning reconstruction after loss is also quite prevalent as in Kumar's (2005) recommendations, "coming to terms with loss mindfully— becoming an active participant in understanding, accepting, and finding meaning in your loss—gives you the power to change your life. Actively finding meaning in loss is the heart of grieving mindfully" (p. 71). In sum, scrutiny of self-help books across a decades-long span showed that constructs of grieving uniquely, in the pursuit of adaptive meaning, and toward objectives consistent with continuing bonds, are gaining traction in the literature offered to readers who struggle to survive their loved ones.

With less intention perhaps than the authors of self-help books, writers of another subset of literature convey to readers many ways that grief may be experienced and survived. The genre of the "grief account" (Dennis, 2008) includes "written and published tales of fiction or nonfiction that prominently feature grief, its meanings, and its inevitable mystery" (p. 802) and includes books such as Calvin Trillin's *About Alice* (2006), Bill Valentine's (2006) *A Season of Grief*, and Mitch Albom's *The Five People You Meet in Heaven* (2003). Thematic analysis of a small sample, two fiction and two non-fiction grief accounts, yielded a total of six narrative dimensions of bereavement (i.e., restorative, affective, evaluative, interpretive, affirmative, and transformative) that extend the constructs that have received attention in the grief scholarship and therapy communities (Dennis, 2008).

The *restorative dimension* features grieving protagonists attempting to take action that distracts from their losses, reinstates a happier past, or even brings the deceased back. Joan Didion's (2005) acclaimed memoir, *The Year of Magical Thinking*, features many of her efforts to create conditions under which her beloved husband can re-emerge into life. The *affective dimension* involves expression of emotions, such as a grief support group meeting where "fluorescent lights buzz overhead. They are bright and cruel, exposing the group's despair: the puffy faces, circles under the eyes like bruised fruit, dampened spirits that no longer want to sing along with the radio" (Winston, 2004, p. 5).

The four remaining dimensions of bereavement in grief accounts hew more closely to meaning making and continuing bonds. The *evaluative dimension* sees "survivors evaluating, assessing, and labeling their situations and the events that led to their losses" (Dennis, 2008, p. 811). The ascription of value to the unwelcome phenomenon of grief, as well as its consequences, both positive and negative, is a fine example of meaning making about loss. Sophie, a young widow, and the main character of *Good Grief: A Novel*, and her friend Ruth, a victim of her own husband's infidelity, encourage each other to focus on the bad things they lost as well as the good, "when life gives you lemons, you make lemonade. When guys break your heart, you conjure nose hairs. Good riddance" (Winston, 2004, p. 249).

The *interpretive dimension* of grief accounts is quintessentially representative of meaning making. By definition, the interpretive entails "making sense of a loss by working it through, identifying causal chains of events, assigning appropriate meanings and even blame" (Dennis, 2008, p. 814) so as to overcome the chaos and confusion that often accompany grief. For example, the unnamed narrator/ protagonist of *Grief: A Novel* wanders the streets of his new hometown, having relocated to escape memories of losing his elderly mother, while wondering what all his time spent visiting her at a nursing home really meant:

> so confused was I still about what all that had meant. What was clear was that I'd become used to going there on Saturdays . . . It was only now that the dimensions of the routine we had established were becoming clear.
>
> *(Holleran, 2006, pp. 3–4)*

The *affirmative* and *transformative dimensions* found in grief accounts foster and feature, respectively, the maintenance and modification of relationships and connections with the deceased. Affirmation in grief accounts takes forms such as revelation or recollection of details of the deceased's "character and experiences . . . to confirm that they were real human beings" (Dennis, 2008, p. 817) and outright assertion of continued bonds. Didion (2005) vividly portrays her husband's favorite robe, television program, and restaurant, and his quirks such as transcribing their daughter's sayings on scraps of paper and storing them in a painted box. Some recollections are less flattering such as Sophie's characterization of her husband Ethan's slovenly car and goofy feet (Winston, 2004). The idiosyncratic qualities of those we have lost are valuable to revisit because they enable efforts to preserve relationships, albeit altered ones, with our loved departed.

Within the *affirmative dimension* of grief accounts the deceased are commonly rendered as present. In *Grief: A Novel*, the protagonist visits "the Gainesville airport . . . the minute I walked inside I felt everything . . . All the happiness came back . . . And I thought: she does exist. She does exist. Where? In my heart. That's where the dead exist—in our hearts. That's where the dead are" (Holleran, 2006, pp. 119–20). Sophie, of *Good Grief: A Novel*, admitted her continued experiencing of Ethan, "I honestly thought I would run inside and tell him to turn on the radio because they were playing an old recording of Flip Wilson, whom he just loves . . . if I hurried, we could tape it" (Winston, 2004, p. 5).

Finally, the *transformative dimension* of grief accounts depicts continuing bonds with those who have left us as inspiring adaptations in our identities, roles, and relationships with others, including the deceased. The plot of *Grief: A Novel* follows the narrator's transition in identity as he loses his mother:

> One of the odd aspects of caring for someone for a long time is that you grow accustomed to a certain intimacy—but as I walked down the dark, tree-lined block . . . I realized I belonged to no one now and no one belonged to me; I was like a crab that has shed one shell but not found another.
>
> *(Holleran, 2006, p. 9)*

Didion's (2005) role transformation from wife to widow was especially problematic as she clung to her husband, John, especially in his absence. In fact, she recalled, when he had once predicted that she would marry again after he was gone:

> You don't understand, I would say . . . we were equally incapable of imagining the reality of life without the other. This will not be a story in which the death of the husband or wife becomes what amounts to the credit sequence of a new life, a catalyst for the discovery that "you can love more than one person."
>
> *(p. 197)*

Experimental Disclosure Texts About Grief: Insight Into Types of Meaning Making

As scholars of communication, we continue to look for connections between the cognitive, emotional, and expressive manifestations of grief. The first dozen or so years of our research program featuring analysis and interpretation of eulogies, elegies, grief self-help books, and grief accounts yielded considerable evidence that constructs including, but not limited to, positive reappraisal, emotional expression, and problem-focused coping are relevant to these texts of grief-related discourse. We produced schemes for understanding and coalescing these observations such as the dimensions of bereavement (e.g., affirmative, interpretive; Dennis, 2008). We also desired, however, to further cast our findings within the context of what we think of as the "new grief paradigm," prominently featuring "the reconstruction of a world of meaning" as "the central process in grieving" (Neimeyer, 1998, p. 65), as well as the phenomenon of continuing bonds with the dead (see especially Klass, 2006; Klass, Silverman, & Nickman, 1996).

Park (2010) provides a perspective on meaning making in the context of distress that we find amenable to experiences with grief (see Kunkel, Dennis, & Garner, 2014). Park's (2010) central tenet is that big-picture "global meanings" such as beliefs may contradict the evaluation of particular situations, thus producing discrepancy and distress. For instance, when a wonderful person is felled by tragedy, the appraisal of that unfortunate event is discrepant from a belief that bad things (should) only happen to bad people. Park's model (2010) of meaning making focuses on efforts to reduce such discrepancy and includes two important distinctions.

The first distinction is between searching for comprehensibility and searching for significance (Park, 2010). When something regrettable has happened, we often strive to understand causality in the form of reasons for its occurrence (i.e., searching for comprehensibility, like in a fatal car crash brought about by inattentiveness and distraction by cellphone texting). We also frequently seek to identify the impacts and consequences that result from its occurrence (i.e., searching for significance, like in the case of children having to grow up without their father).

A second major distinction in the Park (2010) model is between assimilation and accommodation. Assimilation transpires when the meaning of a specific event is assessed in a way that is amenable to global beliefs and meanings (e.g., to avoid having to tolerate the otherwise unacceptable and absolute senselessness of a loss, the founding of a related charity to prevent future losses is recognized as the good to come from it). Accommodation is the alteration of global beliefs and meanings to incorporate events that would otherwise contradict them (e.g., resolving that sometimes, unfairly or even inexplicably, bad things do happen to good people).

We came to understand, through interpretation of a unique database of grief-related texts (Kunkel et al., 2014), that many meanings made by survivors may be located at the intersections of the different levels of Park's (2010) distinctions and that a sizable portion of these meanings speak directly to the notion of continuing bonds. A sample of undergraduate students were recruited for a study of the benefits accrued from disclosing thoughts and feelings about distressing experiences in a controlled manner. The nature of the distress considered was left to the participants' choosing and they wrote or talked about a wide range of events (e.g., domestic abuse, alcoholism, criminal activities) for sessions across four consecutive days. Of the over 200 students in the sample, 16 in the experimental condition focused exclusively on their experiences as grieving survivors of relatives, friends, or pets. Their written or audiorecorded disclosures were transcribed to produce 197 pages of double-spaced text.

An iterative process of analysis of the disclosure texts using Strauss and Corbin's (1998) constant comparative method revealed 25 themes (see Table 18.1; also available in Kunkel et al., 2014, p. 628) among four types of meaning reconstruction situated at the intersections of the searching for comprehensibility/searching for significance (i.e., understanding causes, or understanding impacts, of an event) and the assimilation/accommodation (i.e., adjusting situational meaning to better match global meaning or vice versa) dichotomies (see Figure 18.1; also available in Kunkel et al., 2014, p. 624).

Table 18.1 Themes of Meaning Reconstruction Types

Meaning Reconstruction Types	Meaning-Making Processes
Sensemaking	*Searching for Comprehensibility/Assimilation*

- Cause of loss
- Assignment of blame
- Loss as cause
- Reason why/Purpose
- Predictable/Prepared
- Understanding life and death

Acceptance or Resignation Without Understanding	*Searching for Comprehensibility/ Accommodation*

- No reason/No explanation
- Questioning faith or God
- Bad things happen to good people/Unfair
- Unpredictable life and fate

Realization of Benefits via Positive Reappraisal	*Searching for Significance/Assimilation*

- End of deceased's suffering
- Deceased in "better place"
- Survivor appreciation of deceased
- Survivor appreciation of life and others
- Survivor growth
- Favorable contrast to other outcomes

Realignment of Roles and Relationships	*Searching for Significance/Accommodation*

- Survivor realities
- Survivor roles
- Survivor goals
- Survivor values
- Survivors' relationships
- Continuing bonds: Presence
- Continuing bonds: Interaction
- Continuing bonds: Overseeing
- Continuing bonds: Living legacy

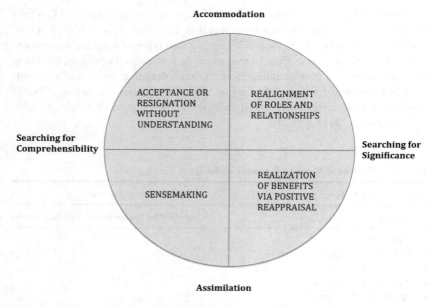

Figure 18.1 Types of meaning reconstruction formed at intersections of meaning-making processes

The first type of meaning reconstruction is *sensemaking*, the assimilation of situational meanings attained when searching for comprehensibility. In attempting to make sense of why losses happen, survivors situate them within pre-existing global frames of reference. There are six themes of sensemaking evident in the discourses of grief: cause of loss, assignment of blame, loss as cause, reason why/purpose, predictable/prepared, and understanding life and death.

The second type of meaning reconstruction is *acceptance or resignation without understanding*, an accommodation of global meanings that may result from the search for comprehensibility. When deaths of loved ones are utterly incomprehensible, survivors may adapt global meanings or worldviews to resolve discrepancy by accepting, or resigning themselves to, a world where explanations are not always available. Other themes of accommodation include questioning faith or God, submitting to a reality of unfairness where bad things happen to good people, and accepting the unpredictability of life and fate.

Realization of benefits via positive reappraisal, the third type, involves assimilation of situational meaning that occurs when searching for significance. To bridge the gap between situational and global meaning, survivors may revisit evaluation of the situational and assess its significance or value more desirably than they did initially. Even when they pale compared to the greater loss, any benefits that are recognized within such positive reappraisal reduce the disturbing discrepancy. Consistently detected versions include the end of the deceased's suffering, arrival of the deceased in a "better place," appreciation of the deceased's life, appreciation of life and other survivors, survivor growth, and favorable contrasts with possible outcomes that did not actually occur.

Finally, *realignment of roles and relationships* is composed of accommodation of global meanings by way of having searched for significance. Survivors may find themselves reconsidering who they are and how they relate to others to address the implications of their losses. Often transformed are survivors' realities, roles, goals, values, and relationships with each other. New meaning is also generated regarding relationships with the deceased. To realign and continue bonds with them, survivors tend to sense their presence, interact with them, feel as though they are overseen by them, and live to honor and impress them as their legacies.

Realignment of Roles and Relationships in Discourses of Grief

Because of its close association with the notion of continuing bonds, we here illustrate the applicability of themes found in our fourth type of meaning reconstruction, *realignment of roles and relationships*, to the discourses of grief (i.e., eulogies, elegies, grief accounts, and grief self-help books), other than grief-related disclosures obtained in experimental settings, wherein they were first discovered.

Survivor Realities

Survivors come to understand the likelihood that they are relegated to a melancholic existence in the absence of their loved ones. Didion (2005) learned that the bereaved:

> searched. They stopped eating. They forgot to breathe. They grew faint from lowered oxygen, they clogged their sinuses with unshed tears and ended up in otolaryngologists' offices with obscure ear infections. They lost concentration. They lost cognitive ability on all scales . . . They blundered in business and suffered sensible financial losses. They forgot their own telephone numbers and showed up at airports without picture ID. They fell sick, they failed, they even . . . died.
>
> *(p. 47)*

Similarly, Stone (2001) wrote, in her elegy *Curtains*, "Memories of a first joyful winter together are contrasted with now cold borscht alone in a bare kitchen" (p. 242).

Survivor Roles

Survivors can find themselves assuming new positions and roles, thus reshaping their own lives and identities. Role labels and changes routinely challenged Didion (2005). She recalled that she once "had trouble thinking of myself as a wife," and wound up having "trouble thinking of myself as a widow" (p. 208).

Survivor Goals

The loss of valued others can inspire new ambitions and goals in those they leave behind. Earl Charles Spencer vowed to accomplish something his sister, Diana, would have loved:

> She would want us today to pledge ourselves to protecting her beloved boys William and Harry from a similar fate. And I do this here, Diana, on your behalf. We will not allow them to suffer the anguish that used regularly to drive you to tearful despair.
>
> *(Spencer, as cited in Kunkel & Dennis, 2003, pp. 34–5)*

Survivor Values

Grief-related events may cause survivors to accommodate values and chief characteristics of identity, accordingly. President Lyndon Johnson eulogized the man he was succeeding, John Kennedy:

> I rededicate this Government to the unswerving support of the United Nations, to the honorable and determined execution of our commitments to our allies, to the maintenance of military strength second to none, to the defense of the strength and the stability of the dollar, to the expansion of our foreign trade, to the reinforcement of our programs of mutual assistance and cooperation in Asia and Africa, and to our Alliance for Progress in this hemisphere.
>
> *(Johnson, 1963)*

Survivors' Relationships

Survivors often turn to each other for support, and may find their relationships with family and friends renewed. In Ronald Reagan's eulogy for the space shuttle Challenger's crew, he asserted:

> To those they have left behind; the mothers, the fathers, the husbands and wives, brothers, sisters, and yes, especially the children; all of America stands beside you in your time of sorrow . . . Across America, we are reaching out, holding hands, finding comfort in one another.
>
> *(Reagan, as cited in Kunkel & Dennis, 2003, p. 37)*

Continuing Bonds: Presence

Maintenance of senses of presence and contact with the departed, even in their overt absence, is a significant manifestation of continuing bonds. In their grief self-help book, Levang and Ilse (1992) devote sections such as "Feeling their presence," "Always a part of me," "Alive in our hearts," "Needing to feel close," and

"The messages of our loved ones" to the appreciation of bond maintenance. Their readers learn that it is acceptable to feel that the deceased "remain an important part of our family" (p. 73) and "they are present in family activities and concerns, encouraging us to help others, enjoy nature's many wonders, and when pressure builds, their examples provide welcome guidance . . . Our loved ones never really leave us" (p. 104).

Continuing Bonds: Interaction

Survivors continue bonds with their cherished lost through visitation and conversation. Graveside interaction is common. More unique, though, was Wood's (2003) father when he "stopped to visit me on his way out of this dimension" in "what the Hawaiians call He ho'ike na ka po—a revelation of the night" and announced that he was happy and relieved "to be released from that body" (p. 161).

Continuing Bonds: Overseeing

The deceased may be represented as watching over their survivors, protecting them, and looking out for their best interests. Kathleen Treanor's daughter, Ashley, promised to "be an angel watching over you" if she were to ever die just days before being killed in the Oklahoma City terrorist bombing at the Alfred P. Murrah Federal Building (Chand, 2003, p. 97).

Continuing Bonds: Living Legacy

In self-help books, DeVita-Raeburn (2004) details a "living for two" phenomenon in which survivors live out the dreams or aspirations of perished brothers and sisters. Likewise, Attig (2000) examines a "practical life" in which we act on the promises, use the advice and counsel, follow in the footsteps, and pursue the cares and interests, of lost loved ones.

Alan O'Day eulogized his mother, Jeannette O'Day: "When you miss her and you remember how much she touched you, she will live on. When you are merciful to an injured animal, when you teach peace and tolerance to a child, she will live on" (Alan O'Day for his mother, Jeannette O'Day; available at www.alanoday.com/jodayeulogy.html).

Conclusion: Applications and Directions

From its earliest conception in the interpretation of eulogy constructs, our research program has evolved with an ever-expanding emphasis on continuing bonds as meaning reconstruction and to include ever-finer distinctions regarding their nature and function. Initially, Kunkel and Dennis (2003) discovered eulogizers sharing direct and detailed observations about the deceased and their relationships with them, and speaking directly to them, or about them in the present tense. We concluded that these phenomena indicated a willingness to both enact and encourage continuing bonds. The same trends were identified in elegy (e.g., Neimeyer, Klass, & Dennis, 2014), though this poetry of lamentation was more likely than eulogies to feature negative impressions of the deceased as vivid reminders of their existence.

Our analysis of self-help books (Dennis, 2012) and introduction of grief accounts (Dennis, 2008) enlarged the roles of meaning reconstruction and continuing bonds. Grief-related self-help books have increasingly advised readers to maintain relationships with the dearly departed. Similarly, grief accounts have offered opportunities to observe bereaved protagonists, in fiction and nonfiction alike, striving for affiliation with the dead. Within instances of what Dennis (2008) called the *transformative dimension*, survivors undergo changes in roles, identities, and relationships, especially with respect to the departed. But it is in the *affirmative dimension* that vibrant and detailed memories of those lost are portrayed so as to enhance connections with them and to render the dead as present in a variety of ways.

To date, our work has provided incontrovertible evidence that grief-related discourse is appropriately marked by processes of meaning making and continuation of bonds with the deceased. It reveals that providers of such discourse (e.g., eulogizers, elegists, writers of grief accounts and grief-related self-help books) offer their audiences a plethora of options for both coping with their own grief and consoling others with theirs. In fact, grief therapists also may benefit their patients by adopting approaches portrayed in the discourses, such as allowing patients to embrace their emotions fully and to recall both positive and negative qualities of their deceased partners, relatives, and friends.

From close inspection of eulogies, we surmised that their creation is a complex set of rhetorical tasks that include memorializing the deceased, expressing one's own emotions, and offering solace to the audience of mourners, and that these ends are accomplished in a variety of ways. Our framework of constructs thus offers not only vantage points for the appreciation and critique of eulogies but also guidance to those charged with addressing these vital responsibilities. Besides relating the positive qualities of lost loved ones, for instance, our work notes the potential value of advising the audience to take up their pet causes or modeling engagement in interaction with them.

Elegies across the centuries appear to be acutely illustrative of the principles of vividly recalling the deceased and embracing the reality and magnitude of losses. Self-help books have, in recent years, been particularly instructive about allowing each grief experience to follow its own course while also promoting mindful meaning reconstruction and maintenance of loving relationships between survivors and the departed. Our research also endorses for the bereaved the utility of reading grief accounts for ideas about adaptive grief coping styles embodied in the six dimensions of bereavement we discerned. These include evaluating causes and consequences of loss; recalling the deceased in sometimes exquisite detail; experiencing the dead in the present; and accepting and pursuing transformative changes in roles, relationships, and identity.

More recently, we discovered, in the disclosure texts of experimental participants, four types of grief-related meaning making and 25 themes across the four types. Located at the intersections of each of searching for comprehensibility, searching for significance, assimilation, and accommodation, the types of meaning reconstruction (i.e., sensemaking, acceptance or resignation without understanding, realization of benefits via positive reappraisal, and realignment of roles and relationships) further highlight the roles of meaning making and continuing bonds in productively contending with grief. We are presently identifying the relevance of the typology and themes to the varieties of grief discourse such as grief accounts and elegies, and did so in the current chapter for the fourth type, realignment of roles and relationships, as it directly captures instances of continuing bonds.

The themes among the types equate with options for arriving at meaning that may be advisable for those striving to manage grief. For instance, within sensemaking, coming to understand that the loss was one that was foreseen, and emotionally prepared for, can provide some comfort. Alternatively, a therapist might assist a patient who cannot reconcile the undeserved horrible death of his wonderful friend to consider accepting, or being resigned to, the fact that an otherwise fair and just world sees exceptions wherein bad things do happen to good people. Or, as a positive reappraisal, noting that a family has become less estranged as it circles together in its time of grief can certainly be of benefit in the coping process. Moreover, sensing the presence of the deceased as a guardian angel of sorts, overseeing and taking care of us, may also be a source of consolation. These are just a few examples of the practical and productive meaning reconstruction processes proffered within our types and themes.

As the world of the living enacts massive shifts in interaction due to the prevalence of digital access and social media, so too does the existence of the dead among the living. The next wave of interpretive analyses seeking to examine discourses of grief is likely to feature data drawn from the font of Internet Protocol servers. Indeed, Pennington (2013) determined that some visitors to the Facebook sites of deceased friends "direct their messages toward the deceased FB friend" as "a way to maintain the connection to the FB friend even after their death" (p. 628). They register disbelief that the friend is gone, express birthday and holiday sentiments, and generally feel like they are communicating with the person who died. As our lives are lived evermore on social media sites (e.g., Facebook, Instagram, Twitter, Snapchat, Periscope, Flicker, Pinterest, Vimeo), so too will our deaths and relationships with the dead be represented on these social platforms. Thus, survivors will continue to learn even more about grieving from the expression of others.

References

Akers, E. (2001). The dead. In S. M. Gilbert (Ed.), *A book of elegies: Inventions of farewell* (p. 146). New York, NY: W.W. Norton & Company.
Albom, M. (2003). *The five people you meet in heaven.* New York, NY: Hyperion.
Attig, T. (2000). *The heart of grief: Death and the search for lasting love.* New York, NY: Oxford University Press.

Chand, C. (2003). Ashley's garden. In J. Canfield & M. V. Hansen (Eds), *Chicken soup for the grieving soul: Stories about life, death, and overcoming the loss of a loved one* (pp. 96–98). Deerfield Beach, FL: Health Communications.

Dennis, M. R. (2008). The grief account: Dimensions of a contemporary bereavement genre. *Death Studies, 32,* 801–836.

Dennis, M. R. (2009). Elegy. In C. D. Bryant & D. L. Peck (Eds), *Encyclopedia of death and the human experience* (pp. 401–404). Thousand Oaks, CA: Sage.

Dennis, M. R. (2012). Do grief self-help books convey contemporary perspectives on grieving? *Death Studies, 36,* 393–418.

Dennis, M. R., & Kunkel, A. D. (2004). Fallen heroes, lifted hearts: Consolation in contemporary presidential eulogia. *Death Studies, 28,* 703–731.

Dennis, M. R., Ridder, K., & Kunkel, A. D. (2006). Grief, glory, and political capital in the Capitol: Presidents eulogizing Presidents. *Death Studies, 30,* 325–349.

DeVita-Raeburn, E. (2004). *The empty room: Surviving the loss of a brother or sister at any age.* New York, NY: Scribner.

Didion, J. (2005). *The year of magical thinking.* New York, NY: Knopf.

Gunn, T. (2001). Death's door. In S. M. Gilbert (Ed.), *A book of elegies: Inventions of farewell* (p. 141). New York, NY: W.W. Norton & Company.

Holleran, A. (2006). *Grief: A novel.* New York, NY: Hyperion.

Hopkins, G. M. (2001). Felix Randal. In S. M. Gilbert (Ed.), *A book of elegies: Inventions of farewell* (p. 284). New York, NY: W.W. Norton & Company.

Johnson, L. B. (1963). Let us continue. Retrieved February 12, 2006 from American Rhetoric site: www.americanrhetoric.com/speeches/lbjletuscontinue.html.

Klass, D. (2006). Continuing conversation about continuing bonds. *Death Studies, 30,* 843–858.

Klass, D., Silverman, P. R., & Nickman, P. L. (Eds). (1996). *Continuing bonds.* Washington, D.C.: Taylor & Francis.

Kumar, S. M. (2005). *Grieving mindfully: A compassionate and spiritual guide to coping with loss.* Oakland, CA: New Harbinger Publications.

Kunkel, A. D., & Dennis, M. R. (2003). Grief consolation in eulogy rhetoric: An integrative framework. *Death Studies, 27,* 1–38.

Kunkel, A., Dennis, M. R., & Garner, B. (2014). Illustrating an integrated typology of meaning reconstruction in discourse: Grief-related disclosures. *Death Studies, 38,* 623–636.

Larkin, P. (2001). The explosion. In S. M. Gilbert (Ed.), *A book of elegies: Inventions of farewell* (p. 146). New York, NY: W.W. Norton & Company.

Levang, E., & Ilse, S. (1992). *Remembering with love: Messages of hope for the first year of grieving and beyond.* Minneapolis, MN: Fairview Press.

Meehan, P. (2001). Child burial. In S. M. Gilbert (Ed.), *A book of elegies: Inventions of farewell* (p. 74). New York, NY: W.W. Norton & Company.

Millay, E. S. V. (2001). Elegy (V), from Memorial to D.C. In S. M. Gilbert (Ed.), *A book of elegies: Inventions of farewell* (p. 286). New York, NY: W.W. Norton & Company.

Neimeyer, R. A. (1998). *Lessons of loss: A guide to coping.* New York, NY: McGraw Hill.

Neimeyer, R. A., Klass, D., & Dennis, M. R. (2014). Mourning, meaning, and memory: Individual, communal, and cultural narration of grief. In P. Russo-Netzer & A. Batthyany (Eds), *Meaning in positivist and existential psychology* (pp. 325–346). New York, NY: Springer.

Park, C. L. (2010). Making sense of the meaning literature: An integrative review of meaning making and its effects on adjustment to stressful life events. *Psychological Bulletin, 136,* 257–301.

Pennington, N. (2013). You don't de-friend the dead: An analysis of grief communication by college students through Facebook profiles. *Death Studies, 37,* 617–635.

Reagan, R. (1986). Eulogy by President Ronald Reagan for the crew of the Challenger Space Shuttle. In A. D. Kunkel & M. R. Dennis (Eds), *Grief consolation in eulogy rhetoric: An integrative framework. Death Studies, 27*, 1–38.

Rich, A. (2001). A woman mourned by daughters. In S. M. Gilbert (Ed.), *A book of elegies: Inventions of farewell* (p. 200). New York, NY: W.W. Norton & Company.

Stone, R. (2001). Curtains. In S. M. Gilbert (Ed.), *A book of elegies: Inventions of farewell* (p. 242). New York, NY: W.W. Norton & Company.

Strauss, A., & Corbin, J. (1998). *Basics of qualitative research.* Thousand Oaks, CA: Sage.

Trillin, C. (2006). *About Alice.* New York, NY: Random House.

Valentine, B. (2006). *A season of grief.* San Francisco, CA: Harrington Park Press.

Winston, L. (2004). *Good grief: A novel.* New York, NY: Wagner Books.

Wood, P. D. (2003). Trailing clouds of glory. In J. Canfield & M. V. Hansen (Eds), *Chicken soup for the grieving soul: Stories about life, death, and overcoming the loss of a loved one* (pp. 160–163). Deerfield Beach, FL: Health Communications.

19

ANCIENT MESOPOTAMIAN REMEMBRANCE AND THE FAMILY DEAD

Renata MacDougal

Introduction

Following the publication of *Dead But Not Lost* (Goss & Klass 2005), I began to look for evidence of continuing bonds in ancient Mesopotamia (broadly modern Iraq and parts of Syria). I was skeptical because the traditional scholarship claimed that the dead were hostile ghosts, lurking about with intent to wreak harm and havoc on living relations. The accepted thinking was that the living employed a periodic ritual to feed and water the spirits of the deceased, to keep them at bay and firmly harnessed to their bleak netherworld existence. However, when we look at the ancient documents and artifacts through the lens of concepts from continued bonds research, another story comes to light. Instead, we find generations of the deceased actively remembered, fêted, and kept present in the embrace of the living family. I focused on the second millennium BCE evidence, as that is when the private, non-royal references to a remembrance ritual began to appear in the texts.

The *kispum* ritual was intended to sustain the deceased in the afterlife. The ritual was a meal, called a *kispum* in Babylonian, usually offered monthly in a private context, and celebrated annually in a public, communal celebration of the mortuary rite. While we know from texts that *kispum* involved offerings, less visible features, such as spoken or sung formulae, gesture, or actions, all important parts of ritual, remain obscure. We do know from texts that *kispum* entailed three actions: performing the care of the dead ritual (*kispa kasāpu*), pouring water (*mē naqû*), and invoking the name (*šuma zakāru*) of the dead. New work in Death and Dying Studies and the archeology of emotion support an alteration of attitudes to the dead in Mesopotamian contexts (Tarlow, 2000, 2011; Harris & Sørenson, 2010).

Traditional View of *Kispum*

In Mesopotamian belief the world was imagined as part of a multilayered cosmos, inhabited by all manner of beings, seen and unseen. In Mesopotamian scholarship, the spirits of the dead, including those of beloved family members, are understood to be either evil or threatening and hostile. The performance of *kispum* in a scheduled ritual context has been broadly portrayed as apotropaic, to keep the dead from re-entering the boundaries of the social world above and interacting in the realm of the living.

In most Mesopotamian as well as biblical scholarship, spirits of the dead, called "ghosts," are characterized as weak and helpless (Scurlock, 1997). Yet the ghost (*eṭemmu*) could act and exhibit a type of power, in that their actions affected lives on Earth. Whether the actions were beneficial (interventions) or somewhat malign (groaning, screams, illness), the ghost nevertheless was able to employ certain forces that enabled results. The behavior of the *eṭemmu*, then, was believed to be controllable by human intervention in the form of post-funerary *kispum* rites. Much of the existing academic literature concentrates on adverse effects, citing particularly incantations that deal with ghost-induced illnesses (Scurlock, 2006). In cases of malign activities, the *kispum* is represented as the preventive cure. However, the question of the identity of the hostile spirits needs to be re-addressed (Skaist, 1980). Mesopotamian family ghosts are reputed to have the same tendency toward mischief as unattached, un-familied *eṭemmū* (ghosts). It is important, however, to distinguish the family deceased from a roving or unattached spirit. These mistreated and neglected ghosts were the vagrants, wanderers (*muttaggišu, murtappidu*), who were likely to interfere with humans.

Incantation texts imply that the living could pacify these wandering ghosts who were not relatives, but who were inflicting harm upon the family members, by performance of certain magico-religious rituals (Castellino, 1955; Bayliss, 1973). These unsettled ghosts were not rancorous family members seeking vengeance, but instead, the spirits of the dead without family or proper funerary rites. The spirit who had no one to speak its name in remembrance or to bury it properly was without family, was truly a "nobody," non-existent. These restless spirits were the ones that caused trouble, that were blamed for disease, or made noises and disruptions in people's houses. According to instructions in incantation texts, an un-familied ghost could receive *kispum* rites, thus ensuring the incorporation of the vagrant ghost within a kin line.

We can infer *kispum* procedures from anti-witchcraft magic substitution rituals to heal the sick (Tsukimoto, 1985, pp. 125–35; Scurlock, 2001). A human figurine or poppet was made from clay and used to transfer the spirit causing the illness from the person into the figure. One of the things used to entice the spirit was the promise of a proper funeral. The substitute figure received an offering display (*taklimtu*), was anointed with good oil, dressed, offered *kispum* by the family, then buried, bewailed, and mourned.

In an anti-witchcraft healing ritual, clay figurines of male and female sorcerers are formed and then treated with the respect due to the family dead. In the text we see glimpses of *kispum* activities, and perhaps some aspects of the normal preparations for burial as well.

> You dress them in makeshift garments. You anoint them with fine oil. Before Šamaš you sweep the ground. You sprinkle pure water. You put down a pure chair for Šamaš. You stretch out a *mišḫu*-cloth on it. You set up a reed altar before Šamaš. In three groups you put out food portions before Šamaš, Ea and Asalluḫi. You scatter dates and *sasqû*-flour. You set up three *adagurru* vessels. You set up three censers (burning) aromatics. You scatter all manner of grain. You put down a chair to the left of the offering arrangement for his family ghosts. You put down a chair for his family ghosts to the left of the other ghosts to the left. You make *kispum* offerings (*kispa takassip*) to his family ghosts. You give them gifts. You honor them. You show them respect. Secondly, you lay out hot broth for his family ghosts . . . You pour out water for them. You make a pure sacrifice before Šamaš. You bring the shoulder, caul fat and roasted meat near to the offering table. You pour out a libation of first quality beer . . . for his family ghosts . . . You recite the incantation "Anything Evil" three times.
>
> *(Tsukimoto, 1985, pp. 167–70; Scurlock, 2001, pp. 195–6)*

Misunderstandings about this genre of incantation texts and those associated with cures for ghost-driven ailments, incorporated with literary passages describing a bleak afterlife, produced a predominant theme of inimical spirits of the dead in the scholarship. However, these texts are only part of the corpus of cuneiform literature mentioning deceased spirits; there were many different kinds of entities believed to inhabit the underworld, including dangerous demons and evil spirits. The evidence suggests that deceased members of the Mesopotamian family were something quite separate from prior interpretations primarily based on myths and disease incantations. Early in the history of the discipline, at the beginning of the twentieth century, classically trained scholars approached the newly translated textual data from Mesopotamia with European cultural filters. They extrapolated ideas from ancient Greek and Roman magical beliefs about ghosts and the spirits of the dead, attributing cross-cultural homogeneity to concepts of the Mesopotamian dead. Thus, the notion of the dead as hostile spirit beings interfering with daily lives of surviving family members found its way universally into Mesopotamian scholarship, and for the most part, persists today. This is reflected in broad generalizations in the literature, which normalize mortuary behaviors and view cross-cultural similarities in practices or material remains as representative of the same ideological phenomena (MacDougal, 2014).

Viewing *kispum* through the lens of continued bonds research, we can instead interpret the ritual as a recurrent magico-religious activity serving as the mechanism for continued emotional bonds with the dead. The meaning of *kispum* rites was different from traditional interpretations in the scholarship; the deceased were incorporated, commemorated, and included in the ongoing existence of the family in a vibrant way. Rather than merely a rite of prophylactic magic, it was a means for expression of grief, for commemoration of the dead through ongoing ritual, and continuing family interaction between the living and the dead.

The Akkadian (Babylonian) word *kispum* comes from *kasāpu*, a verb meaning "to break apart," probably referring to the provision of bread in a communal meal, similar to saying "break bread together." Care for the dead included periodic libations for drink, pouring water, and providing food for sustenance in a commensal ritual. We do know that family members who survived the deceased person were obliged to carry out the *kispum* as a ritual for the ghost (*eţemmu*) of the dead. The heir (*aplu*), usually the eldest son, was designated legally in a will; a few references to a female and legal adoptees as heirs do exist. The designated heir entrusted with the ritual obligations was called the *pāqidu*, "the one who takes care of" the dead. The *pāqidu* bore ritual and symbolic responsibility for the care and well-being of both the living and the dead. The ritual role of the chief heir would also have been symbolically profound for its cosmological effect in the religious sphere, as well as family leadership. In a society in which magic was intertwined with religion and an active part of daily life, the *pāqidu* was more than the "water pourer" (*nāq mê*). The heir assigned this role held great ritual power to intermediate between the upper and lower worlds, which translated to social power in the family structure and so the broader community. In this regard, the leadership of the *kispum* ritual was a role that offered stability and meaning to the family as whole. Through the living, who participated in the *kispum*, the dead continued as family members, thus reinforcing the deeper meaning and identity of the family itself.

Participation in the rituals and in caring for the dead was a serious responsibility for the entire family. A sister chides her recalcitrant brother in an Old Babylonian letter (British Museum 17495):

> As you, my brother know, this year you have sent me neither garlic, nor onions, nor *sirbittum* fish . . . what shall I give the whole year long for the *kispum* offering for the day of the new moon for the house of your family?
>
> *(Kraus, 1964, p. 106)*

According to the Mesopotamian lunar calendar, *kispum* occurred at the *rēš warhim*, the beginning of the month (Whiting, 1987, pp. 62–3). The *ūm bibbulim*, "day of darkness" or "day of the disappearance," appears in cuneiform texts consistently as day of the new moon (Cohen, 1993; Livingstone, 2007, p. 43). Ritually and symbolically, the cusp of no moon/visible moon is significant as a liminal time when the boundaries of the upper and lower worlds are the same. The crucial hours when the moon was invisible enabled the dead to pass from the netherworld to attend the commensal family remembrance ritual.

Kispum could take place at the grave or at home at domestic shrines or in family tomb chapels beneath the house. The continued care of the deceased and the grave connoted a belief in a continued existence of some essential part of being, albeit in a different form as a spirit, and defined as without flesh (*šīru*). The involvement of the whole family in the ritual for the dead was crucial both to the well-being of the deceased and the living family members. The dead were invoked, ritually called forth by name, inviting them to be present with the family at the *kispum* meal. The terms for calling forth and naming carry the sense of making something come into being, a common ancient Near Eastern magico-religious belief. These words were a creative force, pronouncing something into existence, a magical fiat by the power of the word.

The family funerary ritual can be seen as transformative and liminal for both the dead and the living; the living entered into a changed relationship with a family member who was now an *eṭemmu*. The deceased safely transitioned to an alternate existence in a world imagined according to cultural beliefs about the structure of the cosmos. The role of ritual and transformative power in the *kispum* ritual involves ideas of magic, religion, and ritual, which would not necessarily have been separate phenomena in Mesopotamia. However, the family *kispum* ritual must now be seen as distinct from magic rituals that set other types of spirits to rest, particularly incantations against demons and evil spirits, which have been traditionally emphasized in the literature.

Textual Sources

Cuneiform documents that reveal insight into Mesopotamian funerary practices exist in a variety of types (Alster, 1980; Tsukimoto, 1985; Katz, 2003). Here, unlike cultures lacking written documents, we can correlate burial practice to mortuary ideology, at least as far as we can grasp Mesopotamian attitudes from the texts. In examining the archeological written evidence, we can find the earliest mentions of the private *kispum* ritual in the second millennium BC. Therefore, the examples here, as well as other artifactual evidence, are all taken from material dated to the Old Babylonian/Isin-Larsa periods (ca. 2004–1763 BC). Since such primary texts exist, we are potentially able to access at least some of the original meaning of mortuary ritual in the broader human sense, as well as clues to the specific nature of funerary rites in the ancient Near East. No factual treatises exist that spell out for us the properties of Mesopotamian beliefs about life after death. The texts do not provide us with a how-to manual for family *kispum*. Rather, we need to "excavate the texts." Textual sources for *kispum* include a mix of mythological and religious literary works, magic and divination texts, and legal and everyday practical documents. While some excerpts from myths are of a philosophical bent, bewailing the desperation of the netherworld and the nature of the human condition of mortality, some lend different insights. Texts such as laments or prayers mention the *eṭemmu* in a non-hostile way; a cultic calendar hints to us of the date of the ritual; a personal letter reminds a brother to send money for *kispum* observances. Some of the cuneiform texts that discuss goods for the *kispum* ritual occur in list form in accounts or in letters, in both royal and non-royal contexts. These do not lend an aura of despair to the picture of the netherworld that scholars have traditionally deduced from the Gilgamesh and other "descent" texts (Bayliss,

1973; Barrett, 2007). In fact, goods for burials in the texts, while biased toward the elite, include provisions of food and clothing, belying the stark emptiness emphasized in a few pieces of influential literature. Accordingly, Tsukimoto, in his definitive compilation of *kispum* texts, terms the grave offerings *Totenbeigabe*, and deftly translates *kispum* itself as *Totenpflege*, "care of the dead" (1985).

Well-known pieces of literature, such as the *Epic of Gilgamesh*, *Nergal and Ereshkigal*, and *The Descent of Ishtar*, depict a particularly bleak afterlife existence (Dalley, 2000). However, we must be cautious when using isolated primary documents to reconstruct mortuary practices. The Mesopotamian (Sumerian and Akkadian) literary texts, particularly myths, must be considered in light of their purpose, authoring group, genre of literature, and intended audience when correlating references to Mesopotamian attitudes toward death and the afterlife. While the primary texts sometimes present a grim afterlife vision, this view is codependent with the role of their characters, usually engaged in divine or extra-human netherworld journeys. These major epics were dramatic, probably performed, recited, or sung in religious contexts in public festivals, or settings with sacred associations. Suggesting a set cultural tradition, the same state of existence after death is described in nearly word-for-word refrains in several different pieces of literature, suggesting a common (and probably well-known) source. In such passages, a divine or semi-divine character sets out for the realm of the dead, literally the "land of no return" (Sum. *Kurnugi*). In this world, there is no light and the inhabitants dwell in the dark, and seem to be feathered or winged like birds (depicting a soul which has departed the body). Poignantly, the dead eat dust, clay is their bread, and they moan in grief and mourning like doves.

Found among the earliest tablets excavated in the nineteenth century, these texts with similar underworld refrains were part of the earliest corpus of translated cuneiform tablets, from Aššurbanipal's library at Nineveh (Iraq). As noted, these particular passages found their way very early into Mesopotamian scholarship at the end of the nineteenth century; they became the canonical characterization of the afterlife and, indeed, were attributed to an overriding Mesopotamian cultural pessimism. This view became widespread and remains influential in forming our ideas about death beliefs in Mesopotamia. Indeed, the characterization in the underworld journey passages is that of a dark, foreboding land. However, we do not have any other descriptive passages of the world of the dead in the literature of similar nature or length.

We are limited in our vision of the Mesopotamian afterlife by the reliance on this small body of textual references. It is worth remembering that scribes and authors of cultic literature were part of a most elite group. The behaviors and beliefs of the more general population when faced with death almost certainly differed from the divine and semi-divine, larger-than-life heroic experiences reflected in myths and epics.

Allusions and glimpses of the features of the netherworld do occur in other types of texts. Some depict it in rather different ways, for example with solar and stellar circuits passing through and periodically lending it light. The Mesopotamian cosmos was conceived as three-dimensional, expressed horizontally by the plane of the Earth's surface in its extent from the west to the mountains of the east, and vertically from the highest level of heaven and Earth to the very depths of the foundations of an underworld below. The lower realm was probably further divided to house different types of spirits, separating the human ghost from evil demons.

For individuals and family groups, tangible acts involving repetition and practice were the fundamental form of transmission of memory. Ritual actions, such as funerary rites, gained power (often understood as magico-religious results) from their grounding in a common belief system, derived from underlying mythic scenarios, particularly those that delineated the shape of the cosmos. The conception of terrestrial, celestial, and subterranean planes, inhabited by human as well as supernatural beings, is essential to our understanding of the fate and destination of humans after death. The ritual practices associated with the dead, apparent in the archeological data, do not fit well with the grim afterlife picture painted in the scholarly interpretations. Mesopotamian belief in a complex mythological cosmos within an ordered, structured universe affected the relationship of the family with the spirits of the dead, as well as treatment of the body at burial. Archeologically, the care taken to bury the dead and to preserve and protect the tomb or the grave signifies a notion of some type of continued existence in this cosmic setting, and, within the family, a relationship with their dead. The "Land of No Return," the lower world, existed in family memory as a place "below," where the deceased spirits were located. In some cases, this belief was actualized by graves where the dead actually "slept" below the family floors, until called into the terrestrial plane.

Ghosts and the Family Dead

In general, texts portray the family heir responsible and honor-bound to perform the regular *kispum*. But one Old Babylonian period text (British Museum 93766) tells us that *kispum* was not only performed for ancestral family dead. A grieving father, Sin-uselli, reported to an agent of King Hammurapi (1792–1750 BC) that:

> My son Sukkukum disappeared from me eight years ago and I did not know whether he was still alive and I kept making funerary offerings for him as if he were dead (*kispam aktassip*). Now, they have told me that he is staying (dwelling) in Ik-Bari in the House of Ibni-Ea, the "rider" and goldsmith, the son of Silli-Šamaš. I went to Ik-Bari, but they hid him from me and denied his presence to me.
>
> *(Van Soldt, 1994, p. 23)*

The remainder of the letter tells us that King Hammurapi ordered a soldier and a trustworthy man to accompany Sin-uselli to retrieve his lost (enslaved or kidnapped) son, and that the offender be brought to Babylon, presumably for judgment.

This letter seems to turn any idea of *kispum* as restricted to deceased parents, elders, or special ancestors on its head. Here we have clear evidence that other (here a child) family members received the care for the dead ritual, in this case performed even without a body or burial. This father performed *kispum* for his son for eight years, which supports well the claim that the family dead were all provisioned continuously. It also proves that a skeleton in a grave was not necessary to perform spiritual care for the dead. The grammatical form of the verb used (*aktassip*) indicates that the father performed a recurring ritual. Believing in his son's death, he still interacted with and maintained a relationship with his child. The emotion, grief for a lost son, and shock at hearing the boy was alive come through poignantly in this letter. This is not a case concerned with inheritance benefits; it clearly is an expression of grieving and an effort to maintain continued bonds with a deceased family member.

Family identity extended beyond the grave, incorporating the spirits of deceased kin in ongoing remembrance, and reaching back through generations to maintain and curate ancestral bonds. In just this way, therefore, ritual care of the dead served an essential societal function for the living, quite contrary to perceptions of the dead as mere shades or hostile spirits. Preservation of family and clan identity was paramount. The organization of the patriarchal family provided the basic structure of society. Family kinship identity reflected the balance and order of a structured universe, the opposite of "other," enemy rule, destruction, and foreign invasion. Any disruption of family unity or removal from the clan (*kimtum*) earned the curse of the gods. While other identities might exist in relation to the city or larger religious, political, or occupational units as well, this familial or kin grouping is clearly the arena within which mortuary practices were played out. Family, clan, and kin allegiance, loyalty, and honor (adherence to values) amounted to the same thing as family religion, worship, and devotion (Van der Toorn, 1996). Any person associated with a family *kimtum* was never a stranger or an enemy. Ancestors anchored the family identity in their lineage in a real sense, both in the immediate past (remembered relatives) and distant generations.

As we have seen, tending the family ghosts was essential. In a second millennium BC prayer invoking family ghosts, relatives encompassed three generations:

> You, the ghosts of my ancestral family, progenitors in the grave,
> (The ghosts of) my father, my grandfather, my mother, my grandmother,
> my brother, my sister, (The ghosts of) my family, my kin and my clan.
> *(Lenzi, 2011, p. 136)*

The ongoing practice of *kispum* was a powerful factor in the family dynamic. By means of continued remembrance rituals, the dead exerted influence on and interacted with the family. As opposed to state religion and public ritual, what the family did following the death of one its members accomplished not only immediate mourning rituals, rites of passage for the dead, and ongoing *kispum*, but their actions were part of the praxis of common family religion.

On a clay tablet from Nippur (Iraq) from the archives of the Sīn-Naṣir family, probably a well-to-do merchant, a wonderful prayer to the moon god (Sīn) is recorded, which takes us inside an actual family *kispum* ceremony (Wilcke, 1983).

In the earliest hours of the morning of the new moon, in the dark of night, Sīn-naṣir, as the family *pāqidu*, makes a libation of water to the moon god (*In the morning, I am pouring water for you*). He asks the moon god Sīn to set free many generations of his family dead, calling each by name, to partake of bread and drink water with him. This text clearly portrays how the care for the dead through the *kispum* ritual played out. The ritual meal is not lavish. The moon god is invoked, rather than the netherworld judge Šamaš, and it is very interesting that Sīn must allow the *eṭemmī* of all the ancestors to come answer the call for food and water. Mr. Sīn-naṣir calls forth seven generations including several women and an unfortunate fellow who was murdered (Wilcke, 1983, pp. 51–3). Perhaps the family gathered at a house altar in a specially designated room (the *aširtum*) to pronounce the names of the dead. The poor could also pour water in their house, even if there was no built altar. Or this ceremony could easily be done at an extramural grave in a cemetery. It is certainly possible that a long list of names could be memorized, especially in chant or sung format, for families with no tradition of writing or literacy. We have family archives from many elite merchant families showing records of family ancestors going back several generations.

Remembrance and Cultural Memory

As remembered history, remembrance of the dead is a type of cultural memory which can be understood to create social memory (Kansteiner, 2002; Assmann, 2006). Remembering as an act required renewal. *Kispum* as collective memory was a reality and a dynamic part of the social construct (Halbwachs, 1992; Jonker, 1995; Kansteiner, 2002). This includes the more distant ancestral past of cultural memory as well as remembered memory, which applies to the living who had actual remembrances of interactions and events with the more recently deceased. Official state Old Babylonian cultural memory is that preserved in the written word, carried out institutionally by centralized scribal schools and public ritual. The vehicle for the preservation of family memory was ritual commemoration carried out at home or at the grave.

Kispum was also performed in other contexts, outside of the private family. *Kispum* functioned as a remembrance ritual in other non-family groups in society. Members in craft-based occupations, religious clergy, and kings invoked the names of forerunners in recurring ritual.

One record from a professional group comes from a series of prescriptions for the procedure of glassmaking. In tablets from the Library of Assurbanipal at Nineveh (Iraq), the names of past experts in the glassmaking tradition were remembered and recorded (Oppenheim et al., 1970). The instructions in the text stipulate that the first procedure before making glass is *ana ummâni kispa takassip*, "you make *kispum* offerings for the (dead) masters" (pp. 52–3). A sheep is also sacrificed before the chemical recipe for glassmaking begins. The living "descendants" sought benefices from the spirits of their dead predecessors for success in glassmaking. *Kispum* bound the present craftsmen with the legacy and expertise of those who had gone before. In venerating the glassmaking ancestors of the guild family, the living honored bonds with the dead; they remembered, cared for, respected, and interacted with them.

Members of an elite clerical group, the *entu* priestesses, were also known to have performed *kispum* rituals for dead predecessors. The office of *entu* was a powerful religious, economic, and often political one, usually held by the daughter of the king. We know the names of women appointed to this position for over approximately 500 years, from the third millennium into the second. One *entu*, Enanedu (ca. 1834–1763 BC), describes how she restored and shored up the walls protecting the graves of ancestor *entu* priestesses at Ur (Iraq). It was the high priestess's filial duty to offer *kispum*, and care for and honor the deceased forebears of her elite clerical family (Charpin, 1986).

Kispum is well attested in royal documents as well. Another second millennium Babylonian text, *The Genealogy of the Hammurapi Dynasty* (British Museum 80328), states that the tablet was specifically made for performing the *kispum* ritual (Finkelstein, 1966).

The Genealogy is a list of 27 names, with a clause at the end for dead soldiers lost on the battlefields, princes, and daughters of the king. The list adds in all the dead across the land, not naming them as ghosts, but as mankind (*awīlūtum*), who have no one to tend them, and invites them to join with the king in the *kispum*. This text differs from the purely historiographical genre we find in king lists. It is clearly a *kispum* composition meant to be recited for the remembrance of the dead at one of the monthly or annual *kispum* celebrations, or as part of a coronation (p. 117). More than merely legitimizing the ruling dynasty, recitation of the composition *The Genealogy* connected a long-reaching ancestral legacy far beyond familial relatives, with bonds into many generations of rulers past. It clearly has several other underlying purposes, including legitimization of the foundation of the dynasty and systematizing knowledge of the past through genealogies, a well-known form of ancient Near Eastern historiography. The end of the composition identifies its purpose as a true *kispum* document as well as demonstrating the king's largesse, invoking all sorts of untethered dead who do not rest in peace, but rather lack a caretaker to bring them sustenance. In a generic all-call, the king invokes his own family line, his sons and daughters, as well as fallen soldiers on far-away battlefields. All persons, all of the dead of the land, from the rising to the setting sun, who have no *pāqidum* are invited to come forth from the underworld to "Eat this!" and "Drink this!" by royal command (p. 96).

Also notable is that this *kispum* could not have been performed at each grave of so many dead, and therefore was effective just by means of spoken performance. By including the unknown dead as *awīlūtum* in need of remembrance, the king's *kispum* prayer embraces all, reinforcing his royal position as the caretaker of all people, perhaps symbolically uniting all as one national family. The royal *kispum* also joined the king to an exclusive ruling ancestral group hundreds of years before his actual bloodline took power. In this regard, the royal *kispum* was a powerful socio-political ritual act.

Royal performance of lavish *kispum* rituals is well established at Mari (Syria) with extensively detailed studies of food records (Jacquet, 2002). The Mari administrative texts mention provisions *ana kispim ša šarrāni*, "for (all) the kings," referring to a long line of dead predecessors. At Mari, *kispum* invoked the ancient, non-Amorite, Akkadian kings Sargon and Narām-Sin (ca. 2350 BC) as direct ancestors of the Amorite Mari kings hundreds of years after they ruled (Jacquet, 2002, pp. 56–61).

The Assyrian Kinglist, as well, traces ruling ancestors to seventeen kings who famously "lived in tents" as desert tribal sheikhs (Richardson, 1999–2001, pp. 185–90). These names of ancestral leaders spanned centuries and were regarded as true ancestors in the tradition of Mesopotamian historiography. By celebrating *kispum* in a royal context, kings established themselves as directly part of long-exalted family line of sovereigns; blood ties were not required, but created by the *kispum* bonds.

Material Evidence

Beyond archeological evidence for continued bonds in the form of documents on clay tablets, other material remains. Grave types differed widely in ancient Mesopotamia; cemeteries are rare (probably as yet undiscovered). One constant seemed to be the placement of bowls and jars in graves as provisions for the afterlife. While a majority of the population is invisible, we do have abundant mortuary remains from wealthy merchant residential quarters in the city of Ur from the second millennium BC (Woolley, Mallowan, & Mitchell, 1976). Because of a large body of archival texts found, we can determine specific family living quarters and room functions (Battini-Villard, 1999; Brusasco, 2007). Most significantly, family chamber tombs were placed beneath a designated cultic room (*aširtum*), a portion of the house devoted to the maintenance of the family cult of the dead, but also used as a living space (Tricoli, 2014). In many houses, this room contained a wall with cultic furniture: benches, altar-like podiums, offering niches and chimneys (Woolley et al., 1976, PL 44). The symbolism of this placement is profound; the living above co-existed physically and spiritually with the family dead below. It seems clear that the family did not fear their dead; in fact, they remained close to them for eternity.

Known from second millennium houses at Tell Asmar and Ur, altars situated in corners were used for offerings and the worship of the family gods as well (Woolley et al., 1976, pp. 29–30, 146; Delougaz, Hill, & Lloyd, 1967). There were two types of altars: a low, broad dais set into a wall and an offering "table" that is a tall rectangular altar often built upon a brick pedestal. The tables show plastered decoration reminiscent of temple doors and religious iconography. At Ur, offering bowls were excavated *in situ* in front of a few of the altars (Woolley et al., 1976, PL 43, 45). In some of the *aširtu* rooms, adult clay coffin graves were interred directly under the floor, including many infant burial bowls capped with clay covers (PL 39b). Deeper, in a subterranean chamber, some families had large, corbelled, or vaulted tombs in which they placed at least some of the family dead (PL 36–8). Skeletal remains within the tombs do not account for all the family dead; the question of who was afforded burial in the vault is undefined. No texts or markers record the identity of the tomb inhabitants. Perhaps the most compelling deposition was found in an Ur vault where the most recent dead body was at the forefront (PL 48). The remains of the earlier deceased had been swept aside; probably a set period was observed for decay before the tomb was reopened and reused (about two years in the modern Middle East). In any case, the family was clearly "living with the ancestors" (McAnany, 1995).

The graves of family members under house floors, and the care and provisioning in burials, as well as some evidence for post-interment offerings provide very compelling evidence for the concept of continued bonds and remembrance of the dead. The evidence presented for treatment of the dead does not support a belief in the hostile nature of deceased family members. Instead, the dead are kept nearby, accessible and present. The more convincing evidence for *kispum* as a dynamic family remembrance ritual remains in the domestic ritual spaces. These rooms enabled places for *kispum* rituals, private worship of family gods, burial places for the dead, and continued access to deceased family members. The cosmological significance of burial under house floors is undeniable with the image of the dead below, desiring pure water in the grave and the remembrance of their name. In Mesopotamian belief the grave recalls the image of their family members and ancestors dwelling in the netherworld ("below"). In the Ur domestic chapels and graves under the floors, the dead dwelt, apart from the plane of the living ("above"), yet ready to be recalled at the *kispum*. The domestic ritual, or altar, room was the *aširtu*, a sanctuary deep in the heart of the house with protected access. Symbolically and physically, the family dead were kept deep within the heart of the family. These spaces were where the dead and living continued to interact.

Conclusions

Approaching Mesopotamian archeology with newer interdisciplinary theories shows that issues of emotion and belief can be investigated. In Mesopotamian belief, the worlds of the living and the dead were mystically linked for the brief hours when the *kispum* was performed. The ghosts of dead family members were called by name and invited to join in a meal with living family members. As the texts show, ancient Mesopotamian families performed this traditional ritual faithfully, as promised to their loved ones, and according to long tradition. By partaking of food and drink with the family, the deceased symbolically lived on (albeit on another plane of existence).

Fruit pits, animal bones, grains from bread, and perhaps a cup or two near the mouth show evidence of care and providing food for the dead. Some tombs may have been provided with a channel for water to the grave (and perhaps, at least symbolically, into the deceased's cup). Some of the dead were buried with nothing that remains visible in the archeological record. It seems clear that the food and water were not meant to keep the hostile deceased loved ones away and passive; instead the ritual allowed the living to continue interacting with their beloved son or father or grandmother. The long-lasting continuity of the tradition over at least two millennia, and burials beneath house floors, tell us that it was not fear of ghosts that drove this religious rite—it was more productive and positive in that it was bound up with the identity of the family and beneficial results for the living. *Kispum* served as a way to deal with the many human reactions to family death, including grief resolution. Mesopotamian families actually continued before-death relationships with the deceased; the *kispum* formalized continued emotional interaction as an accepted practice. The actual doing of the *kispum* materialized family bonds and seated family identity deep into the past. Bonds with the deceased that continued after life were cohesive and dynamic for group identity. The ritual consolidated self-perception, or who people thought they were, and how they made meaning for themselves in the world of gods, spirits, and men.

References

Alster, B. (Ed.). (1980). *Death in Mesopotamia: Papers read at the XXVIe Rencontre Assyriologique Internationale*. Copenhagen: Akademisk Forlag.

Assmann, J. (2006). *Religion and cultural memory*. Stanford, CA: Stanford University Press.

Barrett, C. (2007). Was dust their food and clay their bread? Grave goods, the Mesopotamian afterlife, and the liminal role of Inana/Ishtar. *Journal of Ancient Near Eastern Religions*, 7(1), 7–65.

Battini-Villard, L. (1999). *L'Espace Domestique en Mésopotamie de la IIIᵉ Dynastie d'Ur à l'Époque Paléo-Babylonienne, Vols. 1 & 2*. Oxford: BAR/Archeopress.

Bayliss, M. (1973). The cult of dead kin in Assyria and Babylonia. *Iraq*, 35, 115–125.

Brusasco, P. (2007). *The archaeology of verbal and nonverbal meaning: Mesopotamian domestic architecture and its textual dimension*. Oxford: Archaeopress.

Castellino, G. (1955). Rituals and prayers against appearing ghosts. *Orientalia*, 24, 240–274.

Charpin, D. (1986). *Le Clergé d'Ur au Siècle d'Hammurabi: (XIXᵉ-XVIIIᵉ siècles av. J.-C.)*. Geneva/Paris: Librairie Droz.

Cohen, M. E. (1993). *The cultic calendars of the Ancient Near East*. Bethesda, MD: CDL Press.

Dalley, S. (2000). *Myths from Mesopotamia: Creation, the flood, Gilgamesh, and others*. Revised edn. Oxford: Oxford University Press.

Delougaz, P., Hill, H. D., & Lloyd, S. (1967). *Private houses and graves in the Diyala region*. Chicago, IL: University of Chicago Press.

Finkelstein, J. J. (1966). The genealogy of the Hammurapi dynasty. *Journal of Cuneiform Studies*, 20, 95–118.

Goss, R., & Klass, D. (2005). *Dead but not lost: Grief narratives in religious traditions*. Walnut Creek, CA: AltaMira Press.

Halbwachs, M. (1992). *On collective memory*, ed. and transl. by L.E. Coser. Transl. from *Les Cadres Sociaux de la Mémoire* and from *La Topographie Légendaire des Évangiles en Terre Sainte: Etude de Mémoire Collective*. Chicago, IL: University of Chicago Press.

Harris, O. J. T., & Sørensen, T. F. (2010). Rethinking emotion and material culture. *Archaeological Dialogues*, 17, 145–163. doi:10.1017/S1380203810000206.

Jacquet, A. (2002). Lugal-Meš Et Malikum; novel examen du KISPUM a Mari. *Florilegium marianum VI; recueil d'études a la mémoire d'André Parrot*, 51–68.

Jonker, G. (1995). *The topography of remembrance: The dead, tradition and collective memory in Mesopotamia*. Leiden; New York, NY: E.J. Brill.

Kansteiner, W. (2002). Finding meaning in memory: A methodological critique of collective memory studies. *History and Theory*, 41(2), 179–197.

Katz, D. (2003). *The image of the netherworld in the Sumerian sources*. Bethesda, MD: CDL Press.

Kraus, F. R. (1964). *Briefe aus dem British Museum. By F. R. Kraus, AbB Heft 1, CT 43 und 44. Altbabylonische Briefe in Umschrift und Übersetzung.* Leiden: Brill.

Lenzi, A. (2011). An incantation-prayer: Ghosts of my family I. In A. Lenzi (Ed.), *Reading Akkadian prayers and hymns* (pp. 133–144). Atlanta, GA: Society of Biblical Literature.

Livingstone, A. (2007). *Mystical and mythological explanatory works of Assyrian and Babylonian scholars.* Winona Lake, IN: Eisenbrauns.

MacDougal, R. (2014). *Remembrance and the dead in second millennium BC Mesopotamia.* Doctoral Thesis, University of Leicester. http://hdl.handle.net/2381/29251.

Mcanany, P. A. (1995). *Living with the ancestors: Kinship and kingship in Ancient Maya society.* Austin, TX: University of Texas Press.

Oppenheim, A. L., Brill, R. H., Barag, D., & Saldern, A. V. (1970). *Glass and glassmaking in Ancient Mesopotamia.* Corning, NY: Corning Museum of Glass Press.

Richardson, S. (1999–2001). An Assyrian garden of ancestors: Room I, Northwest Palace, Kalḫu. In *state archives of Assyria Bulletin* (pp. 145–216). Padova, Italy: SARGON.

Scurlock, J. A. (1997). Ghosts in the ancient Near East: Weak or powerful? *Hebrew Union College Annual,* 68, 77–96.

Scurlock, J. A. (2001 [1995]). Magical uses of ancient Mesopotamian festivals of the dead. In M. Meyer & P. Mirecki (Eds), *Ancient magic and ritual power* (pp. 93–107). Boston, MA: Brill Academic Publishers.

Scurlock, J. A. (2006). *Magico-medical means of treating ghost-induced illnesses in Ancient Mesopotamia.* Leiden and Boston, MA: Brill / Styx.

Skaist, A. (1980). The ancestor cult and succession in Mesopotamia. In B. Alster (Ed.), *Death in Mesopotamia: Papers read at the XXVIe Rencontre Assyriologique Internationale.* Copenhagen: Akademisk Forlag, 123–128.

Tarlow, S. (2000). Emotion in archaeology. *Current Anthropology,* 41, 713–746.

Tarlow, S. (2011). *Ritual, belief and the dead in Early Modern Britain and Ireland.* Cambridge: Cambridge University Press.

Tricoli, S. (2014). The Old Babylonian family cult and its projection on the ground: A cross-disciplinary investigation. In L. Marti (Ed.), *La famille dans le Proche-Orient ancien: réalités, symbolismes, et images: proceedings of the 55th Rencontre Assyriologique Internationale, Paris, 6–9 July 2009* (pp. 43–68). Winona Lake, IN: Eisenbrauns.

Tsukimoto, A. (1985). *Untersuchungen zur Totenpflege (kispum) im Alten Mesopotamien.* Neukirchen-Vluyn: Butzon & Bercker.

Van Der Toorn, K. (1996). Domestic religion in Ancient Mesopotamia. In K. R. Veenhof (Ed.), *Houses and households in Ancient Mesopotamia: Papers read at 40e Rencontre Assyriologique Internationale, Leiden, July 5–8, 1993* (pp. 69–78). Istanbul: Nederlands Historisch-Archaeologisch Instituut de Istanbul.

Van Soldt, W. H. (1994). *Letters in the British Museum.* Transliterated and translated by W. H. Van Soldt, part 2. ABB Heft 13. Leiden: Brill.

Whiting, R. M., Jr., 1987. *Old Babylonian letters from Tell Asmar.* Chicago, IL: Oriental Institute.

Wilcke, C. (1983). Nachlese zu A. Poebels Babylonian legal and business documents from the time of the first dynasty of Babylon chiefly from Nippur (BE 6/2) Teil 1, *Zeitschrift für Assyriologie und vorderasiatische archäologie,* 73, 48–66.

Woolley, L., Mallowan, M. E. L., & Mitchell, T. C. (1976). *Ur excavations. Volume VII. The Old Babylonian Period.* London: published for the Trustees of the two museums by British Museum Publications.

20

CONTINUING BONDS AS A DOUBLE-EDGED SWORD IN BEREAVEMENT?

Candy H.C. Fong and Amy Y.M. Chow

Introduction

Continuing bonds (CB) with the deceased are considered to be natural and may be adaptive in the grieving process (Klass, Silverman, & Nickman, 1996). Recent empirical studies on the role of CB in the adjustment to loss have, however, yielded contradictory findings (e.g., Stroebe, Abakoumkin, Stroebe, & Schut, 2012). Evidence seems to suggest that the relationship between CB and bereavement outcomes is rooted in the forms of CB experienced by bereaved individuals (e.g., Ho, Chan, Ma, & Field, 2013). Some studies further reported that CB can play a mediating role in the relationship between risk factors and standardized grief outcome measures (e.g., Yu, He, Xu, Wang, & Prigerson, 2016a). In addition, Field et al. (2013) included subjectively reported levels of comfort and distress with regard to different forms of CB and observed that some forms of CB were described as both comforting and distressing. Thus, CB appear to be a double-edged sword in bereavement.

Klass (2014–15) examined varieties of CB across culture and over time. He found that the outcomes of CB in some cultures were not necessarily focused on the wellbeing or disruption of the living, but the wellbeing of the deceased in the afterlife. Similarly, Root and Exline (2014) proposed that cultural and religious afterlife beliefs could affect the role of CB in bereavement outcomes. The commonly used measure of CB, the Continuing Bonds Scale (CBS), was developed within a Western cultural context (Field, Gal-Oz, & Bonanno, 2003), although its conceptualization was partly inspired by Asian culture (Klass et al., 1996). This chapter seeks to first describe Chinese cultural perspectives pertaining to the concept of CB. It will then elaborate on the findings of a qualitative study carried out by the authors (Fong & Chow, in preparation) and will then explore other forms of CB that are not currently included in the CBS. The chapter will further discuss the complex role of CB in bereavement adjustment, with implications for research and practice elucidated.

Continuing Bonds with the Deceased in the Chinese Context

Dating back to the Shang dynasty (1750–1027), remains of ancestor worships were found in historic sites in China (Csikszentmihalyi, 2005). The later development of oriental philosophical thought such as Taoism, Confucianism, and Buddhism has further developed ideas on the bonds between the living and the dead. Taoism presents an interconnecting worldview regarding life in the universe. It is believed that all beings, including human beings, are part of a larger unified universe. All beings are seen to be interconnected, in accordance with the Tao, which is the path of nature. Life and death is merely a natural cycle of transformation from the status of "being" to "non-being", following the Tao of nature. Death is a process during which the once concrete life energy (being) diffuses and returns to nature (non-being), which then fertilizes the ground and provides raw materials for other beings to grow and reproduce, like the dead leaves fertilize the breeding ground for the growth of plants and trees. In other words, the life of individual beings may end but the essence of life can live on in the universe to have continuous influence on other lives.

Confucianism specified the ways in which living people related to deceased persons, with a specific focus on family ancestors. Filial piety here entails that descendants have the obligation to provide proper care and respect toward parents and senior members in the family, extending beyond death and into the afterlife (Lakos, 2010). This care can be manifested in various forms of physical, emotional and spiritual care, such as settling down physical remains and treasuring the legacies of a deceased person (Hsu, O'Connor, & Lee, 2009). There are also various occasions specifying the time to commemorate and care for one's ancestors such as the Ching Ming and Chung Yung Festivals, when living people are supposed to visit and clean the gravesites of the deceased. Another important dimension of filial piety is the continuous existence of family ancestors in the family life, biologically by giving birth to younger generations, and spiritually through passing on teachings, values and life wisdoms of deceased family ancestors (Lakos, 2010).

The Buddhist beliefs of predestination and fatalism influence how Chinese people view interpersonal connections including their bonds with deceased persons. The concept of "yuan", which refers to the predestined connections between two people, forms the blueprint for the development of interpersonal relationships (Yang & Ho, 1988). The yuan between two persons is believed to continue even after one person in the relational dyad has passed away, forming CB after death (Chan et al., 2005).

In summary, the philosophical perspectives that characterize Chinese culture reveal a worldview of interconnectedness. As such, there is a continuity perspective in human, family and relational life transcending beyond physical existence. Awareness of this perspective may help us to better understand how Chinese people perceive and experience CB after their family members have passed away.

Continuing Bonds in Relation to Bereavement Outcomes

In their review article entitled "To continue or relinquish bonds", Stroebe and Schut (2005) drew attention to a potential concern about the different role CBs may play in adjustment to bereavement. The authors cautioned that the available studies on correlations of some forms of CB with grief outcomes did not substantiate any causal relationships. Moreover, there are other factors influencing such correlations such as years of bereavement and forms of CB. More recent studies further accounted for the inconsistent findings concerning CB's role in bereavement as stemming from the diversity of definitions and types of CB, individual differences as well as other covariates such as attachment style, pre-death quality of the relationship, suddenness of the death and after-death beliefs (Root & Exline, 2014). Researchers proposed that CB is a multi-dimensional concept, and different dimensions might have different roles in the grieving process (Yu, He, Xu, Wang, & Prigerson, 2016b). The most common classification of dimensions of CB is the two-factors model of externalized and internalized CB as proposed by Field and Filanosky (2010), which has been further validated with a Chinese sample (Ho et al., 2013). Specifically, externalized CB was found to be a positive predictor of grief symptoms, whereas internalized CB was a positive predictor for growth after bereavement (e.g., Scholtes & Browne, 2015). Yu et al. (2016a) also identified the mediating role of externalized CB and internalized CB between insecure attachment styles and post-bereavement growth as well as standard grief measures.

Recent Qualitative Studies on Continuing Bonds in a Chinese Context

It has been reported that Chinese bereaved people adopt some ritualistic ways in bonding with the deceased in addition to the conventional identified bonds such as keeping reminders and memories of the deceased. For example, Pang and Lam (2002) documented the process by which four widowers navigating through prescribed cultural rituals developed personal connections with the deceased throughout their funerals. Chan et al. (2005) identified very specific ritualistic CB in their analysis of clinical interviews with 52 bereaved persons. These included the deceased's spirit revisiting on the seventh day after death and coming back in the form of an insect, as well as regular offerings and settling down of the ashes. CB was generally reported to be potentially normative or even adaptive, with Chinese bereaved people appraising them positively (Chan et al., 2005), and they facilitate the bereavement process through reducing survival guilt (Woo & Chan, 2010).

Forms of Continuing Bonds: Internalized and Externalized Only?

The commonly used measurement of CB is the Continuing Bond Scale (CBS) developed by Field et al. (2005), with validation details reported in Field and Filanosky (2010). The CBS was originally developed from a list of 47 items of CB expressions, as collected by means of a bereavement literature review, and administered to 375 undergraduate students who had experienced a bereavement in the past five years. Exploratory factor analysis reduced the scale to two factors (externalized and internalized CB) of 16 items. Ho et al. (2013) further tested the 47-item CBS through exploratory factor analysis with 71 Hong Kong Chinese people in the first three years of widowhood, and developed a 19-item Chinese version. Scholtes and Browne (2015) considered that the CBS might not be able to capture all CB expressions from a group of bereaved parents. They added three more items related to the Facebook bereavement group and identified a three-factor model with a third dimension of transference, included items related to carry out the deceased's wishes, habits, values, and interests as well as developing a sense of comfort in places related to the deceased.

Exploratory Qualitative Study on Continuing Bond of Chinese Bereaved Persons

To supplement the possible forms of CB among the Chinese population, the authors carried out a qualitative study through in-depth interviews with eight bereaved persons from diverse backgrounds and two funeral professionals. The bereaved participants were asked about the forms of CB they expressed or experienced whereas the professional participants were asked about what they had observed and heard from their bereaved service users. Upon thematic coding, 28 codes were identified and grouped into three themes conceptually: Reflecting in VALUE (V), expressing through ACTIONS (A), and experiencing in SENSATIONS (S). The VAS model of CB experience is proposed as shown in Figure 20.1 (Fong, 2015).

Reflecting in VALUE

CB were sometimes manifested in the form of thoughts, memories, values and attitudes associated with the deceased. These bonds can extend from the past to the future. Bereaved people reminisced about the deceased's life and the fond memories (past). They often realized lessons from the deceased such as personal values and life wisdom, or at least knew more about the preferences of the deceased in different aspects of life. Interestingly, those lessons, values, life wisdom, and preferences were then taken on to guide the bereaved's ongoing life, and could serve as important support for the bereaved in times of difficulties.

Other bonds in the values dimension were dreaming of and thinking about reunion with the deceased. While thoughts about reunion were very much

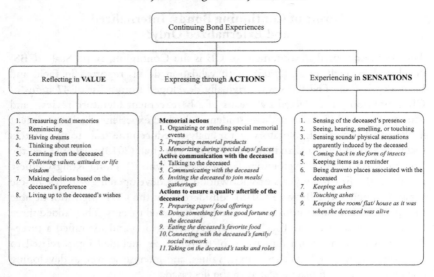

Figure 20.1 Continuing Bond Expressions Among Chinese Bereaved People

dependent on religious beliefs, dreams were quite commonly experienced among our bereaved interviewees. Dreams can manifest in several different contexts conveying messages that can comfort or distress the living persons. There were dreams where the living person visualized the afterlife conditions of the deceased, usually an idealistic life. The deceased can also make efforts to communicate with the living, saying goodbye and final words, or having reminders and foretellings on what would happen to the bereaved. Dreams of an ideal life and those of goodbyes and final words were experienced as comforting by the bereaved, as they were interpreted to signify the deceased's smooth transition to a quality afterlife.

Case Example 1: I am happy to see you in my dream!

Alva is a 55-year-old lady whose father committed suicide by jumping over a cliff edge. She recalled that her father was a quiet, lonely old man who neither got along well with her mother nor had many friends who he could talk to. Alva thought her father must have been very depressed at the time he committed suicide. She regretted not paying enough attention to her father and had been longing to dream of her father, to know more about his afterlife. She eventually had a dream of her father about one year after his death, and the dream consoled her a lot:

"I dreamed of my father several months ago. There are many other people living with him, and he is watching TV . . . I was curious about why he can watch TV with his broken eyes, and he told me that he can smell the TV. He looked very happy. I was really relieved at that time, seeing that he is now living happily with many people around."

By knowing that her father is leading a happy afterlife, Alva gradually moved out of the sense of guilt and regret associated with her father's death and moved on with life.

Expressing through ACTIONS

Connection with the deceased can be experienced in performing actions, behaviors and rituals. They can be largely grouped into three sub-categories including memorial actions, active communication with the deceased and actions to ensure a quality afterlife of the deceased. Memorial actions included efforts to memorialize the deceased person such as setting up special memorial places or dates, organizing or attending events on particular days and/or at particular places, and creating memorial products.

Case Example 2: The miracle dates on Christmas Eve

Bobby is a 36-year-old man whose wife committed suicide. He remembered he and his wife had previously made a promise to each other when they were dating one Christmas Eve that they would meet at an agreed place if they could not see each other. In the first year after his wife passed away, he went to the place as a way to memorialize his wife on Christmas Eve:

> "It was a prior promise with my wife made on Christmas Eve . . . we would meet there [an agreed place] if we could not see each other . . . I started to go there memorializing my wife at Christmas Eve this year . . . I took her graduation albums with me and read them there, and I played the music we liked . . . this gave me a sense of spiritual connection with her, just like she really came and met with me."

Bobby described what was a private time for him and his wife, to experience spiritual connections with his deceased wife. He decided to go on with this miracle date every Christmas Eve, and he will share this with their only daughter, who was 5 years old at the time, when she grows up.

CB in the form of actions can also be integrated into everyday lives; that is, carried out without designated places, times or occasions. Many bereaved people like to engage in activities that the deceased used to do as habits or hobbies. Foods and drinks are very relevant in this context, as many bereaved persons love to consume the favorite dishes or drinks of the deceased from time to time. This may be related to the social meaning of food in Chinese culture. Chinese people like to gather around the dining table with family in times of joy and happiness, for particular festivals, but also in times of sadness and critical family issues. The sense of emotional support, intimacy and connection, and shared precious memories when eating together would be accessed by consuming the deceased's favorite foods and drinks. Some bereaved persons would try to take up the roles and tasks which were previously performed by the deceased. Although this may be a practical way of maintaining optimal functioning of the family and social systems, it is quite possible that the bereaved would also interpret this as doing something for the deceased, continuing the once valuable roles of the deceased.

Actively communicating with the deceased family member can be seen as another action in maintaining CB. The bereaved can verbally or mentally "talk" to the deceased in everyday life, sometimes through connecting objects such as photos, gravestones, diaries and letters. The content of these conversations can be very private, updating about the bereaved's recent experiences, reporting on the conditions of people who the deceased cared for and seeking advice and support in the face of a life crisis. Most bereaved people engaged in such bonding acknowledged the uncertainties about whether the deceased was able to "listen" and "respond" to their messages, yet continuing to communicate with the deceased brought them consolation. Inviting the deceased to join meals and family gatherings is another act of intimacy, reflecting efforts to include the deceased in ongoing family and social interactions and shared lived experience.

Actions to ensure a quality afterlife are very much related to traditional beliefs and rituals within Chinese culture. There is a deep-rooted belief in Chinese culture that people will transition to an afterlife to live in an underworld after death. Their life is somewhat similar to that of living people in the sense that the spirits of the deceased will need "money" and "daily necessities" such as food, housing, clothing, etc., to sustain their "lives". Bereaved people will try to fulfill their family obligations to care for the deceased, through the regular provision of offerings including paper money and food, or on specific occasions, such as the anniversary of the deceased's birth and death, and during the Ching Ming Festivals, which are the culturally prescribed time for the living to connect with the deceased. They will also perform acts of kindness in the name of the deceased, donating the deceased's clothes and financial assets to charities and people in need to facilitate a smooth transition to the afterlife.

Experiencing in SENSATIONS

Sensation-related experiences of CB include bonds in the form of sights, smells, sounds and the sense of touch. These experiences can be further grouped into those initiated either by the deceased or by the bereaved, as proposed by Chan et al. (2005). Deceased-initiated bonds are involuntary and passive experiences of connection with a deceased person. That is, the living people do not have control over when, where and how the connections may happen. Many bereaved people reported occasionally sensing the presence of the deceased, through images, sounds, sense of touch and other forms of physical sensations. Also commonly shared is the experience of seeing insects appear in front of the bereaved, likely to be butterflies and moths. The insects were usually described by the bereaved as having unique features distinguishing them from "normal" insects in terms of their size, color and behavior patterns, making them recognizable. Unlike previous descriptions of such experiences as illusory and hallucinatory (e.g., Field et al., 2005), bereaved people encountering deceased-initiated bonds usually fully acknowledge the deceased's death and would consider such experiences as the deceased visiting them. Some even interpreted the bonds with the concept of "yuan", of which the involuntary bonds reflect a unique and deep predestined connection between the deceased and the bereaved.

Case Example 3: Welcome back, my love!

Joey is a 57-year-old lady who lost her husband in a car accident on the mainland. She shared her experience in which her deceased husband revisited her in the difficult times of the bereavement process:

> I was alone at the first Mid-Autumn festival as I sent my two daughters to study overseas. I could not sleep that night, feeling extremely lonely . . . I missed him very much, tears of loneliness came out from my eyes and I decided to leave the bed to make myself better . . . I walked to the dining room and suddenly, a big moth appeared flying around my waist . . . I know it must be him, he really comes back . . . He was hugging me around me waist to console me!"

Although she felt a bit scared with the moth flying around her, she recalled a sense of sweetness knowing that her deceased husband still made an effort to love and care for her. She looked forward to seeing moths at times of Ching Ming Festivals and Chung Yung Festivals every year, identifying them as her husband revisiting the family.

Bereaved-initiated bonds are voluntary and active experiences of CB among bereaved people. They are efforts which living people actively seek for sensory connections with the deceased. The bereaved may keep the rooms, flat or house as it was before the deceased passed away. Some people would keep items such as photos, key rings, diaries, clothes, writings and work portfolios. Others felt a strong urge to visit places associated with the deceased, such as the locations the deceased previously occupied at home, places where the deceased usually went to or places that contain personal meanings for the bereaved-deceased dyads. There are also people who develop a strong connection with the deceased's physical remains, hoping to ensure the ashes of the deceased are well handled, to keep ashes at home and to touch the ashes.

In sum, the VAS model offers an alternative perspective in understanding Chinese CB manifestations. In contrast to the previous internalized–externalized dichotomy, this model provides a new angle to understand different forms of CB as well as their differentiated impact on the bereaved. This can offer directions for practice, in particular with regard to actions that could be taken to facilitate bereavement adjustment.

The Coexisting Comfort and Distress in Continuing Bond Experience

The newly identified codes from the qualitative study were used to further enrich the original 16-item version of CBS (Field et al., 2005), constructing a 28-item measure of CB. The responding method adopted the methods of Field et al. (2013), asking questions about the presence of each form of CB as well as the level of subjective distress and comfort related to the CB experiences. Findings from 127 bereaved persons aged 18 and above revealed that CB is quite commonly experienced among Chinese bereaved people (Fong, 2015). The overall prevalence of encountering at least one of the 28 forms of CB was 97% and the figures for values, actions and sensations were 92.5%, 93.3% and 79.8%, respectively. Concerning the subjective comfort–distress dimension, our results showed that most bereaved people in the study perceived CB experience as comforting (73.9%), or at least there was a certain degree of comfort that coexisted with distress (19.1%). Only 1.6% found CB experience to be solely distressing.

Continuing Bond as a Protective or Risk Factor to Bereavement Outcomes

In relation to grief symptoms, CB experience was a significant predictor of grief symptoms as well as levels of anxiety and depression. It explained 26.9% of variance ($F(3,83)=17.582$, $p<.01$) in grief symptoms, 8.2% of variance ($F(3,83)=3.733$, $p<.05$) in anxiety level and 10.5% of variance ($F(3,83)=4.453$, $p<.01$) in depression level. Among the VAS dimensions, CB in the form of sensation were predictive of more grief symptoms and higher levels of anxiety and depression; action bonds were predictive of lower levels of depression; and value bonds were insignificant predictors for all measures on bereavement outcomes. The inter-relationships between the three forms of CB were suggested on account of their positive associations with one another, indicating that more experience of CB in any one form was associated with more experience in other forms.

Conclusion

Although this study has been largely exploratory, findings from bereavement outcome measures in terms of subjective comfort–distress and grief symptoms clearly point in the same direction: CB is a double-edged sword in Chinese culture; it can bring comfort and distress; and it can be adaptive or maladaptive in the bereavement process for Chinese bereaved persons. The adaptiveness of CB can depend on whether a person can make meaning from the bond with the deceased (Neimeyer, Baldwin, & Gillies, 2006), and such a meaning-making process is never personal and internal but closely related to the bereaved's interpersonal and socio-cultural contexts (Klass, 2006).

The VAS model offers an alternative perspective in making sense of CB in the Chinese context. Preliminary analysis seems to suggest that CB in the form of sensation and action are particularly relevant to bereavement adjustment. Sensory CB experiences may reveal a need for relational affirmation which induce grief, while action forms of CB provide a channel for proper acknowledgment of grief and collective support. In addition to the forms, the timing and occasions at which CB are experienced can be critical, with Chinese culture emphasizing propriety; that is, doing appropriate things at appropriate times, with appropriate manners and magnitude (Hsu et al., 2009).

References

Carverhill, P. A. (2000). *Bereaved parents of adult children: A discursive study of relationships* (Doctoral dissertation, University of Saskatchewan, Saskatoon, Canada).

Chan, C. L. W. Chow, A. Y. M., Ho, S. M. Y., Tsui, Y. K. Y., Tin, A. F., Koo, B. W. K., & Koo, E. W. K. (2005). The experience of Chinese bereaved persons: A preliminary study of meaning making and continuing bonds. *Death Studies, 29*, 923–947.

Csikszentmihalyi, M. (2005). Confucianism: An overview. In L. Jones (Ed.), *Encyclopedia of religion* (2nd ed., Vol. 3, pp. 1890–1905). Detroit, MI: Macmillan Reference USA.

Field, N. P., & Filanosky, C. (2010). Continuing bonds, risk factors for complicated grief, and adjustment to bereavement. *Death Studies, 34*, 1–29.

Field, N. P., Gal-Oz, E., & Bonanno, G. (2003). Continuing bonds and adjustment at 5 years after the death of a spouse. *Journal of Consultant and Clinical Psychology, 71*, 110–117.

Field, N. P., Gao, B., & Paderna, L. (2005). Continuing bonds in bereavement: an attachment theory based perspective. *Death Studies, 29*, 277–299.

Field, N. P., Packman, W., Ronen, R., Pries, A., Davies, B., & Kramer, R. (2013). Type of continuing bonds expression and its comforting versus distressing nature: Implications for adjustment among bereaved mothers. *Death Studies, 37*(10), 889–912.

Fong, C. H. C. (2015). *The construction and development of a measure on Chinese continuing bond and its correlates with bereavement outcomes.* Unpublished PhD dissertation submitted to the University of Hong Kong.

Fong, C. H. C., & Chow, A. Y. M. (in preparation). *The Value-Action-Senses Model of continuing bond among Chinese bereaved persons.*

Ho, S. M., Chan, I. S., Ma, E. P., & Field, N. P. (2013). Continuing bonds, attachment style, and adjustment in the conjugal bereavement among Hong Kong Chinese. *Death Studies, 37*(3), 248–268.

Hsu, C. Y., O'Connor, M., & Lee, S. (2009). Understandings of death and dying for people of Chinese origin. *Death Studies, 33*(2), 153–174.

Klass, D. (2006). Continuing conversation about continuing bonds. *Death Studies, 30,* 843–858.

Klass, D. (2014–15). Continuing bonds, society and human experience: Family dead, hostile dead, political dead. *Omega, 70*(1), 99–117.

Klass, D., Silverman, P., & Nickman, S. (Eds). (1996). *Continuing bonds: New understandings of grief.* Washington, DC: American Psychological Association Press.

Lakos, W. (2010). *Chinese ancestor worship: A practice and ritual oriented approach to understanding Chinese culture.* Cambridge: Cambridge Scholars Publishing.

Neimeyer, R. A., Baldwin, S. A., & Gillies, J. (2006). Continuing bonds and reconstructing meaning: Mitigating complications in bereavement. *Death Studies, 30,* 715–738.

Pang, T. H. C., & Lam, C. W. (2002). The widower's bereavement process and death rituals: Hong Kong experiences. *Illness, Crisis & Loss, 10*(4), 294–303.

Root, B. L., & Exline, J. J. (2014). The role of continuing bonds in coping with grief: Overview and future directions. *Death Studies, 38*(1), 1–8.

Scholtes D., & Browne, M. (2015). Internalized and externalized continuing bonds in bereaved parents: Their relationship with grief intensity and personal growth. *Death Studies, 39*(1), 75–83.

Stroebe, M., & Schut, H. (2005). To continue or relinquish bonds: A review of consequences for the bereaved. *Death Studies, 29,* 477–494.

Stroebe, M. S., Abakoumkin, G., Stroebe, W., & Schut, H. (2012). Continuing bonds in adjustment to bereavement: Impact of abrupt versus gradual separation. *Personal Relationships, 19,* 255–266.

Woo, I. M., & Chan, C. L. (2010). Management of survival guilt by a Chinese widower through the use of continuing bonds. *Mortality, 15*(1), 38–46.

Yang, K. S., & Ho, D. Y. (1988). The role of yuan in Chinese social life: A conceptual and empirical analysis. *Asian Contributions to Psychology, 263,* 281.

Yu, W., He, L., Xu, W., Wang, J., & Prigerson, H. G. (2016a). How do attachment dimensions affect bereavement adjustment? A mediation model of continuing bonds. *Psychiatry Research, 238,* 93–99.

Yu, W., He, L., Xu, W., Wang, J., & Prigerson, H. G. (2016b). Continuing bonds and bereavement adjustment among bereaved mainland Chinese. *The Journal of Nervous and Mental Disease, 204*(10), 758–763.

21

CONTINUING BONDS WITH NATIVE CULTURE

Immigrants' Response to Loss

Hani M. Henry, William B. Stiles, and Mia W. Biran

In this chapter, we use the continuing bonds model of mourning to examine the process of loss and mourning associated with immigration and understand some of the psychological changes associated with immigration. We begin by explaining our use of the continuing bonds model to understand immigrants' experiences and we review the losses often suffered by immigrants. We then explain how we integrated the assimilation[1] model, which was developed to describe how psychotherapy clients come to terms with their problems, with the continuing bonds model of mourning to characterize individual differences in how immigrants deal with the internal representations of their lost native culture. We then illustrate our conceptual tools by summarizing the results of a series of case studies based on interviews with immigrants. Finally, we offer some clinical recommendations to mental health professionals seeking to help immigrants cope with loss and mourning of native culture.

The Continuing Bonds Model of Mourning as Applied to Immigration

The view that mourning culminates in a continuing bond with what was lost is a counterpoint to grief work theory and its assumption that bereaved individual must detach themselves from the lost objects to reinvest in new relationships. Instead of "letting go" of lost objects and separating from them, the continuing bond model proposed by Silverman and Klass (1996) suggests that the bereaved person continues to integrate, identifies with, and creates a bond with these objects. In this view, mourning is not a contained, time-limited event with an end point when detachment has been achieved. Rather, the lost object is integrated and, as Murray (2001) put it, "becomes part of us" (p. 225). For example, in an eight-year ethnographic study of bereaved parents, Klass (1989) observed that the parents did not withdraw energy from the relationship with their child. Rather, they transformed the inner representation of the child in ways that allowed them to maintain the relationship.

Like bereaved parents or spouses, immigrants suffer numerous losses, whether they immigrate to avoid strife in their native country, to pursue advantages in the new country, or for some other reason. They often lose shared values, traditions, native songs, and familiar food, as well as social status, significant relationships, and in some cases, financial security. Seeking to characterize this loss, Marlin (1994) argued that immigration involves massive losses of loved elements in the abandoned culture, such as the familiar patterns of relating to people. Lijtmaer (2001) argued that immigrants may lose the holding functions that their mother countries provided, such as feelings of safety and connectedness to others. Marcus (2001) argued that they may lose a "home world" that had provided a sense of security and direction in their lives. Mirsky (1991) argued that a deep sense of loss of self-identity may result from the loss of the mother language. Mehta (1998) argued that cultural change and upheaval heightens the risk of disruption in immigrants' identity development because of the incorporation of new cultural norms. And Alvarez (1999) argued that an immigrant's cultural identity is challenged by frequently used labels such as "minority," "alien," and "immigrant."

As we applied it, the continuing bonds model of mourning suggests that immigrants incorporate the lost elements of their native culture, such as personal identity, families, friends, language, values, and traditions, into their life structure in the new host culture. As in the case of bereavement, Russac, Steighner, and Canto (2002) suggested that the loss does not end a relationship; rather, it redefines the relationship in ways that emphasize symbolic interaction. Like people mourning the loss of a loved one, immigrants preserve some inner representation of their native culture, history, and emotional ties to help them manage the challenges of immigration.

The extent and severity of the cultural and familial losses vary widely, depending on the circumstances of immigration and the differences between the native and host cultures. Immigrants' responses to these losses also vary. For many, the mental representations of their native culture are full of life and vigor and continue to inspire them and provide them with solace. Some immigrants thrive in their new home, integrating their former experiences in ways that enrich their new life. On the other hand, some may become confused and challenged.

Integrating the Continuing Bonds Model with the Assimilation Model

To study and describe these individual variations in the process of loss and mourning associated with immigration, we used an interpretive frame that combined the continuing bonds model with the assimilation model, described by Stiles (2002, 2011; see note 1). The assimilation model describes the process of integrating psychologically problematic experiences (memories, wishes, thoughts that are painful or threatening) into the person's usual repertoire of thinking and acting.

Stiles (2011) has argued that people's experiences are understood as active agents that have voices and respond by speaking and acting when they are addressed. Unassimilated voices tend to be problematic, whereas assimilated voices are resources that are available to be used by the clients as circumstances call for them. Emotional pain reflects discrepant voices coming into contact with each other, as when some situation triggers a memory or response that is discrepant from the person's usual way of thinking or acting.

In integrating the continuing bonds model of mourning with the assimilation model, we suggest that immigrants have continuing bonds with their native culture in the form of an internalized constellation of voices of that culture, representing experiential traces of their culture's values, traditions, and people. These voices are activated or triggered by signs or linking objects such as cultural artifacts, native art, physical beauty, language, proverbs, songs, food, and cultural and religious practices. To a degree that varies across individuals, these voices may be incompatible with the newly growing constellation of voices of the host culture. In theoretical terms, the voices of the native and host cultures may be mutually unassimilated. Encounters between such incompatible constellations of voices— occasions that address both constellations at once—make both try to respond at the same time, in incompatible ways. Stiles, Osatuke, Glick, and Mackay (2004) have explained how such encounters are experienced as psychologically painful, producing loneliness, fear, alienation, or self-disgust.

We also suggest that through the process of psychological assimilation, voices of immigrants' native culture can become resources in their new host culture. Assimilation between constellations of internal voices—personal or cultural— requires building meaning bridges. In the assimilation model, a meaning bridge is a sign (such as a word or a story or an image) that has the same or similar meaning from the perspective of both author and addressee (e.g., speaker and hearer). Meaning bridges label or formulate experiences in ways that are acceptable to and accessible by voices representing both cultures. By talking with others, engaging in cultural practices and rituals, and other such expressions, immigrants can discover ways to integrate disparate experiences of native and host cultures.

A series of intensive case studies reviewed by Stiles (2002) has suggested that psychotherapeutic assimilation proceeds along a developmental sequence described in the Assimilation of Problematic Experience Scale (APES). The eight-level sequence, numbered 0 to 7, characterizes the changing relation of the problematic voice to the person's usual self: 0) warded off/dissociated 1) unwanted thoughts/active avoidance, 2) vague awareness or emergence, 3) problem statement and clarification, 4) understanding or insight, 5) application/working through, 6) resourcefulness/ problem solution, and 7) integration/mastery. In successful therapy, clients advance through this sequence of recognizing, formulating, understanding, and eventually resolving the problematic experiences that brought them into treatment. Wilson (2011) has applied a version of the APES in bereavement counseling.

We sought to characterize the process of acculturation by adapting the APES to describe the mutual assimilation of the internal voices representing immigrants' experiences of their native culture and their experiences of the host culture. Our adaptation is shown in Table 21.1. The seemly divergent variety of manifestations of immigrants' continuing bonds can be understood as ordered along this continuum of assimilation. The integration of models also fills in details of the processes by which acculturation may take place, placing an emphasis on the degree of dialogue between internal voices of native and host cultures and finding continuing bonds that can serve as meaning bridges between former and current lives.

Table 21.1 The Assimilation of Problematic Experience Scale (APES) as Applied to the Process of Loss and Mourning in Immigration

APES Stage	Immigrant's Response
Stage 0 Warded off/ Dissociated	Immigrant wards off loss of native culture and is dissociated from this loss. Two possible scenarios may occur: A. Denial of the effects of loss of native culture, manifested by conformity to host culture and marginalization of native culture. Denial of native culture may alternate with clinging to it. B. Clinging to the lost culture, manifested by separation from host culture and idealization of the native culture. Continuing bonds may provide solace and prompt avoidance of host culture.
Stage 1 Unwanted thoughts/ Active avoidance	Immigrant becomes uncomfortable with and may attempt to repress thoughts of native culture. When occasionally exposed to racism and xenophobia, immigrant may examine his/her relationship with host culture. Immigrant may also experience fear of dealing with the loss of native culture and worry about this painful experience. Affect is intensely negative but episodic and unfocused; he/she does not understand why reminders of native culture create such intense emotions. The immigrant continues to deny or cling, and voices of one culture still dominate those of the other. Continuing bonds with native culture continue to provide solace in the case of clinging.
Stage 2 Vague awareness/ Emergence	Immigrant may now be aware of the pain resulting from loss. Pain is acute and feels unavoidable. Immigrant is unable to examine the loss of native culture and may experience acculturation stress and blame his/her pain on the new country. Solace from the continuing bonds may help immigrant ameliorate pain.
Stage 3 Problem statement/ Clarification	Voices of native culture (in case of denial) or host culture (in case of clinging) may emerge and may gradually assert and differentiate themselves from each other. Voices may contradict each other and the immigrant may experience turmoil. Immigrant may recognize that there is an alternative position to clinging or denial (i.e., integration of host and native cultures), and this realization may be problematic. Continuing bonds may continue to provide solace that is associated with clinging but it may also exacerbate this conflict. Affect is manageable but not panicky.

Stage 4 Understanding/ Insight	Understanding between two cultural voices takes place and meaning bridge between them is constructed. Immigrant may proudly exhibit native cultural values instead of dissociating from them (in case of denial). Alternatively, the immigrant may integrate host cultural voices instead of blocking them (in case of clinging). When voices are assimilated to one another, continuing bonds are manifested as resources to be called upon as needed. Affect may be mixed with unpleasant recognition, but also some pleasant surprise.
Stage 5 Application/ Working through	Continuing bonds may provide solutions for possible acculturation problems. Meaningful inner cultural dialogue takes place, which immigrant feels enriched by and functions better as a result. Assimilated lost culture may link immigrant to his/her past and may provide him/her with memories and faith. Affective tone is positive and optimistic.
Stage 6 Resourcefulness/ Problem solution	Immigrant is proud of continuing bonds with his/her culture to the extent that he/she is secure in own cultural identity and may now transmit useful cultural values to the new country. This may then allow him/her to contribute to the welfare of its citizens.
Stage 7 Integration/ Mastery	Native culture and host culture are totally assimilated into one another. Cultural repertoire of immigrant may expand as he/she develops a transcendent identity containing elements from both cultures.

Case Studies of Immigrants' Continuing Bonds with Their Native Culture

We used our adaptation of the APES to characterize the range and variety of immigrants' experiences with loss and mourning of native culture. In this section of our chapter, we illustrate our approach by reviewing four sets of case studies based on interviews with immigrants. The first set of case studies was based on broadcast interviews with immigrants that were available on the broadcaster's webpage. In the other three sets of case studies, the researchers conducted interviews that each took 70–90 minutes to explore the immigrants' responses to departing their home countries and the personal changes they had experienced as a result of immigration. Interviewees signed a consent form and institutional review board (IRB) approvals were secured from the universities where the research was conducted. Transcripts of the interviews were subjected to intensive qualitative analyses based on either assimilation analysis as described by Stiles and Angus (2001) or thematic analysis as described by Braun and Clarke (2006). This involved steps of (1) familiarization with the transcripts and indexing, (2) identifying themes related to loss and mourning of the native culture, (3) selecting passages that represented those themes, and (4) characterizing the process of mourning and assimilation with reference to the models. Details of the procedures along with quotations substantiating the theoretical interpretations are available in the full reports of the studies, cited later.

In the next four subsections, we provide narrative summaries of cases of individuals drawn from each of these four sets of interviews. These case studies were intended as theory-building case study research. As described by Stiles (2009), theory-building research evaluates theories not by separately testing isolated hypotheses against observations of a particular variable in many cases, but rather by comparing theoretical accounts with many observed details in particular cases. As the theory is adjusted and extended to account for more cases, the new observations permeate the theory, making it gradually more general, precise, and realistic. Our aim was to assess and elaborate our integration of the continuing bonds and assimilation models.

Arab Immigrants to Europe and North America

The first set of cases, reported by Henry, Stiles, and Biran (2005), were drawn from broadcast interview transcripts to examine the process of loss and mourning of Arab immigrants who had lived in Europe and North America for long periods. We summarize three cases:

Mr. Badleky was a Syrian artist who had been forced to leave his country and seek refuge in France 15 years earlier. The level of assimilation between his Syrian and French cultural voices could be described as APES 0-B, warded off (see Table 21.1). He seemed to experience a deep sense of confusion and sadness and shielded himself from experiencing the new reality of immigration and its potential for personal growth. His continuing bond with his native culture seemed not to be a source of problem solution and he had extreme difficulties adjusting and adapting to his new country of immigration. He also yearned to reunite with his old home town of Humas as shown in the following quote:

> So you would ask me if staying in Paris is the same as staying at Humas (Syrian town) and I will say it is totally different.

Mrs. Bondoky was an academic who had emigrated from Jordan to Canada 33 years earlier. At the time of the interview, the level of assimilation between her Jordanian and Canadian cultural voices could be described as APES 3, problem statement. Her appreciation of her losses and her continuing bonds with her native culture seemed to have created emotional conflict with the host culture, causing her significant emotional pain and discomfort. The following quote illustrates how she experienced an inner conflict between wanting to stay in Canada and wanting to go back home:

> What really hurts is that during the 33 years of immigration my heart was divided into two parts: Love for my home country and love for Canada. I do love Canada. The last 33 years in Canada were the most beautiful years in my life. I like to go back to my country, but I also love Canada.

Dr. Khoury was a surgeon who had emigrated from Palestine to the U.S. 25 years earlier. The level of assimilation between his Palestinian and American cultural voices could be described as APES 5, application of understanding. A meaningful inner dialogue between the two cultures seemed to have enriched his life. He seemed to use his continuing bond with his own culture as a source of solace and problem solution in the land of immigration. His assimilated memories of his lost culture linked him to his past and served as a resource. He seemed to have reached a stage of assimilation in which meaning bridges had been established between the voice of native and host cultures, as shown in the following quote:

> The American people are the kindest people in the world and the American people do not know what happens in the Arab world. And if the media is accurate, the American people will support Arabic people . . . the problem is that Americans do not know about Arabs and vice versa.

Non-European Immigrants to the United States

The second set of cases were drawn from interviews with immigrants to the U.S. from non-European countries, reported by Henry, Stiles, Biran, Brinegar, Mosher, and Banarjee (2009). We summarize three cases:

Fen had come to the U.S. from China eight years previously to join her husband. She was married and enrolled as a part-time graduate student. The level of assimilation between her Chinese and American cultural voices could be described as between APES 1, avoidance, and APES 2, (painful) emergence. The voices of her native and host cultures were at odds with each other. Fen found contact with American culture painful; she spoke with the voice of her native Chinese culture and clung to it. Her continuing bonds provided her with solace and helped her tolerate her immigration-related losses, but she also used it to retreat from the host culture for which she lacked interest. Fen's inner voices of her native culture were addressed by Chinese art and the natural beauty of China, and her response to these was her solace—a safe place to retreat when graduate school became too stressful. Fen wanted to take the values she learned from the U.S. and its citizens back to China without assimilating them into her own experience as an immigrant or a U.S. citizen. She resisted including a U.S. voice in her daily life activities, as shown in the following excerpt:

> I do not know exactly but they will never understand you. I think there are boundaries. I do not want; I do not want to; I could not; I am not able to break this boundary. Nobody will help break this boundary.

Muhammad was a 30-year-old single Iraqi man who had immigrated to the U.S. 12 years previously. He originally fled Iraq with his family in 1991 to avoid the oppressive regime of Saddam Hussein. After spending 18 months in a refugee camp in Saudi Arabia, he and his family were allowed to come to the U.S.

as refugees. The level of assimilation between his Iraqi and American cultural voices could be described as between APES 2, emergence, and APES 3, problem statement. He seemed to compartmentalize the loss of his native Iraqi culture. He had never fully assimilated some portions of his Iraqi voices culture to his U.S. voices, particularly those associated with the traumatic circumstances surrounding his decision to come to the U.S. As a result, the voices of Muhammad's native culture conflicted with those of the voices of U.S. culture, and encounters between them (i.e., circumstances that addressed both simultaneously) were negative and painful. His continuing bonds with his native culture provided him with solace in dealing with cultural losses; however, unlike Fen, his solace was not a retreating one. Rather, it was accompanied by a sense of inner conflict between the old and new cultures, as shown in the following quote:

> I am split into two parts. I am confused. I feel torn now. When I first came, I was so happy and settled. I now hope that things come back the way they were when I first arrived to America.

Diego was a 54-year-old male college professor who had emigrated from Mexico 24 years previously. The level of assimilation between his Mexican and American cultural voices could be described as APES 6, problem solution. He acknowledged and accepted the loss of many elements of Mexican culture, such as his friends and the way he used to live. He felt that his cultural losses had influenced his life but asserted that they were not irreversible. Diego said that he responded to loss of his native culture by carrying an "emotional backpack" that included his ideals, values, and moral beliefs. Diego maintained his bonds with his culture by his visits to local Mexican restaurants, by speaking in Spanish with his daughters, and by making new friends in Mexico even after his departure. The voices of Diego's two cultures seemed to be linked and the continuing bonds seemed to be a resource that enriched his life in his new culture, as shown in the following excerpt:

> So, when I go to Mexico I speak in English to my sister. To me this is perfectly normal and I feel kinda weird speaking Spanish to my sister. In other words, the mental switch between speaking English and speaking Spanish and thinking in either language to me it is totally transparent. The feelings, the understanding of the culture is totally transparent: When I am down there, I feel like a total Mexican doing what the Mexicans would do: yelling and screaming playing the guitar and acting like a Mexican. When I am here I feel as a complete American and do whatever Americans do.

African Immigrants to Egypt

The third set of cases, reported by Henry (2012), examined the influence of pre-immigration trauma on the acculturation process and continuing bonds with native cultures of African refugees in Egypt. We summarize two contrasting cases.

Abubakr was a 37-year-old Somali male refugee who reported that he had to flee his country 7 years earlier to save his life after the collapse of the central government. Before his departure, he experienced many incidents of discrimination and harassment by members of a different ethnic group. The level of assimilation between his Somali and Egyptian cultural voices could be described as APES 5, application and working through. He had transcended the traumatic experiences surrounding immigration in part by assisting members of the ethnic group that had discriminated against him through his involvement in a Somali development organization that helped them adjust to life in Egypt. Abubakr acknowledged and mourned his cultural losses, and he actively decided not to cling to these losses and move on with his life. For example, he said that loss should not be the only fact in his life and should not prevent him from living. He maintained a continuing bond with his native culture through his religion, which helped ameliorate the intensity of his negative emotional experiences, providing him with solace and helping him integrate himself into Egyptian culture. As a way of building meaning bridges, he focused on similarities between Somali and Egyptian culture, such as their Arab and Islamic roots. This made him feel close to the Egyptian culture and allowed him to make new friendships. He also used this meaning bridge to help his fellow Somalis adjust to Egyptian society, as seen in the following excerpt:

> So when they arrive in Egypt we help them study first in their native language, and also the Arabic language, which is very important because if you don't know this language there will be no communication with Egyptians. So to bridge this wall between the people, we make it easy for them to learn the Arabic language and we also give them some mathematics. Also, the mothers have a group called Established Mother Group. We were teaching these mothers Arabic because the mother is the only one who is going to the market to buy something for the children.

Melke was a 24-year old Ethiopian female refugee who had lived in Egypt for more than 4 years. She had a very different response to pre-immigration trauma. The level of assimilation between the Ethiopian and Egyptian cultural voices seemed best described as APES 1, avoidance. She was not interested in integrating Egyptian culture into her life because she felt "stuck" in Egypt. Her traumatic departure from Ethiopia caused her to abandon her future plans and prevented her from reaching several anticipated milestones in her life, such as finishing her high school diploma. Melke's inability to assimilate her pre-immigration trauma seemed associated with her inability to mourn her cultural losses, as shown in the following excerpt:

> I have been here for 4 years without [anything] and so on. I feel that nothing can possibly happen. I just kill them and I am living day-to-day [eyes well up with tears]. I can't live with that. I saw my friends still

dreaming about the future, but when I saw them, that's my future, you know? I saw people here for 8 years, 10 years and so on, and they don't even finish their high school.

However, she maintained a continuing bond with her native culture through her memory of her carefree days as a teenager. She marginalized the influence of Egyptian culture on her life and seemed unable or unwilling to reconcile the difference between this culture and her native culture.

U.S. Immigrants to Egypt

The fourth set of cases, reported by Henry, Hamdi, and Shedid (2009), was drawn from interviews with U.S. expatriates who were living in Egypt. These immigrants had very different experiences from the ones who had come to Egypt from Africa. They enjoyed many privileges and were welcomed and appreciated due to their skills or expertise. However, their continuing bonds with their native culture seemed to have a major influence on how they mourned their cultural losses and adapted to Egyptian culture, and there was significant variation in how they assimilated their contrasting cultural voices. We summarize two contrasting cases:

Sean was a 27-year-old Caucasian American and a practicing Muslim who had moved to Egypt at the age of 15 with his father. The level of assimilation between his U.S. and Egyptian cultural voices could be described as APES 4, understanding/insight. He had a clear understanding of his position between the two cultures, and his internal cultural voices could communicate with each other, though he had not applied the meaning bridges to produce an integrated cultural identity, as shown in the following excerpt:

> It is easier for me to pinpoint what effect having an American background and a certain kind of education has had on me than it is to say what kind of effect Egypt has had on me. But that's probably because now I've found myself in an Egyptian context, so the particularities of my personality that I have because I'm American stand out more, whereas I think probably if I was in America, it would be easier to see what aspects of who I am have come from my Egyptian experience.

Sean had completed a master's degree in Egypt and worked for a government-sponsored Islamic institution. He maintained a continuing bond with his native culture through his cherished memories of his childhood in New York. He said that New Yorkers, including himself, usually identify themselves as New Yorkers before identifying themselves as U.S. citizens. Sean felt that the influence of the U.S. on him surpassed that of Egypt. However, he also acknowledged the influence of Egypt on him, especially when he visited the U.S.

John was a 53-year-old Caucasian American male who had lived and worked as a college professor in Egypt for 10 years. The level of assimilation between his American and Egyptian cultural voices could be described as APES 1, avoidance. He expressed disappointment in the Egyptian culture and believed that it did not welcome the integration of foreigners. John tried to immerse himself in his U.S. culture while in Egypt. For example, he spent most of his leisure time in U.S. settings, associated exclusively with U.S. citizens, watched U.S. sporting events, and drank imported beer. John blamed the Egyptian culture for his lack of integration but he also acknowledged the role he played in that, as shown in the following excerpt:

> Uh well my integration never really happened. I mean this is not a complaint. I just don't think it's a culture that really integrates people from an entirely different environment. The Egyptians that I know in the U.S., it's such a different movement from here to there than there to here. My impression is they get to the U.S. and instantly begin to want to become absorbed and integrated. It just doesn't seem to me that it's the kind of culture that is set up for that. And there's certainly no disappointment on my part about that because I didn't make the effort.

Clinical Recommendations

To effectively deal with immigrants who may be undergoing the process of mourning associated with departing their countries, therapists need to examine their clients' worldviews, including their perceptions of loss and their reactions to both host and native cultures. In addition to providing information, this process of examining can promote a constructive dialogue among clients' inner cultural voices. According to Boulanger (2004), many therapists do not engage their immigrant clients in discussions about the difficulties inherent in fitting between two cultures. Acknowledging the presence of the continuing bonds may be the first step to facilitate such discussions. A client's continuing bonds with the native culture should not be seen as a threat to mourning losses and adjusting to the host culture. Rather, the continuing bonds can become resources for integrating elements of the two cultures as a way of facilitating therapeutic progress.

Therapists may want to conduct a full assessment of the losses experienced by their immigrant clients and examine possible differential responses to this loss. Some losses may be readily mourned, whereas others may not. Therapists should be aware of the possibility of regression in assimilation of loss. For example, one of the interviewed immigrants had productively mourned the loss of native culture only to face new life circumstances that seemed to reverse this mourning process. Finally, Sue and Sue (2003) argued that therapists can easily become a part of an establishment that oppresses immigrants and turns its back on them. If the immigrant's mourning of native culture is influenced by oppression or racism, therapists would do well to monitor their own possible discomfort in discussing these issues so that they can be effective with their immigrant clients.

Note

1 As used in this chapter, the term *assimilation* refers to psychological assimilation as described in the assimilation model. The unmodified term assimilation has had different meanings in the psychotherapy and immigration literatures. In the psychotherapy literature assimilation refers to a process of integrating experiences into one's thinking and behavior. By contrast, as used by Berry (1997) and other contributors to the immigration literature, assimilation refers to the immigrant's full acceptance/idealization of the host culture and total rejection and devaluation of the native culture. Ironically, very high levels of cultural assimilation may reflect very low levels of psychological assimilation. Total rejection and devaluation of the native culture represents a form of warding off (APES 0-A; see Table 21.1).

References

Al Jazeera (2004). *Appointments with immigrants.* Retrieved January 2004 from www.alja zeera.net/programs/date-with-mahjer.

Alvarez, M. (1999). The experience of migration: A relational approach in therapy. *Journal of Feminist Family Therapy, 11,* 1–27.

Berry, J. W. (1997). Immigration, acculturation and adaptation. *Applied Psychology: An International Review, 46,* 5–68.

Boulanger, G. (2004). Lot's wife, Cary Grant, and the American dream: Psychoanalysis with immigrants. *Contemporary Psychoanalysis, 40*(3), 353–372.

Braun, V., & Clarke, V. (2006). Using thematic analysis in psychology. *Qualitative Research in Psychology, 3,* 77–101.

Henry, H. M. (2012) African refugees in Egypt: Trauma, loss and cultural adjustment. *Death Studies, 36,* 583–604.

Henry, H. M., Hamdi, N., & Shedid, N. (2009). The cultural continuing bonds of US expatriates living in Egypt. *International Journal of Intercultural Relations, 33,* 1–10.

Henry, H. M., Stiles, W. B., & Biran, M. W. (2005). Loss and mourning in immigration: Using the assimilation model to assess continuing bonds with native culture. *Counselling Psychology Quarterly, 18,* 109–119.

Henry, H. M., Stiles, W. B., Biran, M. W., Brinegar, M. G., Mosher, J. K., & Banarjee, P. (2009). Immigrants' continuing bonds with their native culture: Assimilation analysis of three interviews. *Transcultural Psychiatry, 46,* 257–284.

Klass, D. (1989). The resolution of parental bereavement. In D. Kalish (Ed.), *Midlife loss: Coping strategies* (pp. 149–178). Thousand Oaks, CA: Sage Publications.

Lijtmaer, R. M. (2001). Splitting and nostalgia in recent immigrants: Psychodynamic considerations. *Journal of the American Academy of Psychoanalysis, 29*(3), 427–438.

Marlin, O. (1994). Special issues in the analytic treatment of immigrants and refugees. *Issues in Psychoanalytic Psychology, 16,* 7–16.

Marcus, P. (2001). Loss and renewal. In P. Suedfeld (Ed.), *Light from the ashes.* Detroit, MI: The University of Michigan Press.

Mehta, P. (1998). The emergence, conflicts, and integration of the bicultural self: Psychoanalysis of an adolescent daughter of South Asian immigrant parents. In S. Akhtar & S. Krammer (Eds), *The colors of childhood.* Northvale, NJ: Jason Aronson, Inc.

Mirsky, J. (1991). Language in migration: Separation and individuation conflicts in relation to the mother tongue and the new language. *Psychotherapy, 28,* 618–624.

Murray, J. (2001). Loss as a universal concept. A review of the literature to identify common aspects of loss in adverse situations. *Journal of Loss and Trauma, 6*(3), 219–241.

Russac, R. J, Steighner, N. S., & Canto, A. L. (2002). Grief work versus continuing bonds: A call for paradigm integration or replacement? *Death Studies, 26,* 463–478.

Silverman, P. R., & Klass, D. (1996). Introduction: What is the problem? In D. Klass, P. R. Silverman, & S. L. Nickman (Eds), *Continuing bonds: New understanding of grief.* Philadelphia, PA: Taylor & Francis.

Stiles, W. B. (2002). Assimilation of problematic experiences. In J. C. Norcross (Ed.), *Psychotherapy relationships that work* (pp. 357–365). Oxford: Oxford University Press.

Stiles, W. B. (2009). Logical operations in theory-building case studies. *Pragmatic Case Studies in Psychotherapy, 5*(3), 9–22. doi: 10.14713/pcsp.v5i3.973. Available: http://jrul. libraries.rutgers.edu/index.php/pcsp/article/view/973.

Stiles, W. B. (2011). Coming to terms. *Psychotherapy Research, 21*, 367–384. doi: 10.1080/ 10503307.2011.582186.

Stiles, W. B., & Angus, L. (2001). Qualitative research on clients' assimilation of problematic experiences in psychotherapy. In J. Frommer & D. L. Rennie (Eds), *Qualitative psychotherapy research: Methods and methodology* (pp. 112–127). Lengerich, Germany: Pabst Science Publishers. Also published in *Psychologische Beiträge, 43*, 570–585.

Stiles, W. B., Osatuke, K., Glick, M. J., & Mackay, H. C. (2004). Encounters between internal voices generate emotion: An elaboration of the assimilation model. In H. H. Hermans & G. Dimaggio (Eds), *The dialogical self in psychotherapy* (pp. 91–107). New York, NY: Brunner-Routledge.

Sue, D. W., & Sue, D. (2003). *Counseling the culturally different: Theory and practice* (3rd edition). New York, NY: John Wiley & Sons.

Wilson, J. (2011). The assimilation of problematic experiences sequence: An approach to evidence-based practice in bereavement counseling. *Journal of Social Work in End-Of-Life & Palliative Care, 7*, 350–362. doi: 10.1080/15524256.2011.623468.

SUBSECTION IV.2

A New Cultural Context
Social Media

The final three chapters in the book describe the culture created on Facebook as a new frame for continuing bonds.

The chapter by David Balk and Mary Alice Varga is the only one in this book that is directly connected with a chapter in *Continuing Bonds: New Understandings of Grief.* Balk wrote a chapter in the 1996 anthology about bereaved adolescents and early adults. In their more recent data, he and Varga find differences between those who use social media, and those who do not. Social media, they say, is a cultural development that changes the way people continue their bonds and share their bonds with the deceased with a community of others.

Melissa Irwin analyzes the themes she finds on "technologically situated ritualized spaces." She notes that only 20 years ago bereavement scholars, including one of this book's editors, were saying that contemporary continuing bonds are in the private sphere, not the public. She argues that Facebook provides a new kind of public space in which individuals' private bonds can be more widely socially shared.

The Section and book ends with a wide-ranging chapter by Elaine Kasket. She recasts the literature on continuing bonds within the new cultural frame. She says social media is changing where our memories of the dead are stored. Younger bereaved people who are used to "telepresence" now find presence of the online. Durable biographies are now constructed online. Social media allows users to share their continuing bonds within a community that is quite different from the face-to-face world before social media.

22

CONTINUING BONDS AND SOCIAL MEDIA IN THE LIVES OF BEREAVED COLLEGE STUDENTS

David E. Balk and Mary Alice Varga

Introduction

The power of the Internet and the overwhelming influence of social media in the lives of college students was not a consideration when the chapter on attachment and bereaved college students was written for the book *Continuing Bonds: New Understandings of Grief*. Since then the Internet and social media have become dominant features in both the development of late adolescents and their day-to-day experiences. We contend that examining bereaved college students' use of social media offers dramatic possibilities for examining attachment in the lives of college students coping with grief. We provide in this chapter (a) a quick overview of the psychosocial developmental notions that undergird the central importance of attachment in the lives of college students and (b) the role and influence of social media in the lives of college students. In addition, in response to requests from one of the editors, we have offered a brief summary of that earlier chapter on attachment and bereaved college students.

Psychosocial Development and Attachment in the Lives of College Students

The psychosocial developmental framework provides a persuasive structure for examining development during the college undergraduate years. Typical college undergraduates are in what psychosocial developmental theorists have termed "late adolescence" or "young adulthood." Major developmental achievements expected of late adolescents/young adults are (a) becoming autonomous, (b) making clear choices about how to earn a living, and (c) entering into and maintaining close, intimate friendships. The ultimate outcome is to achieve a distinct identity during the late adolescent years.

Identity formation, though following common patterns, occurs in varying trajectories, and clearly not all late adolescents become autonomous individuals with a clear sense of occupational direction and the skills and courage to be a friend. Being adrift as to purpose and goals can create enduring concern in late adolescents; at times such persons are late bloomers and go on to make noticeable contributions as adults. We have witnessed the gnawing anxiety displayed by late adolescents who are adrift, the empty stares in their eyes as they contemplate their lack of direction.

Identity formation is not simply an inner, psychological urge. Societal expectations about becoming an adult imbue the push toward greater maturity. Thus, the journey toward identity formation has both psychological and social influences. The journey varies not only with each individual but also within various cultures. It is not the intent or within the scope of this chapter to examine cross-cultural issues with identity formation, but we do recognize that overarching patterns have been found in self-concept development during adolescence and that variations are present across cultures – for instance, about what autonomy means and about what makes for secure attachments (Cong, Spector, Ying, & Shi, 2011; Rothbaum, Weisz, Pott, Miyake, & Morelli, 2000).

One of the chief developmental markers of identity formation involves lasting relationships. The notion of entering into and maintaining stable relationships alludes to the practice of becoming attached to others. Research done with adolescents indicates that the majority maintains and expresses emotional ties with their parents while negotiating the course of separating from them. As they proceed through their undergraduate years, most college students invest their time and interests in a select group of peers, spend increasing amounts of time with one or two persons, and become cognitively, emotionally, and interpersonally more skilled in making and keeping friends.

As adolescents grow into young adults, interpersonal relationships grow, mature, and change. College students at this level begin to engage in more intimate relationships and less approval-seeking from parents and even friends. These emerging adults begin to embrace individuality, diversity, and self-sufficiency. Researchers are now examining the role of social media in the development of interpersonal relationships and are suggesting that increased social media use can lead to less developed relationships (Masin & Foubert, 2014).

Role and Influence of Social Media in the Lives of College Students

Social media platforms are now an everyday occurrence in the lives of college students. Nearly 90% of young adults (ages 18–29) use social media, with educated students more likely to do so. The very great majority of traditional-aged college students comprise a group known as digital natives; they have never known a time when computers, the Internet, and nearly instantaneous access to the world were not realities; they are familiar with computers, and engaging in social media platforms is an integral part of their lives (Prensky, 2001).

We also know that social media platforms are used for a variety of reasons, including entertainment; information seeking; information sharing; needing to belong; self-presentation; approval and support; and interpersonal connections and social interactions. College students, in particular, primarily use social media platforms for social interactions (Nadkarni & Hofmann, 2012; Pempek, Yermolayeva, & Calvert, 2009; Urista, Dong, & Day, 2009).

Social media is also gaining popularity as an environment college students use to deal with bereavement. College students are using social media sites, such as Facebook, to express their grief, seek grief support, and stay connected to the deceased (Egnoto, Sirianni, Ortega, & Stefanone, 2014; Frost, 2014). Facebook is an optimal outlet, especially for students unable or unwilling to express their grief in face-to-face interactions. College students stay connected to the deceased through social media, often talking with the deceased directly, memorializing them, and using these platforms as an important tool in mourning. Bereaved adolescents also continue ongoing relationships with the deceased via social media. They will visit the Facebook page of the person who died, often commenting on their pictures, posting memories, and talking directly with the deceased (Pennington, 2013).

Although it is speculated that the majority of college students use social media as a means to express grief, cope with loss, and stay connected to the deceased, such use is not always the case. Findings from a bereavement study conducted on a college campus illustrate the alternative perspective students have of social media platforms and their roles in bereavement. Instead of all college students using social media during bereavement, students' perspectives of the place of social media in grief fall along a continuum that ranges from social media considered an inappropriate venue for expressing grief to social media accepted and used as an outlet for communicating one's grief. These differing perspectives also challenge the notion of the role social media plays in continuing bonds.

A Summary of the 1996 Chapter

The attachment findings reported in the 1996 edition of *Continuing Bonds: New Understandings of Grief* emerged from a larger research project funded by National Institute of Mental Health (NIMH) to determine whether a series of social support interventions would benefit bereaved college students. The intervention study began with 110 bereaved students and 70 not bereaved. A total of 141 students remained in the study for its duration: 80 bereaved and 61 not bereaved. The bereaved students were randomly assigned either to intervention or control groups. The study gathered both quantitative and qualitative data: quantitative from standardized self-report measures of distress and the qualitative from responses to Thematic Apperception Test (TAT) cards. Data were gathered on three separate occasions approximately 6 weeks apart.

The examination of attachment looked at influences that attachment to the deceased had on bereavement responses as measured by answers to three self-report measures of distress (the Beck Depression Inventory (BDI), the Impact of Event Scale, and the SCL-90R) and two self-report measures of grief (the Texas Inventory of Grief and the Grant Foundation Bereavement Inventory). An attachment scale was devised from 29 items in the Grant Foundation Bereavement Inventory. Each item was prefaced with the phrase "How often during the past month have you . . .", and each item was answered on a 1 to 5 scale ranging from "never" to "all of the time." Examples of the 29 items include "thought about how he/she died," "avoided going to places that might remind you of him/her," "asked questions to find out more about his/her life," "pictured him/her in your mind," and "made a special effort to visit places that remind you of him/her." Higher responses to the scale indicated greater attachment to the person who had died.

Discriminant function analysis determined that attachment scale responses grouped into three distinct categories: students with little attachment (n = 15), students with some attachment (n = 49), and students with much attachment (n = 16). Levels of attachment were not correlated to age, gender, religious affiliation, or intervention/control group membership. A statistically significant relationship was found between level of attachment and duration since the death, with greater attachment linked to less time since the death. A majority of the students indicated an ongoing attachment (that is, some or much attachment) to the person who died. In addition, students with much attachment reported more distress than did students with some or little attachment. Over the course of the intervention study, distress significantly differed according to the students' level of attachment. In all but one case, it was always students with much attachment that reported significantly higher signs of distress.

Discriminant function analysis allows clinically meaningful profiles to be developed about the bereaved students grouped according to level of attachment. These profiles are provided directly below.

Profile of a Bereaved Student with Little Attachment

Students with little attachment had low depression scores, were not bothered by intrusive thoughts and feelings, and did not make efforts to avoid reminders of the death. They did not report acute grief. Their responses to the measures of distress resembled the responses of a normal, nonclinical population. They basically looked like their nonbereaved peers.

Profile of a Bereaved Student with Some Attachment

These students' BDI depression scores were for all intents and purposes like the scores of the students with little attachment. They engaged in avoidant behaviors and reported being troubled by intrusive thoughts and feelings about the death.

Their grief scores were more acute than the scores reported by students with little attachment but significantly less than the grief scores of the students with much attachment. Their SCL-90R responses indicated somatic issues, anxiety, and obsessive-compulsive behavior almost a standard deviation above responses of peers who are not in clinical treatment. Their SCL-90R scores for psychotic distress and for depression reached one standard deviation above the norm.

Profile of a Bereaved Student with Much Attachment

The responses of these students identified persons with the most distress of all participants in the study. Their scores on the BDI suggested mild mood swings. These students worked hard to avoid reminders of the death and reported intrusive thoughts and feelings occurred often. Their grief was acute throughout their time in the study. Nearly all of their SCL-90R distress scores were one standard deviation above the norm for a nonclinical population, and they were particularly troubled by anxiety, paranoia, psychotic symptoms, depression, and obsessive-compulsive behavior.

Method

Since the 1996 chapter on college student bereavement and attachment was published, research into how college students use thanatechnology (the use of the Internet for grief purposes) has been conducted in various capacities (Deatherage, Servaty-Seib, & Aksoz, 2014; Pennington, 2013; Sofka, Cupit, & Gilbert, 2012; Vicary & Fraley, 2010). This chapter presents findings from a university-wide grief study conducted to explore college students' use of social media during bereavement. After receiving institutional review board (IRB) approval, approximately 10,000 undergraduate students were contacted about participating in a survey using both closed-ended and open-ended questions about social media use as a form of grief support. Students were asked to indicate a) whether they used social media as a grief support and b) whether they found social media grief support helpful. They were invited to expand on their experiences and thoughts on using social media as a grief support.

Findings

Participants included 829 undergraduate students, including 664 (80%) females and 154 (19%) males. The mean age was 20 years (SD = 8.72) and the majority of students identified as white (n = 496, 60%) and Christian (62%, n = 516). Most students (74%, n = 613) reported experiencing a loss within their lifetime. Of these, the death occurred in the past 6 months (15%, n = 92), 7 to 12 months ago (12%, n = 74), 13 to 24 months ago (15%, n = 93), 25 to 36 months ago (12%, n = 74), and more than 36 months ago (45%, n = 273). These data correspond closely with incidence and prevalence findings in other published reports about college student bereavement.

When the 613 students who experienced a loss were asked about the relationship of the person they lost, most students reported grandparents (43%, n = 265), followed by parents (16%, n = 101), aunts/uncles (13%, n = 82), and friends (11%, n = 65). When asked about their perceived closeness to the deceased, 58% (n = 355) reported their relationship as "very close," 25% (n = 154) reported being "close," 14% (n = 88) reported being "somewhat close," and only 1.8% (n = 11) reported the relationship as "not close at all." Most frequent causes of death included illnesses (65%, n = 399) and accidents (12%, n = 74). The majority of students also reported the death as unexpected (64%, n = 395).

Of the 613 students who experienced a loss, only 26% of students (n = 157) reported using social media as a means of grief support (see Table 22.1). Most students used Facebook (84%, n = 132), followed by Instagram (30%, n = 47) and Twitter (20%, n = 32). Sixty-three percent (n = 389) explicitly indicated they did not use social media as a grief support. When the 157 students who used social media as grief support were asked how helpful it was, the majority of them (54%, n = 84) reported it as helpful (see Table 22.1).

All 613 students who experienced a loss were also asked 1) to share if and how they used social media during their grief, and 2) what types of information they posted. These 165 open-ended comments were extracted and analyzed using thematic analysis and the constant comparative method. Three themes were identified and are outlined below along with excerpts from students (see Table 22.2).

These themes identify three points on what we conceptualize as The Bereavement and Social Media Use Continuum that illustrates the degree to which college students use social media during bereavement (see Figure 22.1). The first theme addresses the point on the continuum that identifies students who widely use social media to express grief, to receive support, and to facilitate

Table 22.1 Social Media Use by Bereaved College Students

Usage	n	Percentage
Use social media as a grief support	157	26
(Found support helpful)	(84)	(54)
(Did not find support helpful)	(73)	(46)
Did not use social media as a grief support	389	63
No response	67	11

n = 613

Table 22.2 Degree of Social Media Use by Bereaved College Students

Degree of Usage	n	Percentage
Vast social media use	104	63
Limited social media use	44	27
No social media use	17	10

n = 165 open-ended qualitative comments from students

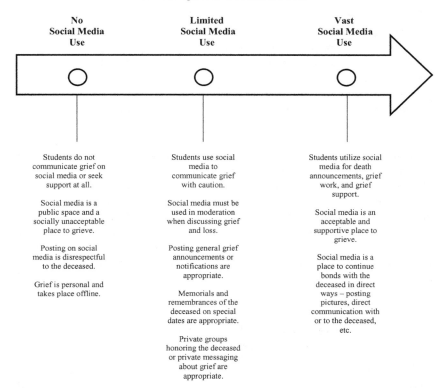

Figure 22.1 College Student Use of Social Media During Bereavement Continuum

continuing bonds. The second theme addresses the point on the continuum of students who use social media in limited capacities. The third and final theme identifies students who reside on the point of the continuum where using social media for grief is socially unacceptable.

Themes around continuing bonds were also examined. When re-analyzing data specific to students who used social media vastly or in limited amounts, three themes were outlined. These themes include emotional expressions, memories of the deceased, and speaking directly to the deceased.

Vast Social Media Use: Openly Grieving, Receiving Support, and Continuing Bonds

Although the majority of undergraduate students indicated they did not use social media for grief support, those who did were very specific about their uses. Of the 165 qualitative comments students provided, nearly two-thirds (63%, n = 104) indicated use of social media in very public ways to express grief. One student said, "I released my feelings. I told how I felt about me and my great grandmother's relationship, and also posted pictures of her." While students reported expressing their feelings on social media, they also mentioned gaining support. One student shared, "I just post pictures and talk about memories. My 'friends' encourage and empathize." Another student said, "I just posted that my grandfather passed and I was really upset. Everyone's comments is [sic] what really helped me. Several messaged me and asked if I needed anything. It was really sweet." The notion of community and support in this unique online capacity serves as a comfort for grieving students.

In addition to sharing grief emotions and receiving support, students also shared how they directly connected to the deceased using social media. One student shared, "I use Facebook to talk to Sammie even though she's gone. Helps me feel like there's still an open line of communication, even though she's gone." Direct contact with the deceased's existing social media account was not an uncommon phenomenon. Another student said, "I would post on his Facebook wall as if he could read what I was saying and so his family members knew I still care for him."

Students use social media as a tool to stay connected to the deceased in very therapeutic ways. Whether they are verbalizing things they never got to tell their lost loved one, or striving to keep their memory alive, these students use social media as a way to connect with the deceased and continue bonds.

Limited Social Media Use: Announcements, Anniversaries, and Special Events

In the middle of The Bereavement and Social Media Use Continuum are students who use social media in a limited capacity. When examining the open-ended comments about their social media use specific to grief, 27% (n = 44) of students fell on this area of the continuum. These students used social media to post brief messages about their loss, static information such as death announcements or funeral arrangements, or posts only on specific dates or events. One student said, "I just updated everyone on the situation and the inevitable loss." Another student shared that, "I posted one status about my grandfather's sudden death." Social media was used as a way to communicate information as well. For example, one student said she posted, "Informing every one of the loss and funeral arrangements, received many condolences in return." Other students shared that posting announcements in this mass manner reduced the number of people they had to individually speak with about the death event.

Students also used social media to communicate specific information about certain causes of death and events surrounding the loss. One student said, "Because suicide is such a big issue to me, I posted on Tumblr that I am always here to talk if someone needs me. I can't handle losing more loved ones." Another student shared, "Because he was killed in a public tragedy, I put his story out there for people to hear from our side." Having social media as a platform to communicate these grief events and perspectives was an important part of the student grief experience in these instances.

In addition to grief announcements and information sharing, students readily reported using social media as a way to remember or memorialize their deceased loved ones on important days. These important days included birthdays, holidays, anniversary of death, and others. One student said, "I post a status around the anniversary of his death." Another student shared that, "I recognize the birthdays of both my dad and mom as well as important days such as Mother's Day and Father's Day." Other students explicitly stated how much they missed the deceased during these important dates.

The 27% of students within this part of the continuum find it socially appropriate to post these "remembrance statuses" via social media to remember the deceased and remind the online universe of their existence; however, 70% of students identified with the "No Social Media Use" of the continuum; they specifically did not use social media to communicate their grief and considered it inappropriate to use social media for such personal matters.

No Social Media Use: Grieving Is Socially Unacceptable in Social Media

A large number of students shared that they did not use social media as a grief support (70%, n = 545). When examining the 165 qualitative responses, 10% (n = 17) of students explicitly shared their viewpoints on social media as a place that is inappropriate to talk about grief. One student said, "I think social media is NOT a place for personal issues as sensitive as grief." Expanding on this idea, another student shared that:

> I didn't use social media because I believe that my grieving is on such a personal level that I don't wish to seek help or comfort from a very public place. I would rather communicate with those closest to me than share my grief with the world.

The personal nature of grief contrasted with the perceived public nature of social media – and some students felt very strongly about this notion. One student said, "I do not like when people post stuff like that on social media. The only thing I posted was the location of the funeral and to not send flowers because we were taking donations to the lung association instead." Another student expanded on this idea and shared:

> I understand how social media can be useful when it comes to finding many people to help reassure you. If a lot of people know about your pain, then there will be more people who will be able to help you through your pain. However, I feel that social media is not the place to post things like, "My cat died today" or "My husband died of cancer" or whatever an individual is suffering through. That really doesn't seem appropriate to me and is really odd in my mind.

Another student echoed this sentiment, "I did not use social media. I feel like that would have been disrespectful to the deceased. If I was going to tell anyone or talk about it, I would do it face-to-face or over the phone, but not texting."

Alternatively, there were some students who view social media as a place you can grieve with restrictions. One student said, "I mentioned my loss on Facebook, but minimally. I posted with friends who knew him. On Tumblr I made one rather long post expressing my grief because it was more anonymous than Facebook." Another student shared what happened when others on social media are nonresponsive to grief postings:

> I abused the ability to talk online when I should have not been online. I said things and I thought people would respond but honestly they didn't, so I thought the world hardly cared when it first happened. It didn't help me get over it.

Social media platforms are public spaces, despite the façade of privacy that comes with various user settings. These are also very sociable environments that function around "posts" and "responses." If a student posts about grief and a response is not triggered, such as the student presented here, this experience of being ignored can exacerbate feelings of loneliness.

Facilitating Continuing Bonds Through Social Media

Further examination of the qualitative comments students provided illustrates the specific ways in which they engage in continuing bonds with their deceased loved one. The comments of 148 students who reported they used social media as a bereavement tool were analyzed. Findings indicated that students used social media in three distinct ways: 1) emotional expression; 2) posting memories of the deceased; and 3) speaking directly to the deceased (see Table 22.3).

Emotional Expression

Approximately 38% (n = 56) of the 148 comments illustrated various ways in which students used emotional expressions on social media as a connection to the deceased. One student shared, "I posted an angry status due to the fact that I

Table 22.3 Continuing Bonds Strategies Used via Social Media

Strategy	n	Percentage
Emotional expression	56	38
Memories of the deceased	44	30
Speaking directly to the deceased	10	7
No strategies used	38	25

n = 148 open-ended qualitative comments from students who reported using social media vast or limited amounts hadn't forgiven the person that died." Comments centered around sadness, anger, and confusion, which are all common feelings young adults experience during bereavement. Social media provides a platform for students to express these emotions in explicit ways and often indicate a continued bond with the deceased, as these students have illustrated.

Memories of the Deceased

In addition to emotional expression, social media also serves as a space where students can share memories of the deceased. Thirty percent (n = 44) of the 148 comments made a notation about using social media in a memorial capacity. Students often post pictures, poems, and specific memories of the deceased or positive times they shared together. One student said, "I put a picture of my cousin as my profile picture and a status about all the good times we shared." Sharing memories was also intertwined with emotional expression. For example, one student shared that "I created a Facebook group. Posted pictures, feelings, and stories." Many other students specifically referenced anniversaries or holidays as when they posted memories to stay connected to their loved one. Students often shared that they would "Post on the anniversary of the death" or pay tribute on special holidays. Similar to what other studies have found, college students use social media in a variety of ways as not only a grief support, but as a memorial tool as well.

Speaking Directly to the Deceased

Using social media to directly to the deceased is one of the most explicit ways in which college students stay connected to their lost loved ones (Krysinska & Andriessen, 2015). Approximately 7% (n = 10) of the 148 qualitative comments mentioned how the student used social media to directly speak to the deceased. Half of the 10 students spoke about how they specifically posted on the deceased's social media page. One student shared that "I post to my mom's wall about events and it helps to continue to feel connected with them." In these instances, social media pages of lost loved ones transform into a memorial page for students post-death. Similar to visiting cemeteries, students can "go to" the social media page of their loved one to visit their "profile," post memories of them, and even speak directly to them.

Summary of Empirical Study

Of the 613 students who experienced a loss, only 26% of students (n = 157) reported using social media as a means of grief support. The majority of these students (54%, n = 84) also reported social media as a helpful grief support. Open-ended comments about if and how students used social media illustrate a continuum of use, which we have named The Bereavement and Social Media Use Continuum. This continuum demonstrates the ways young adults conceptualize the role of social media during bereavement. Of the 165 qualitative comments, the majority (63%, n = 104) are from students who fall within the "Vast Social Media Use" on the continuum, where grief is expressed very publicly and explicitly on social media. Other students (27%, n = 44) reside closer to the middle of the continuum, "Limited Social Media Use," and are intentional about limiting the ways they use social media when grieving. Finally, the remaining students (10%, n = 17) practice "No Social Media Use." This area on the continuum pertains to students who view social media as an inappropriate place to express their grief. When examining social media behavior specific to continuing bonds, we learned that college students engaged mostly in emotional expression (38%, n = 56), posting memories of the deceased (30%, n = 44), and speaking directly to the deceased (7%, n = 10).

Discussion

Sofka, Cupit, and Gilbert (2012) assert that "Technology has expanded the ways that we as a society think about dying, death, and grief" (p. 3), and this change is particularly true for young adults. Young adults in college use social media for all facets of their lives, including their grief experiences; however, results from this study indicate that is not always the case. In fact, there appears to be a continuum of students and their use of social media during grief experiences (see Figure 22.1). It is widely known, and this study confirms, that the majority of students (63%) use social media to post death announcements and information. Students also turn to social media on anniversaries, holidays, and other special dates to memorialize the deceased. However, there is still also a population of students (10%) who conceptualize grief as a personal, private experience, while social media is a very public environment, and mixing the two is viewed as inappropriate or should be used with caution. Our quantitative results indicate that 70% of young college students did not use social media as a grief support. The limited qualitative data from 17 young adults provide us with initial insights into this phenomenon; however, additional information is needed to explain why these results conflict with what research reports regarding the vast use of social media.

The continuum of use of social media during grief experiences offers interesting implications for continuing bonds. Many students may find solace in using social media as a medium to their lost loved one and feel comfortable doing so in a public space (Irwin, 2015). Thus, social media can be an important resource for students with difficulty communicating their grief in face-to-face interactions or who lack support elsewhere in their lives. Social media also assists students with continuing bonds. College students can perceive social media as an explicit way to stay connected to the deceased and facilitate continuing bonds in a new technologically advanced way.

While it is assumed that college students are using social media to stay connected to the deceased, this assumption may not always be accurate. Reflecting on findings related to the continuum of social media use during grief, we learned college students may only use social media in a limited capacity. These instances include death notifications, announcements about funeral or burial arrangements, and pointed posts on specific holidays or important dates. As students pointed out in the study, some also prefer to communicate via private messages.

On the other end of the spectrum are students who do not use social media for grief purposes – a topic not widely discussed in the literature. As students shared, they are engaging in mourning practices offline and do not conceptualize the public online environment as an appropriate place to grieve. Students who were interviewed illustrated how these digital natives are engaged in continuing bonds offline in a more personal way. One student has her grandmother's scarf in her living room on a table that keeps her grandmother in her life. Another student kept a box of mementos after her boyfriend's murder. While the online environment provides a space for college students to grieve and establish continuing bonds in a virtual way, the offline way of connecting with the deceased should not be ignored. Students still find value in privatizing their experiences and respecting their lost ones in more traditional ways. Once again, the continuum of how students perceive the role of social media in bereavement sheds light on their multiple perspectives about use of social media. Educators, clinicians, researchers, and university officials should keep this continuum in mind as they support bereaved college students.

References

Cong, L., Spector, P. E., Ying, L., & Shi, L. (2011). The interaction of job autonomy and conflict with supervisor in China and the United States: A qualitative and quantitative comparison. *International Journal of Stress Management, 18*(3), 222–245.

Deatherage, S., Servaty-Seib, H. L., & Aksoz, I. (2014). Stress, coping, and Internet use of college students. *Journal of American College Health, 62*(1), 40–46.

Egnoto, M. J., Sirianni, J. M., Ortega, C. R., & Stefanone, M. (2014). Death on the digital landscape: A preliminary investigation into the grief process and motivations behind participation in the online memoriam. *Omega, 69*(3), 283–304. doi: 10.2190/OM.69.3.d.

Frost, M. (2014). The grief grapevine: Facebook memorial pages and adolescent bereavement. *Australian Journal of Guidance and Counselling, 24*(2), 256–265.

Irwin, M. D. (2015). Mourning 2.0: Continuing bonds between the living and the dead on Facebook. *Omega, 72*(2), 119–150. doi: 10.1177/0030222815574830.

Krysinska, K., & Andriessen, K. (2015). Online memorialization of grief after suicide: An analysis of suicide memorials on the Internet. *Omega, 71*(1), 19–47.

Masin, R. C., & Foubert, J. D. (2014). Effects of gender and Facebook use on the development of mature interpersonal relationships. *Journal of Student Affairs, 23*, 51–58.

Nadkarni, A., & Hofmann, S. G. (2012). Why do people use Facebook? *Personality and Individual Differences, 52*(3), 243–249. doi: 10.1016/j.paid.2011.11.007.

Pempek, T. A., Yermolayeva, Y. A., & Calvert, S. L. (2009). College students' social networking experiences on Facebook. *Journal of Applied Developmental Psychology, 30*(3), 227–238. doi: 10.1016/j.appdev.2008.12.010.

Pennington, N. (2013). You don't de-friend the dead: An analysis of grief communication by college students through Facebook profiles. *Death Studies, 37*(7), 617–635.

Prensky, M. (2001). Digital natives, digital immigrants Part 1. *On the Horizon, 9*(5), 1–6.

Rothbaum, F., Weisz, J., Pott, M., Miyake, K., & Morelli, G. (2000). Attachment and culture: Security in the United States and Japan. *American Psychologist, 55*(10), 1093–1104.

Sofka, C. J., Cupit, I. N., & Gilbert, K. R. (2012). Thanatechnology as a conduit for living, dying, and grieving in contemporary society. In C. J. Sofka, I. N. Cupit, & K. R. Gilbert (Eds), *Dying, death, and grief in an online universe: For counselors and educators* (pp. 3–15) New York, NY: Springer Publishing Company.

Urista, M. A., Dong, Q., & Day, K. D. (2009). Explaining why young adults use MySpace and Facebook through uses and gratification theory. *Human Communication, 12*(2), 215–229.

Vicary, A. M., & Fraley, R. C. (2010). Student reactions to the shootings at Virginia Tech and Northern Illinois University: Does sharing grief and support over the Internet affect recovery? *Personality and Social Psychology Bulletin*, 1–9.

23

MOURNING 2.0

Continuing Bonds Between the Living and the Dead on Facebook— Continuing Bonds in Cyberspace

Melissa D. Irwin

People we leave behind mourn our deaths – although differing in terms of ways, degrees, and duration. Friends, family, and others create meaning in their grief, as they celebrate our lives and mourn our passing. Through memorialization, the living find comfort in the memories of and in continuing bonds with those they have lost. Klass and Walter (2001) find that in contemporary Western culture, individuals lack the cultural framework in which to incorporate the presence of the deceased into their lives. The continuing bonds thesis is flexible in its application to various populations and activities, and this study expands its application to cyberspace and social media. In this chapter, I argue that Facebook users' public expression of their ongoing experiences with the deceased is a burgeoning phenomenon, regardless of a possible lack of cultural framework or performative script for doing so. Despite lacking a collective Western cultural framework for incorporating the deceased's presence within people's lives, interactions with a deceased individual's Facebook page constitute a new public form of continuing bonds.

These continuing bonds between the living and the dead exist in cyberspace and have expanded beyond dedicated (and more private) memorial websites. Individuals supplement traditional bereavement rituals (such as funerals), which often signaled the termination of bonds, with new technologically situated ritualized spaces (such as Facebook) for continuing bonds with the deceased. Online memorial pages constitute a novel, ritualized, and public space for maintaining continued bonds. As such, individuals have transformed Facebook into a technologically mediated ritualized space where they can continue bonds with the deceased.

Melissa D. Irwin

Mourning 2.0: From Private to Public Ritual, Memorialization, and Continuing Bonds

Facebook memorial pages constitute a novel, ritualized, and public space for maintaining continued bonds, and individuals exhibit several types of bonding interactions with the deceased. While Klass and Walter (2001) found that in contemporary Western culture, individuals lack the cultural framework in which to incorporate the experiences of continuing bonds, Facebook users in this study's sample chose to express publicly their ongoing experiences with the deceased, regardless of a possible lack of Western cultural framework or performative script for doing so.

Giddens (1991) argues that one possible reason for the decline of formal rituals, and by extension knowledge of performative scripts related to death rituals, is the post-modern focus on increasing individualism where ritual has been replaced by discourse. Klass and Walter (2001, p. 440) also argue that "the sacred reality of ritual may not mesh with the personal constructions of the varied individuals who participate in them today." This study demonstrates that ritual has not necessarily been replaced by discourse but rather that online discourse is now being used to supplement traditional, terrestrially bound death rituals. Such stark, personalized individualism and the increasing focus on discourse, which supplements traditional ritual, are publicly displayed on the Wall postings for the deceased in this study, lending credence to both Giddens' (1991) and Klass and Walter's (2001) arguments related to ritual behavior and its importance in post-modern Western society.

Although Klass and Goss (1999, p. 561) argue that continuing bonds serve a private, rather than a public, function where "the bond with the dead is relegated to the private sphere of the family or a community of friends that is separated in modernity from the sphere of public discourse," social media analysis reveals that individuals are now able to continue their relationships with the deceased in a new, public online space, such as Facebook. These burgeoning practices challenge longstanding notions regarding "appropriate" memorialization and bereavement which were traditionally viewed as private, individualized experiences. Many individuals continue to perform traditional rituals, perhaps not knowing any other alternative or simply adhering to traditional Western norms regarding death ceremonies. In light of technological advances which now offer online, virtual spaces for memorialization and the potential to create new rituals associated with the dead, both traditional and innovative rituals will continue to serve an important function for those who remain.

In this study, individuals use Facebook as a ritualized memorial space and publicly recount their experiences with their deceased loved ones via their Wall postings. The central theme found throughout many Wall postings is that of a presence of the deceased felt by bereaved individuals in their daily lives. Many individuals who posted on Facebook memorial page Walls appear to share some belief in life beyond death and are aware of their loved one's presence, albeit in varying degrees. The three primary thematic sub-categories represented in this sample illustrate individuals' belief in the presence of their deceased friends and family members, and these categories demonstrate how these Facebook members use this belief to continue their bonds online in a public venue after death. Some postings directly exemplified the feeling of presence, while others included various other communications with the deceased – ranging from natural phenomenon symbolizing messages from the deceased to "conversations" with the dead.

Mourning and memorialization 2.0, including Facebook memorial pages, have more permanence and can function to indefinitely immortalize the deceased and provide an unbounded online space for interactions between the living and the dead. Thus, bereavement periods can extend long after the internment and decay of the physical body. The dead now live among us in the virtual sphere, transcending both time and space, where they can virtually live forever in cyberspace. The potential for ongoing ritualistic interaction and continuing bonds with the deceased in cyberspace is palpable in our technologically dominated era.

Of the 1,260 Wall postings, a total of 579 individuals wrote on the deceased's Walls. Of the 579 writers, 436 were female, 130 were male, and 13 were indeterminable. Judging solely from the Wall posters' profile pictures attached to their comments, the age of the majority of writers appeared to be 18–25 years old. One main Wall posting thematic category, presence of the deceased, and three thematic sub-categories emerged that demonstrate various types of continuing bonds: messages and visitations from the deceased, guidance from beyond and reunion with the deceased, and "conversations" with the deceased. These public, online interactions demonstrate how individuals create and continue bonds with the dead on Facebook and how individuals have transformed Facebook into a public, ritualized bereavement space.

This study demonstrates that the practice of continuing bonds has moved beyond the traditional private sphere and into more public realms, such as cyberspace and social networking sites, like Facebook, which share both collective and individualistic characteristics and can serve as a wholly secular space. A plethora of online spaces, including Facebook, now exist where the continuation of bonds extend indefinitely and where the bonds are not necessarily bound by traditional physical limitations for their creation and practice (e.g., cemeteries, bedrooms).

Cybermemorials on Facebook: Social Networking Between the Living and the Dead

There is a growing trend for the bereaved to create memorial pages and extend interaction via personal profiles of the deceased on popular social networking sites such as Facebook.com. Unlike cemeteries, which are the predominant physical memorialization space for the dead, Kastenbaum (2007, p. 421) notes that cybermemorials provide a "nearly dimensionless form of memorialization [that] occupies no fixed space. It is everywhere and nowhere." On Facebook, a member can create a group or page dedicated to almost any topic. Site members have created dedicated memorial pages to the deceased, as well as "live" deceased member profiles.

When the deceased's profile remains "live," friends can continue to post messages on the decedent's Wall and often address the deceased as though they are still alive.

In a country such as the United States where individuals rarely discuss death or its performative scripts or behavioral expectations for people when someone has died, cybermemorial pages on Facebook appear to have emerged as a constructive way for both the younger and mid-life generations to confront and make meaning out of someone's death, even if they have never met the deceased. Within the first eight years of Facebook's launch, over 30 million users had died, and over 300,000 users die every month, leaving millions of profile pages abandoned or memorialized and curated by others (Quora, 2015). Issues related to deceased members' profiles are so pervasive that Facebook now has official policies related to them, including a Legacy Contact designation for those who wish their profile pages to be curated by others, post-death.

Characteristics of Memorial Pages' Writers and Content

Most of the memorial pages were created by friends of the deceased, although a few were created by family members. Additionally, 29 of the 1,260 Wall postings were posted by complete strangers:

> I don't know you Janece but ur story made it all the way 2 Cali and I felt bad.
>
> *(Wall posting for an 18-year-old African American female,*
> *possible homicide victim)*

> Even Though I dnt Know You Imma Give my Respect . . . R.I.P
>
> *(Wall posting for a 16-year-old Hispanic male,*
> *possible homicide victim)*

Individuals who chose to post on the 12 Facebook memorial pages had many different approaches to doing so, with posts including topics such as blaming someone for and/or questioning the death, references to religion (e.g., heaven, angels, God), marking passage of time since death (e.g., "Happy birthday!" and "It's been 3 months now . . ."), expressions of love, loss, sadness, and missing, and information related to funeral arrangements and donations. The style and tone in which individuals wrote range from formal to very informal:

> Brother, tomorrow is going to be the hardest day of my life. I don't want it to come, but I know I have to. I'm so sad that this happened. I love you.
>
> *(Wall posting for a 27-year-old male written by his brother)*

> Lovelovelove youuu! Miss youu, and your always in my heart and on my mind<3333.
>
> *(Wall posting for an 18-year-old female written by*
> *a young adult female)*

Many Wall postings address the deceased in the present tense, further confirming the generally non-explicit notion that posters believe a presence of the deceased exists. Additionally, the use of non-standard, informal language and slang suggests a lack of general sense of "appropriate" and expected public mourning behavior and may indicate how correspondence related to death (e.g., formal, traditional condolence postings) has become less ritualized and scripted.

Thematic Categories of Facebook Wall Postings

Presence of the Deceased: Messages, Visitations, and "Feelings"

Bereavement can bring a wide array of individual experiences – some ordinary and some extraordinary – including "sensing" the presence of the deceased. One main theme that emerged in all 12 Facebook memorial pages and on many of the Wall postings is that bereaved individuals felt the presence of the deceased in their daily lives. Simon-Buller, Christopherson, and Jones (1988) note that the sensing of the presence of the deceased is often pathologized in our society. Consequently, many individuals are reluctant to discuss their experiences, even though scholars consider experiencing a presence as a normal part of grief (Parkes, 1972). According to Klass and Walter (2001), people are reluctant to discuss said experiences with others, because in contemporary Western culture, individuals lack the cultural framework in which to incorporate the presence of the deceased into their lives, unlike in other cultures where the spirit world is regarded as real.

Many bereaved individuals experience presence of the deceased as after-death communication. Kwilecki (2011, p. 241) defines after-death communication (ADC) as "spontaneous communications from the dead [which] introduce the possibility of constant, ongoing contact outside of ritual settings," and "believers may experience continuing bonds through faulty electrical equipment, passing cars, stray coins, and so on." Often happening in tandem with the identifiable sensing of a presence, afterlife "conversations" with the deceased continue, although little research has been dedicated to the extent of the practice. The bereaved may have a variety of ADC experiences, including experiencing a presence, dreams, odors, voices, and "meaningfully timed appearances of animals, rainbows, and other symbolic natural phenomenon" (Kwilecki, 2011, p. 220). Botkin and Hogan (2005) and LaGrand (2006) conclude that the bereaved's experience of ADC is primarily a beneficial experience. In 633 Wall postings, individuals expressed their experiences related to presence, which supports the research of Klass et al. (1996) in relation to continuing bonds and which also supports other research related to presence and ADC.

Many individuals who posted on memorial page Walls appear to share some belief in an afterlife and are aware in varying degrees of their loved one's presence. The following examples demonstrate how these Facebook members continue their bonds online in a public venue after death. Twenty-six Wall postings specifically exemplified individuals' ADC experiences with the deceased. These Wall postings directly referenced messages or visitations from the deceased, and these experiences appear to be overwhelmingly positive in nature for the recipients. The following excerpts best exemplify this thematic sub-category, and the excerpts presented are representative of patterns found across the 1,260 Wall postings.

Several ADC experiences focused on a natural phenomenon that was interpreted as a message sent directly from the deceased. For instance, one woman posted on the Wall of her 27-year-old deceased male friend, where she recounted her experience with a butterfly and interpreted it as a message from him: "P.S. I know that you sent that butterfly to attack my dress. It was totally you!! It worked. It totally made me laugh." This interaction suggests that the woman believed that her deceased friend was contacting her from beyond via her interaction with the natural world, the butterfly. This experience prompted her to not only think of her friend but also indicates her belief in some type of life beyond death in which her friend can control natural phenomenon and can directly communicate with and impact the lives of others. The interaction was positive and reassuring to her and indicates a continuing bond extending beyond the mortal plane.

In another example of a natural phenomenon being interpreted as interaction with the deceased, a young woman interpreted snow in winter as a message from her deceased 12-year-old female cousin, writing, "i know its not true haha but i just wanted to say thanks for the snow!!" She appears to be somewhat skeptical ("not true haha") but generally believes (or at least, wants to believe) that her deceased cousin sent her a message (or a gift) via the snow. The enthusiasm expressed in the posting suggests that the snow itself and interpreting the snow as being sent from somewhere beyond and directly from her deceased cousin were a pleasant amalgam of natural and paranormal experiences.

Another young adult woman recounted her indirect experience interpreting a natural phenomenon as a message from the deceased and posted on her 18-year-old deceased friend's Wall, "<3 your mama told me you made a pretty rainbow for her a week after you passed." This posting is particularly relevant in exemplifying the belief in a presence of the deceased and the ability of the deceased to control the rainbow. Although the mother of the deceased did not directly post anything related to this experience on her daughter's Wall, the fact that someone else, who had spoken to the mother and who had understood the importance and impact of the experience, did post is significant. It not only demonstrates that the writer believes in this ability of the deceased to make and send "a pretty rainbow" directly to those with whom she wishes to communicate but also that the mother believes the same. Although the experience of the pretty rainbow was second-hand, her willingness to post it suggests that the experience was overwhelmingly positive for both the deceased's mother and for herself and that she felt comfortable enough within the page and with fellow posters to do so.

A final example of a Wall poster interpreting an everyday occurrence as a sign from his deceased 27-year-old brother relates to a seemingly random song occurring on the radio at precisely the right time to impact him:

Like today, I was dealing with a situation and I was in the middle of making a choice. Lo and behold a song came on the radio from when we lived in Memphis on Caravel. I haven't heard that song in so long, but I know it was him helping me out.

Although he is not speaking directly to his deceased brother, as in the previous examples where writers are directly engaging the deceased, the sentiment is the same: The man believes that his brother is not only capable of but did directly interact with him via a song on the radio that seems to be significant to both of them. His posting indicates that when he needed guidance, his brother was able to transcend the limitations of death to come to his brother's immediate aid. In posting this experience on his deceased brother's Wall, the writer is publicly stating that the deceased can not only communicate with those who remain but that the deceased are charged with providing guidance and aid. Thus, the experience continues and reinforces the siblings' bonds. The willingness to share this experience so publicly with others also suggests that the experience was a positive one that can serve to reinforce others' beliefs related to similar phenomena.

Other Wall writers experienced visitations of the deceased. These visitations occurred during either dreams or waking hours. One Wall poster recounted a directly interactive experience with the deceased in her dream writing: "You were in my dreams last night. It was so good to see that pretty smile and talk to you. We had so so much to talk about. Thanks for the visit, love you and miss you so much!" This young woman was posting directly to her deceased 16-year-old female friend. Her appreciation toward the deceased for visiting her indicates that she viewed this experience as positive and reassuring. By publicly posting about her direct experience with the deceased, she reinforces the belief that the deceased are able to interact with the living and that the possibility of continuing one's bonds with them is not only possible but assured, even if said interaction is restricted to the dream state.

While several posters expressed experiences related to natural phenomena and dream visitations, others described their direct experiences related to presence which occurred during their waking hours. One woman recounted her direct experiences with not only her 30-year-old male deceased friend (on whose Wall she was posting) but also with other deceased relatives during a fund-raising walk, writing:

At the NAMI walk yesterday I felt Jason walking with me! I felt his spirit with me encouraging me to keep walking. My daughter Rosanna (R.I.P.) and my Dad (R.I.P.) were with me too. I had the strength to keep going! I am so grateful for my Guardian Angels looking out for me!

Several salient themes are represented in this posting. First, the woman is publicly expressing her belief that this particular friend, her father, and her daughter who have died are capable of visiting and interacting with the living. Second, her post heavily implies that the support she "felt" from the deceased individuals provided her with the encouragement and strength she required for completing the task at hand. Her use of the term "felt" also implies the direct experience of presence, as in she literally "felt" the deceased loved ones there with her. Her reference to "Guardian Angels" also indicates her religious belief(s) and the expectation that there are such beings that aid, guide, and "watch over" the living. Her experience of the friend who died recently and of other deceased family members being "there" is also suggestive of longstanding continuing bonds with them.

In yet another example, a young woman asked her deceased 18-year-old female friend to: "Leave me hints to know when you are with me. i know you were with us the other night in pauls car. i could feel it. ☺" Not only is she recounting the experience of her friend being with her and others in another friend's car, but it also demonstrates her desire and expectation to continue to "feel" her friend's presence, although she is unsure as to how she will be notified that the deceased is "with" her. This writer believes that her deceased friend can be "with" her and others but also that continuing the bond with her friend is not only possible but likely. Her use of the smiley face emoticon indicates that she is looking forward to continuing their bond, especially if she "feels" her friend's presence.

Guidance from Beyond and Reunion with the Deceased

Writing on and reading the posts of others on the deceased's Wall is a public, group experience. Many Wall posters chose to include references to religion, and this suggests that their public declaration of their particular religious beliefs (e.g., existence of an afterlife) serves to strengthen their group bond during their respective bereavement periods. There were 267 Wall postings that directly referenced the deceased providing guidance from beyond, survivors requesting such guidance, the possibility (inevitability) of the bereaved being reunited with the deceased in the hereafter, and other religious sentiments. Many of the Wall postings specifically referred to religious symbols or tenets – in most cases, vernacular Christian (e.g., heaven, angels, and/or God). The following excerpts best exemplify this thematic sub-category, and the excerpts presented are representative of patterns found across the 1,260 Wall postings.

There were 40 requests for the deceased to watch over individuals (or groups) from an afterlife or statements that show the Wall posters believe that the deceased is currently watching over those who remain. For example, an adolescent teammate of a deceased 16-year-old female expressed her desire for the friend to "watch over" their team writing, "Watch over us next season. We can do anything with our guardian angel looking out for us. Were doing this for you! <3" By asking the deceased to watch over the team's next season, the young woman is publicly expressing her belief that there is an afterlife and that in that afterlife, we have some type of sway or control over what does or does not happen to those left under our charge as "guardian angels." She is speaking directly to the deceased, imploring her to "watch over us" and indicating that she and her teammates will continue their bonds with the deceased young woman by vowing, "Were doing this for you!"

In another example which incorporates the themes of religion, an afterlife, and being under the watchful eye of the deceased, a young woman speaks directly to her deceased 18-year-old female friend:

> But I know you are looking after me up in heaven. Hopefully, I can make sense of all this craziness one day.i know yr looking out for me and keeping me on track. thank you. thank you for everything youve done for me and continue to do for me.

The deceased died of a drug overdose, and the writer had completed drug rehab. The call for the deceased to look after and keep her friend "on track" is akin to the sponsor/addict relationship, albeit one between the living and the dead. Simply knowing and believing that her deceased friend is actively looking out for her is suggestive that this continuing bond is beneficial and may provide the writer with needed support, so that she does not relapse into drug use.

There were 49 Wall postings related to the bereaved being reunited in the future with the deceased (most often, in heaven). Many writers expressed desire and anticipation in being reunited with their deceased friends and family. Most writers expressed these reunions in religious terms. One young woman expressed her desire to see her deceased 17-year-old female friend in the afterlife, writing: "Someday baby girl im gonna meet at the cross roads and I Know u gonna be there waiting on me with open arms and that distinctive grin u have." This posting does not simply express the potential that a reunion might occur but, rather, the certainty that it will. The writer is secure in her faith that her friend will be waiting for her with open arms "at the cross roads" – a thought that is wholly reassuring and positive for the writer. She writes directly to her friend, publicly indicating her belief that there is an afterlife and that those who have died are there waiting for us. The writer believes that not only is the continuation of bonds with the deceased possible for the living but that these bonds will continue in the afterlife, as well.

Another example of respondents' security and faith that bonds will continue in the afterlife is exemplified in a post by a young woman to her deceased 16-year-old male friend, writing, "Seee You Sooon MyNigga ; UnTill Then Save Me Ah Spot Uhp Ihn Thuggs Mansion k (:" This post exemplifies the anticipation that one day soon the two friends will be reunited – in something that they refer to as "Thuggs Mansion." This term suggests that God is a "Thugg" (used positively) and that He resides in a "Mansion" (heaven) where those who are accepted into it will reside in luxury. This post also suggests that, although their conception of heaven and God may be unorthodox, the writer has publicly announced her belief in a definite, unifying religion – most likely Christianity. The use of the smiley face emoticon also indicates that the writer is looking forward to said reunion with the deceased in "Thuggs Mansion" and that the deceased will "Save [her] Ah Spot" there, indicating that whatever bond they shared (and continue to share) in this life will be continued in the next.

Melissa D. Irwin

"Conversations" with the Deceased

Three hundred and forty Wall postings contained "conversations" with the deceased. These conversation-based postings were often the longest, in that individuals wrote of experiences in which they wished the deceased could have participated or provided accounts of daily activities. Some writers expressed wishing that the deceased could be there to see or to experience something specific. Others wrote of everyday activities that might mean something to the deceased, while others explained to the deceased what they missed or loved about him or her. The following excerpts best exemplify this thematic sub-category and show patterns found across the 1,260 Wall postings.

In 29 Wall postings, the bereaved wished that they and the deceased could experience something together. Many writers expressed their longing to see the deceased one last time, as in the case of the young man who wrote the following to his 16-year-old girlfriend:

> you are on my mind again tonight.. listening to a song that reminds me
> of you. just wishing I could see your face one more time.. Its not easy to
> let go..but i know im never alone. see you soon babe.

The bereaved boyfriend is expressing his desires, wishes, and experiences to the deceased. By doing so, he is continuing his bond with her, via his experiences of presence, especially as he hears "a song that reminds me of you." By choosing to continue his "conversations" with his deceased girlfriend – emoting and expressing his frustrations – he is publicly demonstrating not only his belief that she is where she can also communicate with others but that his public "conversations" with her serve some purpose or hold some meaning for himself and others. He is also expressing his belief that he is "never alone," suggesting that his deceased girlfriend is "with" him somehow – indicating his belief in presence – and that one day, they will be reunited where their bond will continue in the afterlife.

There were 220 combined references to everyday activities or memories that the bereaved wanted to share with the deceased and explanations regarding what the bereaved missed or loved about him or her. The Wall postings related to everyday activities or memories that the writers wanted to share with the deceased (and others) were the longest postings and often consisted of one or more lengthy paragraphs. Many postings were directed primarily toward the deceased, while others were reminiscent of speaking out loud to no one in particular.

One example of directly addressing and engaging in "conversation" with the deceased demonstrates how the sister of a 27-year-old male suicide victim feels compelled to share her emotional difficulties with him:

> I too call your phone to hear your voice. I know one day it will be
> gone like you are. I cry often. I yell at you and myself . . . We made it
> to southaven today. The first thing I did was take your urn picture and

angel out. I love you so much. I miss talking to you. Well actually I talk
to you all the time, you just don't talk back.

This posting was in response to their mother, who had posted that she often
calls her deceased son's cell phone to listen to his disembodied voice, which she
also finds somehow comforting. In his sister recounting that she also calls her
deceased brother's cell phone and that she and her family visited "southaven" (the
cemetery) describing their activities there, she is re-affirming her own and her
family's connection to her brother. Their visitation to the cemetery is indicative
of a more traditional post-death ritual, and his family's and her continued communication online with their deceased son/brother indicates their willingness to
supplement traditional rituals with new, technological ones. His sister writes to
him as though he can hear her and admits that "I talk to you all the time, you
just don't talk back," indicating that she also believes that there is some type of
existence beyond. However, she is frustrated that "you just don't talk back." We
do not know if she believes he is capable of directly talking back to her, or if he
just does not reply.

Another example of writing directly to the deceased about life bereft of their
physical presence is from a young woman written to a 16-year-old male, writing:

> I Just Wish There Was A Way To See You One More Time &; Just
> Hear Your Voice , Tellinq Me Everythinq Will Be Ohkay . I Know I
> Dont Go Visit You Often But Dont Think I Forqot About You .Its Just
> Hard For Me To Know That Your Under Me &; Then I Cant Help But
> Look At The Picture Of You That They Have Showinq Your Smile &;
> It Just Makes Me Cry Knowinq I Wont Be Able To See That Smile For
> A Whilee . But We Have So Many Good Memories Toqether&; Thats
> What Gets Me ThroughEverday . But Untill I See You Aqain I Just
> Want To Let You Know That I Miss You , Everyone Do

She is publicly expressing her longing for his corporeal presence and remembering how he would emotionally support her when he was alive. Her statement, "I
Know I Dont Go Visit You Often But Dont Think I Forqot About You" indicates that she believes her friend is able to discern whether she visits his grave and
that he can hear her, wherever he may be, thus demonstrating her belief that some
type of existence beyond death is not only possible but in this case, at least, definitive. In writing, "I Wont Be Able To See That Smile For A Whilee" and "But
Untill I See You Aqain," she is also expressing her belief that some other realm of
being exists and that she will be reunited with her deceased friend at some point
in the future. In choosing to publicly express her longing, she has demonstrated
not only her belief that there is some type of existence after death, albeit in more
secular terms than in some other postings. She has also demonstrated her desire
to continue a bond with the deceased. Believing that he is watching over her and
that she can "speak" with him via online communication is suggestive that she
also anticipates that this bond will continue online and in the "hereafter."

Melissa D. Irwin

Thanatechnology and Continuing
Bonds in the 21st Century

The tenuous balance between tradition and technology and its ever-evolving impact on our lives ensure that the interactions between the living and the dead will continue to be negotiated. It remains to be seen if online memorialization, such as on Facebook, will have a positive or a negative impact on our relationships with one another and with the dead. This study demonstrates that, despite lacking appropriate cultural frameworks related to the deceased, increasingly, individuals supplement traditional bereavement rituals, such as funerals, with new, technologically situated ritualized and public spaces (such as Facebook) for continuing bonds with the deceased. Despite being a nascent phenomenon, the use of thanatechnology for continuing bonds with the deceased, especially on sites such as Facebook, is firmly entrenched as cultural practice in the second decade of the 21st century.

According to the data, Facebook memorial pages constitute a novel, ritualized and public space for maintaining these continued bonds, and individuals exhibit several types of bonding interactions with the deceased. Some bereavement experts view Facebook as a positive addition to grieving for the internet savvy generation, because younger users are not hesitant to show their feelings and vulnerability, even in the public sphere (Katims, 2010). Hence, the younger internet generation could catalyze the development of a new model of grieving and the solidification of this burgeoning bereavement ritual, and future research could address how the younger generation of mourners has influenced traditional rituals and grieving models. With so many individuals creating and visiting cyber-memorials on Facebook, this usage implies that these pages serve a vital function for those who are left behind and who find comfort in the continuing interaction they can have – with not only someone who has died but also with the broader online friend community who can potentially provide some degree of emotional support, whether it be akin to Durkheim's collective effervescence or a more secular experience. Additionally, as evidenced in this study, online participation would also suggest that younger individuals are more inclined to mourn openly and publicly than previous generations were generally apt to do and potentially, for longer periods of time.

Because Facebook members can create, maintain, and interact with others on pages dedicated to the deceased, memorial page participants can create a type of virtual immortality – ensuring that their deceased friends, family members, and others are not forgotten. So long as the internet exists, individuals can and will continue their bonds online with the deceased. Regardless, one certainty remains: every minute of every hour of every day, people die, and with their deaths come sorrow and mourning. We miss those who are no longer with us. Although we have memories of them, those memories too fade with time. Without death rituals and memorialization, traditional or burgeoning, technology-based or otherwise, and our loved ones to maintain our memories, those who have died would be forgotten – simply lost to the sands of time.

It is through these rituals and memorials that we hope to provide potentially everlasting meaning to their lives and to perhaps make sense of our own. Although death rituals and memorials have both remained the same and have evolved over time, they function to ease the grief of those who remain. Death rituals, memorialization, and continuing bonds between the living and the dead, whether on Facebook or elsewhere, provide a valuable function not only for the living but also for the deceased who many believe remain present with us, even after death.

References

Botkin, A., & Hogan, R. C. (2005). *Induced after-death communication: A new therapy for healing grief and trauma.* Charlottesville, VA: HamptonRoads.

Durkheim, E. (2001). *The elementary forms of religious life* (C. Cosman, Trans.). New York, NY: Oxford University Press. (Original work published in 1912.)

Giddens, A. (1991). *Modernity and self-identity.* Oxford: Polity.

Kastenbaum, R. J. (2007). *Death, society, and human experience* (9th ed.). Boston, MA: Pearson.

Katims, L. (2010). Grieving on Facebook: How the site helps people. *Time Magazine,* January 5 (www.time.com/time/business/article/0,8599,1951114,00.html).

Klass, D., & Goss, R. (1999). Spiritual bonds to the dead in cross-cultural and historical perspective: Comparative religion and modern grief. *Death Studies, 23*(6), 547–567.

Klass, D., Silverman, P. R., & Nickman, S. L. (Eds). (1996). *Continuing bonds: New understandings of grief.* Washington, D.C.: Taylor & Francis.

Klass, D., & Walter, T. (2001). Processing of grieving: How bonds are continued. In M. S. Stroebe, R. O. Hansson, W. Stroebe, & H. Schut (Eds), *Handbook of bereavement research: Consequences, coping, and care* (pp. 431–448). Washington, D.C.: American Psychological Association.

Kwilecki, S. (2011). Ghosts, meaning, and faith: After-death communications in bereavement narratives. *Death Studies, 35*(3), 219–243.

LaGrand, L. (2006). *Love lives on: Learning from extraordinary encounters of the bereaved.* New York, NY: Penguin Group.

Parkes, C. M. (1972). *Bereavement: Studies of grief in adult life.* London: International Universities Press.

Quora (2015). How many Facebook profiles exist for people who are now dead? (www.quora.com/How-many-Facebook-profiles-exist-for-people-who-are-now-dead).

Simon-Buller, S., Christopherson, V. A., & Jones, R. A. (1988). Correlates of sensing the presence of a deceased spouse. *Omega, 19,* 21–30.

Stroebe, M. S., Hansson, R. O., & Stroebe, W. (Eds). (1993). *Handbook of bereavement research: Theory, research, and intervention.* Washington, D.C.: Taylor & Francis.

24

FACILITATION AND DISRUPTION OF CONTINUING BONDS IN A DIGITAL SOCIETY

Elaine Kasket

In your mind's eye, place yourself in this scenario. You have a dear friend, someone from back home, from your childhood. At school you diverted yourselves from lessons by surreptitiously exchanging notes, full of in-jokes and just-us secrets. You took innumerable photographs of one another and of the two of you together. Since growing up and moving further apart geographically, you have maintained contact and have saved all of your communications, for such is the importance of the relationship to you both. Now well into adulthood, you store all of these memories, the legacy of a lifelong friendship, in a large shoebox.

Now imagine this. Your friend dies unexpectedly, to your utter devastation. The connection you had was an integral part of your identity. In the wake of the death, you experience an overwhelming urge to feel that thread of connection again. You dig the shoebox out of the attic, and indeed its contents are richly resonant of not just who your friend was, but what the two of you were together. Especially initially, you spend a lot of time poring over letters and photos. After a while you do this less – the impulse comes and goes – but it's all right. The shoebox isn't going anywhere, and you know where to find it, by your bed where you can easily reach it. Having this treasure trove of memories, and knowing you can access it any time you wish, is a great comfort to you, a way of continuing to feel connected to someone who you will always refer to as your best friend, even though they are no longer here.

One day, a few months after your friend's death, there is a knock at the door. Opening it, you are surprised to see your friend's parents, who have driven thousands of miles to get to you. Without a word, they enter your home and walk through to your bedroom, straight to the shoebox. Bundling it up, they walk back out, get into their car, and drive away. Helpless and shocked, you are unable to protest, but when the numbness wears off, panic sets in. That shoebox is everything you have that connects you to your friend, and you are frantic to retrieve it. When you finally manage to reach your friend's parents, they have horrifying news: they have destroyed the shoebox. You can almost feel your friend's hand slipping from the grasp of your own. There is a thudding noise in your ears, like a door closing.

You might think this a preposterous scenario. Who would bother to do something like this, and who would support their right to do it? That shoebox was *yours*, and you should have been left alone to grieve the way *you* needed and wanted. Legally, their actions constitute trespass and theft – you could have these people arrested. Morally and ethically, this wanton destruction of property would be considered unconscionable. Psychologically, and in terms of continuing bonds, it would be impactful indeed, for with the loss of the shoebox, you have lost something of your ability to find comfort and meaning through a continued connection.

If you are a digital immigrant (Prensky, 2001), whose early memories stretch back before the mid-1980s, the idea of boxes full of paper memories will not seem odd at all. If you are a digital native, however, you may have never clapped eyes on a roll of film, much less taken one to be developed, and may never have sent a handwritten letter through the mail. Today, however, we transmit messages to anyone across the globe instantly and store them indefinitely, and there is little need to print photographs that are always accessible, from the cloud, on ready-to-hand smartphones. If you accept the proposition that "the realm of the dead is as extensive as the storage and transmission capabilities of a given culture" (Kittler, 1999, p. 13), our strongly technologically infused culture has significant implications for how the dead persist among us, and how we experience their presence in our lives.

The rise of digital technologies has been one compelling reason for a new book on continuing bonds at this juncture, and three of the chapters in this book focus in some way upon on the experience of continuing bonds in the digital era. This chapter will highlight several phenomena that may prove essential for understanding continuing bonds both now and in the years to come. On one hand, our inexorably advancing digital technologies unquestionably facilitate the possibilities for continuing bonds. Collectively speaking, we now capture more information about ourselves than at any point in history, and this information is rendered and conveyed as text, audio, still imagery, and video. We share information more regularly and with far more people than ever before. We store huge amounts of data, intentionally and unintentionally, ably assisted by information systems that save things as their default mode. We can access this stored information from anywhere. The argument has been made, persuasively, that for the first time in history it is harder for societies to *forget* than it is for them to *remember* (Mayer-Schönberger, 2011). So, particularly for people who have grown up hyperconnected to one another through technology, and for whom "telepresence" is as natural as physical presence, the Internet houses not only a digital reflection of their lives and relationships, but also a massive externalised memory bank (Mayer-Schönberger, 2011). For digital natives, there are no shoeboxes in the attic. Visual, auditory, and verbal memories are archived endlessly and constantly, but almost exclusively in digital form.

When digitally stored material relating to a deceased individual is available to significant others and to entire communities, it is easy to see how digital legacies can facilitate continuing bonds. There is, however, a complication. As we increasingly leave our legacies online and consign memory to our hard drives and the Internet, continuing bonds with our dead may be both facilitated and disrupted.

Lost and Found: Facilitating Continuing Bonds Through Technology

In 2009, around the time that Facebook was overtaking MySpace to become the world's most popular social networking platform, I was searching for an old friend online and stumbled upon the profile of a similarly named young woman who had died in an automobile accident. Observing the ways in which her network of friends carried on their interactions with her profile – speaking to her, communicating with one another, evolving her image and her legacy, and continuing conversations they had begun with her in life – I was keen to understand more about the uses of this forum for talking to the dead and undertook a qualitative document analysis on 943 wall posts, drawn from five "in memory of" Facebook pages, groups created specifically to memorialise dead individuals. The term "always-on generation" (Anderson & Rainie, 2012) had not yet entered the lexicon, but I was particularly interested in the experiences of digital natives, for whom immersion in social networking was clearly becoming second nature. To find out more about the experience of continuing to interact with the in-life profiles that deceased individuals had created themselves, and which had remained posthumously persistent and repurposed as sites of mourning and memorialisation, I also conducted three in-depth interviews with bereaved digital natives, all of whom still had access to the in-life profiles of the people they had lost.

The key features and themes that I identified in that study (Kasket, 2012) have been confirmed and extended by numerous research studies since, including that described in the previous chapter, with a strong convergence of themes supporting the emergence of a "new normal" within bereavement, in which multiple continuing-bonds processes are facilitated through interaction with posthumously persistent information stored digitally online. The younger and more accustomed to "telepresence" these mourners were, I observed, the more likely they were to use second-person modes of address, speaking directly to the deceased. Mourners spoke to the community of other grievers as well, negotiating and co-constructing the legacy and durable biography of the deceased (Walter, 1996). Continuing bonds on Facebook were strongly expressed in my participants' accounts of the comfort found in continuing visits and communication; the vividness of the deceased's ongoing digital telepresence; the investment they felt in maintaining contact through the site; and the fear they had of that bond's being broken through profile removal. Finally, it was clear that digital natives in particular felt intuitively that Facebook was a reliable route to feeling that one was *actually getting in touch* with the deceased. The idea that communicating via a Facebook account would be a more effective means than any other of getting a message across seemed to be accepted as an article of faith, even when it offended secularly inclined individuals' sense of what was possible or rational. In observing this latter phenomenon in particular, I felt that I was discovering quite new territory.

Until, that is, the day in 2010 when I presented at St. Mungo's Museum of Religious Art in Glasgow, where I had been invited by the artist Gillian Steel to speak about my research to an audience of members of the public, primarily digital immigrants. Presenting the above findings and noticing that my audience seemed nonplussed, I silently lambasted myself for not providing more context; for example, better defining and describing what social networking profiles actually were. After the talk, an elderly woman approached, and I readied myself to contend with confusion or disapprobation about social media. Instead, she told me in a rather bored fashion that what I was speaking about was nothing new, identified herself as a member of the Glasgow Association of Spiritualists, and handed me an envelope full of faded "spirit photographs" from the late 19th century. I was polite but did not see how my talk on continuing bonds on social media might be linked to this lady's belief that these photographs represented an authentic communion with dead spirits. Now, however, I think that I have grasped the connection.

In the Web 2.0 era, an Internet characterised by sharing, connecting, and user-generated content, anyone can publicise information worldwide in an instant, and anyone can make their voice heard and their opinion known. It is the latest phase in a long line of technologies that humans have invented and employed over the centuries to capture, convey, and retain information and knowledge. The world-changing developments of language, writing, and the printing press emerged over thousands of years, but with the industrial revolution the emergence of new technologies accelerated rapidly, proliferating throughout the late 1800s and early 1900s: the telegraph, the photograph, the telephone, the phonograph, the wireless radio.

Perhaps one of the strongest indicators of our instinct to continue bonds is the fact that as each new technology has emerged, it has been pulled into service as a method of connecting to the dead. In the mid-19th century, the tapping of the telegraph was echoed in the spirit rapping of the Fox sisters' famous séances (Sconce, 2000). As soon as portrait photography become popular, the misty faces of the dear departed materialised on formal photographs of the bereaved. Thomas Edison himself speculated, in a 1920 *Scientific American* article, whether he could produce a sufficiently sensitive version of his phonograph to capture the voices of the dead (Walter, 2015). And in modern-day Japan, Itaru Sasaki, a 70-year-old gardener who had installed an old-fashioned English-style phone box in his garden to help him stay connected to his dead cousin, has received a continuous stream of visitors to his property following the devastating Tōhoku tsunami in 2011.

Inside [the box] is a black rotary phone, rusting on a wood shelf. This
phone connected to nowhere. It didn't work at all. But that didn't matter to Itaru. He just needed a place where he felt like he could talk to his
cousin, where he could air out his grief . . . "Because my thoughts could
not be relayed over a regular phone line, I wanted them to be carried on
the wind," [he said], "so I named it the wind telephone." . . . [A]ter the
tsunami and earthquake happened, word got out about Itaru's special
wind telephone, that he was using it as another way to stay connected
to the dead. Soon people started showing up randomly on his property,
and walking right into the phone booth. This has been going on for
five years now . . . thousands of people from all over Japan have come
to use his phone.

(Meek, 2016)

Taking the historical view, and seeing how every generation of humans has used
the available technologies of the day to search, to call, and to reach out to their
dead, it could indeed be argued that there is nothing new under the sun. On Itaru
Sasaki's wind telephone, visitors sometimes dial the numbers for residences that
were swept away by the tsunami, the usual numbers on which they used to reach
their husbands and wives, the places where their loved ones could last be found.
Likewise, digital natives, thoroughly accustomed to experiencing the Internet as
the "place" where they perhaps most frequently met their friends, continue to
speak to them in that place.

The potential for a more powerful sense of connection seems greater in the latter example, however. When mourners speak to their dead in Itaru Sasaki's phone
booth, they are doing so from a place that their lost loved one never visited; there
is nothing but silence on the line when one picks up the receiver of the wind
telephone, no stamp of the familiar, no image or feel of the deceased. A social
network, however, is a well-known stomping ground, the place where you often
communed with the person, and the vestiges of them are strong and everywhere.
Seeing them there, in the same space as before, one drops into communicating
just as one always has when visiting this place. In a world where to send a communication into the ether is to assume it has been nearly instantly received, it
is not so surprising that this same sense persists after death, not odd at all that a
person might say, "It's strange but part of me just feels like he sees it somehow"
(Kasket, 2012, p. 66).

To fully comprehend the complexity of our digital legacies, one must recognise
that they are not representations of us in isolation, like portraits or autobiographies; their content is forged jointly among ourselves and our communities, and
following the trail of digital footprints will show not just where we walked, but
with whom. The sense when one visits a dead person's social networking profile
is not just "this was him" or "this was her," but "this was *us*" – or even "this *is* us."
As of this writing, the only reason that Facebook removes a dead user's profile is
if it was recorded as the deceased's wish, for example if they ticked the "remove

my profile after death" box in their settings, or had a more comprehensive digital will, and/or if their next of kin go through the necessary request and verification procedures to take the profile down. The default position, however, is preservation of the account in "remembering status." The contributions of the now-dead user are frozen in time, but there is activity all around them as the community of grievers embroider on existing content, on one side of death's divide, and evolve the space on the other, visiting and speaking with the dead, and encountering and conversing with others who also mourn.

Social networking does not constitute the whole of a digital footprint or legacy, however. TripAdvisor reviews written by the now-dead may influence your choice of hotel. That recommendation on Amazon, penned by someone no longer on earth, may have spurred you to purchase a book. Data as mundane as search histories and bookmarked web pages remain behind on computers and other devices, speaking more loudly and personally than you might imagine, as one daughter who inherited her mother's laptop describes: "Her computer activity was like a breadcrumb trail through her inner life: her interests, her hopes and her plans for the future, even those that would never come true" (Brannen, 2016).

So, while physical remains are sequestered and silent behind cemetery gates, digital remains are comparatively vocal and agile. Projections or reflections of the modern-day dead are continuing their existence online, their ranks swelling every day, shifting in precise form but still recognisable, making themselves seen and heard. Never has the argument that continuing bonds are sociologically and communally held (Klass, 2006) been more vividly exemplified than through the persistent, accessible, vivid presence of the dead in society, made possible through contemporary digital technology.

Lost, Found, and Lost Again: Disruption of Continuing Bonds in the Digital Age

Perhaps the fact that we are able to find solace and continuing connection to our dead through our access to rich digital legacies is a comforting thing, but at the same time we cannot take the availability and persistence of these digital remains for granted. While the capacity to store our data seems almost limitless, "[d]igital beings can either endure forever, without any change, or disappear instantly without leaving a trace. [They] have two contradictory possibilities simultaneously: eternal endurance and instant vanishment" (Kim, 2001, p. 101). When access to digital legacies is important for continuing bonds, the idea of eternal vanishment may provoke intense anxiety. While in some ways this is merely a normal manifestation of well-known phenomena – fearing the pain of loss, and faltering when someone that we love and rely upon is taken away – the modern technologically mediated context introduces some novel facets to this natural apprehension.

Once upon a time, when someone died, it was the family or the deceased's closest associates that had privileged access to the dead: to their bodies, to information about them, to their personal effects, to their writings and their photographs. Having access also meant having control over who *else* had access. Family members were the keepers of the gate, presenting a certain image of the dead, feeding information to obituary writers or celebrants delivering the eulogy. Rather than just being about stage-managing the deceased's image for a public audience, however, these activities were part of the individually and collectively undertaken process of idealisation, the building of a durable biography of the deceased that the bereaved can carry forward comfortably (Walter, 1996). In this process, "[m]emories of the negative aspects of the dead are lost and idealization is carried out by most bereaved people and encouraged by society" (Parkes & Prigerson, 2010, p. 81). It is an adjustment and smoothing over of the more difficult or unattractive aspects of the person, of unresolved issues in the relationship, and of troubling memories, and it functions to assist and support continuing bonds.

Also once upon a time, friends were generally situated at the more distant end of the access-and-control spectrum. A continuing bond with the deceased might also have been important to these friends, but they were more vulnerable to becoming disenfranchised mourners, their grief unseen, their relationships with the deceased not realised or acknowledged. The long-time secret mistress who wished for the return of precious correspondence might not have got past the front door of the family home; the school friends might never have heard of the death, or been notified of the funeral that they might have wished to attend.

In an extremely short space of time, we have seen a significant shift in this traditional balance of power. The mistress may have a greater level of access than the mother. A father may have to appeal to friends for photographs to display at the funeral. Family members who have been excluded from a deceased person's social networking profile may not be able to see the digital remains, but friends can access them whenever they like. Often the family is not even able to choose how, when, and to whom their loved one's demise is announced, and a death may be revealed through a news link embedded in a journalist's tweet, or comments made by a friend on a Facebook page – "I can't believe what just happened, RIP Jennifer." A notification by a friend on social networking, in fact, may be how the family themselves come to hear about the death.

In any struggle for control over or access to a deceased person's digital legacy, there are usually at least four stakeholders: family, friends, corporations, and the dead person themselves. Facebook, and its evolving policies around deceased users, is a case study in how these parties' interests can come into conflict with one another. As its first attempt at dealing with its users dying off, the social network introduced a memorialisation feature in 2009 – a one-size-fits-all policy in which Facebook would set all of a deceased user's original posts to "friends only" once notified of the death. Subsequently, in 2014, an amendment to policy was introduced that would give the dead themselves much more control over their posthumously persistent digital selves. "Starting today, we will maintain the visibility of a person's content as is," the announcement read:

This will allow people to see memorialised profiles in a manner consistent with the deceased person's expectations of privacy. We are respecting the choices a person made in life while giving their extended community of family and friends ongoing visibility to the same content they could always see.

(Facebook as cited in Cohen, 2014)

In their statement, Facebook explicitly acknowledged the importance of the site for continuing bonds, a position they have often voiced since, and simultaneously set down certain parameters for who could access the content of an individual profile for these purposes. When it rolled out its "Legacy Contact" settings shortly after this time, allowing users to stipulate removal of the profile after death and/or to appoint a legacy contact to manage the account, it gave the dead even more control over the fate of their digital legacy. In these evolutions we can see Facebook trying to treat users and their families more individually and sensitively, and to be more consistent with American laws that accord the dead ongoing privacy rights (Harbinja, 2013), but ultimately corporate involvement in the control of digital legacies can have disruptive effects for continuing bonds in many cases, as the stories below illustrate. Both involve millennial women, active Facebook users, who died in 2014 and left behind substantial digital legacies that were important to their families and friends.

The first story is that of Hollie Gazzard, an English 20-year-old from Gloucestershire who had shared over 1000 photos on her Facebook account, and who was brutally murdered in her workplace. Hollie's profile was important to the family as a place to remember and to continue to feel connected to her, but nine of her photographs showed her together with her killer, who was her ex-boyfriend. The continued presence of these photos was highly distressing to her family, who requested their removal from the account. Facebook, however, initially stuck firm to its policy that the profile would be preserved just as Hollie had left it, respecting her (assumed) preferences as they were at the point of her death. Her family successfully campaigned to have the photos removed, assisted by UK laws that more strongly support next of kin's taking responsibility for the deceased's privacy rights and their copyrighted material (Harbinja, 2013). After the photos were removed, relieved family described that they were finally able to use the memorialised account, their edit of Hollie's durable biography (Walter, 1996), to recall happy times. Not wanting others to have a similar experience, they pleaded with Facebook to handle each deceased user's account on a case-by-case basis.

The story of Amy Duffield, a 23-year-old young woman from Nottinghamshire, also features the struggle between corporation and family for right to control and access the digital legacy. She too shared much of her life online, and her mother Sharon was on her Facebook friends list. Sometime after her death, Sharon realised that Amy's account been placed into "Remembering" status without her having triggered or consented to this, but what was especially troubling for her was that Amy's name had mysteriously disappeared from Sharon's *own* list of Facebook friends, compromising Sharon's access to Amy's digital legacy.

In a desperate bid to rectify this, and with the additional hope of seeing Amy's private messages, Sharon asked Facebook to grant her this. While the social network absolutely declined her request for access to private messages, the BBC reported that Facebook had claimed Sharon's excision from Amy's friends list was attributable to a "bug" that they were trying to fix (Harris, 2015).

Sharon's description of her experience is an eloquent expression of not just the importance of a digital legacy in being able to continue bonds, but also of the trauma of this bond's being disrupted. "What needs to be changed is, Amy will *always* be my friend, and I don't want her to be obliterated," Sharon said. "They've got to have a proper procedure, and they've got to think about the psychological impact of what they're doing, because it's very very damaging" (Harris, 2015). The families of Hollie and Amy, in pleading for "proper procedures" and "case-by-case" treatment of deceased users, are throwing down a challenging gauntlet indeed, considering that if Facebook's users were a country, it would have the third largest population of any country in the world.

The phrase Amy Duffield's mother chose – *I don't want her to be obliterated* – expresses just how much the digital legacy can be resonant of a deceased loved one. If the digital reflection of a person is lost, or one is denied access to it by whatever means, the impact can be devastating for continuing bonds. "[I]t would feel like I wouldn't be able to talk to her properly," said one of my research participants. "It would be deleting the last bit of her that's still *almost real* . . . the one *last thread of her* that I have. If we lost it, it would be like *losing her all over again*" (emphasis added; Kasket, 2012, p. 66). In mass media reports, in qualitative academic research, and in anecdotes and conversation, we are seeing and hearing more and more anxiety about whether the online legacy of our dead will continue to be preserved.

Perhaps millennials have a particular reason to be concerned with this. In the 2012 *Imagining the Internet* survey, one expert argues that

> memories are becoming hyperlinks to information triggered by keywords and URLs. We are becoming "persistent paleontologists" of our own external memories, as our brains are storing the keywords to get back to those memories and not the full memories themselves.
>
> *(Case, cited in Anderson & Rainie, 2012)*

The younger generation, relying on technology to stockpile their memories for easy search and retrieval later, may not spend their cognitive resources in additionally laying down internal memories. Imagine, then, that you are a young digital native and that your dead friend's online legacy disappears. Someone has entered your home, stolen your shoebox, and destroyed your memories.

The Not-So-Final Word

Our experience of the dead among us, and of our connection to them, is profoundly influenced by the increasing fusion between human beings and the technologies that are becoming extensions of their flesh-and-blood bodies. Millennial digital natives "think with, think into, and think through [their] smart tools" (Chudakov cited in Anderson & Rainie, 2012); physical, mental, and digital selves are knitting together in an increasingly seamless triumvirate. One third of this triad, the digital self, may very well persist after death, conveying echoes and reflections of the other two facets. Alongside this gradual human-technology fusion, our conceptions of privacy and the ways in which we regulate it have significantly changed, and "privacy" has become nearly synonymous with "privacy settings." How we build our digital legacies, and how we manage the privacy settings around them, may eventually determine who will be able to continue their bonds with us, and who will have that ability disrupted, for as they become larger and more complex digital legacies will undoubtedly become even more central for these continuing bonds processes. The vivid digital reflections of ourselves created in life, remaining behind in the ether after our deaths, will continue to bring new dimensions to the word "ethereal," new twists on the "ghost in the machine" (Ryle, 1949).

References

Anderson, J., & Rainie, L. (2012). Milennials will benefit *and* suffer due to their hyperconnected lives (Pew Internet & American Life Project). Available at: www.pewinternet.org/2012/02/29/millennials-will-benefit-and-suffer-due-to-their-hyperconnected-lives.

Brannen, K. (2016, 8 May). Her secret history: I discovered my mother's digital life after her death. *The Guardian*. Available at: www.theguardian.com/lifeandstyle/2016/may/08/secret-history-my-mothers-digital-life-after-her-death.

Cohen, D. (2014). Facebook to leave privacy settings of memorialized accounts unchanged: Create a "A Look Back" for families of deceased users [Online Article]. Available at: www.adweek.com/socialtimes/privacy-settings-memorialized-accounts-a-look-back-deceased-users/432726.

Harbinja, E. (2013). Does the EU data protection regime protect post-mortem privacy and what could be the potential alternatives? *SCRIPTed*, *10*(1), 19. doi: 10.2966/scrip.100113.19.

Harris, A. (Reporter) (2015). Digital legacy report [Television Broadcast]. BBC: East Midlands Today. Available at: www.youtube.com/watch?v=8pi720izNeU.

Kasket, E. (2012). Continuing bonds in the age of social networking. *Bereavement Care*, *31*(2), 62–69. doi: 10.1080/02682621.2012.710493.

Kim, J. (2001). Phenomenology of digital-being. *Human Studies*, *24*, 87–111. doi: 10.1023/A:1010763028785.

Kittler, F. (1999). *Gramophone, film, typewriter* (G. W.-Y. a. M. WUTZ, Trans.). Stanford, CA: Stanford University Press.

Klass, D. (2006). Continuing conversation about continuing bonds. *Death Studies*, *30*, 1–16.

Mayer-Schönberger, V. (2011). *Delete: The virtue of forgetting in the digital age*. Princeton, NJ: Princeton University Press.

Meek, M. (Producer) (2016). One last thing before I go: Really long distance [Radio series episode]. In I. Glass (Executive Producer), *This American life*. Chicago, IL: WBEZ. Available at: www.thisamericanlife.org/radio-archives/episode/597/one-last-thing-before-i-go?act=1.

Parkes, C. M., & Prigerson, H. (2010). *Bereavement: Studies of grief in adult life* (4th ed.). London: Penguin.

Prensky, M. (2001). Digital natives, digital immigrants. *On the Horizon, 9*(5), 1–6. doi: 10.1108/10748120110424816.

Ryle, G. (1949). *The concept of mind.* Chicago, IL: Chicago University Press.

Sconce, J. (2000). *Haunted media: Electronic presence from telegraph to television.* Durham, NC: Duke University Press.

Walter, T. (1996). A new model of grief: Bereavement and biography. *Mortality, 1*(1), 7–25.

Walter, T. (2015). Communication media and the dead: From the stone age to Facebook. *Mortality, 20*(3), 215–232. doi: 10.1080/13576275.2014.993598.

REFLECTIONS AND CONCLUSIONS

Going Forward with Continuing Bonds

Edith Maria Steffen and Dennis Klass

This anthology is a sampling of multi-disciplinary and cross-cultural developments that intersect in the ideas around continuing bonds. We are not (yet) ready for a unified theory of continuing bonds. The model has always been collaborative and crowd-sourced, and so we anticipate developments will go forward on many fronts. In these concluding thoughts we will note some key take-home messages and points for further development.

Continuing Bonds Are Complex and Defy Simplistic Ideas About Adaptiveness

The central message in *Continuing Bonds: New Understandings of Grief* in 1996 was that ongoing relationships with the deceased are normal and that the idea of "finishing" grief was therefore irrelevant (Silverman & Nickman, 1996). The editors and authors of the book showed that people do not simply "resolve" grief but that there is a dynamic ongoing process in which people reorganize their lives following a significant loss. The bonds with the deceased are not fixed or static but are constructed and develop in the light of many different factors that continue to change. Some research in the intervening years has focused on trying to identify which kinds of continuing bonds might be adaptive and which not, but as some of the chapters in this volume show, for example the chapter by Ho and Chan and the chapter by Fong and Chow, there is no simple relationship between, for example, internalized versus externalized continuing bond type and bereavement adjustment; instead this is more likely to vary across individuals and involves a lot of other factors including cultural ones. Research that is interested in teasing out when and how continuing bonds are "adaptive" or "maladaptive" will have to be much more context-sensitive and nuanced to be able to make meaningful claims about their precise role in a given situation.

Continuing Bonds Are Relationally Rich and Call for Relationship-Sensitive Approaches in Therapy

Many chapters in this new anthology also echo the key message of the complexity of the bonds as they are constituted within rich and complex relationships, particularly those that are centered in therapeutic work with the deceased. Thus, Rubin and colleagues highlight the importance of focusing on the *quality* of the relationship rather than on whether the deceased lets go of or holds on to the deceased. Where this quality is characterized by attachment security, as Kosminsky explains, the relationship can become a resource for the bereaved, or even potentially a welcome presence, as Hayes and Steffen describe. However, where the quality of the relationship with the deceased is less wholesome for the bereaved as in the case of an unwelcome presence or where there is an insecure attachment relationship and much unfinished business, new therapeutic practices can respond helpfully to these relationship configurations as several chapters explore. This may involve attachment-informed work as Kosminsky details, person-centered work as in Hayes and Steffen, or even behavioral approaches such as forgiveness interventions as put forward by Gassin. Neimeyer and Hooghe's annotated session transcript demonstrates working in-depth on and with the relationship with the deceased to facilitate the meaningful reconfiguration of the bond in helpful ways. It is noteworthy that the finely grained attention on the specifics of the situation as described by the authors in the clinical section seems to show a way forward toward a greater understanding of continuing bonds in general. Future research efforts, particularly quantitative ones, can follow these promising trails.

The Continuing Bonds Model Helps Us See the Socio-Cultural Dimensions of Grief

The continuing bonds model originally grew out of an appreciation of cross-cultural understandings of bereavement and has been concerned with showing the interconnectedness of people, and the new anthology develops this theme further, with many chapters emphasizing the social and cultural situatedness of human beings and how our cultural scripts and narratives shape our experience of loss and bereavement and our relationships with the deceased.

The term continuing bonds appears sometimes to be used interchangeably with attachment or simply relationship; however, this risks neglecting the culturally grounded view of continuing bonds that the model is built on. While the 1996 book sketched the outlines of the socio-cultural basis of the model, we find that the new anthology adds detail and color. Walter's chapter explores from a sociological perspective how different cultural frames create differences in the attitudes of whole societies toward their dead, for example differences in whether a culture fosters a sense of responsibility or obligation toward the deceased. Valentine applies this broader view to specific Western and Eastern cultures, showing how tensions between the individual and dominant scripts for continuing bonds are negotiated creatively at the level of the person. We also find the theme of scripts and narratives developed by other authors. Dennis and Kunkel's close examination of different types of grief accounts shows how different cultural discourses create, for example, transformative or affirmative continuing bond narratives. Other chapters provide further examples of how culture shapes continuing bonds expression, for example in China, as Fong and Chow present a new model of understanding bonds in this context. Charting not only the horizontal reach of continuing bonds in terms of culture but also their vertical reach in terms of history, MacDougal's chapter provides an account of continuing bonds in Ancient Mesopotamian culture that shows their impact on group identity and cohesion and the importance of family identity in this cultural context. The variety of focal points in these chapters seems to demonstrate the broad applicability of the continuing bonds model, the chapter by Henry and colleagues on continuing bonds as a helpful concept for the situation of immigrants being another such example. Such breadth invites further applications and extensions of the model.

Continuing Bonds Opens up Alternative Ways of Thinking about the Reality of Being

In the 1996 concluding thoughts, the authors spoke about the paradox of death as "[t]he deceased are both present and not present at the same time" (Silverman & Nickman, 1996, p. 351). This theme has been developed, and we found it important to dedicate a section in itself to the ontology of continuing bonds and not to dodge the question of the existential status of the deceased and our bonds with them. If we allow the voices of the bereaved to be heard, we will often hear that the deceased come and visit or that we can communicate with them and how therapeutic this can be. Beischel and colleagues' chapter on forms of healing outside those offered by Western mental health such as medium consultations reminds us that a large proportion of the bereaved population views the deceased as continuing to exist in some form and to be available for communication, but research and scholarship has tended to either dismiss this perspective or avoided the debate.

As Bush puts it vehemently in his chapter, can we take survivors seriously when they say that the bonds are "real"? Some of us may do so more readily than others. A few authors in the book make suggestions as to how we can get on the side of believing survivors in novel ways. One way may be to take a step back from a black-or-white understanding of reality and instead, similar to how Tedeschi and colleagues suggest, embrace the paradox of death through dialectical thinking, thus allowing the deceased to be both alive and present *and* dead and absent. Another approach might be for skeptics to set aside their own assumptions and allow themselves to be ontologically flooded as Hunter proposes, giving space to different explanations rather than insisting on a purely scientific (and often materialistic) worldview. Cooper provides the perspective that it is possible to ask these questions from a positivist-empiricist angle too, as he shows how parapsychology investigates the possibility of survival beyond death. This open and perhaps fearless discussion of the ontological question could be seen as a call to further thoughtful work that can expand the philosophical underpinnings of the continuing bonds model.

Continuing Bonds Opens Us to Include Creative and Innovative Communal Expression

Considering both the cultural dimension of continuing bonds and their paradoxical, dialectical, or even transliminal (Thalbourne, 1991) ontology, there is much room for the creative and possibly transcendent outworkings of their potential. Several chapters seem to capture this as they describe the different kinds of territory that can be charted when giving expression to continuing bonds. The chapter by Scrutton, for example, shows how continuing bonds can help overcome philosophical problems around belief as a linear and logical construct through casting belief as a communal practice or a shared ritual imbued with rich meaning. Hedtke's chapter on re-membering the deceased through re-integrating them into our lives and our communities seems to tap a similar element when she describes how past and present are bridged by anchoring connection in meaning through narratives that can become inspirations for the bereaved. Continuing bonds can also facilitate the symbolization of grief; for example, in "invisible" losses such as pregnancy loss, they can help make the loss more concrete and give permission to grieve, as Lau and colleagues elaborate.

Commemorating the deceased on social media and a variety of digital platforms for mourning can also be counted among the innovative cultural forms of expression. Balk and Varga's, Irwin's, and Kasket's chapters explore this recent and widespread cultural change. Kasket adds an interesting point to the ontological debate as she discusses how our "digital self" will be the part of us that survives our physical and mental selves, constituting a permanent legacy with which others can continue to interact.

This final "take-home" message could also be seen as blending the previous key points and suggests we be on the watch for further novel and creative cultural frames in which people experience and express their continuing bonds.

Closing Thoughts

In the 20 years since the term was introduced into bereavement studies, continuing bonds have gone from being dismissed and pathologized to being a fully recognized and accepted phenomenon in bereavement scholarship and practice. In fact, continuing bonds can now be seen not just as a phenomenon in grief but as a way of characterizing and expanding on grief itself, transcending standard conceptualizations of grief in the process. The model lends a structural perspective to our understandings of grief that draws attention to the relational and contextual as well as the philosophical and spiritual-existential dimensions of grief. Structurally, this allows us to conceptualize our grief in terms of relationships stretching both into the past and into the future, and adding not only a larger temporal element but transcending this at the same time through incorporating our past and our future in the present, but, as such an understanding can be seen to expand the present, it also adds a spatial element to our conceptualizations, broadening the view of the person and of people's identities as embedded in a complex "web of bonds and meanings" (Klass, 1999, pp. 174–6).

The enthusiasm with which these fundamental ideas have been taken up and applied to different disciplines has led to a proliferation of research, scholarship, and practice that can widen our gaze, our horizons, and our experience and, it is hoped, will also inspire us to venture forth into these new possibilities for ourselves. In this volume we have collected just a sample of what has been emerging since the 1996 book was published. We are not yet at the point where we can put forward a "grand theory" of continuing bonds, and maybe this would not even be desirable, given the postmodern roots of the model. We are still collecting and exploring, and there is room for pioneers to probe further, whether into the new avenues that are introduced in this volume or into entirely uncharted territories. It is up to all of us who are engaged in this continued undertaking.

References

Klass, D. (1999). *The spiritual lives of bereaved parents*. Philadelphia, PA: Brunner/Mazel.

Klass, D. (2006). Continuing conversation about continuing bonds. *Death Studies, 30*, 1–16.

Silverman, P. R., & Nickman, S. L. (1996). Concluding thoughts. In D. Klass, P. R. Silverman, & S. L. Nickman (Eds), *Continuing bonds: New understandings of grief* (pp. 349–355). London: Taylor & Francis. New York, NY: Routledge.

Thalbourne, M. A. (1991). The psychology of mystical experience. *Exceptional Human Experience, 9*, 168–186.

INDEX

Index